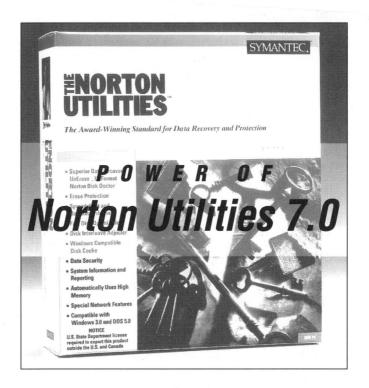

David Doty

A Subsidiary of
Henry Holt and Co., Inc.

Copyright ©1993 David Doty

All rights reserved. Reproduction or use of editorial or pictorial content in any manner is prohibited without express permission. No patent liability is assumed with respect to the use of the information contained herein. While every precaution has been taken in the preparation of this book, the publisher assumes no responsibility for errors or omissions. Neither is any liability assumed for damages resulting from the use of the information contained herein.

Throughout this book, trademarked names are used. Rather than put a trademark symbol after every occurrence of a trademarked name, we used the names in an editorial fashion only, and to the benefit of the trademark owner, with no intention of infringement of the trademark. Where such designations appear in this book, they have been printed with initial caps.

First Edition—1993

ISBN 1-55828-289-0

Printed in the United States of America.

10 9 8 7 6 5 4 3 2 1

MIS:Press books are available at special discounts for bulk purchases for sales promotions, premiums, fund-raising, or educational use. Special editions or book excerpts can also be created to specification.

For details contact: Special Sales Director
MIS:Press
a subsidiary of Henry Holt and Company, Inc.
115 West 18th Street
New York, New York 10011

ACKNOWLEDGEMENTS

Thanks to Carole McClendon of Waterside Productions, Nancy Stevens, Kathy Bonhurst, Robert Kerwin, Vicki Routs, and Frank Arjasbi of Symantec, and Cary Sullivan and Joanne Kelman of MIS:Press, for their invaluable assistance.

CONTENTS

SECTION I: GETTING ACQUAINTED   1

CHAPTER 1: INTRODUCTION   3

What Are Utilities and Why Do We Need Them   3
What's New in the Norton Utilities 7.0   5
How This Book Is Organized   5

CHAPTER 2: RUNNING NORTON UTILITIES   7

Norton Utilities Shell and Menus   7
Keyboard and Mouse Usage   13
Command-Line Usage   16

CHAPTER 3: CUSTOMIZING NORTON UTILITIES   19

Changing Your Configuration   20
Configuration Options   21

SECTION II: PREVENTING DISK PROBLEMS   37

A Note on Backups   38

CHAPTER 4: PROTECTING FILES FROM ACCIDENTAL ERASURE — 41

The SmartCan Method	42
The File Attribute Method	48
Other Erase-Protection Methods	50
Summary	51
Recommendations	51

CHAPTER 5: PROTECTING DISKS FROM ACCIDENTAL FORMATTING — 53

What Does a Format Do, and How Can It Be Undone?	54
Using Image	55
Using Safe Format	57
Summary	65
Recommendations	65

CHAPTER 6: DISK PROTECTION — 67

Viruses: Threat or Menace?	67
Using the Disk Monitor to Control Disk Writes	69
Hard-Disk Head Parking	75
Summary	77
Recommendations	78

CHAPTER 7: CREATING A RESCUE DISK — 79

What Do We Need to Be Rescued From	80
Creating a Rescue Disk	81
Restoring a Rescue Disk	84

SECTION III: CORRECTING DISK PROBLEMS — 85

CHAPTER 8: RECOVERING ERASED FILES — 87

How Files are Written and Erased	87
Running Norton UnErase in Emergency Situations	89
Running Norton UnErase After Installation	90
Running UnErase from the DOS Prompt	97
Using Manual UnErase	98
Summary	104

CHAPTER 9: RESTORING ACCIDENTALLY FORMATTED DISKS — 105

How UnFormat Works 105
Running UnFormat in Emergency Situations 107
Running UnFormat After Installation 108
Summary 115

CHAPTER 10: REPAIRING DAMAGED DISKS WITH NORTON DISK DOCTOR 117

Lost Clusters 118
Cross-Linked Files 119
Starting the Norton Disk Doctor 119
Running NDD from the DOS Prompt 129
Summary 131

CHAPTER 11: REPAIRING DATA FILES WITH FILE FIX 133

Compatibility 133
Running File Fix 134
Running File Fix from the DOS Prompt 146
Summary 146

CHAPTER 12: NORTON DISK TOOLS: RECOVERING FROM THE DOS RECOVER COMMAND, REVIVING DEFECTIVE DISKETTES, AND OTHER REPAIRS 147

Recovering from Recover 148
Reviving a Defective Diskette 150
Marking a Cluster 151
Make a Disk Bootable 152

SECTION IV: PROTECTING YOUR VALUABLE DATA FROM UNFRIENDLY EYES 155

CHAPTER 13: PROTECTING CONFIDENTIAL FILES WITH DISKREET 157

How Diskreet Works 158
Installing the DISKREET.SYS Driver 160
Running Norton Diskreet 164
Running Diskreet from the DOS Prompt 176
Summary 178

CHAPTER 14: PERMANENTLY ERASING FILES AND DISKS WITH WIPE INFO 179

Running the Norton Wipe Info Program 182
Running Wipe Info from the DOS Prompt 188

viii ■ *Power Of...Norton Utilities*

Summary   190

SECTION V: ENHANCING HARD-DISK PERFORMANCE   191

CHAPTER 15: USING CALIBRATE TO IMPROVE HARD-DISK PERFORMANCE   193

What Calibrate Does   194
Calibration Program Limitations   196
Preliminaries   198
Running Calibrate   200
Running Calibrate from the DOS Prompt   207
Summary   208

CHAPTER 16: USING THE NORTON CACHE (NCACHE2) TO IMPROVE DISK-ACCESS SPEED   209

What Is a Cache and Why Is It Useful?   209
Preliminaries   211
Types of PC Memory and How the Norton Cache Can Use Them   214
Installing the Norton Disk Cache   219
Disk Cache Options   228
Installing the Norton Cache from the DOS Prompt   241
Summary   241

CHAPTER 17: UNFRAGMENTING DISKS WITH SPEED DISK (SPEEDISK)   243

Running Speed Disk   246
Running Speed Disk from the DOS Prompt   255
Summary   256
Recommendations   256

SECTION VI: GENERAL HARD-DISK MANAGEMENT TOOLS   257

CHAPTER 18: MANAGING YOUR DIRECTORY STRUCTURE WITH NORTON CHANGE DIRECTORY (NCD)   259

Network Usage   260
Running Norton Change Directory   261
Running NCD from the DOS Prompt   269
Summary   272

CHAPTER 19: SORTING YOUR FILES WITH DIRECTORY SORT (DS)   273

Contents ■ ix

Network Usage	274
Full-Screen Mode	274
Command-Line Usage	277
Summary	279

CHAPTER 20: VIEWING AND CHANGING FILE ATTRIBUTES — 281

Command-Line Usage	283
Summary	285

CHAPTER 21: SEARCHING FOR MISSING FILES WITH FILE FIND (FILEFIND) AND FILE LOCATE (FL) — 287

File Find	288
File Locate	301

CHAPTER 22: MISCELLANEOUS FILE MANAGEMENT UTILITIES — 305

File Size	306
File Size Summary	309
File Date	310
Text Search	312
Searching for Text on a Disk	314
Text Search Summary	317

SECTION VII: ADVANCED DISK REPAIR TECHNIQUES — 319

CHAPTER 23: HOW YOUR DISK SUBSYSTEMS WORK — 321

Disk Architecture	321
Formatting	330
How DOS Organizes and Manages Files	333
Physical Layout of a Hard Disk	343
Disk Controllers	344

CHAPTER 24: RUNNING THE NORTON DISK EDITOR (DISKEDIT) — 351

Running the Disk Editor in Emergencies	352
Starting the Disk Editor	353
The Menu Bar	356
A Walking Tour of Your Hard Disk	385
Summary	392

X ■ *Power Of...Norton Utilities*

SECTION VIII: MISCELLANEOUS FEATURES — 393

CHAPTER 25: TUNING YOUR SYSTEM WITH THE NORTON CONTROL CENTER (NCC) — 395

Running the Control Center	397
Saving Your Settings	415
Running the Control Center from the DOS Prompt	416
Summary	418

CHAPTER 26: COPYING FLOPPY DISKS WITH THE DISK DUPLICATOR (DUPDISK) — 419

Using Disk Duplicator	420
Command-Line Options	422
Summary	423

CHAPTER 27: PRINTING ASCII TEXT FILES WITH LINE PRINT (LP) — 425

Command-Line Operation	426
Printing with Line Print	428
Summary	431

CHAPTER 28: ENHANCING BATCH FILE PERFORMANCE WITH BATCH ENHANCER (BE) — 433

Using Batch Enhancer	434
Batch Enhancer Subcommand Reference	436
Creating and Editing Batch or Script Files	453
Summary	457

CHAPTER 29: EXAMINING CONFIGURATION AND ANALYZING PERFORMANCE WITH NORTON SYSTEM INFORMATION — 459

Network Usage	460
Running System Information	460
The Menu Bar	462
Running Norton System Information from the DOS Prompt	477
Summary	478

CHAPTER 30: TESTING HARDWARE SYSTEMS WITH NORTON DIAGNOSTICS (NDIAGS) — 479

The File Menu	481
System Tests	483
Memory Tests	488
Disk Tests	489
Video Tests	491
Other Tests	493
Comprehensive Tests	494
What If My System Fails the Diagnostics	496
Running the Norton Diagnostics from the Command Line	504
Summary	505

INDEX — 507

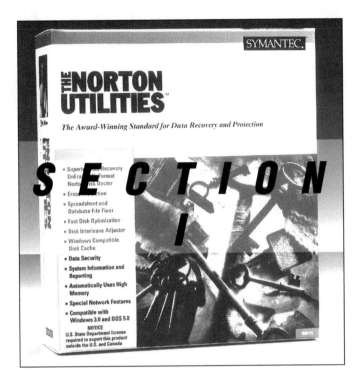

GETTING ACQUAINTED

The chapters in this section describe what the Norton Utilities are, the new features that have been added to Norton Utilities version 7.0, the general procedures for navigating through the program's menus and dialog boxes using your keyboard and mouse, and how to customize the Norton Utilities to suit your system configuration and working style.

Introduction

What Are Utilities and Why Do We Need Them?

If you want your IBM-compatible PC to operate at its maximum efficiency and provide the most trouble-free operation, you should invest in some good utilities. No, I'm not suggesting that you buy stock in the telephone or electric company; I mean that you should buy some utility *software* to help keep your PC in prime operating condition, to manage your file system efficiently, to prevent damage to your valuable data, and to recover missing or damaged files in emergency situations. If you are not familiar with the term, *utilities* are programs that perform the maintenance and housekeeping chores internal to the computer, as distinct from *application* programs—the word processors, spreadsheets, database managers, presentation graphics programs, and the like that we use to accomplish the real work for which we bought our computers in the first place.

Sad to say, your computer, whether it is a trusty XT that has served you for years or the latest '486 speed demon, is not a self-maintaining device. This is particularly true of disk subsystems (floppy-disk drives and hard disks), which

4 ■ *Power Of...Norton Utilities*

involve high-speed moving parts. It may be that, so far, your disks have performed flawlessly, and you have never been confronted with the dreaded "SECTOR NOT FOUND," "SEEK ERROR," "GENERAL FAILURE READING DRIVE C," or any of the other frightening error messages that DOS uses to inform you that something has happened (usually at the worst possible moment) to prevent you from accessing the data that you depend on for your livelihood. No matter. The odds are that someday one of these problems will occur. (Don't believe me; just ask Mr. Murphy.)

Fortunately, in addition to being the most vulnerable to damage, disk subsystems are the most amenable to preventive maintenance and repair by means of utilities software. If your power supply burns out or your RAM chips go bad, there is not much that you can do except take your computer to the shop. Nor is there much you can do, other than using proper power conditioning and operating your computer under the conditions specified by the manufacturer, to prevent such events. There is, however, a great deal that you can do to keep your disk systems operating properly, to protect the integrity of your data, and to correct problems when they occur—provided, of course, that you have the proper tools and know how to use them. That, of course, is where Norton Utilities and this book come in.

In the best of all possible worlds, your operating system would provide all the utilities necessary to manage your file system and maintain your disk subsystems, but in the PC DOS/MS DOS world, this has not been the case, alas. Many necessary utilities were lacking, especially from earlier versions of DOS. For example, the UNDELETE and UNFORMAT commands were not added to DOS until the release of version 5.0, more than 10 years after the initial release. Further, those utilities that were provided were often "unfriendly"—hard for the average user to use correctly and supported by documentation that only a computer wizard could understand. Software developers saw an opportunity in DOS's shortcomings and began creating utility packages to fill the gaps. Among the first such packages to appear (and still one of the most popular), was Norton Utilities. Norton Utilities is a software tool box containing over 30 different tools, the great majority of which are concerned with disk subsystems. Among the most important features of Norton Utilities are the following:

- ◆ repairs most logical and physical disk defects automatically
- ◆ prevents accidental file erasure and accidental disk formatting
- ◆ unerases accidentally erased files
- ◆ recovers files from accidentally formatted disks

Chapter One: Introduction ■ **5**

- repairs damaged files, including 1-2-3 and dBase files
- improves disk performance by "unfragmenting" files and optimizing disk interleave
- transparently encrypts and decrypts sensitive files, with password protection.
- provides extensive information about all aspects of your system's configuration and performance
- adds new commands that enhance the performance and appearance of batch files

WHAT'S NEW IN THE NORTON UTILITIES 7.0

Version 7.0 of Norton Utilities does not depart radically from previous versions of the program. Most of the familiar tools are still there under their familiar names, although they may have undergone some minor modifications. All the features have been rewritten as necessary to make them compatible with the forthcoming (at the time of this writing) DOS 6.0. In addition to these small modifications, Norton Utilities 7.0 includes the following new features:

- The Norton Diagnostics (NDIAGS)—exhaustive diagnostics program for all hardware subsystems.
- The Norton Disk Duplicator (DUPDISK)—an improved replacement for the DOS DISKCOPY command.
- SMARTCAN—an enhanced version of the Erase Protect program found in previous Norton Utilities versions (copies deleted files to a hidden directory so that they can be retrieved easily).

HOW THIS BOOK IS ORGANIZED

In this book, we'll examine in detail each of the tools provided by Norton Utilities, what it's used for and how it works. Wherever possible, we'll provide practical examples of how a tool is used to prevent or solve the problems that you're most likely to encounter in day-to-day operation.

6 ■ *Power Of...Norton Utilities*

The Norton Utilities command menu is divided (by default) into four categories: Recovery, Security, Speed, and Tools. The Norton Utilities documentation is mainly an alphabetical reference. Rather than follow either of these approaches, this book divides the subject matter into eight major sections, including an introductory section, according to function: Preventing Disk Problems, Correcting Disk Problems, Protecting Confidential Data, Enhancing Performance, General Hard-Disk Management, Advanced Disk Repair Techniques, and Miscellaneous Features. Every reader is strongly encouraged to read the "Preventing Disk Problems" section *before* problems occur and implement a regular preventive maintenance program as described there. Doing so may save you a lot of grief later. All readers, but especially those who are new to PC disk management, are also encouraged to read the sections on Enhancing Performance and General Hard-Disk Management. If you are lucky, you will never need the information in the Correcting Disk Problems or Advanced Disk Repair sections, but it cannot do you any harm to be aware of these repair techniques *before you need them*. If you are familiar with the kind of problems that may arise and know how to fix them, you will be less likely to panic in a real emergency. If you want a general introduction to the way in which disk subsystems operate, be sure to read Chapter 23, "How Disk Subsystems Work," in the "Advanced Disk Repair" section. The "Miscellaneous Features" section contains information about a variety of tools and techniques that do not involve disk performance and maintenance. These tools, although not essential for the safe and reliable operation of your system, may occasionally prove useful.

2

RUNNING
NORTON UTILITIES

NORTON UTILITIES SHELL AND MENUS

When you start Norton Utilities, either by typing **NORTON Enter** at the DOS
prompt or by double-clicking the Norton Utilities icon on the Windows desk-
top, you load a menu/shell program that provides easy access to the many features of the Norton Utilities. (The features of Norton Utilities can also be
executed individually on the command line, as described later, but at least for
the novice, running the Norton menu program provides the easiest way to
access the features of Norton Utilities.) The Norton menu screen is shown in
Figure 2.1. It is divided horizontally into two main windows: the Command
window on the left and the Description window on the right. The Command
window lists the various tools and features of Norton Utilities and is used to

select the utility to be executed. The Description window displays a description of the feature currently highlighted in the Command window, along with some of its more commonly used command-line options. At the bottom of the screen is a command line (seen in the figure as a narrow, black window containing a dotted line) that displays the command syntax for whatever feature is highlighted in the Command window. On this command line, you type whatever options, parameters, or switches are required by the utility program that you want to run. At the top of the screen is a menu bar with three pull-down menus, labeled **Menu, Configuration** and **Help.**

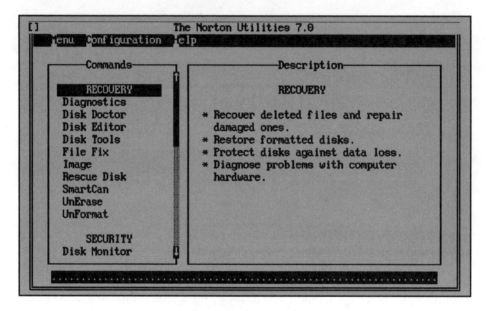

Figure 2.1 Norton menu

The Menu Bar

The Menu Menu

A menu called Menu may seem redundant, but in reality the pull-down menu by this name (Figure 2.2) allows you to modify or customize the menu that appears in the Norton Command window. The five options that appear on this pull-down menu are **Sort by name**, **Sort by topic**, **Add menu item**, **Edit**

Chapter Two: Running Norton Utilities ■ 9

menu item, and **Delete menu item**. The first two commands select the way the utilities are arranged in the Command window, either by name, in alphabetical order, or under four "topic" headings: "Recovery," "Security," "Speed," and "Tools" (the default). If you change the menu-sort order, the results will be displayed immediately and will remain in effect until you change them again.

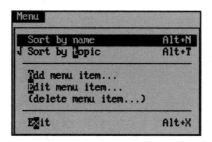

Figure 2.2 *The Menu menu*

N O T E

Topics are not executable commands; they are simply the categories into which the utilities are organized. The default topics are "Recovery," "Security," "Speed," and "Tools," but you can change these or add new ones of your own, as described later.

The third item on the Menu menu, **Add menu item**, allows you to add topics and commands to the Command window. To add a topic to the menu, **Sort by topic** must be selected. Simply type the name of the new topic (up to 14 characters long) in the box provided, then use the arrow keys on your cursor keypad or your mouse to move the new topic to the desired position in the list of topics. You can add a new command to the menu at any time, regardless of what sort method is currently in use. A new command can be anything that can be typed on the DOS command line (e.g., a DOS command, a batch file, or even another application program); it need not be a Norton/Symantec program or have anything to do with Norton Utilities. To add a new command to the menu, first type the name of the command as you want it to appear in the menu (up to 16 characters), then type the DOS command-line string that will execute the command (up to 128 characters, the maximum length of DOS command line). Next, if **Sort by topic** is active, position your new command among the list of topics as desired, by selecting the radio button for the desired topic. Finally, you can choose to add a description that will be displayed in the Description window on the right side of the screen when your new command is highlighted on the menu.

The menu in the Command window is limited to 10 topics and 256 commands.

The fourth and fifth commands on the Menu menu, **Edit menu item** and **Delete menu item** do exactly what their names indicate. **Edit menu item** allows you to change the command name, command-line string, topic position, and optional description of any item currently on the menu. **Delete menu item** allows you to remove any command currently on the menu. It will not, however, allow you to remove a topic that has commands listed under it. If an active topic is highlighted when you pull down the Menu menu, the **Delete menu item** command will be dimmed (displayed in a lighter text color) to indicate that this command is not currently available.

Obviously, the **Edit menu item** and **Delete menu item** commands give you the power to modify the Norton menu in ways that are not particularly useful (e.g., by removing commands that you may want to use later or by changing command names so they are no longer recognizable). Unless one is possessed of a compelling need to do so (and I can't think why one would be), the novice is advised to leave the existing menu items alone. However, in the event that you do modify the Norton menu in ways that you find unsatisfactory, you can easily restore the menu to its default condition by reinstalling Norton Utilities from your original diskettes.

If you want to ensure that you can restore the Norton Utilities to their default setup without going to the trouble of reinstalling the program, you can do so by making a copy of the file that holds the configuration information, NORTON.INI, under another name, such as NORTON.OLD. (Type **COPY NORTON.INI NORTON.OLD** at the DOS prompt.) To restore the old configuration, just reverse the process (**COPY NORTON.OLD NORTON.INI**).

If you are configuring Norton Utilities for a novice user and you want to disable menu editing, you can do so with the **Enable/Disable Menu Editing** command on the Configuration menu (see "Customizing the Norton Utilities," later).

The Configuration Menu

The second of Norton Utilities' pull-down menus, the Configuration menu (Figure 2.3), allows you to customize the appearance and operation of many aspects of Norton Utilities. The options offered by the Configuration menu are the same as those that can be configured when Norton Utilities is initially installed on your system. The options offered by the Configuration menu will be explained under the heading "Customizing the Norton Utilities" later.

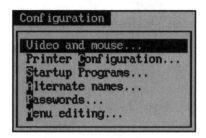

Figure 2.3 *The Configuration menu*

The Help Menu

The third pull-down menu on the Norton Utilities menu bar is the Help menu (Figure 2.4). The Help menu provides general information on getting around in the Norton Utilities menus and dialog boxes, tips on keyboard and mouse usage, and the like. Additional, context-sensitive help for each of the utilities can be obtained by highlighting the utility in the Command window and pressing **F1**. The Help menu also provides access to the Norton Advisor (accessible through a menu of its own in previous versions of Norton Utilities). The Norton Advisor is an on-line reference system for disk problems and common PC error messages. It contains information about common disk problems, DOS error messages, error messages issued by the DOS CHKDSK utility, and error messages issued by three popular applications—Lotus 1-2-3, WordPerfect, and dBase. It also allows you to search for a reference to an error message without knowing what program issued the message. You can scroll through a list of messages under each of the preceding categories and the Advisor will display an explanation of what conditions may have caused the highlighted problem or error message and indicate what steps you may want to take to correct or recover from the error. The suggested solutions proposed by the Advisor are accompanied, where appropriate, by buttons that allow you to run the Norton Utility suggested to solve the problem without leaving the Advisor.

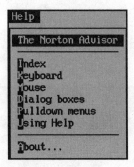

Figure 2.4 *The Help menu*

Launching a Utility

The procedure for starting any of the Norton Utilities from the Norton menu is straightforward:

1. Move the highlight in the Command window, using either the cursor control keys or the mouse, to the name of the utility you want to run.
2. Type any required options, switches, or parameters on the command line at the bottom of the screen. (The Description window on the right side of the screen will display some of the most commonly used command-line options for the highlighted utility. The complete command-line options for the various utilities can be found in their respective chapters or in the *Norton Utilities User's Guide*.)
3. Press **Enter** or double-click either mouse button to load the utility.

Context-Sensitive Help

In addition to the information provided by the descriptions of the various utilities in the Description window, the Norton menu provides more extensive information by means of its context-sensitive help system. To get help with any of The Norton Utilities, highlight the utility in question in the Command window and press **F1**. (You can also get help with the items on the pull-down menus on the menu bar via this method.) Once you are in the Help system, you can move forward or backward through the help screens or select help on any aspect of the Norton Utilities from a list of topics.

KEYBOARD AND MOUSE USAGE

All the features of Norton Utilities can be accessed either from the keyboard or with a mouse. Keyboard and mouse usage in Norton Utilities is consistent with most contemporary PC programs, so experienced PC users shouldn't have much difficulty finding their way around the program. The same keyboard and mouse conventions are used in the Norton menu and in the various utilities.

NOTE The following detailed descriptions may make navigating in the Norton menus and dialog boxes appear more complex than it actually is. Getting around in a program takes more time to read about than to do. Unless you've never used a computer program before, you'll probably find that the easiest way to learn how to operate the Norton Utilities is just to load the Norton menu and explore.

Pull-Down Menus

Keyboard Usage

The pull-down menus at the top of the screen can be accessed either by pressing **F10** or by pressing the **Alt** key plus the first letter of any of the three menu titles (i.e., **Alt+M** for "Menu," **Alt+C** for "Configure," or **Alt+H** for "Help." Pressing the **Alt** key alone highlights the first menu title on the menu bar but doesn't pull down a menu. Once you have done this, you can use the **Left** and **Right** arrow keys to move along the menu bar and the **Down** arrow key to open a menu. Once a pull-down menu has been opened, you can move among the items on the menu using the **Up** and **Down** arrow keys on your cursor-control keypad and move among the menus using the **Left** and **Right** arrow keys. When you have highlighted the menu item that you want, press **Enter** to execute it.

You can also execute a menu item by pressing its "hot key," the highlighted letter—usually but not always the first letter, in the item's name as it appears on the menu. For example, to select the **sort by Name** option on the Menu menu, first press **Alt+M** to open the menu, then press **N** to select the **sort by Name** option. To close a pull-down menu without executing a command, press **Escape**.

Mouse Usage

To access the pull-down menus with the mouse, move the mouse pointer to the desired menu title on the menu bar and click once with either mouse button. To execute a command on a menu, move the mouse pointer to the command and click once with either mouse button. To close a pull-down menu without executing a command, move the mouse pointer to a blank area outside the menu area and click once with either mouse button.

General Keyboard Usage

The following are some keys and their uses:

> **Enter**—executes the currently highlighted item or button in a dialog box.
>
> **Tab**—moves among the options in a dialog box in sequential order.
>
> **Shift+Tab**—moves among the options in a dialog box in reverse sequential order.
>
> **Escape**—leave a dialog box without accepting changes.
>
> **Arrow keys**—move to the nearest item in the chosen direction.
>
> **Home** or **Page Up**—moves to the first item in a dialog box.
>
> **End** or **Page Down**—moves to the last item in a dialog box.
>
> **Hot keys (highlighted letters in dialog boxes or menus)**—press and hold the **Alt** key, then press the highlighted letter to perform the action associated with the highlighted letter.

Radio Buttons

Radio buttons are used to select from among a number of mutually exclusive options in a dialog box. They behave like the station selection buttons on older car radios; only one button can be selected at a time, and selecting a new button automatically deselects the old one.

Use the **Up** and **Down** arrow keys to move to the next radio button. Pressing the spacebar selects the radio button at the cursor position (and deselects the button that was previously selected). Pressing the spacebar when the cursor is on a button that is already selected deselects the button. Radio buttons may also have "hot keys," indicated by a highlighted letter in the name associated with the button. To select a button by means of its hot key, press and hold the **Alt** key; then press the highlighted letter. To select a radio button with the mouse, move the mouse pointer to the button and click either mouse button.

Check Boxes

Check boxes are used to select options that are not mutually exclusive. With the keyboard, use the **Up** and **Down** arrow keys to move to the desired check box, then press the spacebar to check or uncheck it. With the mouse, move the mouse pointer to the button and click once with either mouse button to check or uncheck it.

Control Buttons

Dialog boxes have rectangular control buttons that select and execute actions. Most have, at minimum, an **OK** button, which is used to exit the dialog box and accept the current settings, and a **Cancel** button, which is used to exit the dialog box and ignore any changes that were made while it was open. Additional buttons that open other dialog boxes to control special features may also be present. You move among the buttons in a dialog box using the **Tab** and arrow keys, in the same manner that you move among the other controls. If a button is currently selected, it will be highlighted and will have two indicator arrows at the ends. Pressing **Enter** executes the action associated with the highlighted button. If no button is selected, the default button (usually the **OK** button) is indicated by the arrows. If you press **Enter** when no button is selected, the action associated with the default button will be performed.

16 ■ *Power Of...Norton Utilities*

Text Boxes

Some features of the Norton Utilities, such as the Help system, display a window full of informational text, with additional invisible text outside the window. To scroll the text in a Help window, use the **Up** or **Down** arrow keys to move line by line, the **Page Up** and **Page Down** keys to advance by one screenfull, and the **Home** and **End** keys to move to the beginning or end of the text. Text windows are also equipped with scroll bars that can be manipulated with the mouse. To scroll up or down using the mouse, move the mouse pointer to the arrow at the top or bottom of the scroll bar and press either mouse button and hold it until the text has scrolled by the desired number of lines. Alternately, you can scroll the text by placing the mouse pointer on the highlighted block on the scroll bar, pressing and holding either mouse button, and dragging the highlighted block up or down on the scroll bar.

The Command Window

The Command window displays the list of utilities that can be executed. To select and load a utility using the keyboard, use the **Up** or **Down** arrow keys, the **Page Up** or **Page Down** keys, and/or the **Home** and **End** keys to move the highlight to the desired utility, type any necessary switches or options on the command line at the bottom of the screen; and then press **Enter.** To select and load a utility using the mouse, use the scroll bars to scroll the list in the window if necessary, move the mouse pointer to the desired item, type any necessary switches or options on the command line, and then double-click with either mouse button.

COMMAND-LINE USAGE

Each utility in Norton Utilities not only can be started from the Command window, but also can be executed from the DOS command line. To start any of the utilities from the command line, simply type the command name, followed by any necessary options or switches, and press **Enter.** To find the correct command-line syntax for each utility, consult the *Norton Utilities Command Line Usage Guide* or the appropriate chapter of this book.

Chapter Two: Running Norton Utilities ■ 17

Why start utilities from the command line when the Norton menu is so convenient? First, it is slightly faster. If you're an experienced PC user and are comfortable with typing cryptic commands with switches and options to start your programs and you know the utility and options that you need to solve your problem (which you surely will by the time you finish this book), you can save a few seconds by bypassing the Norton menu and starting utilities from the command line. For most users, however, the extra few seconds needed to start the Norton menu will be well rewarded by the support and advice that the menu provides.

Starting individual utilities from the command line also allows the utilities to be executed from batch files. Combined with the new commands provided by NU's Batch Enhancer (BE), described in Chapter 28, this permits some truly powerful commands.

NOTE

When launching individual utilities form the command line, you can get a limited amount of help by typing **COMMAND-NAME /?** where "COMMAND-NAME" is the command-line name of the utility of interest.

CUSTOMIZING NORTON UTILITIES

When you first install Norton Utilities, the Norton Install program automatically configures the program based on what it finds from examining your hardware. Except for display type and the programs to be installed in your AUTOEXEC.BAT and CONFIG.SYS files, it doesn't consult you about your preferences. Once the installation is completed, you can examine and change many aspects of the configuration selected by the Install program.

Changing Your Configuration

Once you have installed Norton Utilities, there are three different ways to modify your configuration: You can open the Configuration menu on the top menu bar of the Norton menu (Figure 3.1) and select any of the options listed there; you can select the **Configuration** option in the Command window and then select any of the options listed in the dialog box that appears (Figure 3.2); or you can run the Norton configuration program, NUCONFIG, from the DOS command line, which displays the same Configuration dialog box. These three methods operate in exactly the same way; that is, all three allow you to configure the same aspects of Norton Utilities' operation.

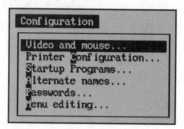

Figure 3.1 Configuration menu

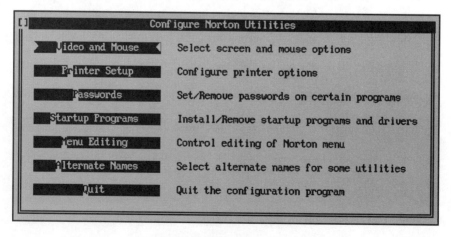

Figure 3.2 Configuration dialog box

Chapter Three: Customizing Norton Utilities ■ 21

NOTE We shall describe the configuration options in the order in which they appear on the Configuration menu (Figure 3.1). The options appear in a different order in the dialog box that appears when you select **Configuration** in the Command window or run Nuconfig from the DOS command line.

CONFIGURATION OPTIONS

Video and Mouse

The Video and Mouse Configuration dialog box (Figure 3.3) allows you to customize the appearance of the Norton Utilities screens and the behavior of your mouse. This dialog box is divided into two major subsections, **Screen Options** and **Mouse Options**. The first item under **Screen Options**, **Screen Colors**, allows you to select (via a list box) from among a number of predefined color settings for laptop (LCD) displays, black-and-white or monochrome (i.e., green or amber) displays, CGA colors (for the original IBM Color Graphics Adapter), two sets of colors for EGA or VGA displays, and a custom color set of your own design.

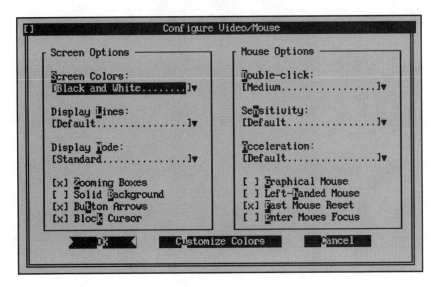

Figure 3.3 *Video & Mouse Configuration dialog box*

Customizing Screen Colors

To customize your screen colors, select the **Customize Colors** button at the bottom of the Video and Mouse Options dialog box. This opens another dialog box (Figure 3.4) with a window on the left listing the various screen features that custom colors can be applied to and a window on the right showing an example of the currently selected feature in the currently selected color(s). To change the color of the currently selected feature, select the **Color** button at the bottom of the dialog box. This pops up yet another dialog box (Figure 3.5) with a window showing the 16 × 16 possible background/foreground color combination available, assuming you have a VGA- or EGA-type display. Move the two pointers to choose your colors from the **Background** and **Foreground** color bars, then select the **OK** button to accept your choice or **Cancel** to exit the dialog box without accepting your changes. To restore the colors that were used when you first installed Norton Utilities, select the **Default** button. There are over 50 different screen items that you can apply different colors to and 16^2 = 256 different color combinations that can be applied, so you could easily while away an afternoon customizing your screen colors. (Isn't it wonderful how computers make us more productive?)

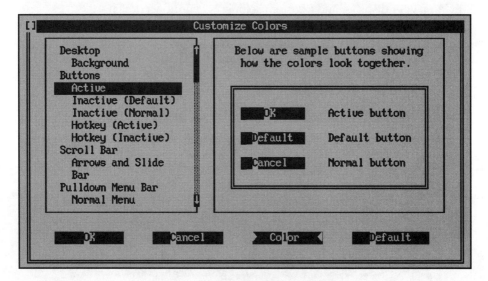

Figure 3.4 Customize Colors dialog box

Chapter Three: Customizing Norton Utilities ■ 23

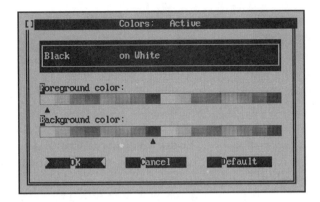

Figure 3.5 Color Selection dialog box

After you have finished customizing your colors, be sure to select the **Save** button when exiting the Customize Colors dialog box. Back in the main Video and Mouse Options dialog box, select **Custom Colors** in the Screen Colors list box, if you have not already done so, to turn on your custom colors.

It is possible to create a great many different color combinations that are wholly or nearly illegible. If you inadvertently select such a combination, you can restore your custom colors to the default colors that were in effect when you first installed the Norton Utilities by selecting the **Default** button in the Customize Colors dialog box. You can also use the Screen Colors list box in the Video and Mouse Options dialog box to select one of the predefined color combinations that is appropriate for your display. In the unlikely event that you mess up your screen colors so thoroughly that you can't find the **Default** button or the Screen Colors list box, you should probably reinstall Norton Utilities from your original diskettes.

NOTE

For even more color variety, you can use the Norton Control Center to create a custom palette of colors (see Chapter 25).

NOTE

The second option on the Screen Options menu, **Display Lines**, allows you to select the number of text lines displayed on the Norton Utilities' screens. The available options are 25, 43, or 50 lines. Whether you can take advantage of the

24 ■ *Power Of...Norton Utilities*

extended 43- or 50-line screens will depend on the type of display adapter installed in your system.

The next item under Screen Options, **Display Mode**, allows you to control the appearance of your Norton Utilities screen. The available options are **Standard**, **Some Graphical Controls**, and **All Graphical Controls**. In the Standard configuration, the screen is displayed in text mode. Text characters such as square brackets and parentheses are used to represent check boxes and scroll bars. The second option, **Some Graphical Controls**, draws square, shaded check boxes. The third option, **All Graphical Controls**, adds graphical scroll bars and other details to dialog boxes. The two graphical control options serve only to make the Norton screens appear a bit more Windowslike, or Maclike, and have no practical effect on the program's operation. Their selection is strictly a matter of personal taste.

Below the Display Mode menu are four check boxes that affect various aspects of the Norton screens. The first check box, **Zooming Boxes**, determines how dialog boxes appear on the screen. If this option is selected (the default), dialog boxes zoom onto the screen; that is, they start small and rapidly grow to full size. If this option is not selected, dialog boxes pop onto the screen at full size. In practice, this makes very little difference, although if you have a very slow display adapter, you might save a few milliseconds by turning this option off. The second check box, **Solid Background**, selects between a solid (the default) or a stippled background for the Norton Utilities screens. This option is strictly a matter of personal preference.

The third check box, **Button Arrows**, affects the appearance of the buttons that appear in dialog boxes and is used to select actions. By default, two inward-pointing arrows appear at the ends of the default or currently selected button, whose action will be executed when you press **Enter**. If you deselect this option, no arrows will appear. Depending on your screen type and color selection, this can make it very hard to determine what button is currently selected, so it is probably best to leave this option on. The fourth and final check box, **Block Cursor**, allows you to substitute a large block cursor for the default underline cursor on the Norton Utilities command line.

Mouse Options

The first three Mouse Options use list boxes to select your double-click speed (slow, medium, or fast), mouse sensitivity (the ratio of mouse movement to mouse pointer movement—default, low, medium, or high), and mouse acceleration rate (default, low, medium, or fast). Below these are four check boxes, for **Graphical Mouse** (the mouse pointer appears as a graphic arrow rather than as a rectangular block), **Left-Handed Mouse** operation, **Fast Mouse Reset** (recommended for use with serial mice and IBM PS/2 and Compaq mouse ports for optimal performance), and **Enter Moves Focus**. This last item doesn't really involve mouse operation. Rather, it changes the keys that move among the items in a dialog box and exit the dialog accepting the current settings. Normally, the **Tab** keys move sequentially through the items in a dialog box and the **Enter** key exits the dialog box with the current settings activated (equivalent to selecting the **OK** button). However, if you check **Enter Moves Focus**, you can move through the items in the dialog box sequentially by pressing **Enter** and accept the current settings by pressing **Ctrl+Enter**. Note, however, that pressing **Enter** when the **OK** button is highlighted also exits the dialog box and accepts the current settings.

NOTE

If you have problems using your mouse in Norton Utilities, try deselecting **Fast Mouse Reset**.

Printer Configuration

The **Printer Configuration** option, new in Norton Utilities 7.0, is used to create configuration files for use with the Line Print utility (see Chapter 27). When you select **Printer Configuration** from the menu, the Configure Printer dialog box (Figure 3.6) appears. It shows a list of the currently available configuration files in a scroll box. A series of six buttons along the right side of the dialog box can be used to create new configuration files or modify existing ones. The six buttons are as follows:

Close—leave the Configure Printer dialog box.

Select—select a default file for use with the LP utility.

Add—create a new configuration.

Edit—modify an existing configuration.

Delete—delete the highlighted configuration.

Rename—rename the highlighted configuration.

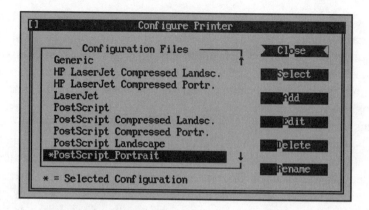

Figure 3.6 *Configure Printer dialog box*

NOTE

The configuration names displayed in the scroll box are *not* DOS file names; they are descriptive names of up to 30 characters. When you create a printer configuration file, it is automatically named CONFIG*n*.NPC, where *n* is the sequential number of the configuration file, in order of creation. The Configuration program stores the descriptive names of the files and their associations with the CONFIG file names in a hidden file called DESCRIPT.ION.

When you select the **Add** button, a dialog box appears in which you type the descriptive name of the configuration. When you type the name and press **Enter** or select **OK**, a new Printer Settings dialog box (Figure 3.7) appears. Most of the options in the dialog box correspond to command-line options used with the Line Print utility. The purpose of Print Configuration is to save a set of options in a file so that you can use Line Print without having to type a long string of options on the command line.

The options are the following:

Compressed Print—use compressed type (132 text columns). The default is uncompressed (80-column) type.

Wrap Lines—automatically wrap text lines at the specified margins (on by default).

Number Lines—print line numbers (useful for program listings; off by default).

Printer Type—one of the following:

Chapter Three: Customizing Norton Utilities ■ 27

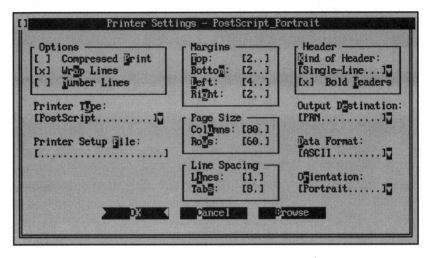

Figure 3.7 *Printer Settings dialog box*

- Teletypewriter
- Formatted teletypewriter
- Epson/IBM dot matrix
- IBM Proprinter
- IBM Quietwriter
- Toshiba dot matrix
- HP LaserJet
- PostScript

Printer Setup File—a file containing a setup string to send to the printer before printing the specified file (not to be confused with the Configuration file; see Chapter 27 for an example). Use the **Browse** button at the bottom of the dialog box to search for printer setup files.

Margins—the top, bottom, left, and right page margins, expressed in characters.

Page Size—expressed in text columns and rows.

Line Spacing—lines (1 = single-spaced, 2 = double-spaced, etc).

Tabs—horizontal tab spacing, expressed in characters.

Header—specify a single-line header (file name, current date and time, page number) or double-line header (the preceding plus file creation date and time.

Bold Header—use bold type (off by default).

Output Destination—a DOS logical device name (i.e., PRN or any LPT or COM port), or a file name.

Data Format—ASCII, EBCDIC, or WordStar.

Orientation—portrait or landscape (available only for LaserJet or PostScript printers).

When you have set all the options to your satisfaction, select **OK** to save your configuration and return to the initial dialog box or select **Cancel** to exit the dialog box without saving your settings, then select **Close** to end printer setup. For a more detailed description of the printer options, consult Chapter 27.

Startup Programs

The Startup Programs dialog box (Figure 3.8) allows you to select from a number of Norton programs and drivers that can be added to your CONFIG.SYS or AUTOEXEC.BAT files and automatically run or installed when you boot up your system.

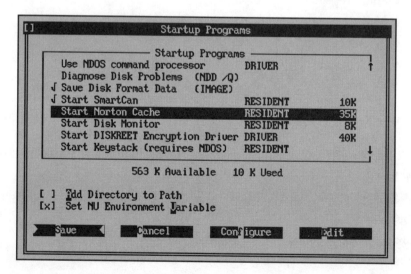

Figure 3.8 *The Startup Programs dialog box*

The available options include the following:

- The NDOS.COM command-line shell—a more powerful replacement for COMMAND.COM.
- The Norton Disk Doctor (NDD) with the /QUICK option—tests the system area of your hard disk.
- The Image utility (IMAGE)—saves a copy of the system area of your hard disk as a file, so that it can be used by the Unformat utility to reconstruct the disk in the event of an accidental format and by the UnErase utility to restore highly fragmented files.
- SmartCan—saves erased files in a hidden directory for easy recovery.
- The Norton Cache (NCACHE2)—a disk-caching program, improves the speed of disk reads and writes.
- The Disk Monitor utility (DISKMON)—protects some or all areas of your disks from unauthorized writes; also provides head parking and "disk light" services.
- The DISKREET.SYS driver—for file encryption.
- The KEYSTACK.SYS driver—used in conjunction with NDOS to store and play back command-line activity.

To select any of these options, move the highlight to the desired command then press the spacebar or double-click the mouse to select it. In many cases, it is possible (and necessary) to configure the programs or drivers selected in this dialog box. If this is the case, the text in the **Configure** button at the bottom of the dialog box will be darkened when the item is highlighted. (For items that don't need configuration, the text in the button is dimmed.)

NOTE We recommend that you consult the chapters describing the various features listed earlier to gain a thorough understanding of how they operate before adding them to your AUTOEXEC.BAT or CONFIG.SYS files. This is especially recommended if you are a new Norton Utilities user.

In addition to adding the programs described earlier to your AUTOEXEC.BAT or CONFIG.SYS file, the Startup Programs dialog box has two check boxes that add your Norton Utilities directory to the DOS PATH statement and create an NU environment variable. A PATH statement is part of the DOS environment. It enables DOS to find and execute programs that aren't in the current directory. Assuming that you have Norton Utilities installed in the \NU directory on drive C (the default), the program will add the line "PATH C:\NU," to your AUTOEXEC.BAT file. If your AUTOEXEC.BAT file already includes a path statement, the NU directory will be added to the path. This allows you to type **NORTON Enter** at the DOS prompt to load the Norton menu regardless of what the current directory is, rather than having to type **C:\NU\NORTON Enter** or **CD\NU Enter**; **NORTON Enter**. An environment variable is an abbreviation for a DOS command that is stored as part of the DOS environment. Again assuming that your Norton Utilities directory is C:\NU, the program adds the line SET NU=C:\NU to your AUTOEXEC.BAT file. Norton Utilities uses this variable to locate initialization and help files for various programs.

NOTE

To see your current PATH and any active environment variables, type SET **Enter** at the DOS prompt.

Editing AUTOEXEC.BAT and CONFIG.SYS Files

After you have selected the options you want, you can view and, if necessary, edit your AUTOEXEC.BAT and CONFIG.SYS files by selecting the **Edit** button at the bottom of the dialog box. A new dialog box displaying your AUTOEXEC.BAT file will pop up (Figure 3.9). You can toggle between your AUTOEXEC.BAT and CONFIG.SYS files by selecting the list box at the top of the dialog box. In the dialog box, move the highlight to a line that you want to move or delete and press the spacebar or double-click the mouse to select it. Then you can either move or delete the selected line, using the appropriate button at the bottom of the dialog box. If you select the **Move** button, the text on the button will change from "Move" to "Drop." Move the line using either the cursor keys or the mouse, then select the button again to drop the line at the new location. If you select the **Delete** button, you will be asked to confirm that you want to delete the line. When you are satisfied with the state of your AUTOEXEC.BAT and CONFIG.SYS files, select the **OK** button. If you want to exit the dialog box without accepting any changes you have made, select the **Cancel** button.

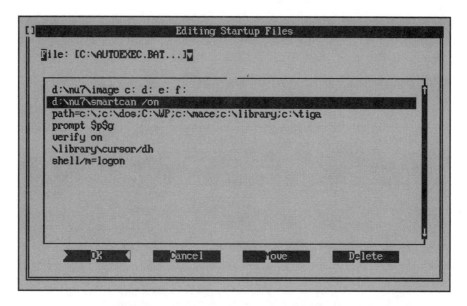

Figure 3.9 Edit AUTOEXEC dialog box

You cannot add new lines to your AUTOEXEC.BAT or CONFIG.SYS files or modify the text or existing lines in the Edit dialog box. To do this, you must use a text editor or a word processor that can load and save ASCII files.

For changes made in your AUTOEXEC.BAT or CONFIG.SYS files to take effect, you must reboot your system.

Alternate Names

The Alternate Names dialog box (Figure 3.10) allows you to change the names of several Norton Utilities programs to shorter forms for quicker command-line loading. The long and short names are listed later. You can select short forms for any of the names by pulling down their respective list boxes, or you can select short forms for all by using the **All Short Names** button at the right side of the dialog box. The Safe Format utility (SFORMAT) is a special case, in that it can be given two other names, SF or FORMAT. The latter should be chosen if you want to replace the DOS FORMAT command with SFORMAT (recommended). In this case, the DOS FORMAT command is renamed XFORMAT.

Table 3.1 Long and Short Names

Function	Long Name	Short Name
Disk Editor	DISKEDIT	DE
File Find	FILEFIND	FF
Safe Format	SFORMAT	SF or FORMAT
System Information	SYSINFO	SI
Disk Duplication	DUPDISK	DD

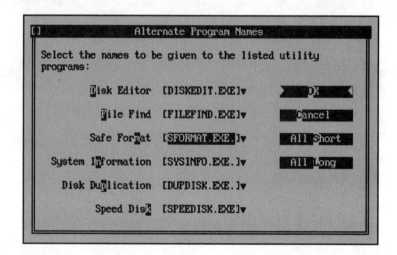

Figure 3.10 Alternate Names dialog box

Passwords

Many of the Norton Utilities can damage or destroy your data, or even render your hard disk unbootable if they are used carelessly or maliciously. The **Passwords** option allows you to use a password to protect these dangerous

Chapter Three: Customizing Norton Utilities ■ 33

tools from unauthorized use. If you share a computer with other, less experienced users, or if you are an MIS manager or systems administrator with responsibility for a number of PCs or a network, you will probably want to take advantage of this feature. The Password dialog box (Figure 3.11) displays all the programs that can be protected. (For the complete list, see later.) Press the spacebar or double-click with the mouse to select the programs that you want to protect, or use the **Protect All** or **Remove All** buttons to select or deselect all the programs, then select the **Set Password** button. (Only one password is selected to control access to whatever group of utilities you have selected.) A dialog box will pop up for you to type your password in. Your password can be up to 15 characters long and can consist of any collection of letters, numbers, and symbols. When you type your password, it will be displayed on the screen as a string of *'s. You will then be asked to type the password a second time for verification. If the second password matches the first, it will be set for all the utilities you selected. If the second password doesn't match your first, a beep will sound and you will be asked to type the password again. Be sure to remember your password, as you won't be able to run the selected utilities or remove password protection without it.

NOTE You want your password to be something easy for you to remember but hard for others to guess. You would not, for example, want to use your name, your spouse's or child's name, your car's license number, or some other piece of publicly available information as a password.

Table 3.2

Password Protectable Programs

Calibrate	Disk Editor
Disk Tools	File Fix
Norton Disk Doctor	Diagnostics
Configuration	Safe Format
Speed Disk	UnErase
Unformat	Wipe Information

34 ■ *Power Of...Norton Utilities*

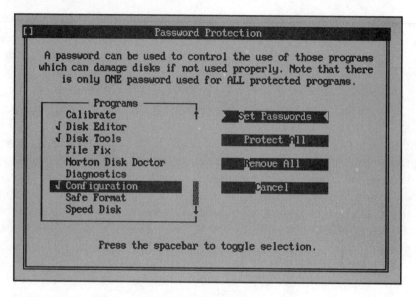

Figure 3.11 Password dialog box

NOTE If you do lose or forget your password, you'll have to reinstall Norton Utilities from the original diskettes in order to regain access to the protected utilities.

Menu Editing

By default, users are able to add or delete items freely from Norton Utilities menus by using the **Add** menu item, **Delete** menu item, and **Edit** menu item options on the Menu menu. This is a powerful feature that enables you to customize the Norton menus to fit your needs, but if you are setting up Norton Utilities for inexperienced users, you might want to remove this feature to keep them out of trouble. You might, for example, want to remove from the menu those utilities that could damage or destroy data in inexperienced hands, then disable menu editing so that they cannot easily be restored.

NOTE Disabling menu editing doesn't hide the disable/enable menu editing option, so if you really want to prevent a user from editing the menu, you must take an additional step. The configuration information for Norton Utilities is stored in a file called NORTON.INI, which resides in your Norton Utilities directory. You can prevent a user from reenabling menu editing, or otherwise modifying the Norton Utilities configuration, by changing the attribute of this file to Read-Only using the Norton File Attribute utility (FA). The syntax for this operation is:

    FA NORTON.INI /R+

We recommend that you consult Chapter 20 for a detailed account of the File Attribute utility before performing this operation. Of course, any person expert enough to do this operation could change the attribute back to read/write and then reenable menu editing, so one must hope that a person with sufficient understanding to do so will behave responsibly.

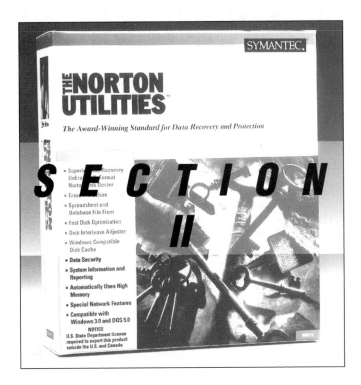

SECTION II

PREVENTING DISK PROBLEMS

A variety of potential problems threaten the integrity of your valuable data. The biggest of these is probably you. In a moment of fatigue or inattention, you may type **ERASE *.*** when you meant **ERASE *.TMP**, or **FORMAT C:** when you meant **FORMAT A:**. Anyone who has never experienced the shock and embarrassment of making such an error is fortunate indeed. Moreover, data can be damaged and destroyed by viruses, software bugs, hardware failures, physical wear and tear on disks, and glitches caused by voltage surges and spikes, brown-outs, and other power problems. Fortunately, with proper precautions, the likelihood of data loss from these causes can be reduced greatly, if not eliminated completely.

38 ■ *Power Of...Norton Utilities*

◆ The SmartCan utility (Chapter 4) protects erased files by keeping copies of them in a special hidden directory for a period of time that you specify. Files protected in this fashion can be recovered with total certainty within the specified time limit.

◆ The Safe Format utility (also in Chapter 4) formats disks so that they can be unformatted easily. It is also much faster than the DOS FORMAT command.

◆ The File Attribute (FA) utility (Chapters 4 and 20) can be used to make your program files and other "permanent" files "read-only," so that they cannot be erased accidentally or overwritten.

◆ The Image utility (Chapter 5) preserves copies of the system area of your hard disk that can be used to restore the disk in the case of an accidental format. The Image files are also used when unerasing highly fragmented files and can be used to make selective repairs on the system area.

◆ The Disk Monitor utility (Chapter 6) can protect all or part of your disk from damage by viruses or bug-ridden software. The Disk Monitor also includes a head-park feature that can help protect your disk from damage resulting from physical impacts.

◆ The Rescue utility (Chapter 7) creates a rescue disk that can be used to boot your system in the event of a hard disk failure and to restore your CMOS setup memory and repair the system area.

Unfortunately, many PC users don't learn the importance of taking precautions such as these until after they've experienced serious data loss. If you take the time to read Chapters 4–7 and use whichever of the techniques apply to your system configuration and work habits, you may save yourself hours of unnecessary work in manually re-creating lost data, plus an unmeasurable amount of stress and anxiety. If you don't, it is likely that, sooner or later, you will learn the hard way that a kilobyte of prevention is worth a megabyte of cure.

A NOTE ON BACKUPS

The most important component of any disk maintenance program is one that is not handled by the Norton Utilities, and hence not discussed in detail in this

Section II: Preventing Disk Problems ■ 39

book: a regular backup program. This cannot be stated too strongly: *If you depend on the data on your hard disk for your livelihood, you must back up your hard disk regularly.* It takes time, it is boring, and it is all too easy to neglect, but regular backups are absolutely essential. Unfortunately, many computer users learn this only after the sad experience of a hard-disk crash or failure. Don't wait for this to happen to you. Your hard disk may give you years of flawless operation, or it may fail catastrophically tomorrow. There's no way to be sure.

Many excellent backup programs are available today. Symantec, publisher of Norton Utilities, also offers Norton Backup, and many other software vendors offer comparable products. If haven't already done so, get one and use it regularly. The least expensive way to back up your hard disk, but also the most time-consuming, is to use floppy disks. Floppies can be used in conjunction with a commercial backup program or with the DOS BACKUP and XCOPY commands. As hard disks grow ever larger, the number of floppies required to back them up grows proportionally. A 100Mb drive requires 70 1.44Mb floppies for backup. A 1Gb drive (1 gigabyte = 1,024 megabytes) would require nearly 700! Backing up to floppies is, therefore, becoming increasingly unwieldy and inconvenient, and a job that is inconvenient is, alas, one that is unlikely to be done regularly. Fortunately, the price of backup devices such as quarter-inch cartridge (QIC) tape drives, magneto-optical drives, and WORM (Write-Once/Read-Many) drives has declined steeply in the last few years, so there is really no excuse *not* to get a dedicated backup device. External drives that attach to the parallel or serial port and do not require a controller card to be plugged into an expansion slot offer an economical solution for the backup of several PCs.

How often should you back up your hard disk? That depends on how much work you do on your computer. Ask yourself how much work you would be willing to re-create from scratch in the event of a hard disk failure and act accordingly.

Protecting Files from Accidental Erasure

There are several ways to use Norton Utilities to protect files from accidental erasure. One method involves using the SmartCan program (called Erase Protect, or EP, on Norton Utilities version 6.x or earlier), which creates a special hidden directory on the disk it is protecting and moves erased files there and maintains them for a period of time that you specify. Another method involves using the File Attribute utility (FA) to set the attributes of selected files to Read-Only, so that they cannot be modified, deleted, or erased at all without first resetting the attribute to Read/Write. These two techniques are best suited to different situations; the SmartCan utility works best with data files (i.e., word processor documents, financial worksheets, database files, and other files that are frequently created and modified and that would therefore be impractical to protect with the Read-Only attribute). The SmartCan program can be easily configured, as described later, to protect files with some extensions while ignoring others. The Read-Only attribute setting is better suited to protecting files that you expect to keep on your hard disk more or less "permanently," and seldom or never modify. Good candidates for this kind of protection include the executable files used by your various application programs (e.g., .COM, .EXE, and .OVL files) and data files that are used as templates by your word processing, desktop publishing, spreadsheet, and database programs. Of course, making a template file Read-Only doesn't preclude your loading the file, modifying it, and saving it under another name.

NOTE Using an erase-protection method doesn't excuse you from doing regular hard-disk backups. Other kinds of disk problems might still damage your erase-protected files. Or your system might be stolen or damaged by a fire, flood, or other disaster. Regular backups are your best protection against all kinds of disk problems.

THE SMARTCAN METHOD

SmartCan is a memory-resident program that watches for commands that erase or delete files and stores those files in a hidden directory that it creates for this purpose. Although, like all the Norton Utilities programs, you can load SmartCan from the Norton menu or from the DOS command line, the most effective way to use the program is to install it in your AUTOEXEC.BAT file, so that it loads automatically whenever you boot up your system. To do this, add the line "SMARTCAN /ON" to your AUTOEXEC.BAT file. You can do this using the **Startup Programs** option on the Norton Utilities Configuration menu.

Configuring SmartCan

When you install SmartCan for the first time, you need to configure the program to specify the drives to protect, the types of files to protect, the amount of time to save protected files, and the like. To do this, select SmartCan from the Norton menu or type **SMARTCAN Enter** at the DOS prompt. This will load the program and display the configuration dialog box in Figure 4.1.

The check box in the upper left-hand corner of the Configure SmartCan dialog box will be checked if you have run the program with the /ON option,

Chapter Four: Protecting Files from Accidental Erasure ■ 43

whether from the Norton menu, the DOS command line, or your AUTOEXEC.BAT file. The three radio buttons allow you to protect all your files from erasure, to select particular classes of files for protection by their extensions, or to select a group of file extensions to *exclude* from protection, with all other types of files being protected. The default setup protects all files except those with the extensions .TMP, .SWP, and .INI, which programs typically use for files that they create for temporary use while the program is running and then automatically delete when the program terminates.

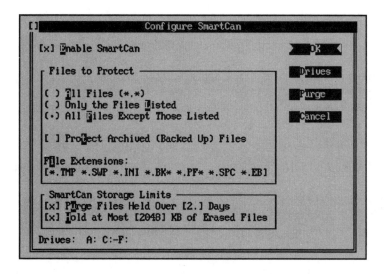

Figure 4.1 SmartCan configuration dialog box

N O T E After you have used SmartCan for a few days, check the Purge dialog box (described later) and you may see a great many saved files that you never knew existed. These will be temporary or swap files created by various applications that do not use the preceding extensions. You should add these file extensions to your exclude list (if you are using this method to specify which files to protect), so that your SmartCan directory is not cluttered with these useless files.

The default SmartCan setup saves erased files for five days or until 2048Kb (2Mb) of disk space is used by the SmartCan directory, whichever comes first. Once either of these limits has been exceeded, SmartCan will begin automatically purging the saved files, beginning with the oldest. The default setup does not protect files that are "archived" (i.e., files that have the archive bit in their attribute byte set). The archive bit is set by commercial backup programs and by the DOS BACKUP and XCOPY commands, so it is assumed that you have back-up copies of any files that have this attribute set. You can, however, change the setting to protect archived files if you wish by checking the box in the Configuration dialog box.

To select the drives to be protected, select the **Drives** button to display the dialog box in Figure 4.2. You can select the drives to be protected individually, by drive letter, or you can select all the drives of a particular class: floppy drives, "local drives" (i.e., hard disks or logical volumes physically present in the system where the installation is taking place), or network drives.

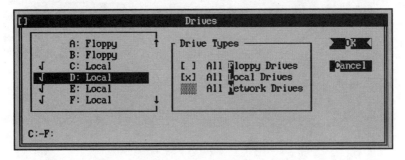

Figure 4.2 *SmartCan drive select dialog box*

NOTE

The network administrator is responsible for setting up and configuring SmartCan on network drives.

NOTE

If you select your floppy drives for protection with SmartCan, the saved files are kept in a hidden directory *on the floppy from which they were deleted.* Thus, before you can recover the lost files, you must find the floppy from which you deleted them (not always an easy task!).

Purging Files

Normally, SmartCan automatically purges files when the specified protection time has elapsed, or when the specified amount of disk space has been filled, and there

Chapter Four: Protecting Files from Accidental Erasure ■ 45

is no need for you to intervene actively in the process. You can, however, manually purge files from the SmartCan directory by opening the SmartCan Configuration dialog box and selecting the **Purge** button. This opens a dialog box that displays a list of files that the program is currently protecting on the selected drive (Figure 4.3). Scroll through the list and tag the files that you want to delete by pressing the spacebar or double-clicking with the mouse. You can also select the **Tag** button and type the names of the files that you want to delete, or a file-spec using the DOS wildcard characters. When all the files you want to delete are tagged, select the **Purge** button to delete them. To leave the Purge dialog box without deleting any files, untag the files or select the **Cancel** button.

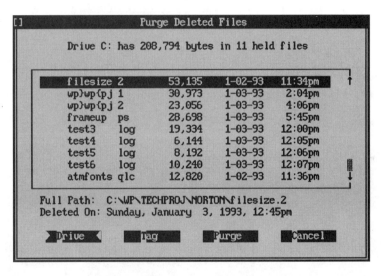

Figure 4.3 SmartCan Purge dialog box

NOTE On network drives the network administrator should be responsible for manually purging files, if it should prove necessary. This should be done during off-hours, because when the SmartCan Purge dialog box is open, SmartCan is *not active*, and any files that are erased during this time *will not be protected*.

SmartCan Command-Line Options

SmartCan accepts the following command-line options:

/STATUS   Reports the current status of the program; A typical status report is shown in Figure 4.4, below.

/ON   Enables SmartCan.

/OFF   Disables SmartCan, and, if possible, removes it from memory (see note).

/UNINSTALL   Same as /OFF.

/SKIPHIGH   Prevents the program from loading into high memory (used in conjunction with /ON).

/CONVERT   Searches for and converts Erase Protect trash cans (use this option the first time you run SmartCan if you have been using the Erase Protect utility from Norton Utilities version 6.x or earlier).

NOTE To be removed from memory by the /OFF or /UNINSTALL options, SmartCan must be the last memory-resident program loaded.

```
SmartCan Status:      Enabled
Drives Protected:     C: (SmartCan contains 430K in 14 files)
                      D: (SmartCan contains 6K in 2 files)
                      E: (SmartCan is empty)
                      F: (SmartCan contains 40K in 9 files)
Files Protected:      All files except those with these extensions
                      TMP, SWP, INI, BK*, PF*, SPC, EBF, DIR
Archive Files:        Not Protected
Files Deleted After:  2 days
```

Figure 4.4 *SmartCan Status Report*

Advantages and Disadvantages of SmartCan

The SmartCan method of file protection involves a trade-off between file security and disk space conservation. The larger the disk space you allow for

Chapter Four: Protecting Files from Accidental Erasure ■ 47

SmartCan's hidden directories and the longer the period that you allow it to save files before it purges them, the safer you'll be from the possibility of accidentally erased files. On the other hand, disk space is not free, and if you're like me, you're always struggling to find enough of it to accommodate your latest project without buying a new hard disk. So how much space to allot and how long to save files before purging them is a judgment call. If you're an experienced user, are well organized and seldom make mistakes, and no one else shares your system, then a day or two might be as long as you'd want to save erased files. On the other hand, if you're a new computer user and you are nervous about accidentally erasing something important, or if you share your system with other, less experienced users, you might prefer to use the default five-day/2Mb setup, or perhaps even more. Some trial and error may be required to determine what types of files are most important to save and how long to save them.

Another concern about SmartCan is that it is a memory-resident program. At 10Kb, SmartCan is relatively small, but if your memory is already stuffed with device drivers and memory-resident programs, an extra 10Kb could be the straw that breaks the camel's back. Moreover, compatibility is *always* an issue where memory-resident programs are concerned. It is impossible to be sure that a given memory-resident program, however carefully written, will give trouble-free operation in every possible PC environment. Another concern is that copying erased files to the hidden directories *takes time*. In particular, it may increase the apparent time of disk operations in some applications, because operations may be taking place that you are not aware of. For example, when you save a file from your word processor, replacing another file of the same name, the program may not simply write a new file beginning at the same starting cluster as the old file and add new clusters if necessary to accommodate the new file. It may first make a backup copy of the old file, then write the new file, and, after the new file has been successfully saved, delete the backup copy. If you haven't configured SmartCan to ignore the backup files, you can add to this process the time it takes for SmartCan to copy the deleted backup file to its hidden directory. In any case, SmartCan at least uses up some processor time in watching for deletions and checking to see whether the deleted files match its specification. If you are using a disk cache, such as the Norton Cache, to speed up disk operations, you may find that using SmartCan sometimes vitiates the time saved in disk writes by using the cache.

48 ■ *Power Of...Norton Utilities*

THE FILE ATTRIBUTE METHOD

The File Attribute method of protecting files has the advantage of being simple to use and relatively permanent; that is, it stays in effect until you (or someone knowledgeable) deliberately changes it.

The File Attribute utility is a command-line utility. It can be run either from the DOS command line or from the Norton menu, but it has no menus, dialog boxes, or full-screen mode. Its operation is controlled by the options you type on the command line, and its action is executed immediately after you press **Enter**. The syntax for setting the Read-Only attribute for a file or group of files using the FA command is as follows:

```
FA [filespec] /R+ [/S]
```

where [filespec] represents the directory, path, and the file or files for which you want to set the Read-Only attribute. The DOS wildcards * and ? can be used in the filespec (the /S switch will be explained later). If no filespec is included, FA works on all files in the current directory. For a full description of the FA utility and its other applications, consult Chapter 20. For example, to set the Read-Only attribute for all of the .EXE files in your C:\WORD directory you would type:

```
FA C:\WORD\*.EXE /R+
```

Perhaps you don't know what all the extensions of the files in the WORD directory are that the program uses. There might be a couple of dozen different files, with nearly as many different extensions, but you know that the files that you *don't* want to protect in this way are your documents, which are subject to frequent modification and deletion (you'll use the SmartCan method to protect them). Assuming that your document files all use the extensions .DOC or .TXT, it's a simple, three-step process to set the attributes of all the files *except* the .DOC and .TXT files to Read-Only:

```
FA C:\WORD\*.* /R+
FA C:\WORD\*.DOC /R-
FA C:\WORD\*.TXT /R-
```

The /S switch allows you to set the attributes for all the files in the subdirectories in one operation. For example, typing

```
FA C:\*.EXE /R+ /S
```

would set the Read-Only attribute for every .EXE file in the root directory and all the subdirectories on drive C. To see what files have the Read-Only attribute set, use the /R switch without the plus sign. For example,

```
FA C:\WORD /R
```

would show all the files in the WORD directory (regardless of their extensions) that have the Read-Only attribute set.

Advantages and Disadvantages of the File Attribute Method

The only real disadvantage to using the file attribute method for protecting files from erasure is that you will eventually want to erase the files you have protected. For example, you may want to replace an old version of an application with a newer release, which entails writing over the old files with the newer versions. This is no problem, provided that you remember that some of the files have the Read-Only attribute set and clear it before trying to install the new files. The syntax for clearing the Read-Only attribute is the same as that for setting it, except that a minus sign is used instead of a plus sign. For example,

```
FA C:\WORD\*.EXE /R-
```

clears the Read-Only attribute for all the .EXE files in the WORD directory. If you forget that you have Read-Only files in a directory and try to install an updated version of a program in that directory, you'll end up with an aborted or botched installation and probably some pretty rude error messages, so if you're going to use this technique, it's a good idea to get in the habit of checking the attributes of the files in a directory *before* doing any installations, mass deletions, and so on.

NOTE Some application programs modify their own .EXE or .COM files to store changes in configuration. Such programs will not work properly if these files have their Read-Only attributes set. It may take some trial and error to discover which files associated with a given application can be safely protected. In general, any file with a date

50 ■ *Power Of...Norton Utilities*

earlier than the date when you first installed the program is probably a safe bet. However, if you do accidentally set the attribute for an inappropriate file, it is easy to clear it again.

OTHER ERASE-PROTECTION METHODS

If you share your computer with others, there is yet another way to prevent *them* from accidentally erasing your files (or examining or modifying them, for that matter). This is to use the DISKREET encryption driver to create an "NDISK," a hidden, password-protected "virtual drive" to store your most important and/or confidential files. Consult Chapter 13 to learn how to use this technique.

Another, more drastic method for protecting files from erasure (or modification) is to use the Disk Monitor utility (DISKMON) to watch in the background for attempts to modify or erase certain files or classes of files. The Disk Monitor is potentially useful for protecting disks from viruses or from buggy programs that attempt to write to areas of the disk that should be left alone (see Chapter 6), but as a general-purpose erase-protect tool, it's probably a bit heavy-handed. If you were to set up DISKMON so that it protected *all* the files on your disks, you would have to give permission for *every* disk write operation. Most people want fast performance from their computers, including fast disk operations. Having to confirm every disk write would be akin to running your disk with training wheels and would probably be too annoying for anyone to tolerate for very long. In addition, DISKMON can only ask your permission to allow a disk write operation when the program you are running is in character mode. It cannot ask in graphics mode programs, such as Windows and all Windows-specific applications. Its solution to this problem is to beep and disallow *all* disk writes when the screen is in graphics mode. This is obviously an impractical solution, so you would have to disable DISKMON before running Windows or other graphics mode programs. Given the increasing popularity of Windows and other GUI's, DISKMON's utility for erase-protection purposes is obviously limited. SmartCan is probably a better choice for erase-protecting data files in most situations.

Chapter Four: Protecting Files from Accidental Erasure ■ 51

SUMMARY

The Norton Utilities offers a number of different methods for protecting files from accidental erasure. The SmartCan program is a good way to protect work files that are frequently modified or deleted. Setting the Read-Only attribute with the File Attribute utility is a good way to protect program files that you intend to keep more or less permanently on a disk. The Diskreet encryption program can protect important files from accidental erasure by other users by hiding them in a password-protected directory. The Disk Monitor utility can be used to protect files from erasure or modification but is not very practical for this purpose, although it has other uses.

RECOMMENDATIONS

If you're an experienced PC user and seldom or never erase files by mistake, the precautions described in this chapter may be overkill and you may prefer to conserve memory and disk space by not using SmartCan. If you're a novice or if you share your system with other, less experienced users and you can spare the memory and disk space, you may find that your peace of mind is increased by installing SmartCan in your AUTOEXEC.BAT file and using it to protect at least all your hard disks/partitions. Setting the attributes of all your program files to Read-Only, although not absolutely necessary, consumes no memory or additional disk space, takes only seconds, and is just as easily reversed if you change your mind, so it couldn't hurt.

THE NORTON UTILITIES™

5

PROTECTING DISKS FROM ACCIDENTAL FORMATTING

The accidental formatting of a hard disk is rare, like a nuclear meltdown, a tidal wave, or an 8.0 earthquake. However, like these other disasters, it has such drastic consequences (the potential loss of *all* your programs and data) that it is well worth taking whatever steps are feasible to deal with the results. The accidental formatting of a floppy disk, although more common and less catastrophic, is also worth preventing, if possible. Fortunately, Norton Utilities provides a simple method to protect your disks so that they can be easily restored in the unlikely event that an accidental format does occur.

Two different Norton Utilities are useful in protecting disks from accidental formatting: Image and Safe Format (SFORMAT). Using the Image utility daily will save an up-to-date copy of your system area in a file that the Norton UnFormat utility can use to restore your disk to its former condition. Using Image regularly will also help the Norton UnErase utility to recover severely fragmented files. The other step you should take to avoid accidental formats and make all formats, accidental and intentional, recoverable, is to delete or rename

54 ■ *Power Of...Norton Utilities*

the DOS Format command (FORMAT.COM) and use only the Norton Safe Format utility (SFORMAT) for all your formatting. This is especially important for systems using earlier DOS versions. (In DOS 3.1 and earlier, if you type **FORMAT Enter** without specifying a drive, the program will format the current drive without asking for confirmation, even if the current drive is a hard disk.)

What Does a Format Do, and How Can It Be Undone?

Formatting a disk is the process of preparing the disk for use. A formatted disk has two main areas: the system area and the data area. The system area contains the information DOS uses to keep track of where files are stored. The data area is where your programs, files, and data reside.

There are two levels of formatting, low-level (also called hard or physical) formatting and high-level (or logical) formatting. Low-level formatting creates the physical layout of the sectors on the disk. High-level, or logical, formatting creates the system area used by DOS.

Low-level formatting destroys all data on a disk, including the system area. High-level formatting merely resets the information in the system area. It leaves all the data in place, but by removing all the reference information for the data, it makes it impossible for DOS to find. On hard disks, low-level formatting is normally performed at the factory. The DOS FORMAT command and Norton Safe Format perform only high-level formatting on hard disks. The DOS FOR-MAT command performs both low-level and high-level formatting on floppy disks. Norton Safe Format can perform both formats or a high-level format alone when reformatting a floppy disk that was previously formatted.

The key to protecting a disk from accidental formatting is to avoid perform-ing a low-level format and to keep a copy of the system area elsewhere on the disk, where an appropriate program (such as the Norton UnFormat utility) can find and restore it. Since the data on a disk that has received only a high-level format have not been altered or erased, it is only necessary to restore the system area to restore the whole disk to its previous condition. Both the Norton Image and the Norton Safe Format utilities create a copy of the DOS system area that the UnFormat utility can use to restore the system area. Safe Format also makes every effort to prevent you from low-level formatting a floppy disk that may contain useful files (or from formatting a hard disk at all).

Chapter Five: Protecting Disks from Accidental Formatting ■ **55**

USING IMAGE

How Image Works

Image protects disks by taking a "snapshot" of the system area (boot record, file allocation tables [FATs], and root directory) and saving it to a file called IMAGE.DAT in the root directory. (IMAGE.DAT must be stored in the root directory to be effective.) Image also keeps an index file, IMAGE.IDX, with an entry in the root directory. This file is stored as a hidden file in the last (or end) cluster of the disk. The IMAGE.IDX file is located in the last cluster of the disk because the UnFormat operation begins working at the end of the disk.

Running Image Daily

For it to be of benefit, you must run Image regularly, preferably at least once a day, so that you will always have a current copy of the system area available in the event of an accident. The easiest way to do this is to add the Image command to your AUTOEXEC.BAT file so that it will be run automatically whenever you boot up your system. Add the following line to your AUTOEXEC.BAT file:

```
IMAGE [drives]
```

where [drives] are the drive letters of whichever drives you want to protect, separated by spaces. For example, if you have a hard disk with three logical drives, C, D, and E, you would add the line:

```
IMAGE C: D: E:
```

When it is run, Image responds by indicating that it is updating the IMAGE.DAT file; it then tells you that it has finished doing so, for each of the specified drives. If you run Image without specifying a drive, it will work on the current drive only. (The preceding example assumes that you have added your Norton Utilities directory to your DOS PATH statement; if not, you would have to include the path in the command—e.g., C:\NORTON\IMAGE.)

You can easily add Image to your AUTOEXEC.BAT by running the Configure program from the Norton menu and selecting **Startup Programs**.

Tag the Image utility in the Startup dialog box, and use the **Configure** button to select the drives you want to protect.

NOTE You can only protect hard disks and/or disk partitions using Image in your AUTOEXEC.BAT file. If you want to protect a floppy disk, you must run Image from the command line or the Norton menu.

Network Usage

You can use the IMAGE.DAT file on a network, but it can only protect the drives in your system; it cannot protect network drives external to your system.

Command-Line Options

Normally when you run Image and a previous copy of IMAGE.DAT exists, the old version will be renamed IMAGE.BAK. You can prevent this by running Image with the /NOBACK switch. However, since Image is quite fast and renaming the old file does not add appreciable time to its operation, there seems to be no obvious reason for doing so. You can also prevent Image from displaying its messages by using the /OUT command-line switch.

NOTE The IMAGE.DAT file created by Norton Utilities 7.0 Image command is compatible with the Norton Utilities 4.5 FRECOVER.DAT file. All the Norton Utilities 7.0 programs can use either the IMAGE.DAT or FRECOVER.DAT files. When you run Image, it renames the FRECOVER.DAT file to IMAGE.DAT.

Running Image from the DOS Prompt

If you are doing a lot of work on your computer, resulting in the creation of many new files, one run of Image at the beginning of the day may not give you sufficient protection, so you may want to run Image again at the end of the day before you turn off your system, or when you take a break in the course of the workday. You can run Image either from the Norton menu or from the DOS command line. In either case, the command-line syntax and options are the same as those given earlier for the AUTOEXEC.BAT file.

NOTE With version 5.0, DOS has finally caught up with the Norton Utilities where format recovery is concerned. DOS 5.0 has a safe format command, a facility for saving the system area (MIRROR), and an unformat utility.

NOTE You should run Image before loading Windows or DESQview. If you run it from your AUTOEXEC.BAT file, you should have no problems.

USING SAFE FORMAT

The Norton Safe Format utility (SFORMAT) performs three different types of formats on floppy or hard disks: Safe, Quick, and DOS. Both the Safe and the Quick formats analyze the disk to be formatted and warn you about any files present before proceeding with the format. In addition, both can optionally save the system area in an IMAGE.DAT file to allow unformatting. The DOS format option performs both low-level and high-level formatting on floppies, as does the DOS FORMAT command. In so doing, it destroys *all* data on the disk, so that it cannot be recovered. The DOS option *must* be used when a disk is formatted for the first time; the Safe and Quick options can only be used to reformat a disk that has previously been DOS formatted.

Format Options

Safe Format

The Safe Format option uses a Norton formatting algorithm to do the format. It is considerably faster than the DOS FORMAT command because it doesn't erase all the data on the disk. It saves the system area information to an IMAGE.DAT file (if you select the **Save IMAGE Info** option). This file is created as a Read-Only file, so it cannot be deleted. The IMAGE.DAT file is used to recover data in case of accidental formatting. The Safe option can only be used to reformat disks that have previously been low-level formatted with the DOS FORMAT command or with Safe Format's DOS option.

Quick Format

The Quick Format option is a good deal faster than even the Safe option. It places a new system area on the disk but does not reset the tracks and sectors. It also saves the system information to an IMAGE.DAT file (if you have chosen the **Save IMAGE Info** option). This option is useful when you want to remove a large directory tree quickly from a hard disk. The Safe option can only be used to reformat disks that have previously been low-level formatted with the DOS FORMAT command or with Safe Format's DOS option.

DOS Format

The DOS Format option is similar to the DOS FORMAT command. It completely erases all data on the disk. This data cannot be recovered. To establish the structure of tracks and sectors, the DOS Format option must be used when a new disk is being formatted for the first time. It should probably be used *only* to format new disks, or when you deliberately want to destroy the files on a disk for security purposes (an even better tool for this purpose is the Norton WipeInfo utility—see Chapter 14).

Renaming Safe Format

To avoid accidentally running the DOS FORMAT command, it is recommended that you rename Safe Format to "FORMAT" and rename the DOS FORMAT command to "XFORMAT." This can be done using the **Alternate Names** option on the Norton Configuration menu. When you change the name of SFORMAT to "FORMAT," the program automatically finds and renames the DOS FORMAT command to "XFORMAT."

Running Safe Format

You can run the Safe Format program from the Norton menu or from the DOS prompt.

When you start the program, the Safe Format dialog box is displayed, as shown in Figure 5.1.

Chapter Five: Protecting Disks from Accidental Formatting ■ 59

Figure 5.1 Safe Format main dialog box

NOTE

If you start Safe Format under Windows or DESQview, a prompt box appears warning you that multitasking environments keep files open and make frequent disk writes and that running Safe Format in such an environment may cause problems. However, you can use Safe Format to format floppy disks under these environments without any likelihood of such problems occurring. In the unlikely event that you want to reformat your hard disk, you should certainly exit any multitasking environment and reboot your system without any unnecessary drivers or TSRs installed before proceeding. (Anyone who wants to reformat their hard disk in the background while running Windows should probably seek professional counseling at once.)

Formatting a Floppy Disk

The following steps outline the procedure for formatting a floppy disk with Safe Format. (This process is much quicker to perform than to read about.)

1. Insert the disk you want to format into the appropriate drive.

2. Choose the drive where you have placed the disk for formatting in the Drive list box.

NOTE

Initially, only floppy drives are available for formatting. This is done purposely to prevent you from accidentally reformatting a hard disk. If you are sure you want to include hard disks in the choices, you can do so by selecting **Allow Hard Disk Formatting** on the Configure menu (see later). It is best not to do this until you actually need to format a hard disk.

60 ■ *Power Of...Norton Utilities*

3. Use the Size list box to specify the capacity of the diskette that you want to format. The type of floppy disk drives in your computer is automatically checked by Safe Format (although you should verify the settings). Safe Format configures itself to format the highest capacity of each drive, but you can change the setting if you wish to format a disk with a lower capacity. Use the Size list box (Figure 5.2) to change the settings if you wish to do this. The list box will display all the available formats for the type of drive selected. For example, if you have a 5-1/4" 1.2Mb drive, Safe Format by default will format disks in that drive to 1.2Mb, but you can use the list box to select any of the other allowed DOS formats for a 5-1/4" disk, from 160Kb single-sided through 360Kb double-sided.

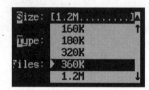

Figure 5.2 *Drive size list box*

NOTE

You cannot use the **Size** option to change the size of a hard disk partition. You must use the DOS command FDISK to do that. The **Size** option applies only to floppy drives.

4. Select the Format Type: **Safe**, **Quick**, or **DOS**.

NOTE

For a new, previously unformatted disk, you must choose DOS formatting. When you reformat a disk at a different capacity than that for which it was formatted previously, you cannot use the **Quick Format** option.

5. Specify whether or not you want to place the system files on the disk. The options are **None**, **Put on Disk**, and **Leave Space**. **None** does not put the system files on the disk (the disk is not made bootable). **Put on Disk** puts the two DOS hidden system files (IBMBIO.COM and IBMDOS.COM or MSDOS.SYS and IO.SYS) and COMMAND.COM on the disk (the disk is bootable). **Leave Space** leaves space in the appropriate location for the system files, which can be added later with the DOS SYS command or Norton Disk Tools.

Chapter Five: Protecting Disks from Accidental Formatting ■ 61

6. Specify whether you want to **Save Image Info**. This is on by default if you have selected the Safe option in step 6. It cannot be selected if you have chosen the **DOS Format** option.

NOTE

You cannot save Image info if you are reformatting a disk at a different capacity.

7. Select the **Format** button to begin the format process. The sequence of screens displayed depends on the **Format Type**, **System Files**, and **Save Image Info** selections you have made.

Safe or Quick format type: If you are using one of these format modes, the disk contents will be analyzed. The next screen you see will resemble the one in Figure 5.3.

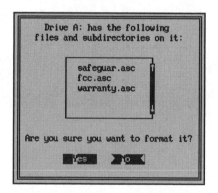

Figure 5.3 *Prompt box showing files on disk to be formatted*

Selecting **Yes** starts the formatting process, and the screen shown in Figure 5.4 will be displayed.

DOS format: When you are performing a DOS Format, you see the warning screen shown in Figure 5.5.

NOTE

Be careful when pressing **Enter** on this screen. The **Yes** button is automatically selected (notice the arrowheads on either side of it). If you press **Enter** without moving the highlight, the formatting will begin and your data will be lost.

62 ■ *Power Of...Norton Utilities*

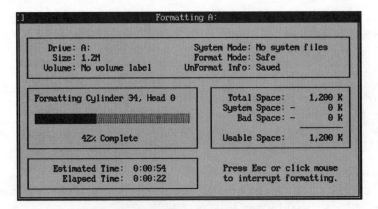

Figure 5.4 Formatting progress dialog box

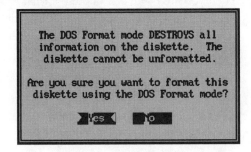

Figure 5.5 DOS format warning screen

Selecting **Yes** begins the formatting process and the screen shown in Figure 5.4 is displayed.

NOTE If you accidentally format a disk using either Safe Format or Quick Format, you can recover the data with UnFormat. It is important to do this as soon as possible so that new data will not overwrite the current data.

Configuring Safe Format

Select the **Configure** button or press **Alt+C** to access Safe Format's Configuration dialog box. The Configuration menu contains three options, as shown in Figure 5.6.

Chapter Five: Protecting Disks from Accidental Formatting ■ 63

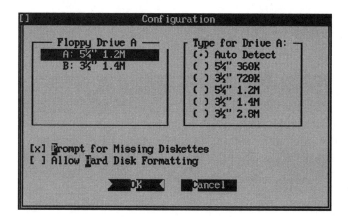

Figure 5.6 Configuration dialog box

Floppy Drives

The two boxes that occupy most of the upper portion of the Configuration dialog box show the floppy drives installed in your system and their maximum formatting capacities. When you first install Norton Utilities, the program detects what kind of floppy drives you have installed, and Safe Format uses this information. Hence, the **Auto Detect** radio button will generally be checked. If Safe Format has correctly identified your drives, there is no need to change the selections; if you want to use a drive to format a disk at a lower capacity, use the Size list box in Safe Format's main dialog box. If Safe Format has misidentified your drive(s), highlight the drive and select the radio button for the appropriate drive size.

Hard Disk Formatting

Normally, Safe Format allows you to format only floppy disks. Selecting this option allows you to format hard disks as well. If you are certain you want to do this, check **Allow Hard Disk Formatting**. If you choose **Allow Hard Disk Formatting** the drive list on the main screen will include all your disk drives (hard disks and floppy disks).

Prompt for Missing Diskettes

The **Prompt for Missing Diskettes** check box is intended to be used with some laptop computers that do not allow Safe Format to detect an unformat-

64 ■ *Power Of...Norton Utilities*

ted floppy disk in the drive. If you have this problem with your laptop, check this option.

Running Safe Format from the DOS Prompt

All the options of the Safe Format program described earlier can also be accessed from the DOS prompt. To run Safe Format from the DOS prompt the syntax is:

```
SFORMAT [drive:] [options]
```

where [drive:] represents the drive letter of the disk to be formatted.

Options

The following options are available:

/A	Automatic mode. The program does not pause during operation and returns to DOS when done. This is useful for batch files.
/S	Copy system files on the disk you are formatting (makes the disk bootable).
/B	Leave room for system files on the disk.
/V:label	Place a volume label on the disk. The label can be up to 11 characters long.
/1	Format a single-sided disk (not used in current PCs).
/4	Format a 360K diskette in a 1.2Mb drive.
/8	Format eight sectors per track.
/N:*n*	Number of sectors per track (*n* can be 8, 9, 15, or 18).
/T:*n*	Number of tracks (*n* = 40 or 80).
/F:size	Disk size in kilobytes (e.g., /720 will format a 720K diskette in a 1.44Mb 3.5" drive).
/Q	Specifies Quick format (reinitialize the system area only).
/D	Specifies DOS format (same as using the DOS FORMAT command—destroys all data on the disk).
/U	Unconditional format (same as DOS format).

To view a list of the available options at the DOS prompt, type **SFORMAT /?**

NOTE

This seems like a large and confusing list of options, but there are several that you will probably never need to use. Many of these options are apparently included only to maintain compatibility with the DOS FORMAT command. For example, you never need to specify the number of tracks or sectors (/N and /T); specify the size, if it is different from the maximum capacity of the drive, and SFORMAT will do the rest. Moreover, it is not likely that you would ever want to use the /1 or /8 options, which format 5.25" floppies with obsolete formats that were used under DOS 1.X.

SUMMARY

If you haven't taken appropriate precautions, an accidental format of a disk can destroy all your data. Two Norton programs, Image and Safe Format, help to prevent data loss from accidental formats. Image takes a "snapshot" of the system area for the drive(s) you specify and stores it in a Read-Only file called IMAGE.DAT. Safe Format can also save an Image file when reformatting a disk and warns you about any existing files on the disk before proceeding with the format. In addition, it's much faster than the DOS FORMAT command.

RECOMMENDATIONS

Install Image in your AUTOEXEC.BAT file and configure it to save the system areas of all of your hard disks or logical disks (partitions). Delete or rename the DOS FORMAT command and use Safe Format for all your formatting. Leave the **Allow Hard Disk Formatting** option in the Safe Format configuration turned off until and unless you actually need to format a hard disk.

6

DISK PROTECTION

In addition to accidental erasures and accidental formats, other forces threaten the safety and integrity of the data on your disks. One that has received a lot of attention in the press in recent years is computer viruses. Another, less sinister but probably more common problem is head crashes—physical damage to the disk surface caused by the disk head striking the platter. Although it cannot absolutely prevent either of these problems, the Norton Disk Monitor (DISKMON) can at least decrease their probability of occurring.

VIRUSES: THREAT OR MENACE?

One hears a lot about computer viruses in the media these days, but as with stories about pit bull attacks and car jackings, it is difficult to judge the true magnitude of the problem. I personally have never suffered from a computer virus attack (knock on silicon), nor have any of my acquaintances. I am inclined to suspect that the problem is not nearly as severe as sensationalistic reporting and the press releases of antivirus software companies would lead you to believe. Nevertheless, I believe that viruses exist and that some have the potential to damage your disks. Should you be worried about virus infections? Should you take precautions to protect your disks? The answer, as to so many questions, is, "It depends."

If you use only shrink-wrapped software, never swap disks with other users, and your system is never connected to the outside world via on-line services or networks, then the chances of your system being contaminated by a virus are near zero. If your only disk swapping involves data files from customers and colleagues, then you're still reasonably safe. To infest your system, a virus must be in a file containing executable code. A virus could sit in a data file (a word processor document, a database file, a graphic image, or whatever) for years, but it would never have the opportunity to take control of the system and do its dirty work. (An important exception is a boot-sector virus on a floppy disk, as described in the note later.) If you limit your BBS contacts to well-known and well-managed commercial on-line services, your chances of escaping infection are still good, as these services are normally quite careful about inspecting up-loaded programs to be sure that they're clean before allowing subscribers to download them. (Imagine what would happen to the business of one of these commercial services if it got around that they had infected thousands of customers with a damaging virus.) Where you've got to be careful is with small, fly-by-night bulletin boards featuring conversations among hacker types and offering cracked versions of copy-protected programs for downloading. Anyone who downloads program files from one of these dubious sources is tempting fate. Also, one would do well to take care with software from loosely structured user groups or swap meets. In short, if you don't know where a program comes from, be careful. What about the office network as a possible source of infection? Again, it depends on the kind of security precautions your network administrator has taken and whether your colleagues take sensible precautions with the programs they introduce into the network through their individual systems. Certainly, any company that relies on a network ought to have sensible policies to avoid contamination by viruses.

NOTE

Boot-sector viruses: I mentioned earlier that if you only swap disks with data files, your system is unlikely to be infected through this route. The exception to this rule involves viruses that reside in the boot record. This is the first sector that is read off a disk that is being used to boot the system, and it includes the code that instructs the system to find and load the other files that make up most of DOS and complete the booting process. If you're like 99% of present-day PC users, you boot your system from a hard disk and seldom or never use a floppy disk for booting. However, on one occasion or another, you've probably left a floppy disk in your A drive, left the drive door closed when booting your system, and been rewarded with the message "Non-system Disk or Disk Error, Replace Diskette and Strike Any Key When Ready." In other words, the system assumed that, because there was a disk in the A drive and the door was closed, you wanted to boot from drive A, but the disk in drive A was not a bootable disk.

So what? You open the drive door, press a key, and the system goes on and boots from the hard disk and you're back to business as usual, right? Well, you are unless the floppy disk in the A drive had a virus hidden in its boot record. (All disks, hard or floppy, have boot records, regardless of whether they are bootable. See Chapter 23 for more information on disk data structures.) In that case, what may have happened is that the computer loaded the infected boot record, which took over the system, copied itself to the boot record of your hard disk, and then called the BIOS routine that displayed the "Non-system Disk ..." message to keep you in the dark about its activities. The Norton Disk Monitor cannot prevent this operation because it is loaded (typically) from your AUTOEXEC.BAT file, which does not happen until long after the boot code is executed. Fortunately, it's simple to prevent this problem. Just make a habit of keeping the door of your A drive open, or if it's a 3.5" drive, of keeping the drive empty, when you're not performing an operation on a disk in the drive, and double-check to be sure that the drive is empty before you power up the system. If you never boot the system with a floppy disk in the A drive, the problem can't occur.

USING THE DISK MONITOR TO CONTROL DISK WRITES

If you have decided that there is some likelihood that you may be exposed to viruses, or just to help maintain your peace of mind, you can greatly diminish the likelihood of a virus damaging your disks by using the Norton Disk Monitor's Disk Protection feature to control disk operations.

70 ■ *Power Of...Norton Utilities*

How Disk Protection Works

The Disk Protection feature of the Disk Monitor uses a memory-resident program (TSR) that watches in the background for disk writes to areas of the disk that you have specified. When a program attempts to write to one of these areas, Disk Monitor pops up a message asking whether you want to allow the write operation. If you are doing something that obviously requires a disk write, such as saving a file in an application, you would allow the write to go ahead, but if you were suspicious or uncertain about the write operation, you could prevent it. From a virus protection point of view, the most important aspect of the Disk Monitor is its ability to protect the system area of the disk, which contains the File Allocation Tables (FATs), boot record, and partition table. Viruses often do their damage by altering these areas.

Running Disk Monitor Automatically

Since if you want disk protection at all, you presumably want it at all times, you will probably want to add the Disk Monitor to your AUTOEXEC.BAT so that it is installed whenever you boot up your system. This can be done easily using the **Startup Programs** option on the Norton Configuration menu. When you check Disk Monitor in the Startup programs dialog box, another dialog box pops and asks whether you want Disk Monitor's Disk Protection or Disk Light feature (described later) installed. (The third feature of Disk Monitor, disk head parking, is not available in this dialog box and should not be installed in your AUTOEXEC.BAT file.) Check the appropriate box, and the line DISKMON /PROTECT+ will be added to your AUTOEXEC.BAT file. However, this procedure *does not* fully configure Disk Monitor. To do this you must run the program from the command line or the Norton menu and follow the procedure described later.

Configuring the Disk Monitor

To configure disk protection, select Disk Monitor from the Norton menu or type DISKMON without options at the DOS prompt. The dialog box in Figure 6.1 will appear. Select the **Disk Protection** button to open the Disk Protection dialog box in Figure 6.2. The Disk Monitor offers four levels of file protection.

Chapter Six: Disk Protection ■ 71

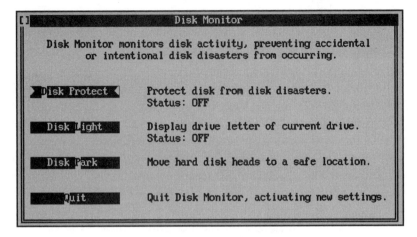

Figure 6.1 Disk Monitor main dialog box

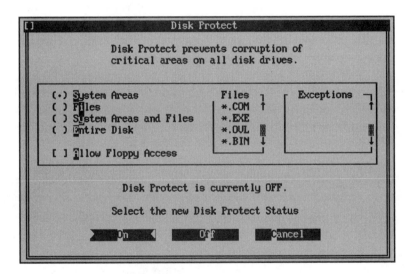

Figure 6.2 Disk Protect dialog box

1. *System Area:* protects the Partition Table, Boot Record, and both copies of the FAT (File Allocation Table). When this option is on, none of these areas can be modified. Even the Norton Disk Editor cannot write to these areas without your permission. This prevents damage from viruses or from a buggy

program that attempts to write to the wrong areas. In addition, protecting the system area prevents the accidental deletion of the system files.

2. *Files:* this option blocks all programs from writing to the files you have designated. These protected files cannot be deleted or changed in any way without your permission. You select groups of files for protection by listing their extensions in the Files box. The default setting is to protect all .COM, .EXE, .OVL, .BIN, and .SYS files. This is a good starting place, as it includes most of the types of files that include executable code. (Remember that a virus must infest an executable file to get control of the system.) You can alter the default list as needed and add other extensions. You can have up to nine extensions in the list. You can also list specific files that you want to except from protection. This may be necessary because some programs modify their own executable files while running in order to store updated configuration information. These programs may not operate properly if not allowed to perform these write operations, and you may find it unnecessarily annoying to have to give permission for every such write operation. You can add up to 20 files to the Exceptions box. Exceptions must be specific complete file names (i.e., you cannot use wild-card characters in the Exceptions box).

NOTE

Since only files are selected for protection with the Files option, no directories or unused clusters are protected. This means you can copy files or add new files to the disk without permission.

3. *Systems Areas and Files:* protects both the system area and designated files. The procedure for selecting files for protection is the same as that described earlier.

4. *Entire Disk:* allows no alterations to any portion of the disk without your permission. All files, the systems area, and unused clusters are protected. You cannot specify any file as an exception to this level of protection and you cannot add new files to the disk.

5. *Allow Floppy Access:* overrides the selected protection option in one specific instance: when you are formatting a floppy disk. You can format a floppy disk using any format program and the process will not be interrupted. If you do not select this option, you will be interrupted often with requests for permission to proceed. The exact number of interruptions depends on the size of the floppy disk and what protection option is in effect.

Chapter Six: Disk Protection ■ 73

After you have selected the level of protection you want and entered any file extensions or exceptions to the boxes, select **ON**. You will be returned to the main Disk Monitor dialog box. To turn off the options, return to the Disk Protect dialog box and select **OFF**. Even if you turn off protection DISKMON saves your configuration (protection level, file extensions, and exceptions) and will use them the next time you turn protection on.

The first time you use Disk Monitor, it creates a file called DM.INI, containing all the disk protection choices you have selected. This file is stored in the directory where the DISKMON.EXE file is stored. If you delete the DM.INI file from the directory, there is no immediate effect, but the next time you run the program, all the settings will be reset (all protection off). You will then have to choose new settings.

NOTE

The disk protection level you have selected applies to all the disks in your system. You cannot specify different protection levels for different disks.

Working with Disk Protection

When Disk Monitor is installed with some level of protection turned on, the program keeps track of all attempts to write to any disks. It notifies you if an attempt is made to write to a protected item. If you are in the text mode, you will see a dialog box resembling the following example:

```
Disk Monitor
A write operation was attempted on a protected file.
Do you wish to allow this operation?
Yes          No          Disable Protection
```

Press **Y** if you want to approve the write. You can avoid having to answer this question frequently by pressing **D**. This disables the protection for the duration of the procedure. You can make these choices even if you only hear the beep and do not see the dialog box. Remember to turn the protection back on when you finish.

If a protected write is attempted while you are in a graphics mode (working in Windows, for example), Disk Monitor automatically rejects the write. The program that was attempting to write will probably issue a "write protect" or "access denied" message. This is something of a problem if you do much of your work in Windows, or in other graphics-oriented programs. You can select system area protection only, which will give you protection against the worst effects of many viruses, or you can, through trial and error, develop a list of file types and extensions that allow you to get your work done while protecting files that are not normally written to.

Windows and other bitmapped, multitasking environments present a particular problem because they create temporary files for use in managing the environment and write to these files frequently and unpredictably. When you load the Disk Monitor with Windows or DESQview installed, the program displays a dialog box warning you of this situation.

NOTE

To find out which of your programs create temporary files and what extensions they use, install SmartCan in your AUTOEXEC.BAT file (see Chapter 4) with no files excepted from protection. After going about your normal work routine for a few days, check the list of files SmartCan has saved. You may be amazed by the variety of files that are created and erased by your programs without your ever knowing they existed. Be sure none of these extensions are included in the list of files you want the Disk Monitor to protect.

You may want to turn off disk protection before running graphics programs that need to write to disks (such as Windows, or any desktop publishing, presentation graphics, draw, paint, or CAD program). You can simplify this by creating a batch file that turns off the Disk Monitor, starts your graphics program, and reactivates your selected protection when the program is finished. To create such a batch file, emulate the following example, substituting the command-line name of the program you wish to run:

```
DISKMON /PROTECT-
PROGNAME    (substitute the command to start the particular program)
DISKMON /PROTECT+
```

Network Usage

The Disk Monitor's disk protection works on individual PCs and on networks (with some limitations). It protects files on either local or network drives, but it cannot protect the system area of a network server.

Hard-Disk Head Parking

Hard-disk heads are not intended to touch the disk surface; normally they ride on a thin cushion of air just 0.3–0.6 microns above the surface of the spinning disk. However, when you turn off your system the heads do come to rest on the disk surface. Many hard disks have a mechanism that automatically moves the heads over a safe area, where no data is stored whenever the system is turned off. These disks are said to be self-parking. Other hard disks, particularly older models, do not have this feature. If you have such a disk, you should use a disk-parking program to move the heads to a safe location and prevent potential damage to the disk surface. The Disk Park function of the Norton Disk Monitor performs this function.

Using the Disk Monitor's Park Feature

Unlike the Disk Protection feature you should not run the Disk Park feature from you AUTOEXEC.BAT file—you want to park the heads when you turn your computer *off*, not when you turn it on. Parking the heads should be the last thing you do before switching off power. This is one of the situations where it is most convenient to use the command line—just type DISKMON /PARK at the prompt to park the heads. The program responds with a message indicating that the heads of all drives have been parked and advises you to turn off your system, as shown in Figure 6.3. You should do so at once without running any other programs, as any operation that involved disk access would move the heads back to the active surface of the disk. If you change your mind and want to go on computing, you don't have to do anything special to unpark the heads; any operation involving disk access will do this.

If you prefer, you can also park the disk heads by loading the Disk Monitor, either from the command line or from the Norton menu, and selecting the **Park** button in the dialog box. when you do this the program will behave exactly as described earlier.

The Disk Monitor cannot park the heads of a network drive.

NOTE

76 ■ *Power Of...Norton Utilities*

Figure 6.3 The Disk Park dialog box

The Disk Light Feature

The third feature of the Disk Monitor, and one that is, at most, of minor interest, is the Disk Light feature. This feature displays an indicator in the upper right corner of the screen when a drive (hard disk or floppy) is being accessed and shows the drive letter. This is intended particularly for systems that don't have drive lights that are visible on the outside of the case. This would be useful if you had a hard disk on a card, for example, although these disks usually come with a TSR program that performs the same function. If you're already using the Disk Monitor for disk protection, it doesn't consume any additional memory to use the Disk Light feature, so you might save a little RAM by using it instead of the utility that came with your disk. It is also potentially useful if you have a system with a "tower" case that is hidden under your desk, so you can't see the disk lights. As with the Disk Protection feature, the Disk Light does not operate if you are running a program in graphics mode, such as Windows, which greatly diminishes its potential usefulness.

If you are going to use the Disk Light feature, you will presumably want it on all the time, so you should add the /LIGHT+ option to the DISKMON line that you added to your AUTOEXEC.BAT file for disk protection. You can, of course, also activate the Disk Light feature by typing **DISKMON /LIGHT+** at the prompt or by loading DISKMON either from the prompt or from the Norton menu and selecting the **Light** button.

Command-Line Options

Except for selecting a level of protection and creating lists of files for inclusion or exclusion from protection, all the Disk Monitor's features can be turned on or off with command-line options, which can be used either at the DOS prompt or

Chapter Six: Disk Protection ■ 77

from the Norton menu, thereby bypassing the Disk Monitor dialog box. The available options follow.

DISKMON /?
Displays a list of the available command-line options.

/STATUS
Displays the Disk Monitor status on the screen, including the ON/OFF status of the disk light and disk protection. If protection is on, the level of protection is shown.

/PROTECT+ (or /PROTECT-)
Enables or disables disk protection. When enabled, whatever protection level you selected previously is used.

/LIGHT+ (or LIGHT-)
Enables or disables the Disk Light feature.

/PARK
Parks heads on all local hard drives.

/UNINSTALL
Removes Disk Monitor from RAM.

NOTE You can disable Disk Monitor by turning the options to **OFF**, but the 8K of RAM memory it uses will not be freed. Since Disk Monitor is a TSR program, you cannot uninstall it unless it was the last TSR program loaded into memory. If it was not the last TSR program loaded and you decide to deactivate both the protect and light features of Disk Monitor, you see a message saying that Disk Monitor cannot be removed. This is misleading, since the protect and light items are turned off as you specified.

/SKIPHIGH
Prevents Disk Monitor from being loaded into high memory (the memory area between 640K and 1024K).

SUMMARY

Disk Monitor offers three features that help protect your disks from damage (either accidental or deliberate). The Disk Protect feature prevents writes to

78 ■ *Power Of...Norton Utilities*

areas of the disk that you specify. Disk Light keeps you from accidentally turning off your computer while writing is in progress. Disk Park parks the heads in a safe area, preventing damage to your hard disk.

RECOMMENDATIONS

Using the Disk Monitor program is a trade-off between protection level and convenience. At minimum, you should probably install system-area protection if your think that there is any likelihood of your system being infested by a virus. This is unlikely to cause much inconvenience, as normal applications have no need to manipulate the system area; all such operations are managed by the operating system. Choosing the files plus system protection level may also be manageable, but it will probably take some trial and error to develop a list of files and exceptions that will allow you to get your work done without perpetual interruptions while protecting those files that ought not to be modified. Selecting protection for all files is probably not a practical option, particularly if you do much of your work in graphics mode programs. It is somewhat akin to living in an underground bunker to protect yourself from meteorites—it is probably effective, but the price is more than most of us would want to bear.

You definitely should use the Disk Monitor's head-parking feature if your hard disks aren't the self-parking variety. You should *always* park the heads before you move your system, and it is not a bad idea to park them at the end of the workday.

THE NORTON UTILITIES™ 7

CREATING A RESCUE DISK

A rescue disk is a diskette that contains the files necessary to boot your computer and to restore important information that may have been lost or corrupted. In Norton Utilities versions 6.x and earlier, the Disk Tools program created and restored rescue disks that contained only the boot record and partition table of your hard disk and the contents of your CMOS setup memory. This was potentially useful if the data in any of these areas was lost or corrupted but did not provide a way to boot your system if your hard disk had become unbootable (an essential preliminary step before restoring the lost or corrupted data). Norton Utilities 7.0 features an independent Rescue Disk utility with greatly expanded features. A rescue disk created with NU 7.0 includes, in addition to the items previously listed, the files required for booting your system, AUTOEXEC.BAT and CONFIG.SYS files, the Rescue utility, and a number of other Norton programs useful for restoring a malfunctioning hard disk to proper working order.

80 ■ *Power Of...Norton Utilities*

WHAT DO WE NEED TO BE RESCUED FROM?

A number of mishaps can result in the inability to boot your system. One of the most common, and one that *must* happen if you keep your system long enough, is failure of the battery that runs your CMOS setup memory. Your setup memory contains information about your system's configuration, but the most vital item is a description of your hard disk—the number of cylinders, tracks, sectors, and so on. If you loose this information (your battery dies or you inadvertently dislodge the battery while installing an expansion board), your system no longer knows that you have a hard disk. If you're like a great many users, you always boot your system from drive C and haven't thought about booting from a floppy for years. So you start thrashing around looking for a bootable diskette that you can use to start your system. What's that? Your dealer installed DOS on your hard disk before you bought the system and didn't give you a set of DOS disks? Uh oh. Now you can see why some people call these rescue disks "panic disks." If you can't boot off your hard disk and can't find a floppy disk with the necessary files, panic is not too strong a word.

In addition to the lost CMOS problem, other common situations can put you in the no-boot state. For example, you may have just installed some new hardware device in an expansion slot and installed a device driver for it in your CONFIG.SYS file. The first time you boot your system after the installation, your systems passes POST but stalls somewhere in the boot process. Your new device driver may be conflicting with some other driver, or the driver and/or hardware device may not be configured properly and may not recognize one another. Whatever the cause, you want to get in and edit your CONFIG.SYS file to remove the driver and see if that is the source of your problem. But your system won't boot to allow you to correct the problem that's preventing your system from booting. Catch 22! Here is another system where a bootable floppy with minimum AUTOEXEC.BAT and CONFIG.SYS files is essential.

In addition to the two scenarios described, there are many other situations where a rescue disk can come in handy. A virus may have damaged your boot sector or partition table. Or a buggy program or head crash could have done the same thing. Or one of those unknown evil forces that come out when the moon is full or Saturn is in retrograde may have taken control of your system. Whatever the cause, if your computer suddenly fails to boot from its hard disk, you'll be glad to have a rescue disk within reach.

CREATING A RESCUE DISK

To create a rescue disk, select **Rescue Disk** on the Norton menu or type **Rescue** at the DOS prompt. When the dialog box (Figure 7.1) appears, select **Create**. This brings up another dialog box, shown in Figure 7.2. The top two lines of the dialog box indicate the drive where the rescue disk is to be created and the capacity of the diskette. Below this is a pair of check boxes that specify that the rescue disk is to be formatted (necessary when creating the disk for the first time) or that only changed files are to be updated. The scrolling list that occupies the lower half of the box shows the files that will be stored on the rescue disk. Those marked with an asterisk (*) are mandatory, whereas those marked with a check are optional and can be selected or deselected by the user. If you want to deselect some of the files the program has chosen, move the highlight to the file name and press the spacebar.

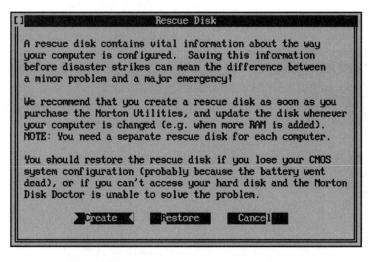

Figure 7.1 Initial Rescue dialog box

If you wish, you can add files to the rescue disk other than those the program initially chooses. To do this select the **Browse** button near the upper right corner of the dialog box. This will open a new dialog box, shown in Figure 7.3. Initially, this will show the files in the current directory, but you can view files in any directory on any drive by using the Drive list box to change the drive and the directory box to select a different directory on the drive. The scrolling

82 ■ *Power Of...Norton Utilities*

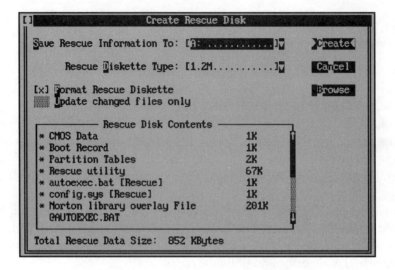

Figure 7.2 Create Rescue Disk dialog box

list box on the right side of the screen contains a list of the files in the current directory. Move the highlight to the file you want to select, then select the **OK** button and press **Enter.** You will be returned to the main Rescue dialog box with the selected file added to the file list and checked.

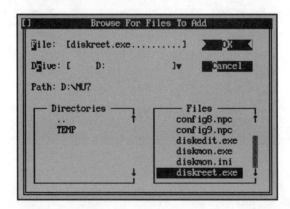

Figure 7.3 Browse dialog box

When you have selected all the files you want to add to the rescue disk, select the **Create** button to begin the process. The program will format the disk (if appropriate) and copy the necessary files. When the program has finished cre-

Chapter Seven: Creating a Rescue Disk ■ 83

ating the rescue disk, label the disk and store it in a safe place. (But not so safe that you can't find it if and when you need it!)

Table 7.1 shows the files on a typical 1.2Mb rescue disk.

Table 7.1 Contents of a typical Rescue Disk

COMMAND.COM	
AUTOEXEC.BAT	Minimal AUTOEXEC.BAT
CONFIG.SYS	Minimal CONFIG.SYS
BOOTINFO.DAT	Data from hard-disk boot record
PARTINFO.DAT	Data from hard-disk partition table
RESCUE.EXE	Rescue utility
NLIB100.RTL	Norton library overlay file
NDD.EXE	Norton Disk Doctor
SFORMAT.EXE	Norton Safe Format
UNERASE.EXE	Norton UnErase utility
UNFORMAT.EXE	Norton UnFormat utility
FDISK.EXE	DOS disk partition utility
NDIAGS.EXE	Norton diagnostics

If you examine the AUTOEXEC.BAT and CONFIG.SYS files on a rescue disk, you will see that they are not the same as those that reside in the root directory of your hard disk. Instead, they are minimal versions, including only the information necessary to get your system up and running. You could edit them to add other drivers, TSRs, and so on, but it is probably better not to do so. When you are trying to diagnose a cranky system, you normally want a "plain vanilla" configuration, with no unnecessary device drivers or TSRs to complicate matters.

NOTE Because one of the purposes of the rescue disk is to be able to boot your system when you are unable to boot from your hard disk, you should save the rescue disk on your A drive if you have more than one floppy drive with different sizes/capacities. For example, if you have a 5.25" 1.2Mb A drive and a 3.5" 1.44Mb B drive, the Rescue utility will let you create a rescue disk on either drive. However, you should use only drive A for this purpose. If you created a rescue disk on drive B, it would be good for some purposes, but you could not use it to boot from. If your A drive is a 5.25" 360Kb floppy, you will have to deselect most of the optional files, but you will still be able to create a rescue disk that contains all the mandatory files plus one or two useful tools or drivers.

NOTE

You should update your rescue diskette whenever you change the settings in your CMOS setup memory, upgrade your operating system, install a new hard disk, or repartition an existing disk.

Restoring a Rescue Diskette

You need to use the rescue disk when all or part of your hard disk becomes inaccessible (i.e., when you attempt to boot your system and receive an error message, such as "Hard Drive Not Found" or "Missing Operating System"). The process of restoring a rescue diskette is quite simple. Boot your system with the rescue disk, if necessary. Once the system has booted, try to access your hard disk via DOS (i.e., by typing the drive letter at the prompt). If you can access the drive, then run Norton Disk Doctor (see Chapter 10), either from the rescue disk or from the Norton directory of your hard disk, if it is accessible, to see whether it can diagnose and correct the problem. If you can't access the hard disk, run the Rescue utility and select the **Restore** button. This displays the dialog box in Figure 7.4. Indicate the drive to restore the Rescue information from, and check the appropriate items to restore (CMOS information, Boot Records, and/or Partition Tables), and select the **Restore** button to begin the restoration process.

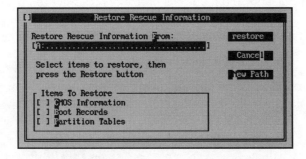

Figure 7.4 Rescue Disk restore dialog box

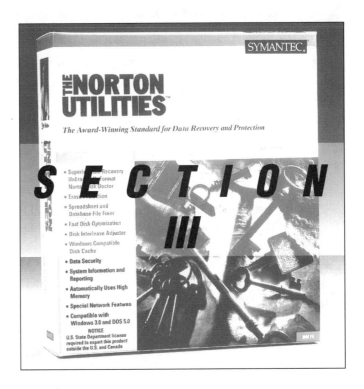

Correcting Disk Problems

If you failed to take the precautions described in Chapters 4–7 in time or if, despite your best efforts, the forces of chaos still managed to gain possession of your disks, there is still hope. Norton Utilities offers an assortment of intelligent tools that can solve most disk problems automatically, with a minimum of user intervention. Several of these tools work best in conjunction with the prevention methods described in the previous section, but even if you haven't taken such precautions, you may be able to recover all or some of your lost or damaged data if you act promptly.

- ◆ The UnErase utility (Chapter 8) restores accidentally erased files.
- ◆ The UnFormat utility (Chapter 9) restores accidentally formatted hard and floppy disks.

- The Norton Disk Doctor (Chapter 10) diagnoses and automatically repairs a variety of common disk problems, such as lost clusters, cross-linked files, and file allocation table errors. In addition, it tests the disk surface to detect bad sectors, recovers data from those sectors, and relocates it to safe areas.
- The File Fix utility (Chapter 11) repairs defective spreadsheet, database, and WordPerfect files.
- The Norton Disk Tools (Chapter 12) perform a variety of tasks, including repairing disks trashed by the DOS RECOVER command and restoring the low-level format on unreadable diskettes.

WARNING The key to the successful repair of most disk problems is that you must not write any new files to the problem disk until the problem is solved. Doing so may overwrite the data that you are trying to recover. If you have just purchased Norton Utilities to solve a particular hard-disk problem, *do not install Norton Utilities on your hard disk*. Run it from the Norton emergency disk, as described at the beginning of the Norton Utilities documentation.

Recovering Erased Files

If, despite your care and precautions, you manage to erase a file accidentally that you intended to keep, do not despair. If you installed SmartCan, as described in Chapter 4, you will be able to recover the file completely, provided you act before it is purged from SmartCan's protected directory. Even if you haven't been using SmartCan, you will probably be able to recover the file perfectly, and with a minimum of effort, if you use the Norton UnErase program immediately, before clusters belonging to the erased file are overwritten with new data.

How Files are Written and Erased

When you save a file on a disk, information about it is written to the system area of the disk. A directory entry is created in the root directory or a subdirectory, as appropriate, containing the file name, the starting cluster number, the file size, and other information. File Allocation Table (FAT) entries contain information that tells DOS where it should go to find the remaining clusters of the file. The data comprising the file is stored in the data area of the disk, beginning in the cluster indicated in the directory entry.

When you erase or delete a file, the data comprising the file is not removed from the disk; it remains intact until it is overwritten by new data. The erase command writes a σ (sigma) character to replace the first letter of the file name in the directory entry. In addition, the FAT entries for the file are changed to zeros, indicating that the clusters occupied by the file are available for use. Hence, it is possible to recover an erased file completely, provided that it has not been overwritten by new data and provided that you can locate all the clusters that belonged to the file. This is the task that the Norton UnErase program performs.

Obviously, then, the most important step in recovering an erased file is: *Don't write any other files to the disk until you have recovered the erased file(s)*. If you're in an application and need to save your work before you try to recover the erased file, *save your work on another drive*—either on a floppy disk or on a different logical drive on a hard disk. Saving the file to a different directory doesn't help, because different directories are not segregated physically on the disk. In short, the less work you do on your system between the time you erase the file and the time you attempt to recover it, the more likely you are to be completely successful. And don't forget, many applications open temporary files when they are running and delete them when they are closed, so even loading and exiting an application without saving any files may interfere with the recovery of erased files.

NOTE If you have followed the advice in Chapter 4 and installed the SmartCan program in your AUTOEXEC.BAT file, your chances of completely recovering erased files are greatly improved. If you remember to UnErase the file before SmartCan purges it, your recovery will be 100% successful. It is also a good idea to include the Image program in your AUTOEXEC.BAT file (see Chapter 5), so you will always have up-to-date backup copies of your disks' system areas available. This will be useful if you need to recover a fragmented file.

A Note on Image and SmartCan vs. Mirror

UnErase can use data saved by either the Norton Image utility or the Mirror program in DOS versions 5.0 or later, if available, in recovering files. (Mirror

Chapter Eight: Recovering Erased Files ■ 89

is a utility similar to Image; it too saves a copy of the DOS system area in a file for unformatting a disk or recovering fragmented files.) UnErase checks for both Image and Mirror data. If both are found, it uses the one with the most recent information.

The Mirror program has an option called Delete Tracking. This loads a memory-resident program that keeps track of files that are deleted and records the clusters that they occupied in a file. Delete Tracking is intended to serve the same function as SmartCan: to make it possible to recover erased files easily. SmartCan, however, is superior in several ways. First, it actually moves the erased files to a protected directory; Delete Tracking records the clusters that were occupied by the deleted file but cannot prevent those clusters from being overwritten by newer files. Hence, SmartCan can guarantee 100% recovery of erased files, whereas Delete Tracking cannot. Second, SmartCan purges its holdings after a specified interval, whereas Delete Tracking keeps its list of erased files indefinitely, long after the information has ceased to be useful. Third, SmartCan works on network drives, whereas Delete Tracking doesn't. For these reasons Norton Utilities users will probably prefer to use SmartCan rather than Delete Tracking. Nevertheless, the Norton UnErase program will use Delete Tracking information if it is present. You can prevent UnErase from using Delete Tracking data by typing the **/NOTRACK** option on the DOS or Norton menu command line when starting the program. (For more information on Mirror and Delete Tracking consult your DOS manual.)

RUNNING NORTON UNERASE IN EMERGENCY SITUATIONS

WARNING

If you have an emergency and need to restore erased files on your hard disk, and you have just purchased the Norton Utilities for this purpose, *do not install the Norton Utilities (or any other program) on your hard disk in order to recover the files!* Installing the Norton program files might overwrite the erased files you are trying to recover. In an emergency use the following procedure: Insert the Norton Utilities Emergency Disk into floppy drive A or B, as appropriate for the disk size/type, log on to that drive, and type **UNERASE Enter**.

You will see the UnErase main dialog box (Figure 8.1) with an empty list box displaying the message "No Files Found," indicating that there are no erased files on the Emergency disk; this is as it should be. Use the **Change Drive** and **Change Directory** commands on the File menu to change to the drive and directory on your hard disk where the file(s) that you want to recover is located. Now you can follow the instructions beginning in the second paragraph under the heading "Running Norton UnErase After Installation."

Running Norton UnErase After Installation

If you have already installed Norton Utilities, you can run the UnErase program either by loading the Norton menu and selecting **UnErase** or by typing **UNERASE Enter** at the DOS prompt. You may include a path and/or file name on the command line when you start the UnErase program. If you include a file name, UnErase will go straight to the task of unerasing the specified file without displaying any menus or dialog boxes. (If you have more than one file to recover from the same disk, it is better not to do this. See later.) Otherwise, the main UnErase dialog box (Figure 8.1) will appear, showing a list of the erased files in the current directory or the directory you entered on the command line. The following description applies equally to running the UnErase program from the Emergency disk or from a hard disk.

NOTE The UnErase program will not run under a multitasking environment, such as Windows or DESQview. If you attempt to run the program in one of these environments, a message will appear to inform you of this fact and to recommend that you change to a single-tasking environment (i.e., DOS) before running the program.

The UnErase main dialog box shows file names (with a "?" substituted for the first letter), file lengths, date and time stamps, and a fifth column labeled "prognosis." (Files that are protected by SmartCan show complete file names.) The prognosis is the program's estimate of the probability of a successful recovery. Files that were protected by SmartCan (or the Erase Protect program from Norton Utilities versions 6.x or earlier) receive a prognosis of "excellent." Other files are rated "very good," "good," "average," or "poor."

At the bottom of the UnErase main screen are three buttons: **Info**, **View**, and **UnErase**. At the top is a menu bar with four pull-down menus: File, Search, Options, and Help.

Chapter Eight: Recovering Erased Files ■ 91

```
┌[ ]────────────────────────────UnErase─────────────────────────────┐
│ File  Search  Options  Help                                       │
│   ┌[ ]──────────────────Erased Files in A:\──────────────────┐   │
│   │   Name              Size      Date       Time   Prognosis │   │
│   │  ┌───────────────────────────────────────────────────────┐│   │
│   │  │ ?enov718 let       757    8-17-88    11:48am  poor    ││   │
│   │  │ ?enoves2 let     1,738    8-17-88    12:02pm  poor    ││   │
│   │  │ ?erps817 let     2,432    8-17-88    10:59am  good    ││   │
│   │  │ ?erpstra 318     2,322    3-18-88    10:55pm  poor    ││   │
│   │  │ ?est     bat       541   12-29-92     4:04pm  excellent││   │
│   │  │ ?g1013   let     1,164   10-13-88    10:46pm  poor    ││   │
│   │  │ ?halm830 let     1,348    8-30-88    12:22pm  poor    ││   │
│   │  │ ?henry2  let     2,294    1-09-88     5:58pm  poor    ││   │
│   │  │ ?hild822 let     1,277    8-22-88     2:53pm  poor    ││   │
│   │  │ ?holz818 let     1,158    8-22-88     3:01pm  excellent││   │
│   │  │ ?iegel   let     3,286    6-21-88     9:58pm  poor    ││   │
│   │  │ ?ilk817  let     1,054    8-17-88    11:11am  good    ││   │
│   │  └───────────────────────────────────────────────────────┘│   │
│   │        ▶ Info ◀        ▶ View ◀         ▶ UnErase ◀       │   │
│   └──────────────────────────────────────────────────────────┘   │
└───────────────────────────────────────────────────────────────────┘
```

Figure 8.1 *UnErase main dialog box*

Use the **Info** button to learn more about the condition of the highlighted file. Selecting this button displays a dialog box similar to that in Figure 8.2. This dialog box shows the date and time the file was created or last modified, the file size and attributes, the starting cluster, and the number of clusters needed. Below these is a brief explanation of the prognosis and a description of the probable result of the recovery attempt. If there is more than one erased file on the list, you can go to the next or previous file using the buttons at the bottom of the screen.

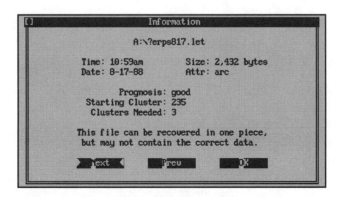

Figure 8.2 *Info dialog box*

The **View** button displays the contents of the currently highlighted file (see Figure 8.3). You can scroll up or down through the file using the arrow keys or the mouse. If you want to scroll left or right in the file, use **Ctrl+Left** arrow key or **Ctrl+Right** arrow key. If the file has been partially overwritten, the program will display a message to this effect and you will not be able to view the file. If there is more than one erased file in the list, use the buttons at the bottom of the screen to go to the next file or the previous file. You can also toggle the file display between ASCII text and hexadecimal.

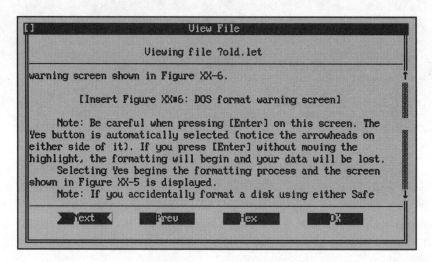

Figure 8.3 The View box

Selecting the **UnErase** button automatically recovers the highlighted (or tagged) file(s).

A Simple Recovery

If you know the name and location of the erased file and if you have not done any work that overwrote any of the clusters belonging to the file, you will most likely be able to recover the file completely by highlighting it on the screen and selecting the **UnErase** button. This will open a dialog box where you can supply the missing first letter of the file name (Figure 8.4). If you know the correct letter, enter it. Otherwise, any letter will do; you can always rename the file later. When you type the letter, the program will immediately begin unerasing the file. When the operation is completed it will change the label in the prognosis column to "Recovered." You should, of course, load the file into the appropriate application in order to verify that the file was recovered correctly.

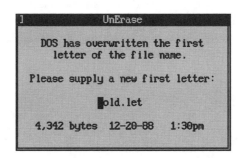

Figure 8.4 Supply missing first letter dialog box

Even if a file is highly fragmented or partially overwritten, or if it has an otherwise bad prognosis, you should attempt a simple, automatic recovery, before you try the more difficult manual one. At worst, the program can only fail to recover the file, in which case you're no worse off than when you started. More likely, it will succeed in recovering at least some of the clusters belonging to the file, in which case you have a starting point for a potentially successful manual recovery. Of course, if it turns out that *all* the clusters belonging to the file have been overwritten with new data, then recovery will be impossible, in which case there's nothing to be done but re-create the lost file from scratch.

 If the erased file is a program file (e.g., an .EXE, .COM, .OVL, .BIN, or .SYS file) rather than a data file, it is better to reinstall it from the original disks or from a backup than to try to Unerase it. This is the case because a program file that was imperfectly recovered might misbehave in unpredictable ways when it is executed. If the program is large and complex, problems resulting from an imperfect recovery might not show up immediately. It is therefore preferable to avoid the risk and reinstall a known clean copy of the program.

 Unerasing more than one file from the same disk can result in the first recovered file overwriting parts of other erased files. To avoid this you should *always* use the **UnErase To** option on the Files menu (see later) if you have more than one erased file to recover. (This warning does not apply if *all* the erased files were protected by SmartCan.)

94 ■ *Power Of...Norton Utilities*

Advanced Features

If the erased file you want to recover is not shown in the directory where you expected to find it, if the file was located in a subdirectory that was erased, or if the automatic UnErase operation failed to recover the file completely, you will need to try some of the more advanced features described later.

The Menu Bar

When you load the UnErase program, the menu bar at the top of the screen displays four items: **File**, **Search**, **Options**, and **Help**. You can access the menu bar by pressing **Alt** or **F10**.

The File Menu

The File menu provides you with options for viewing and selecting erased files. Many of the options also have shortcut keys, which are listed on the right side of the menu. In the following description, the shortcuts are listed in parentheses after the menu item. You can also select a menu item by typing its hotkey (the highlighted letter in its name).

View Current Directory (**Alt+C**)—displays the erased files in the current directory (the default display mode).

View All Directories (**Alt+A**)—lists all erased files on the current drive.

Change Drive (**Alt+D**)—displays a dialog box with a list of available drives. Selecting a drive changes the display to the erased files on the selected drive.

Change Directory (**Alt+R**)—opens a dialog box similar to that shown in Figure 8.5. This dialog box displays the directory tree for the current drive with the current directory highlighted. To change the directory, highlight the directory you want and press **Enter**. The UnErase screen will now display the directory you selected.

Select (**Spacebar**)—selects or unselects the highlighted file. Selected files are marked with two inward-pointing arrowheads. If the highlighted file is already selected, this option appears on the menu as **Unselect**. Pressing the spacebar when the highlighted file is already selected unselects the file.

Chapter Eight: Recovering Erased Files ■ 95

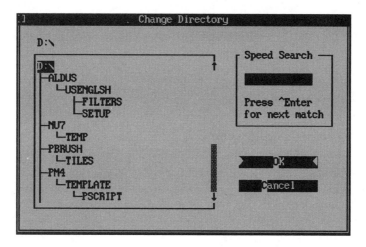

Figure 8.5 *Change Directory dialog box*

Select Group (**+** on numeric keypad)—opens a dialog box with a space for you to enter a file specification. You can include a range of files by using the DOS wild-card characters * and ?. For example, you might enter the filespec ***.LET** if you wanted to recover a group of erased letters.

Unselect Group (**-** on numeric keypad)—opens a dialog box where you can enter the file specification for files to untag. All tagged files matching the file specification are untagged. This can be used only if you have previously selected files.

Rename—allows you to enter a new name for the recovered file or directory. This command is available only if a recovered or non-erased file is highlighted. Use this command to change the name of a file if, for example, you want to recover an erased file with the same name.

UnErase To—allows you to send the recovered file to the another drive. A dialog box with a list of available drives appears. After you have selected a drive, the UnErase To dialog box is displayed. This dialog box allows you to select a directory and file name for the recovered file. *It is highly recommended that you use this option whenever you have more than one file to recover from a given disk, as it eliminates the possibility of a recovered file overwriting portions of other erased files awaiting recovery.* There is no shortcut for this option.

Append To—can be used only after you have recovered a file. When a recovered file is highlighted, selecting **Append To** takes you to the Manual UnErase screen (next menu item). You can add free (unallocated) clusters to the recovered file if you wish. (Free clusters include those in other erased files or unused clusters.) This is useful if you have recovered a file and later discover that you did not include all the clusters belonging to it.

Manual UnErase (Alt+M)—allows you to try to put an erased file back together manually if the automatic UnErase procedure cannot recover the file. (This feature will be described in detail later.)

The Search Menu

The Search menu provides a variety of methods for finding data belonging to files that cannot be located by file name. There are no keyboard shortcuts for the items on this menu.

For Data Types—scans the disk, searching for clusters containing data of the specified type(s). Four options are offered:

- Normal text
- Lotus 1-2-3 and Symphony spreadsheet data (also works with other spreadsheet data, such as Quattro Pro)
- dBASE data
- Other—includes all other types of data, including graphics

Check the appropriate check boxes to make your selections.

NOTE If you have erased spreadsheet or database files, just using UnErase to recover the file may not be sufficient. If the file does not perform as expected when loaded into the appropriate application, use FileFix (see Chapter 11) to repair it.

For Text—displays a box where you can enter a text string for which to search. By default, the search is not case sensitive, but you can specify a case-sensitive search by unchecking the **Ignore Case** box.

For Lost Names—locates inaccessible filenames of erased files. These names belong to files that were deleted from directories, after which the directories were themselves deleted. After the files are found, they can be recovered as usual.

Chapter Eight: Recovering Erased Files ■ **97**

Set Search Range—in the unlikely event that you know the range of sectors in which a lost file may be found, use this command to restrict the search to those sectors by entering the starting and ending cluster numbers. This works for any of the three search methods described earlier.

Continue Search—you can interrupt a search using any of the three methods on the Search menu by pressing **Enter** or **Esc** at any time during the search. If you have interrupted a search, use this command to resume where you left off.

The Options Menu

The Options menu gives you six choices for sorting the listed erased files on the UnErase screen.

Sort by Name—sorts alphabetically by name, using the second letter of the filename (since the first letters are missing).

Sort by Extension—sorts the list of files alphabetically by extension.

Sort by Time—sorts according to the date and time of the latest modification, from earliest to most recent.

Sort by Size—sorts according to file size, from smallest to largest.

Sort by Directory—groups the files by directory, if you have erased files from two or more directories. To use this option, you must first select **View All Directories** on the File menu.

Sort by Prognosis—lists files according to their recovery prognosis, from best to worst. The possibilities are "Excellent," "Very Good," "Good," "Average," "Poor," "Non-erased," and "Recovered."

Include Non-erased Files—includes the names of all files on the disk, both erased and non-erased. This option is active only if the disk contains non-erased files; it can be selected regardless of which of the six sort options are active.

RUNNING UNERASE FROM THE DOS PROMPT

You can run UnErase from the DOS command line. The command-line syntax is as follows:

```
UNERASE [file spec] [option]
```

where [file spec] is the filename and path of the file(s) to UnErase. The file spec can include the DOS wild-card characters, * and ?. Several options are available for use with this command:

/IMAGE	Use Norton Image information for file recovery (do not use DOS Mirror information).
/MIRROR	Use Mirror information for file recovery (do not use Image information).
/NOINFO	Exclude both Image and Mirror recovery information.
/NOTRACK	Do not use Delete Tracking information for file recovery.
/SMARTCAN	Recover only files saved by SmartCan.
/NOSMARTCAN	Exclude files saved by SmartCan.
/SKIPHIGH	Do not use high memory.

NOTE

If you have badly fragmented or partially overwritten files, you must use Manual UnErase in the full-screen mode to recover them (if possible).

Using Manual UnErase

The Manual UnErase feature allows you to select a group of clusters and assemble them in any order you wish in an attempt to reconstruct a file that the automatic UnErase feature could not recover. If UnErase fails to recover a file completely, it is usually because one or more of the clusters that belonged to the file have been overwritten by another file or because the file was badly fragmented and an up-to-date IMAGE.DAT file was not available to enable it to find all the clusters (a good reason to run Image daily in your AUTOEXEC.BAT and to unfragment your disks weekly with SpeedDisk). You can use Manual UnErase either to add clusters to a partially recovered file (via the **Append To** option on the File menu) or to construct a complete file from scratch.

Chapter Eight: Recovering Erased Files ■ 99

NOTE

If the unrecovered file is on a floppy disk, make a copy of the disk using the DOS DISKCOPY command. Do your manual recovery work on the copy.

When you select **Manual UnErase**, a dialog box similar to that shown in Figure 8.4 will appear, prompting you to supply the first letter of the file name. Enter the letter (or any letter if you do not know the actual letter). The Manual UnErase screen shown in Figure 8.6 will then be displayed.

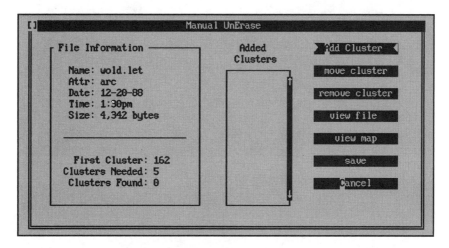

Figure 8.6 Main manual UnErase screen

The left side of the UnErase screen contains information about the file. You can see the file size, the attributes, the beginning cluster number, the number of clusters needed, and the number of clusters found so far. In the center of the Manual UnErase dialog box is the Added Cluster list, which displays the cluster numbers that have been selected for the file. This will be empty when you begin if the file is still erased. (If you are working with a recovered file using the **Append To** option, the clusters belonging to the file will be listed.) You can move up and down the list using the arrow keys or mouse. Select (highlight) a cluster by pressing the spacebar. Highlighted clusters can be moved or deleted using the buttons on the right side of the dialog box.

At the right of the screen are seven buttons: **Add Cluster**, **Move Cluster**, **Remove Cluster**, **View File**, **View Map**, **Save**, and **Cancel**.

If you did not come to the **Manual UnErase** option via the **Append To** option, the first thing you must do is **Add Clusters**, since no clusters have yet been selected and added to your file. When you select the **Add Clusters** button, you will see a new dialog box (Figure 8.7) with five buttons for adding clusters via different methods:

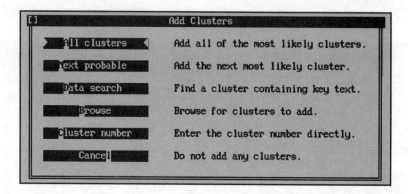

Figure 8.7 Add Cluster dialog box

All Clusters—adds all the most likely clusters for the file to the Added Clusters list. This is the place to begin in reconstructing your file. When you select this command, you will be returned to the main Manual UnErase dialog box and the selected clusters will be listed in the Added Clusters window. (Use the **View File** option to confirm that the clusters belong to the file you are trying to recover.)

Next Probable—adds the next most likely cluster to the list of clusters. If the **All Clusters** option failed to find all the clusters needed to reconstruct the file, try this option next.

Data Search—allows you to search the free clusters on the disk for a data string, which can be specified in either ASCII or hex format. You can also specify whether the search is to be case sensitive and/or specify a cluster offset at which to begin the search. If search string is found, the contents of the cluster containing it are shown with the search string highlighted. At the bottom of the screen are four choices:

Chapter Eight: Recovering Erased Files ■ 101

- **Add cluster**—add the cluster to the list on the Manual UnErase screen.
- **Find Next**—locate the next occurrence of the search string.
- **Hex**—toggle between hex and ASCII displays for viewing the cluster.
- **Done**—return to Manual UnErase main dialog box.

Browse—allows you to step through the free clusters on the disk and view their contents. Using the buttons at the bottom of the dialog box (Figure 8.8), you can browse through the clusters sequentially, either forward or backward, or jump to a particular cluster number. You can also toggle the display between the hex and ASCII formats. Use the **Add** button to add the displayed cluster to your file and use the **Done** button to return to the main dialog box.

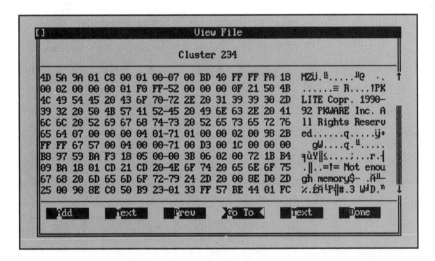

Figure 8.8 Browse dialog box (hex view)

Cluster Number—for use in the unlikely event that you have an idea of which clusters are required for the file. A dialog box appears where you specify a range of clusters by its beginning and ending cluster numbers (Figure 8.9). If all the clusters in the range you specify belong to non-erased files, you will be returned to the dialog box so that you can try again. If some of the clusters in the range you selected are in use by a non-erased file, the program will offer you a choice of **Adjust Range** or **Continue**. If you select **Adjust Range**, the program will truncate the range you selected to one that consists of free clus-

102 ■ Power Of...Norton Utilities

ters. Select **Continue** if you want to specify a different range. When have selected a range that includes only free clusters, use the **Done** bu add those clusters to the list.

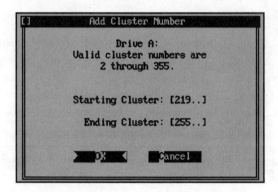

Figure 8.9 Cluster numbers dialog box

Once you have added some clusters to your list, you can use the ren buttons on the right side of the main dialog box to view and manipula covered data.

Use the **Move Cluster** button to move the highlighted clus new location in the list. When you select this button, inward-pointing ads appear around the selected cluster number and the label on the bu nges to **End Move**. Use the **Up** and **Down** arrow keys or the mouse the selected cluster to a new location, then press **Enter** or click the bu lrop the cluster.

Use the **Remove Cluster** button to remove the highlighted clu n the list. The cluster will be removed immediately when you select the b you change your mind, use the **Next Probable** option in the Add C alog box to restore it.

Use the **View File** button to view the contents of the clusters st to determine whether they all belong to the file and whether they ar ight order. You can scroll through the file using the arrow keys or th and toggle the display between hex and ASCII format.

The **View Map** option displays a map of the physical layout lisk, similar to that in Figure 8.10, showing the locations of the selec ters, other free clusters, and clusters belonging to non-erased files.

Chapter Eight: Recovering Erased Files ■ 103

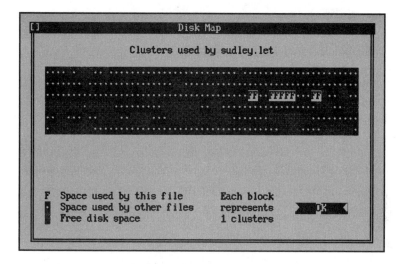

Figure 8.10 Disk map

When you have finished selecting the clusters for your file, use the **Save** button to write the restored file to the disk. If you have fewer clusters in your list than the directory entry indicates were in the original file, the program will warn you and give you the options of **Save Anyway** or **Resume**. Select **Save Anyway** to write the file as it is, or select **Resume** to add more clusters to the file.

Is Manual UnErasing Practical?

The Manual UnErase procedure outlined earlier seems fairly simple and straightforward, and so it is. In practice, however, manually unerasing a file that the UnErase program has failed to recover automatically may or may not be feasible. If clusters belonging to the file have been overwritten, no amount of searching the disk will recover them—they're gone for good. If this is the case, a partial recovery is the best you can hope for. For text files or other files consisting primarily of alphanumeric data, this may be useful, but for other types of files, such as bitmapped images, program files, or files that have been compressed, a partial recovery may be the same as no recovery at all. For data files that require a header or prologue to identify the file for the application that uses it, such as database or spreadsheet files, the Norton File Fix utility (see Chapter 11) may be able to restore partially recovered files.

104 ■ *Power Of...Norton Utilities*

Even if all the clusters belonging to the file still exist on the disk, manual recovery may not be practical if the file is large and/or severely fragmented. If the file is an ASCII file or a word processor file and if you are familiar with its contents or have a hard copy to guide you, with sufficient time and patience you will probably be able to recover it. Before attempting to do so, however, it is worth pausing to ask whether this is the most efficient way to restore the file. If you have a recent backup, you may be able to restore the file and type in the changes in less time than it takes to UnErase the file manually. Or it may be more cost effective to have a professional typist retype the file from the hard copy than for you to spend hours trying to recover it cluster by cluster.

Non-text files are much more difficult. Almost every different application uses a different file format for storing data. To restore a non-text file successfully, you must first be able to recognize data belonging to the file (or, at least, belonging to the correct application) when it is displayed in hex format. A detailed presentation of the formats currently in use would require a book in its own right. You can obtain the file formats used by most applications from their vendors for a modest fee, and it is not a bad idea to do so (before you have trouble) if you depend on the safety of data from a particular program for your livelihood or if you want to make a career in data recovery. However, frequent backups, combined with the systematic use of the Image and SmartCan utilities, can spare you the necessity of ever having to deal with these arcane matters.

SUMMARY

The Norton UnErase utility can help you find and recover deleted files. Even data from fragmented or partially overwritten files may be recovered by using UnErase in its manual mode.

THE NORTON UTILITIES™

9

RESTORING ACCIDENTALLY FORMATTED DISKS

If you have accidentally formatted a floppy disk, or even (horror of horrors) your hard disk, all is not lost. The Norton UnFormat utility can probably restore most or all of your programs and data. This is especially true if there is an up-to-date copy of the system area stored in an IMAGE.DAT file on the disk (see Chapter 5).

HOW UNFORMAT WORKS

All disks are divided into two areas, the system area and the data area. The information used by DOS for keeping track of files is stored in the system area; the files themselves are kept in the data area. Before a new disk can be used for the first time, it must be divided into sectors and tracks, and the data structures that comprise the system area must be created. This process is called *formatting*.

106 ■ *Power Of...Norton Utilities*

There are two types of formatting that must be performed before you can use a disk, low-level and high-level. (Refer to Chapter 23 for a detailed discussion of formatting.)

Low-level formatting establishes the sectors and tracks on a disk. In the process, it destroys all data on the disk. High-level formatting establishes (or, when a previously formatted disk is reformatted, clears) the system area. The DOS FORMAT command performs both low-level and high-level formatting on floppy disks. It does only high-level formatting on hard disks. Most hard disks are low-level formatted at the factory. High-level formatting does not destroy data. It merely resets information in the system area to indicate that the data area is free for use.

Since only high-level formatting is done on hard disks, the data on a reformatted hard disk remains intact until it is overwritten by new data. The same is true of floppy disks that have been formatted with the **Safe** or **Quick Format** options of the Norton Safe Format utility or with the FORMAT command in DOS 5.0 or later. This means you can recover your files if you can find out where the data is stored. This is the purpose of the Norton UnFormat utility.

You can greatly simplify UnFormat's task and greatly enhance its chances of success by running the Image utility daily (see Chapter 5). When you run UnFormat, it searches for the IMAGE.DAT file created by the Image utility. If it finds this file, it uses the data to restore the system area to its condition when the file was saved, as described later. It can also use the MIRROR.FIL file saved by the Mirror program in DOS versions 5.0 or later for this purpose. However, even if you have not used Image or Mirror, you may still be able to recover most of your data. In this case, the final result will depend on the amount of file fragmentation and on the number of large versus small files, among other factors. You can't expect a 100% recovery, and you may not get anything useful. At a minimum, the files in the root directory will be lost, although you may be able to recover them with the UnErase command (see Chapter 8).

As with unerasing erased files, successfully recovering an accidentally formatted disk requires prompt action. If you copy or save new files to the disk before attempting recovery, those files will probably overwrite clusters containing data belonging to old files that you want to restore. Once new data has been written to the clusters, there is no way that the old data can be recovered. When UnFormat restores the system area from the IMAGE.DAT file, the old directories and files will be restored, but some of the files may contain corrupt data from the files that were written after the disk was formatted.

Chapter Nine: Restoring Accidentally Formatted Disks ■ 107

NOTE Some versions of DOS, including AT&T DOS 2.11 and Compaq DOS 3.1, overwrite information when formatting a hard disk. UnFormat cannot recover this data. Newer versions of DOS supplied with these systems do not have this problem. If you are using one of these versions of DOS, you should replace the FORMAT.COM command with the Norton Safe Format command. (It is a good idea to do this if you are using any DOS version prior to 5.0 from any vendor. See Chapter 5 for details.) To replace the FORMAT.COM command, select **Configuration** from the Norton menu, then choose the **Alternate Names** item from the Configuration menu. The **Alternate Names** dialog box will appear. Find **Safe Format** among the names listed in the dialog box; then open the list box and select FORMAT.EXE as the new name. This causes Safe Format to be renamed FORMAT (the DOS command will be renamed XFORMAT).

Network Usage

You can run UnFormat from a network, but you cannot unformat a network drive.

RUNNING UNFORMAT IN EMERGENCY SITUATIONS

WARNING If you have an emergency and need to recover the data on your hard disk, *do not install Norton Utilities (or any other program) on your hard disk*. Run UnFormat from a floppy disk, as follows:

1. Reboot the computer with a bootable floppy disk, using the same version of DOS as you used to format the hard disk. (If you made a Rescue disk, as described in Chapter 7, it is ideal for this purpose.)

2. If you used a Rescue disk, leave it in the drive; otherwise, remove the diskette and insert the Norton Utilities Emergency Disk in the drive.

3. Type **UNFORMAT** and press **Enter**. The UnFormat Introductory Screen will be displayed (see Figure 9.1). Go to step 2 under "Running Norton Utilities After Installation," and proceed as indicated.

Running UnFormat After Installation

You can run the UnFormat program from the Norton menu or from the DOS command line. The program will guide you through the following procedure by prompting you for the necessary information.

1. To start UnFormat, type **UNFORMAT** at the DOS prompt or highlight **UnFormat** on the Norton menu and press **Enter**. (You can skip step 2 (next) by including the letter of the drive to be unformatted on the command line when you start the program.) The UnFormat introductory screen will be displayed (see Figure 9.1).

NOTE If you start the UnFormat utility from a multitasking environment such as Windows or DESQview, a message will appear warning you that the program might not be safe to run in such an environment. You can safely unformat floppy disks in this situation, but you should not try to unformat a hard disk while running Windows or DESQview.

Figure 9.1 UnFormat introductory screen

2. Select **Continue**. A screen similar to that in Figure that in 9.2 will prompt you to select the drive to unformat. Highlight the drive you want and select **OK** or press **Enter**.

3. A message will appear stating that the program is analyzing the disk. After the disk is analyzed, a dialog box will appear to ask if you have saved an IMAGE.DAT file. Select **Yes** if you are not sure.

Chapter Nine: Restoring Accidentally Formatted Disks ■ 109

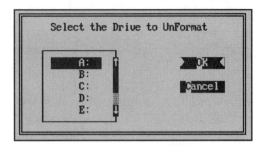

Figure 9.2 *Drive-selection box*

NOTE

Norton Utilities 4.5 creates a file called FRECOVER.DAT, which is compatible with the IMAGE.DAT file. UnFormat searches for either one; if it finds a FRECOVER.DAT file, it renames it IMAGE.DAT.

4. UnFormat analyzes the disk and displays a list of the current files on the disk (if any are found), as shown in Figure 9.3. A warning message appears indicating that the current contents of the disk will be lost and asking if you are sure you want to recover the disk.

Figure 9.3 *Files on disk warning*

110 ■ *Power Of...Norton Utilities*

You can save the current files to another disk and then proceed with the unformat procedure to recover the previous files. If no current files are found, you will see only the message asking if you are sure you want to unformat the disk.

5. Select **Yes**. The program will search for the IMAGE.DAT file. If only one IMAGE.DAT file is found, the screen in Figure 9.4 will be displayed. If more than one IMAGE.DAT file is found, a screen similar to Figure 9.7 will be displayed. Refer to the section titled "Unformatting When Two Image Files Exist" later in this chapter.

Figure 9.4 *One Image file found*

If there is no IMAGE.DAT file on the disk, the search will take longer. When UnErase finishes the search, you are told that no Image information exists for that drive. Refer to the section "Recovering a Disk without an IMAGE.DAT File," later in this chapter. You will be warned that restoring the Image information removes the current contents.

6. Select **OK**. A screen will appear asking you to select a full or partial restoration (see Figure 9.5). A partial restore gives you a choice of restoring specific parts of the system area. You can select either the boot record, the file allocation table (FAT), or the root directory. Do not choose a partial restore unless you are certain where the problem is. For example, if you know that file names in the root directory have been altered, you could choose to restore only the root directory. The full restore selection restores the entire system area. If you are not sure which type of restoration you want, select **Full**.

Chapter Nine: Restoring Accidentally Formatted Disks ■ 111

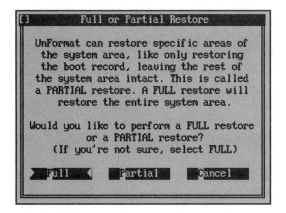

Figure 9.5 Full or partial restore dialog box

7. After selecting a full or partial restoration, a message "restoring Image Info to drive N" will be displayed while the restoration proceeds. When the restoration is completed, the message screen shown in Figure 9.6 appears.

Figure 9.6 Successful recovery message

8. Quit UnFormat and select **Disk Doctor** from the Norton Main Menu or run it from the DOS prompt by typing:

```
NDD [drive:] /Quick
```

112 ■ *Power Of...Norton Utilities*

The screen notice in Figure 9.6 does not mean there was necessarily a problem with the restoration. The Norton Disk Doctor can, however, clean up any disk problems that may have been caused by changes made to the disk after you made the last IMAGE.DAT file, and it is a good idea to do so as a precaution (see Chapter 10).

Unformatting When Two Image Files Exist

If your disk was accidentally damaged (by a virus or by a power failure during a disk operation, for example), you might not realize immediately that your data was corrupted. If you subsequently ran Image, the new IMAGE.DAT file would contain a copy of the corrupted system area plus information about any new files that had been written since the accident. The new Image file is named IMAGE.DAT file, and the previous file, which contains the old, uncorrupted information, is renamed IMAGE.BAK.

When UnFormat searches for Image information, it finds both versions of the Image file and displays the screen in Figure 9.7. This screen indicates when the most recent and the previous versions Image Info were saved, and you are offered a choice of which version of the Image file to restore. If you choose **Recent**, UnFormat uses the IMAGE.DAT file and restores the corrupted version of the system area, while preserving any files that have been written since the accident. This is probably not what you want, as the whole object of running UnFormat was to restore the disk to its uncorrupted state from before the accident. Choosing **Previous** restores the data from the IMAGE.BAK file. In this case, files that were saved after the accident will be lost, but the uncorrupted version of the system area will be restored. Copy the new files to another disk before proceeding with the restoration.

Recovering a Disk Without an IMAGE.DAT File

If a disk is accidentally formatted before you have used the Image command to create an IMAGE.DAT file, you may still be able to recover most of your data. The first three steps are the same as those described earlier. When you get to step 4, the Restore Image Info progress screen shown in Figure 9.8 appears. UnFormat searches the disk, beginning with the last sector, for the Image data. You can watch the progress on the map. The cluster being searched is shown at

Chapter Nine: Restoring Accidentally Formatted Disks ■ 113

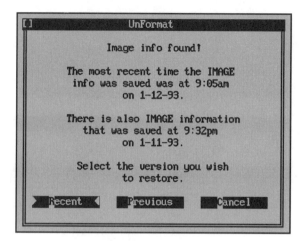

Figure 9.7 *Two Image files found*

the lower left; at the right is a legend box explaining the symbols on the map. After the search for Image data is completed and no Image data is found, the screen shown in Figure 9.9 appears.

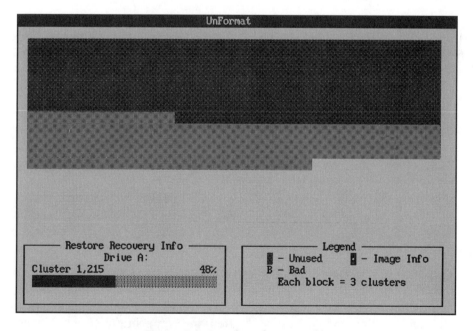

Figure 9.8 *Searching for Image file*

114 ■ *Power Of...Norton Utilities*

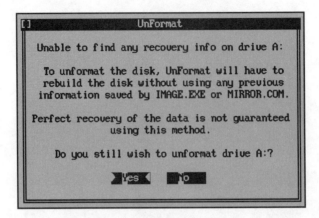

Figure 9.9 Image file not found message

The program warns you that perfect recovery of data is not guaranteed because no Image data exists and asks if you still want to UnFormat the drive. If you select **Yes**, the progress of the unformatting is displayed, followed by a notice that the drive has been unformatted. After you press **OK**, the screen shown in Figure 9.10 appears.

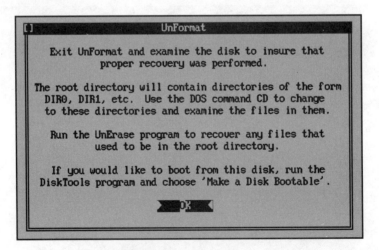

Figure 9.10 Rename subdirectories message

The subdirectories directly under the root directory are renamed sequentially as DIR0, DIR1, DIR2, and so on. Use the **Rename** command in Norton Change

Directory to restore the names. Refer to Chapter 18 for information on the **Rename** command. Files that were in the root directory are lost, but you may be able to recover them using the UnErase utility. Refer to Chapter 8 for details on the UnErase procedure.

Command-Line Options

UnFormat is a full-screen utility; regardless of whether you start it from the Norton menu or form the DOS prompt, the program operates as described earlier. You can, however, affect some aspects of its operation by typing options on the command line when you start the program. The command-line syntax for UnFormat is as follows:

```
UNFORMAT [drive:] [option]
```

where [drive:] is the drive you want to unformat and [option] is one of the following:

/IMAGE   Use Image recovery information (exclude Mirror information).

/MIRROR   Use Mirror recovery information (exclude Image information).

SUMMARY

Norton UnFormat recovers hard disks that have been accidentally formatted. It also works on diskettes that were formatted with Norton Safe Format or DOS 5.0 or later. In addition, it can be used on disks that were corrupted by a power failure or damaged by a virus. A nearly perfect recovery can be made if the disk contains a recent copy of the system area stored in an IMAGE.DAT or MIRROR.FIL file. Even if no copy of the system area exists, it may be possible to recover most of your data.

10

REPAIRING DAMAGED DISKS WITH NORTON DISK DOCTOR

In addition to major disasters such as accidentally erased files and accidentally formatted disks, a number of common, minor problems can afflict your disks on a daily basis. These problems result from software errors, user errors (such as turning off the power when a file operation is taking place, or turning off or rebooting the system without properly closing active programs), and physical damage to disks from ordinary wear and tear or trauma. Often these minor problems are invisible in daily operation, but if they are not diagnosed and corrected promptly, they can reduce the amount of storage space available on your disks or make some of your files unreadable. The Norton Disk Doctor is a program that tests disks for a number of these common problems, and, in most cases, repairs them automatically. You should certainly run Disk Doctor whenever an attempt to read from or write to a file on your hard disk fails or results in a cryptic DOS error message. (Consult Norton Advisor on the Help menu of the Norton Utilities menu shell for

118 ■ *Power Of...Norton Utilities*

the meanings of DOS error messages.) But don't wait for a problem to occur before becoming familiar with Disk Doctor. Run it regularly (weekly, at least) to verify that your disk subsystems are operating properly and no problems are developing.

The following description assumes that you have a basic understanding of how DOS allocates and manages disk space. If you don't, you should read Chapter 23 for a detailed discussion of these matters.

LOST CLUSTERS

The most common problem detected by Disk Doctor is lost clusters. These occur from time to time on every hard disk; in most cases, they are nothing to worry about. If you are running Disk Doctor on your system for the first time and you haven't previously been using a similar program or the DOS CHKDSK /F command on a regular basis, you're almost certain to have some lost clusters. These are marked in the file allocation table (FAT) as belonging to a file but are not connected to any directory or subdirectory entry. In other words, they are orphaned. DOS cannot use them to store new data because the FAT says they're allocated, but they don't belong to a real file, so they're not serving any good purpose. They're just wasting valuable disk space.

How do lost clusters get lost? There are a number of ways, but most have to do with a file write operation being interrupted before it was completed. This can happen when a program crashes during a write operation, when a power failure occurs, or when you switch off the power during a file operation. Another possible cause is that a program had temporary files open for its internal use and failed to close and delete them on termination, either because of a software error on the part of the program or because you turned off or rebooted the computer without first closing the program properly (a bad habit that you would be wise to eliminate). However they got there, lost clusters need to be removed to free the disk space they occupy. Disk Doctor performs this task (as does the DOS CHKDSK command with the /F option). When it finds lost clusters, NDD asks you whether you want to convert the chains of lost clusters to files or delete them. Usually, lost clusters contain nothing of value and deleting them is fine. However, you may want to let NDD convert the chains to files, so that you can browse through them with a text editor to make sure that they contain nothing of value before deleting them.

Chapter Ten: Repairing Damaged Disks with Norton Disk Doctor ■ 119

CROSS-LINKED FILES

A less common problem, and one that is more serious, because it can result in data loss, is cross-linked files. Files are said to be cross-linked when they share a cluster. A cluster should belong to only one file at a given time. When the FAT entries for two different files point to the same cluster as the next cluster in the file, a problem exists. First, the cluster in question contains only the correct data for one of the two files. Second, although two chains lead to the cross-linked cluster, only one chain leads away from it. If you're very lucky, the cross-linked cluster is the last cluster in one or both files. If both files contain additional clusters, the remaining clusters belonging to one of the files will be lost. Cross-linked files sometimes result from two programs under a multitasking system attempting to save a file at the same time. At other times, they occur for no obvious reason. Fortunately, however, they are uncommon.

Network Usage

The Norton Disk Doctor can be run from a network, but it will not test network drives.

Compatibility Considerations

The Norton Disk Doctor works with a variety of partitioning programs, including Disk Manager, SpeedStor, and the FDISK program from DOS versions 3.3 and later. If you have a partitioning program other than the preceding or those listed in the Norton Utilities documentation, you should check with the Symantec/Norton tech support department to determine whether your partitioning program is supported.

STARTING THE NORTON DISK DOCTOR

You can start the Norton Disk Doctor either by selecting the program from the Norton menu or by typing NDD at the DOS prompt and pressing **Enter**. The program can be run interactively in full-screen mode, or particular operations can be specified with command-line options.

Full-Screen Operation

If you start the program without specifying any options on the command line, the Disk Doctor menu (shown in Figure 10.1) will appear, displaying the following choices:

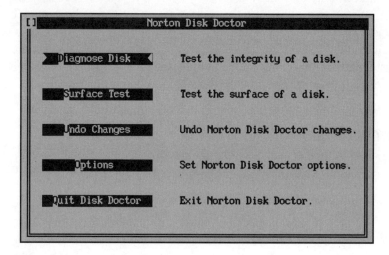

Figure 10.1 *Disk Doctor main menu*

NOTE

You can start Disk Doctor from a multitasking environment, such as Windows or DESQview, and you can diagnose disks, provided that no problems are found. However, Disk Doctor will refuse to repair disk problems, even on floppy disks, when running in such an environment and will display a message to that effect before returning you to the DOS prompt or the Norton menu. Hence, it is best to run Disk Doctor only under DOS.

Diagnose Disk

The **Diagnose Disk** option performs a variety of tests that check the integrity of the data structures on the disk. The areas tested include the partition table, the boot record, the file allocation tables, the directory structure, the file structure, and lost clusters (if present). This testing is one of the two main functions performed by Disk Doctor, and it should be used regularly. You are then offered the option of performing surface tests at a variety of levels (see later).

Surface Tests

The **Surface Tests** option allows you to test the physical characteristics of the disk to determine whether any bad areas have developed. Selecting this option opens the Surface Tests dialog box (Figure 10.2). Several options are available for configuring the surface tests.

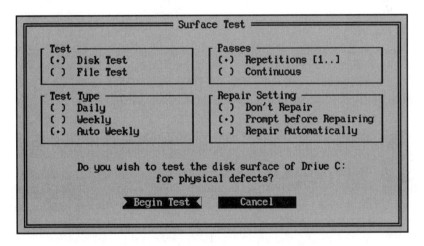

Figure 10.2 *Surface tests configuration dialog box*

Test Type—describes the depth of test to be performed (not the frequency of testing, as the names might lead you to expect). Selecting **Daily** performs a quick test that is designed to be performed every day. Selecting **Weekly** performs a longer and more thorough test. Selecting **Auto Weekly** (the default) performs the Daily test unless the system date indicates that it is Friday, in which case the Weekly test is done.

Passes—selects the number of times the test will be repeated. In most cases, a single pass on each disk will be sufficient, but if you have intermittent problems that are difficult to diagnose or if you want to "burn in" a new drive, you may want to select multiple passes. Either you can select a specific number of repetitions of the test, by selecting the **Repetitions** radio button and entering the number (1–999; the default is 1), or you can have the test repeat indefinitely by selecting **Continuous**. Press **Esc** to interrupt a continuous test.

Repairs—allows you to determine how the program will deal with any bad areas it finds. You can decline to repair the bad area (data about the bad area will be saved and can be printed later in a report), the program can prompt you before making the repair, or it can repair bad areas automatically (recommended).

What happens when a bad sector is found that was not marked previously by DOS as bad depends on whether that sector is being used. If the cluster in which the sector resides is free (not allocated to a file), Disk Doctor simply marks it as bad in the FAT and moves on. If the cluster is in use by a file, Disk Doctor does the best job it can of retrieving the data from the cluster, rewrites that data to a good cluster elsewhere on the disk, and adjusts the FAT entries for the file to point to the new location, before marking the cluster as bad. In either case, the cluster is marked as bad in the FAT, and DOS will not try to use it to store data again as long as the disk is not reformatted.

N O T E

Virtually all hard disks have some bad areas. It is simply not practical, with current technology, to create a disk that is capable of storing dozens or hundreds of megabytes of data and is completely free of flaws. When a hard disk is low-level formatted initially (usually at the factory), the bad areas are marked in such a way that when a high-level (DOS) format is performed, DOS recognizes them and marks them as such in the FAT. Over the life of the disk, new bad areas may develop, either as a result of physical damage to the disk surface (i.e., from head crashes) or as a result of deterioration of the magnetic track and sector ID markers. If your disk develops new bad areas once in a great while, there is no reason to panic. A certain amount of wear and tear is inevitable. If, however, it seems to develop new bad areas frequently, this may be a sign of a serious hardware problem. Back up your disk regularly (if you aren't already doing so) and consult a competent repair person.

Undo Changes

Before Disk Doctor corrects any problems it finds, it offers you the option of creating an UnDo file. This file contains the data from the corrupted or damaged areas of the disk and the information that Disk Doctor needs to restore these areas to their unrepaired condition. If a repair turns out to be worse than the problem, use this command to restore the disk to its previous state from the UnDo file.

Do not UnDo Changes after you have written new files to the repaired disk. Your new files may be lost.

WARNING

Options

You can set the following options for Disk Doctor.

Surface Test—the same options as those described earlier for the surface test.

Custom Message—is intended mainly for systems administrators or PC managers who are configuring Norton Utilities for other users. If you don't want inexperienced users repairing disks with Disk Doctor, you can use this option to configure the program so that when it finds a problem, it will issue a message such as, "Contact PC support at extension 666 for assistance."

Tests to Skip—allows you to skip certain tests whenever you run Disk Doctor. This can be useful if, for example, you have a system with a nonstandard configuration or nonstandard components that cause it to *always* fail a particular test, even though the system is in good working order. You should skip the partition table, for example, if you are using security software that encodes it, or if your disk was partitioned with nonstandard partitioning software.

Save Options—save the options if you want to use your current settings whenever you run Disk Doctor. If you just want to use your settings for the current session, select **OK** instead.

Diagnosing a Disk

When you select **Diagnose Disk**, a prompt box like the one in Figure 10.3 will appear. Press **Enter** to diagnose only the highlighted drive, or use the Spacebar to tag multiple drives for diagnosis. For each drive that is selected, Disk Doctor will perform the following tests in succession on each selected disk:

124 ■ *Power Of...Norton Utilities*

- Partition table
- Boot record
- File allocation table (FAT)
- Directory structure
- File structure
- Lost clusters

N O T E If a floppy disk is being tested, the partition table test is skipped, since floppy disks do not have partition tables.

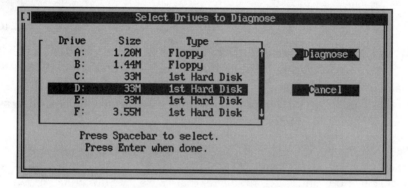

Figure 10.3 Drive selection box

Figure 10.4 shows the Diagnose Progress screen. This example shows that the first two tests have been completed and that the Analyzing File Allocation Tables test is in progress. As the testing progresses, the test description is highlighted and a blinking dot is shown next to it. A check mark is placed next to the test description after the test is complete.

When a problem is found during one of the tests, the program displays a dialog box with an appropriate message, such as that in Figure 10.5, and asks whether you want to correct the problem or cancel the test. This process will be repeated as necessary for each of the tests. Generally, it is advisable to proceed through all the tests and correct the problems as they are found.

Chapter Ten: Repairing Damaged Disks with Norton Disk Doctor ■ 125

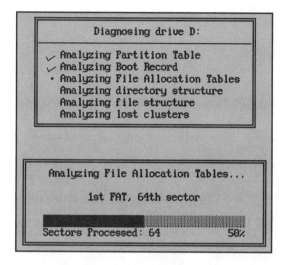

Figure 10.4 Diagnose progress dialog box

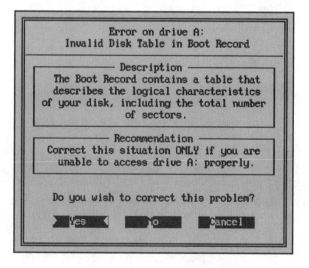

Figure 10.5 Problem found message

If you choose to correct the problems, Disk Doctor displays the dialog box shown in Figure 10.6, asking whether you want to create an UnDo file. An UnDo file permits any changes made to the disk to be undone. The dialog box suggests that the

UnDo files be placed on a newly formatted floppy diskette. The UnDo file *must* be saved to a different disk from the one on which the problem is being corrected. In addition, if you need to save more than one UnDo file (i.e., because problems are being corrected on more than one disk), you should use a separate diskette for each UnDo file, because the UnDo file will always be named NDDUNDO.DAT. Hence, subsequent UnDo files written to a disk will overwrite previous ones.

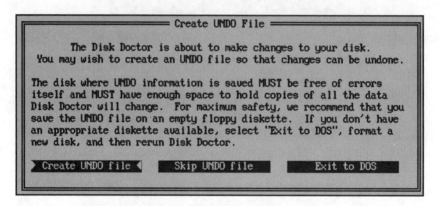

Figure 10.6 UnDo file prompt box

When all the tests are completed, Disk Doctor displays a summary of all the problems that were found, such as that in Figure 10.7.

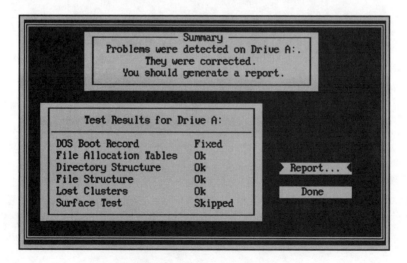

Figure 10.7 Problem summary

Surface Test

After the diagnostic tests are complete, the program offers you the option of performing surface tests. These are designed to check for physical defects on your disk. You should perform surface tests at least once a week to be aware of the onset of subtle problems. If you decide to do the tests, the Surface Test dialog box will appear (see Figure 10.2). Use the dialog box to configure the surface tests, as described earlier in this chapter. When you begin the test, a screen like that in Figure 10.8 appears, showing a map of the disk being tested. You can follow the progress of the tests on the map.

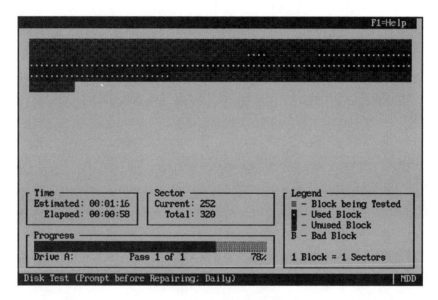

Figure 10.8 Surface test progress

When the tests are completed, the program displays a summary like that shown in Figure 10.6, indicating the problems detected and the actions taken. This screen gives you the option of generating a report with a more detailed account of the test results. The report is displayed initially on the screen in a scrolling text box such as that in Figure 10.9. (Only a small portion of the report is visible in the figure. Use the cursor keys or the mouse to scroll the report.) Use the buttons at the bottom of the dialog box to print the report or save it to a file. A complete report is shown in Table 10.1. Select **Done** to return to the Disk Doctor main menu. This completes the diagnostic procedure.

128 ■ *Power Of...Norton Utilities*

Table 10.1 *A Sample Disk Doctor Report*

```
                    NDD
            Norton Utilities 1.00
           January 11,1993 9:56am

           ┌─────────────────────────┐
           ┊   Report for Drive A:   ┊
           └─────────────────────────┘


                         DISK TOTALS
-----------------------------------------------------------
          362,496 bytes Total Disk Space
          62,464 bytes in 22 User Files
          300,032 bytes Available on the Disk


                 LOGICAL DISK INFORMATION
-----------------------------------------------------------
           Media Descriptor:  FD
            Large Partition:  No
                   FAT Type:  12-bit
              Total Sectors:  720
              Total Clusters: 354
            Bytes Per Sector: 512
          Sectors Per Cluster: 2
           Bytes Per Cluster: 1,024
             Number of FATs:  2
          First Sector of FAT: 1
     Number of Sectors Per FAT: 2
      First Sector of Root Dir: 5
   Number of Sectors in RootDir: 7
  Maximum Root Dir File Entries: 112
     First Sector of Data Area: 12


                 PHYSICAL DISK INFORMATION
-----------------------------------------------------------
              Drive Number:  0
                     Heads:  2
                 Cylinders:  40
         Sectors Per Track:  9
             Starting Head:  0
         Starting Cylinder:  0
           Starting Sector:  1
               Ending Head:  1
           Ending Cylinder:  39
             Ending Sector:  9


                    SYSTEM ARE A STATUS
-----------------------------------------------------------
             No errors in the system


                  FILE STRUCTURE STATUS
-----------------------------------------------------------
          No errors in the file structure


                  SURFACE TEST STATUS
-----------------------------------------------------------
                   Test Settings
                 -----------------
                   Test:  Disk Test
              Test Type:  Daily
         Repair Setting:  Prompt before Repairing
       Passes Requested:  1
       Passes Completed:  1
           Elapsed Time:  31 seconds


         No errors encountered in Surface Test
```

Chapter Ten: Repairing Damaged Disks with Norton Disk Doctor ■ 129

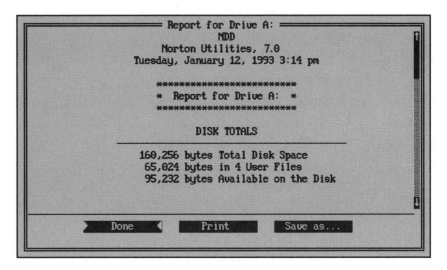

Figure 10.9 Disk Doctor report box

WARNING

Do not save the report file to the disk you are repairing. You may overwrite information you are trying to recover.

RUNNING NDD FROM THE DOS PROMPT

Disk Doctor can be run from the command line, bypassing the menus, by using the /Q, /C, or /DT options (explained later). The command-line syntax is as follows:

NDD [drive(s):] [options]

where [drive(s):] are one or more drives to be tested, separated by spaces. If no drive is specified, the current drive is tested.

The options are as follows:

/Q   Test the partition table, boot record, directory structure, file structure, and lost clusters, but do not perform surface tests.

130 ■ *Power Of...Norton Utilities*

/C	Perform all tests, including surface tests.
/DT	Perform only surface tests.
/R[A]: [filespec]	Write a report to the specified file (use RA to append the report to an existing file).
/X:[d]	Exclude the specified drive from testing.
/REBUILD	Rebuild an entire disk that has been destroyed.
/FIXSPACES	Repair filenames with embedded spaces.
/UNDELETE	Undelete a DOS partition that was previously skipped. For example, suppose NDD detected an old DOS partition, and asked if you wanted to undelete it. If you answered no, you could still go back and undelete it by using this option.
/UNDO	Undo repairs made in a prior session; you will be prompted for the location of the UnDo file.
/SKIPHIGH	Do not use high memory (64Kb to 1Mb).

To view a list of available options, at the DOS prompt type **NDD /?**

Examples:

```
NDD C: /Q /R:A:\TESTRPT
```
performs all tests except the surface tests on drive C and saves a report to the file TESTRPT on drive A.

```
NDD C: D: E: /C
```
This option performs all tests on logical drives C, D, and E.

```
NDD A: /REBUILD
```
This option rebuilds the disk in drive A.

Running Disk Doctor from Your AUTOEXEC.BAT File

Norton Utilities documentation suggests that you add Disk Doctor with the /Q option to your AUTOEXEC.BAT file to test your hard disk(s) daily. You can do this easily via the **Startup Programs** option on the Configuration menu. In

Chapter Ten: Repairing Damaged Disks with Norton Disk Doctor ■ 131

most situations, however, this may be overkill, and a weekly test will probably be sufficient. However, if you've been experiencing mysterious disk errors that you haven't been able to diagnose successfully or if you've corrected a problem and want to be sure it's completely fixed, a daily test can be useful.

Summary

Disk Doctor tests and repairs floppy disks and hard disks. It tests the system and data areas of the disk for logical errors and inconsistencies and can correct most such problems automatically. It also tests the disks for physical defects (surface tests) and recovers data from bad areas.

REPAIRING DATA FILES WITH FILE FIX

Your spreadsheet and database files can become corrupted in many ways. The leading causes are loss of power during a file save and damage to the disk. A partial recovery of an erased file (see Chapter 8) can also result in a corrupted file. File Fix is a file repair utility designed to fix spreadsheet (1-2-3, Excel, Quattro Pro, or Symphony), database (dBASE and Clipper), and WordPerfect files. The File Fix program creates a new copy of the damaged file, leaving the original intact. The new file contains as much recoverable data as possible.

Network Usage

You cannot perform UnZapping on a network or on a substituted or assigned drive.

COMPATIBILITY

Norton File Fix supports Lotus 1-2-3 versions through 3.1; Symphony versions 1.0 and 1.1; dBASE III, dBASE III PLUS, and dBASE IV; Microsoft Excel versions through 4.0; WordPerfect versions through 5.1; and any other product that uses a file format identical to one of these.

Running File Fix

To load the File Fix utility, select it on the Norton menu or type **FILEFIX Enter** at the DOS prompt. You can optionally include the name of the file you want to repair on the command line. Before repairing a file, File Fix checks your disk for cross-linked files and other FAT and directory errors. If it detects an error, the program displays an error message indicating that you need to run Norton Disk Doctor. If this occurs, exit File Fix and run Norton Disk Doctor to correct the problem, then start File Fix again.

If you do not specify a file to repair on the command line, File Fix responds with a dialog box such as that in Figure 11.1, which shows a list of the possible file formats to repair. (If you specify a filename of an appropriate type, the program goes directly to the repair dialog box for the specified file format, skipping this and the following step.) The available options are the following:

- Lotus 1-2-3
- Symphony spreadsheet files
- Quattro Pro
- Excel
- dBase and Clipper
- WordPerfect

Figure 11.1 *File Format dialog box*

Chapter Eleven: Repairing with File Fix ■ 135

Highlight the type of file you want to repair, then select **Proceed** to continue (selecting **Exit** terminates the program).

Next, the program displays a dialog box like that in Figure 11.2, showing the files in the current directory with the appropriate extension (unless you selected WordPerfect, in which case all the files are displayed, because WordPerfect files can have any extension). You can type a filename on the **File** line at the top of the dialog box, use the **Drive** list box to select a new drive, or select one of the directories on the current drive in the **Directories** box on the left side of the dialog box. The files of the specified type in the selected directory are displayed in a scroll box on the right side of the dialog box. Highlight the name of the file that you want to fix and press **Enter**. The program will then open the appropriate dialog box for repairing the type of file you selected, as described next.

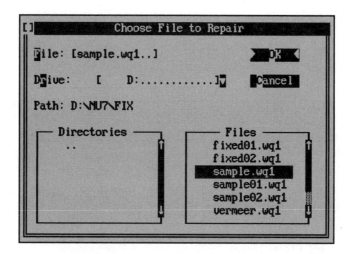

Figure 11.2 File Selection dialog box

Repairing Spreadsheet Files

The following example uses a Quattro Pro file, but the file repair procedure is the same for other spreadsheet files (i.e., 1-2-3, Symphony, or Excel files).

When you select a spreadsheet file from the file selection dialog box or specify a spreadsheet file name on the command line, a spreadsheet file repair dialog box such as that in Figure 11.3 appears.

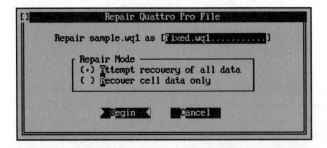

Figure 11.3 *Spreadsheet Repair dialog box (Quattro Pro)*

Specify a file name for the corrected file, or accept the default: "fixed.xxx," where "xxx" is the file's original extension. If there are erased files that you want to recover from the drive where the damaged file is located, you should save the repaired file on a different drive. You can do this by adding a drive letter and optional path before the file name (e.g., B:FIXED.WQ1). There's ample room for a long path; the text in the box will scroll right or left to make room.

Select the Repair Mode. There are two repair modes: **Attempt Recovery of All Data** or **Recover Cell Data Only**. You should always try the **Attempt Recovery of All Data** option first, because it attempts to reconstruct the entire file, including column widths, printer settings, range names, and graphic options. If this method does not work, try the **Recover Cell Data Only** option. The spreadsheet will not be able to read a file recovered by this method, as the formatting data contained in the file header will be lost, but you will be able to view the contents of the file and save the data. Whichever mode you select, File Fix automatically fixes the file and displays its progress.

After the repair process is complete, the number of bytes recovered and unrecovered are displayed. You can generate a report of the corrective actions from this display and send it to your printer or save it as a file.

Repairing dBASE Files

When you select a dBASE file from the file selection dialog box or specify a dBASE file name on the command line, a dBASE file repair dialog box such as that in Figure 11.4 appears.

The box shows the file you selected for repairs and the default name for the repaired version (FIXED.DBF). Specify a file name for the corrected file or accept the default. If there are erased files that you want to recover from the drive where the damaged file is located, you should save the repaired file on a different drive. You can do this by adding a drive letter and optional path before the file name (e.g., C:\TEMP\FIXED.DBF). There's ample room for a long path; the text in the box will scroll right or left to make room.

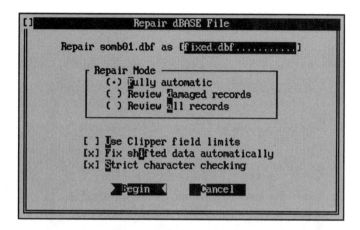

Figure 11.4 *The dBASE File Repair dialog box*

The dBASE repair dialog box offers three repair modes and has three configuration check boxes. The check boxes have the following functions:

Use Clipper Field Limits—this option should be unselected (Off) unless the file was created by Clipper. Clipper allows longer character fields, more fields per record, and larger records.

Fix Shifted Data Automatically—you should usually leave this option on to check data alignment. File Fix works faster with this option off, but it does not check data alignment in this mode. Turn this option off only if you believe the file contains just a few garbled characters.

Strict Character Checking—this option should be selected (On). Turn this option off only if the file you are repairing was created by a program that uses special graphics characters, such as the SBT accounting program. If you are in the manual mode and this option is on, File Fix stops so you can view records with nonstandard characters. In the automatic mode, any incorrect character is automatically replaced by a space.

Your first choice for the repair mode should always be the **Fully Automatic** mode. You should use the semiautomatic **Review Damaged Records** mode or to the manual **Review All Records** mode only if the Fully Automatic repair mode fails. The **Fully Automatic** mode automatically repairs the files. When you select automatic repair, the program first asks whether you want to review the fields. If you answer yes, the fields are shown in a scroll box such as that in Figure 11.5. When you approve the fields, the program proceeds with the repair. When the repair is completed, the program offers you the option of printing a report or saving it to a file.

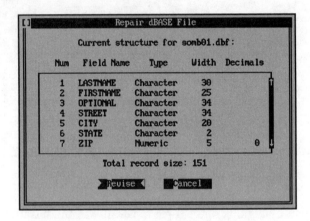

Figure 11.5 Review dBASE Fields dialog box

After you repair a file automatically, you should verify its integrity by loading it into the appropriate application. If the program fails to repair the file automatically (i.e., you attempted to load the repaired file into dBASE and the contents were not displayed properly), try again with the **Review Damaged Records** option. Again, the program will try to repair the file automatically, but if it comes to a record that it can't fix, it will display the record in a dialog box such as that in Figure 11.6. There are five buttons at the bottom of the dialog box:

Accept—keep the record without modification.

Reject—discard the record.

Shift—move the data relative to the field structure of the record, using the **Left** and **Right** arrow keys. (Use this option if the correct data appears but is improperly aligned.)

Mode—switch to a different repair mode.

Cancel—abort the repair process.

After you accept or reject the current record, the program goes back into semi-automatic mode until it finds another unfixable record. This process continues until the end of the file is reached.

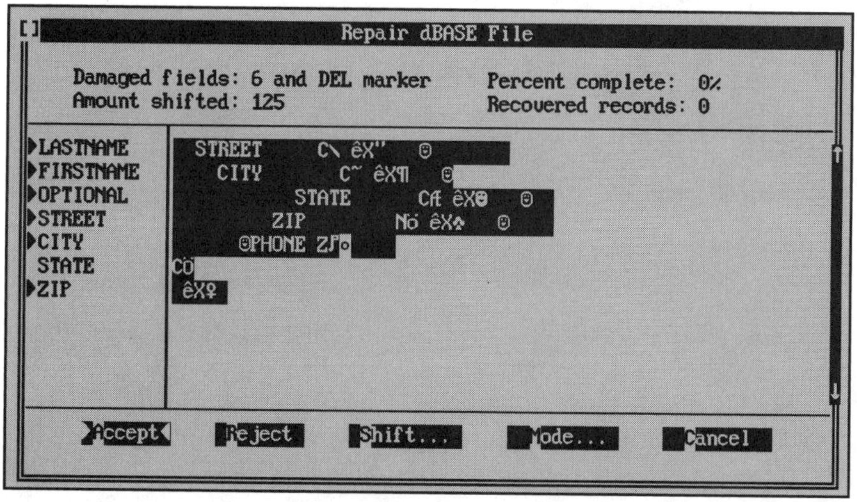

Figure 11.6 Damaged Record dialog box

If the Review Damaged Records mode still fails to repair the file completely, as a last resort you should try Review All Records. This method is essentially the same as the Review Damaged Records method, described earlier, but rather than showing you only the records that it regards as damaged, the program shows you *every* record in the file. The same options as those described earlier are available to modify the records. Obviously, this method can take a long time on a file with many records.

Damaged File Headers

The data in a dBASE file is useless without the file header that describes how the fields in a record are structured. Regardless of which file repair method you select, if the file header is damaged or missing, the program will inform you of this fact by displaying a dialog box such as that in Figure 11.7 and will ask you to review the fields. The fields are shown in a second dialog box, such as that in Figure 11.5.

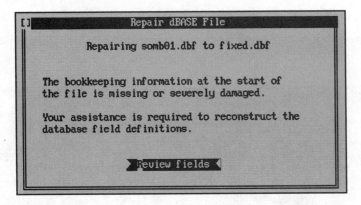

Figure 11.7 Damaged dBASE File Header dialog box

After you review the fields, you have two options: you can import a header from another dBASE file that has the same field structure, or you can reconstruct the fields manually. If another file with an appropriate field structure is available, you should use the import option, as it is quicker and much easier. If you select this option, another dialog box will appear where you select the file to import from. After you select the file, the program will display the fields of the imported header. Use the buttons at the bottom of the dialog box to accept the new header, revise (go back and choose a new file to import from), or cancel the operation. If you accept the imported header, the program proceeds with whichever repair method you have selected.

Manually Repairing a File Header

If you don't have another database file with the same record structure available, you must manually reconstruct the header. Select the **Edit** button in the Repair dBASE File dialog box and use the following steps (use a printout of the database as a guide if one is available):

1. Find the beginning of the actual data. Use the **Left** and **Right** arrow keys to shift the data so that the first character of the first field is aligned with the left side of the box, as shown in Figure 11.8. You can also use the mouse to drag

Chapter Eleven: Repairing with File Fix ■ 141

the data into position or type a position number. Make sure you are aligning the actual data and *not* the field name. When you think you have the data aligned correctly, select **OK** and another dialog box will appear (Figure 11.9).

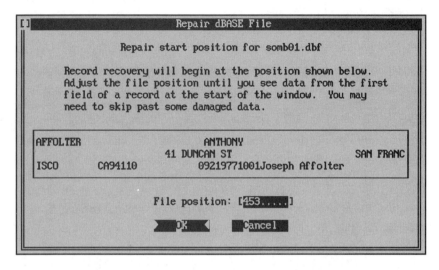

Figure 11.8 Starting Field Alignment dialog box

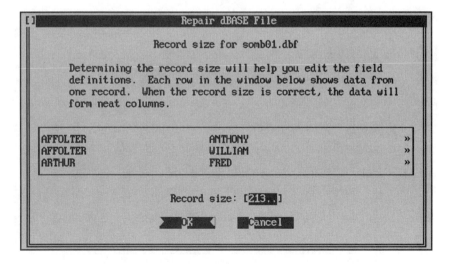

Figure 11.9 Record Alignment dialog box

2. The three rows in the text box represent three records. The object is to align the first character of the first field in each record with the left side of the box. Use the **Left** and **Right** arrow keys to do this. When the first characters of all three records are properly aligned, File Fix knows the correct length of a record in the file that you're trying to repair. Select **OK** to go on to the next step.

3. A new dialog box appears (Figure 11.10), in which you can set the size, name, and type of the fields in the record. Use the **Left** and **Right** arrow keys to make the fields larger or smaller, or select the **Edit** button to open the dialog box in Figure 11.11, in which you can edit the name and data type of the field, as well as the size. Use the **Up** and **Down** arrow keys to move among the fields. If the damage to the header was such that fields are missing or spurious fields were created, you can add or delete fields with the **Insert** and **Delete** keys. To delete a field, move the highlight to the desired field and press **Delete**. To add a field, move the highlight to the position *above* where you want the new field and press **Insert**. When you add a new field, select the **Edit** button to give it the proper name and to change the data type and width, if necessary. When you have set all the fields to the correct sizes, the figures for current record size and desired record size should match. Select **OK** to proceed.

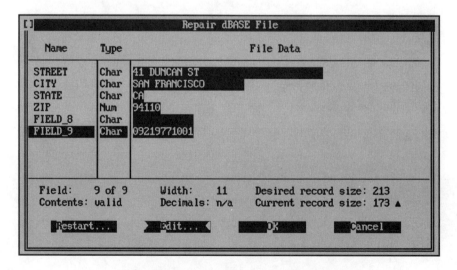

Figure 11.10 Field Adjustment dialog box

Chapter Eleven: Repairing with File Fix ■ 143

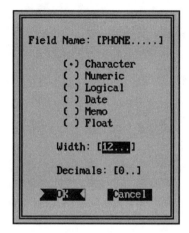

Figure 11.11 *Field Edit dialog box*

You will have to repeat the preceding three steps if you receive either of the following messages:

"The sum of the fields sizes does not agree with the record size used to align the data."

"The field definitions do not agree with the displayed data, perhaps due to some incorrect field types."

N O T E

If you don't get either of these error messages, you'll be shown the field structure of the record again. Accept it to begin the repair using whichever of the three repair methods you selected.

The number of fields File Fix can handle in dBASE files is the maximum number of files permitted by the database program used to create the file:

Program	Fields
dBASE III, III+	128
dBASE IV	256
Clipper	1024

File Fix can handle the maximum record size permitted by the program (except for Clipper). With Clipper you can have huge records, with up to 1024 character fields with a maximum width of 64Kb. File Fix can handle Clipper records up to 65,519 bytes (slightly less than 64Kb).

Repairing WordPerfect Files

WordPerfect files include a prefix that contains information about document formatting, such as what printer the document is set up for and what fonts to use. A very important item in the prefix is the offset, which tells WordPerfect where the prefix ends and the text begins. If the file prefix is damaged, WordPerfect may refuse to load the file.

When you select WordPerfect as the file format and select a file to repair, the program displays the dialog box in Figure 11.12. Specify a file name for the corrected file or accept the default. If there are erased files that you want to recover from the drive where the damaged file is located, you should save the repaired file on a different drive. You can do this by adding a drive letter and optional path before the file name (e.g., C:\TEMP\FIXED.WP5). There's ample room for a long path; the text in the box will scroll right or left to make room.

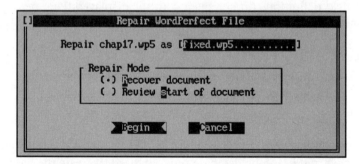

Figure 11.12 WordPerfect File Repair dialog box

After you specify the file name, choose one of the two repair modes: **Recover Document** or **Review Start of Document**. You should always try the **Recover Document** option first, as this method checks the file and automatically repairs any errors it finds. If any errors in the prefix are found, the program displays the Repair Prefix dialog box (Figure 11.13). (This is the same dialog box you will see if you select **Review Start of Document** from the initial dialog box, and the procedure that follows is the same, regardless of how you arrived at this point.) At the top of the dialog box is a scroll box showing the beginning of the file. Use the cursor keys to move the cursor in the box to the beginning of the document (the place where the actual text begins), then use the radio buttons to select one of the three repair methods: **Repair Document Offset**, **Build Simple File Prefix**, or **Import File Prefix**.

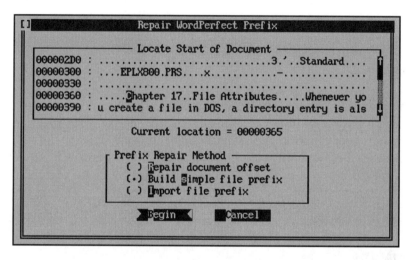

Figure 11.13 WordPerfect File Prefix Repair dialog box

If you have another WordPerfect file that was set up with the same printer, fonts, initial settings, and so on, the **Import File Prefix** option is a good choice. Selecting this option displays a dialog box where you can select a file to borrow a prefix from. Select the file and you will see a message indicating that the prefix was successfully imported. Select **OK** and the program will proceed with the automatic repair of the rest of the file. If a file with an appropriate prefix is not available, try one of the other two options. **Repair Document Offset** will probably work if only the offset is corrupted and the rest of the prefix is undamaged. This method will preserve most of the formatting options in the original prefix. If the **Repair Document Offset** option doesn't work and WordPerfect still won't open the file, other parts of the prefix are probably corrupted. In this case, you must use the **Build Simple File Prefix** option. This option will create a minimal prefix that will allow WordPerfect to open the file, but you will have to re-create formatting data that was in the original prefix manually in WordPerfect.

146 ■ *Power Of...Norton Utilities*

Unlike the other repair procedures, the WordPerfect repair process does not generate a report.

RUNNING FILE FIX FROM THE DOS PROMPT

File Fix is not a command-line utility. You can start File Fix from the DOS prompt by typing

```
FILEFIX [filespec]
```

on the command line, but the result will be the same as running the program from the Norton menu. If you enter a filespec, the program will select the appropriate repair option based on the file extension (except in the case of WordPerfect files) and will then proceed as described previously. You cannot bypass the program's prompts and dialog boxes by using command-line options, as you can with many of the Norton Utilities.

SUMMARY

With the File Fix utility, you can diagnose problems in damaged spreadsheet, database, and WordPerfect files. Whenever possible, File Fix automatically rebuilds an error-free copy, recovering as much data as possible. If it cannot automatically repair the file, it provides tools with which you can perform the file repair manually.

Norton Disk Tools

Recovering from the DOS RECOVER Command, Reviving Defective Diskettes, and Other Repairs

The Norton Disk Tools (DISKTOOL) lists four single-purpose tools on one menu. The tools can be used to recover a disk that was trashed by the DOS RECOVER command; to revive the tracks and sectors on a diskette that has become unreadable, without destroying data; to mark clusters on a disk as good or bad, and to install the DOS system files on a disk that already contains data files. Two other tools that resided on the Disk Tools menu in Norton Utilities 6.x—Make a Rescue Disk and Restore from a Rescue Disk—have been removed and made a separate utility called Rescue (see Chapter 7).

148 ■ *Power Of...Norton Utilities*

RECOVERING FROM RECOVER

The best way to avoid having to recover from Recover is to prevent the problem from ever occurring. This is easily done: *Don't use The DOS Recover command! Ever! Under any circumstances!* In fact, go to your DOS directory *now* and delete the RECOVER.COM file so that there will be no chance that anyone ever attempts to use it on your system. There is nothing that RECOVER.COM does that Norton Utilities can't do better and more safely.

What exactly is the DOS RECOVER command and why should you avoid it like the plague? It is intended to recover files with damaged clusters. It is not too dangerous if it is used on *single files only*, although the Norton Disk Doctor (see Chapter 10) is much better and safer. When it is used on a single file, RECOVER recovers all the good clusters in the file and saves them as a new file. In the process, *it discards any data that was in the bad cluster(s)* and marks those clusters as bad in the FAT. It is far better to use Norton Disk Doctor, which stands a good chance of recovering some or all of the data in the bad cluster(s), or, if that fails, to use Norton Disk Editor to manually copy as much data from the bad cluster(s) as possible. The real problem comes when you attempt to use RECOVER on a whole disk. If, for example, you type `RECOVER C:`, RECOVER assumes that your directory structure is bad and copies *all your files* to the root directory. In the process, it rounds up all the file lengths to correspond to their lengths in full clusters, it destroys your entire directory structure, and it renames all your files with cryptic, machine-generated file names of the form FILE*nnnn*.REC, where *nnnn* is a number. To make matters worse, the root directory has room for only 512 entries. Hence, if the disk holds over 512 files, those over 512 are lost. If this isn't a situation where the cure is worse than the problem, it is hard to imagine what would be.

The Solution

If the preceding advice has come too late and you have already mangled a disk with the RECOVER command, do not despair; Norton Utilities has a solution. The **Recover from DOS's Recover** option of the Norton Disktools program can restore your disk to a condition close to what it was before you ran the DOS RECOVER command. To use this tool, load the Norton Disktools from the Norton menu or type `DISKTOOL` **Enter** at the prompt;

Chapter Twelve: Recovering from the DOS RECOVER Command ■ 149

then select **Recover from DOS's Recover** from the menu, or type `DISK-TOOL /DOSRECOVER` at the DOS prompt. Select the disk that you want to recover from the list box that appears. The program will ask you to confirm that you want to perform this operation. While the recovery process is going on, you will see a screen such as that in Figure 12.1, indicating the progress of the recovery process.

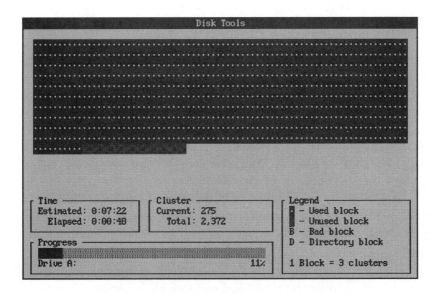

Figure 12.1 Recovery Progress screen

The **Recover from DOS's Recover** option reconstructs the lost directories. It cannot recover the directory names, however, so it gives them names of the form DIR*nnnn*, where *nnnn* is a number. It does replace the files in the proper directories with their original names and correct lengths, but it does not restore the original names of the files that were in the root directory, although it can sometimes restore their correct extensions. When it has finished working, the program gives you a cautionary prompt to remind you to rename the files in the root directory.

NOTE

Use the Norton Change Directory utility (NCD) to restore the correct names to the subdirectories. See Chapter 18 for details.

WARNING Do not save any new files on the disk that you want to restore. The process of recovering from the DOS RECOVER command will destroy the new files. If you have saved new files on the disk, copy them to another disk before performing the recover.

REVIVING A DEFECTIVE DISKETTE

Diskettes (and hard disks too, for that matter) are divided into sectors and tracks when they are initially formatted. The Format program places track and sector ID markers on the disk to enable the disk controller to position the drive's read/write heads so that the appropriate track/sector can be written to or read from. If anything happens to the track/sector ID markers, the disk becomes partially or wholly unreadable. Track/sector IDs on a diskette can be damaged in a number of ways. Over time the magnetic strength of the markers will simply fade, as with any magnetically recorded data. Exposure to magnetic fields can damage both the markers and the data on the disk. Physical damage to the disk, such as abrasion or contamination with foreign substances, can also damage the ID markers or make them impossible to read correctly.

Of course, you could easily restore the tracks and sectors by doing a new low-level format of the disk, either with the DOS FORMAT command or the DOS option of the Norton Safe Format utility. Unfortunately, this would wipe out any files currently on the disk. What is needed is a program that will restore the low-level format of the disk without wiping out the data or system areas of the disk. This is exactly what the Revive feature of Norton Disk Tools does. (The Norton Calibrate utility can perform the same trick for some hard disks. See Chapter 15.)

If you have a diskette with valuable files that cannot be read by DOS or repaired by Disk Doctor, try using the Revive feature to restore the tracks and sectors. Start the Disk Tools by selecting them from the Norton menu and select **Revive a Defective Diskette** on the Disk Tools menu, *or* you can type `DISKTOOL/REVIVE` at the DOS prompt. In either case, the program will prompt you to specify the drive to be revived and to place the defective diskette in the drive. The program will then begin the reviving process and will display its progress on the screen as shown in Figure 12.2. The revival process can take several minutes and make quite a bit of noise, so go make yourself a cup of coffee.

Chapter Twelve: Recovering from the DOS RECOVER Command ■ 151

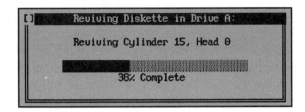

Figure 12.2 *Diskette Revival progress screen*

When the process is completed, it is a good idea to run Disk Doctor (see Chapter 10) on the revived diskette to correct any damage to the system area. The revival process may or may not succeed in making all the files on the disk readable, depending on the nature of the damage, but it will probably at least make the disk readable so that you can use other Norton tools, such as the Disk Doctor, File Fix, and Disk Editor, to attempt to recover damaged files.

MARKING A CLUSTER

A cluster is the minimum amount of disk space that can be allocated by DOS for use by a file. (For a detailed discussion of clusters and other aspects of disk organization, consult Chapter 23.) Each cluster on a disk has a corresponding entry in the file allocation table (FAT), indicating that the cluster is either allocated to a file, free, or bad. When a disk is initially formatted, DOS marks clusters that cannot be read or written properly as bad in the FAT. If other clusters on the disk become bad later on, tools such the Norton Disk Doctor (see Chapter 10) can find and mark the defective clusters. The **Mark a Cluster** option in the Disk Tools menu allows you to manually mark any cluster on a disk as good or bad. If a cluster has been giving you intermittent problems, mark it as bad. This prevents DOS from using it. You can also remark bad clusters as good. Suppose you want to retrieve data from a bad cluster. You will not be able to access the cluster unless you change its status to good. Marking a cluster as good makes it accessible by DOS. (If you remark a bad cluster as good in order to retrieve data, be sure to mark the cluster as bad again when you're finished, so DOS doesn't attempt to use it to store data.

To use this tool, select **Mark a Cluster** from the Disk Tools menu or type `DISKTOOL /MARKCLUSTER` at the DOS prompt. In either case, the program will prompt you to enter the drive where you want to mark a cluster. When you have specified the drive, the program will display a dialog box such as that in Figure 12.3, indicating the valid range of clusters and prompting you to enter the cluster to mark. Use the radio button to indicate whether you want to mark the selected cluster as good or bad. (You can only mark a cluster as good if it was previously marked bad.) If a cluster you are marking as bad currently contains data, the program will copy the data to a good cluster before marking the specified cluster as bad.

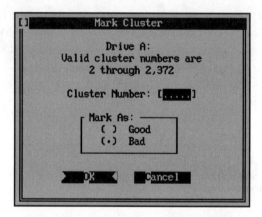

Figure 12.3 Cluster Selection dialog box

NOTE   In most cases, users should refrain from marking clusters manually and should rely instead on the intelligence of the Norton Disk Doctor or similar programs that can evaluate the condition of the disk surface and determine which clusters need to be marked.

MAKE A DISK BOOTABLE

A bootable disk contains the system files IBMBIO.COM and IBMDOS.COM (or MSDOS.SYS and IO.SYS). In DOS versions prior to 5.0 these files must be in specific locations on the disk. If they are not in the expected locations, the boot code cannot find them and the disk will not be bootable. Normally, one makes a disk bootable by formatting it with the /S option. DOS also allows you to format a disk and leave space so that the system files can be added later (via the

Chapter Twelve: Norton Disk Tools ■ 153

SYS command) by using the /B option with the FORMAT command. There is really no point in this, however, because using the /B option takes up as much space as actually installing the system files. If you have formatted a disk without using the /S or /B option and have saved files on the disk and you later try to install the system files with the SYS command, the SYS command will fail and display a "No room for system files" error message.

The **Make a Disk Bootable** tool in the Disktools avoids this problem by physically moving any files found in the area required by the system files to an empty location on the disk. (There must be enough free space available on the disk to make this possible.) After the area has been cleared, it copies the two system files to the appropriate locations. Then it copies COMMAND.COM, which is also required on a bootable disk but is not position sensitive, to a vacant location in the data area of the disk. If you have a floppy disk that contains useful files, using this tool saves time compared to copying the files to another disk, reformatting the disk with the /S option, and copying the files back on to the disk. It can also make a hard-disk partition bootable in the event that you have a formatted hard disk without a bootable partition.

To use this tool, select **Make a Disk Bootable** from the Disk Tools Menu, and press **Enter** or type DISKTOOL /MAKEBOOT at the DOS prompt. The program will prompt you to specify the disk that you want to make bootable. It will then copy the required files, displaying its progress on the screen as it does so.

Protecting Your Valuable Data from Unfriendly Eyes

In the previous sections, we discussed how to protect your data from loss due to user error (your own or others'), viruses, glitches resulting from power loss, and the general wear and tear that affects every computer. We have also seen how several of the Norton Utilities can be used to repair the damage in the event that you fail to avert any of these mishaps. Depending on how you use your computer, your disks may need another kind of protection as well—you may need to protect your confidential data from those who have no business seeing it. Two Norton Utilities serve this purpose:

156 ■ *Power Of...Norton Utilities*

◆ Diskreet (Chapter 13) allows you to encrypt individual files and to create password-protected virtual drives called NDisks, where large groups of files can be hidden and protected with a single password.

◆ Wipe Info (Chapter 14) gets rid of the telltale data that is left behind when you erase files by ordinary means. As you may have learned in previous chapters, erasing or deleting files with DOS commands doesn't actually remove the data; it remains in place until it is overwritten with new data. Anyone with the right tools can easily retrieve your erased files. The last time you sent a floppy disk with a few files to a client or associate, did you think about what was on that disk previously? It is better to be safe; use Wipe Info to remove confidential files and you won't have to worry about your confidential data falling into the wrong hands.

13

PROTECTING CONFIDENTIAL FILES WITH DISKREET

Whatever the purpose for which you use your PC, you probably have some files that you consider confidential, that you wouldn't want just anyone to access. They might be CAD files containing plans for a new product, program files for a piece of software under development, legal briefs, tax and financial records, unpublished articles or screenplays, your client and prospect databases, or just your personal correspondence. The possibilities are as varied as the purposes for which people use their personal computers.

Of course, the simplest way to keep your files confidential is to keep other people from getting their hands on your computer, but that topic is outside the scope of this book. If you work in an environment where it is not practical to make your system physically inaccessible, or if your files are of such value that you think others may be willing to break into your home or office to get at them, then another approach is necessary. That approach is encryption. This is the process of algorithmically scrambling or encoding a file so that it cannot be

157

158 ■ *Power Of...Norton Utilities*

read or otherwise manipulated. Encryption involves the use of a "key," a word or phrase that is used by the encryption software in the encoding process. Anyone who has the key and the appropriate encryption/decryption software can unscramble the file and read it or use it. Without the key, it is impossible to unscramble the encrypted file. If you have chosen your key carefully and protected it from discovery, the possibility of anyone discovering it through trial and error is also virtually nil.

How Diskreet Works

The Norton Diskreet program offers you two methods for encrypting files:

1. You can encrypt or decrypt individual files by giving them their own passwords. Encrypted files can be copied, moved, or transmitted, but they can't be opened, examined, or printed in an intelligible form unless they are first decrypted using the correct password.

2. You can create an encrypted, password-protected "virtual disk" called an NDisk, where you can store files that you wish to protect. When an NDisk is open, you can copy files to or from it and perform any other file operation that can be performed on any normal drive. Files stored in the NDisk can be freely loaded, examined, printed, or modified. When an NDisk is closed, no one can perform any operation on the files stored in it without first using the proper password to open it. This option has the advantage of requiring only one password to access many files.

NDisks can be created on hard disks or floppy disks. You can create multiple NDisks on a single physical or logical disk. Each NDisk is assigned its own drive letter and behaves like an independent disk drive. An NDisk looks to DOS like a hidden file, so you will not see it in a normal directory listing (although you can see it using the Norton FA utility or other utilities that can be used to manipulate file attributes). This is done so that you will not accidentally delete an NDisk.

To create and manipulate NDisks, you must have the DISKREET.SYS encryption driver installed in your CONFIG.SYS file. (The driver is not required for encrypting and decrypting individual files.)

Chapter Thirteen: Protecting Confidential Files with Diskreet ■ 159

Regardless of whether you encrypt individual files or encrypt groups of files by storing them in an NDisk, you have a choice of two levels of encryption:

- ◆ Norton's proprietary method, which is fast but not as secure as DES encryption;
- ◆ The Data Encryption Standard (DES) method, approved by the federal government, which takes more time but is very secure.

If all you want to do is to prevent someone who shares your computer from reading your files, the proprietary method will suffice. To secure files against espionage, the DES method is recommended.

NOTE

File encryption technology and the DES standard are subjects of controversy in the computer industry at present. In particular, some encryption experts claim that the DES standard was deliberately made weaker than the current technology would allow, and some have even suggested that a "trap door" has been built into the DES algorithm to allow government agents to examine your encrypted files. I am not qualified to judge these matters, but if you need the highest possible level of security for your files, including security from the eyes of Uncle Sam, I suggest you consult a qualified security expert.

Network Usage

You can encrypt and decrypt individual files on a network, but you cannot create or access an NDisk on a network drive. You can, however, copy an NDisk to a network drive for storage.

Passwords

The key to the security of Diskreet is the way it uses your passwords. Diskreet uses two kinds of passwords: *main* and *specific*.

- ◆ The main password protects general Diskreet functions such as unlocking the keyboard, changing system settings, and changing the automatic close times for NDisks. The main password is set to null when the pro-

160 ■ *Power Of...Norton Utilities*

gram is installed; press **Enter** when the main password is first requested. For the best protection, select a master password as soon as you begin using Diskreet.

◆ Specific passwords are used to protect individual files or NDisks. They are used for encrypting and decrypting files and for accessing an NDisk.

Each NDisk and each individual file encrypted outside an NDisk requires a password. Use the NDisk passwords to open, edit, or adjust the size of an NDisk. You also must supply the NDisk or File password to change the password. You can use the same password for all the NDisks and/or files you encrypt, but it is probably safer to use a different password for each file.

The specific password you use to encrypt a file or create an NDisk must be at least six characters long. This password is used as the encryption key. The longer it is, the more secure your files are. Diskreet accepts passwords up to 40 characters long. When Diskreet performs the encryption, the process is governed by the encryption key. The encryption procedure used depends on which method you chose (Proprietary or DES).

Encrypted data is only as secure as your password. If anyone guesses or discovers your password, your data is compromised. You should therefore avoid any words or numbers that could easily be connected with you. For example, stay away from your phone number, birth date, addresses, and close relatives' names. Use obscure information that you can easily remember, such as your high school colors or a historical character. If your data requires extreme security, a nonsense phrase is the best.

INSTALLING THE **DISKREET.SYS** DRIVER

To use the NDisk option of the Diskreet program, you must load the DISKREET.SYS encryption driver by adding the following line to your CONFIG.SYS file:

`DEVICE=[path]DISKREET.SYS`

where [path] is the drive/directory where Norton Utilities is installed. If you did not do so when you initially installed Norton Utilities, you can easily add this line to your CONFIG.SYS file using the **Startup Programs** option on the

Configuration menu or in the Norton Configuration program (NUCONFIG). See Chapter 3 for details. The DISKREET.SYS driver occupies approximately 46Kb of RAM. Depending on how your system is configured and what software you use, you may be able to load much of the driver into the high memory area or upper memory blocks (see later), thus maximizing the amount of regular DOS memory available for your applications.

Device Driver Options

Device driver options are for use with the corresponding line in your CONFIG.SYS file only. To add any of these options, you must edit your CONFIG.SYS file with a text editor; you cannot add them from the Startup Programs screen. There is a separate set of command-line options for use with the DISKREET.EXE program, which will be described later in this chapter.

/SKIPHIGH   Prevents the driver from loading itself into an upper memory block. If you are using a memory manager to load programs into high DOS memory, you may want to use this option.

/NOHMA   Prevents the driver from using the high-memory area, leaving it free for use by Windows or other programs.

/A20   Use this option only if you are working on a network and are having problems with your network drive, or if you are losing characters during serial communications.

/QUIET   Disables the Windows warning message (see the following note).

 If you run Windows in standard or enhanced mode after installing the Diskreet driver, you will see a message telling you that Diskreet's auto-open, quick-close, and auto-close timeout features (described later) will be disabled during the Windows session. These features are disabled to protect your data from Windows. You must manually open and close your NDisks when using Windows.

Loading the Driver in High Memory

The DISKREET.SYS driver can be partially loaded into high DOS memory (also known as upper memory blocks or UMB—free memory located between the

640Kb limit of conventional memory and the top of the 1Mb DOS address space) or into the High Memory Area (HMA—the first 64Kb of extended memory above the 1Mb DOS limit). (For a detailed discussion of the different types of memory, consult Chapter 16.) If possible, you should load the driver into one of these areas in order to conserve conventional memory for your applications. Which memory area will be potentially available depends on the type of system you use:

Computer Type	High DOS (UMB)	HMA
8086/8088	No	No
80286	No	Yes
80386	Yes	Yes
80486	Yes	Yes

NOTE Just because you have the processor type indicated in the table does not mean that you have the memory available to load the driver in one of the specified memory areas; it simply indicates that your computer *can access* the specified type of memory if it is available.

For the driver to load into the High Memory Area, the HMA must be free of any other drivers or TSRs. Many DOS 5.0 users use the DOS=HIGH command to load a portion of DOS into the HMA. If you do this, you cannot also load the DISKREET driver into the same area. You might want to experiment with alternately loading DOS and the DISKREET driver into the HMA to see which gives you the most free conventional memory.

To load the driver into the high DOS memory area (UMBs) you must have a '386 or '486 machine with at least 1Mb of RAM and you must have installed a memory manager, such as 386MAX, QEMM386, or the HIMEM and EMM386 programs that are included with DOS 5.0 and Windows. If you have a system that meets these requirements, this is probably the best place to load the driver. To load the driver in high DOS memory, make sure the device line for your memory manager appears *before* the device line for the driver in your CONFIG.SYS file. For more information on the correct way to install a driver in high DOS memory, consult the documentation that came with the memory manager that you are using.

Chapter Thirteen: Protecting Confidential Files with Diskreet ■ 163

NOTE This business of loading TSRs and drivers into different areas of memory is one of the more confusing issues facing PC users today. The only reliable advice I can offer is "Experiment!" If you load a new driver and it doesn't work properly, or if you begin experiencing unexplained system crashes, try changing the order in which drivers are loaded, or change the specification of which drivers go in conventional memory and which go in the HMA or UMBs. There are so many possible combinations of drivers, TSRs, operating environments, and system configurations that it is impossible to predict with much certainty what will work and what will cause problems. Norton Utilities alone offers five different TSRs and drivers, which, if all were loaded, would consume over 90Kb of memory.

After you install the DISKREET driver, you must reboot your system to load the new CONFIG.SYS file and install the driver. After you reboot, a message similar to the following will appear:

```
No Diskreet CONFIG file to read (DISKREET.INI).
Diskreet's main password has been cleared.
Instant close keys have been reset to LEFT + RIGHT shift keys.
AUTO-CLOSE TIME-OUT interval has been set to five minutes and DISABLED.
Keyboard lock & screen blank has been DISABLED. [sic]
NDISK drive count set to one.
* * * * PRESS ANY KEY TO CONTINUE * * * *
Diskreet's logical drive is F.
```

Note that the first line says "No Diskreet CONFIG file to read (DISKREET.INI)." Diskreet keeps your current setup parameters in a file called DISKREET.INI, which has not been created at this point. The next five lines tell you what the default values for the various options will be. Pressing any key will cause Diskreet to write a DISKREET.INI file using the default values. You can change the values later using the NDisks and Options menus in the Diskreet program dialog box.

Removing the Driver from Memory

Because the DISKREET.SYS driver is installed via the CONFIG.SYS file, it cannot be removed from memory except by editing the CONFIG.SYS file and rebooting the system. You may want to do this if you know that you're not going to work with NDisks in a particular work session and you want to make more memory available for your applications.

SHORTCUT Rather than editing your CONFIG.SYS file every time you want to install or remove the driver, make two versions of it, one with the driver and one without. Give them different extensions, such as CONFIG.DSK (for Diskreet) and CONFIG.NRM (for normal). When you want to install or remove the driver, copy the appropriate file to the CONFIG.SYS file (e.g, COPY CONFIG.DSK CONFIG.SYS), and reboot the system.

RUNNING NORTON DISKREET

Start Diskreet by selecting it from the Norton menu or by typing **DISKREET Enter** at the DOS prompt. The dialog box shown in Figure 13.1 will appear. The Diskreet dialog box has a menu bar with four menus at the top of the screen, and two windows, one showing the NDisks currently installed and the other describing the configuration of the highlighted NDisk. The Diskreet menu bar contains four choices: **File**, **Disk**, **Options**, and **Help**. You can access the menu bar by pressing **Alt** or **F10** or by using the mouse.

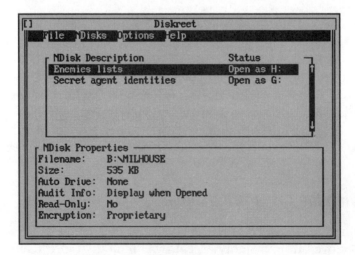

Figure 13.1 *Diskreet main dialog box*

Chapter Thirteen: Protecting Confidential Files with Diskreet ■ **165**

The Files Menu

Open the Files menu to encrypt and decrypt individual files. Each file must have a password (although you can use the same password for all files if you like). Once a file has been encrypted, it cannot be viewed, printed, or loaded into the application that created it without the proper password. It can, however, be copied, moved, deleted, transmitted, or otherwise manipulated by DOS or Norton Utilities file commands.

Encrypting a Single File

The Files menu has two options: **Encrypt** and **Decrypt**, plus **Exit** to terminate the program. Select **Encrypt** to encrypt a single file. (The file will be encrypted using the settings specified on the Options menu, described later.) The program will open a dialog box such as that in Figure 13.2, displaying the files in the current drive and directory. You can type a file name on the File line near the top of the dialog box or select a file by highlighting it in the scrolling text box on the right side of the dialog box. You can also change the drive and/or directory if necessary. When you have selected the appropriate file to encrypt, press **Enter** or click **OK.** A new dialog box, such as that in Figure 13.3 appears, where you can enter the name that you want to give to the encrypted file and your password. The default name for an encrypted file is the original file name with the extension changed to SEC, but you can enter any name you choose. After you have specified the file name, type your password, which must be at least six characters long. The password will be echoed by a string of *'s, so that passersby cannot read it. Type your password again to confirm it. If you don't enter the second password correctly, the program will notify you and ask you to type it again.

After you have typed the password correctly for the second time, the encryption process will begin and the screen will display a series of messages as the operation progresses. Another message will appear indicating that the file has been encrypted successfully. Then, depending on the settings in the Options menu, you may be prompted to indicate whether you want to delete the original, unencrypted file.

Decrypting a Single File

The process of decrypting a single file is analogous to the encryption process. When you select **Decrypt** on the File menu, a dialog box showing the

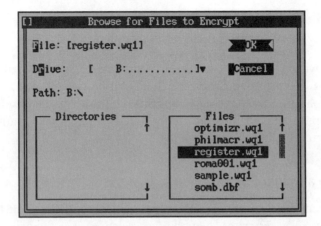

Figure 13.2 File Selection dialog box

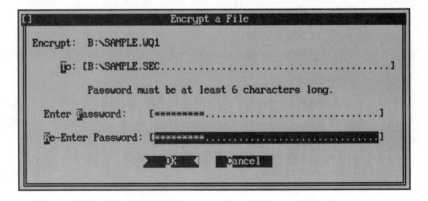

Figure 13.3 File Encryption dialog box

encrypted files in the current drive/directory appears. Select the file to decrypt and press **Enter** or select **OK**. Another dialog box will prompt you to type the password. If you type it correctly, the file will be decrypted. The progress of the operation will be shown in a series of screen messages, and a final message will indicate that the operation was successful. Type the wrong password and an error message will appear indicating that you entered the password incorrectly. Once the file is decrypted, you can work on it like any other file.

The NDisks Menu

Use the commands on the NDisks menu to create, open, close, or modify NDisks. As stated previously, an NDisk is a hidden file, located in the root directory of any drive, that behaves like a password-protected disk drive. The DISKREET.SYS driver (described earlier in this chapter) *must* be loaded before you can perform any work involving NDisks. To open an NDisk, you must supply the proper password. Once an NDisk is open, you can work with the files it contains just as if it was an ordinary disk drive. Close the NDisk after you have finished working, and no one without the proper password will be able to access the files.

Open—open the NDisk highlighted in the window in the main dialog box.

Close—close the highlighted NDisk, assuming it is currently open.

Close All—close all the NDisks currently open on all system drives.

N O T E

If you are working under DOS, NDisks can be configured to open automatically when you boot up or when you first try to access them. They can also be set up to close automatically after a fixed timeout or when you press a selected hot-key combination. These auto-open and -close features are set with the **Edit** option (see later) and the Options menu, described later in this chapter. If you are working under Windows, however, you must manually open and close all NDisks.

Create—before you use an NDisk for the first time, you must create it. When you select **Create**, a dialog box such as that in Figure 13.4 appears. Enter the name you want to give the file (eight or fewer characters, with no extension—the extension .@#! is automatically added to all NDisks), the drive you want to create the NDisk on, and a description of the contents of the file. The description is particularly important, because NDisks are listed in the Diskreet dialog box by description, *not* by file name. Enter a description that you will be sure to recognize. Next, select the size for the NDisk, in kilobytes. The dialog box will show you the amount of space available on the drive that you have selected, and you can give any amount of space from 32Kb up to the maximum space available on the drive to the NDisk (a maximum of 32Mb on a hard disk). Use the list box to select your encryption method (fast proprietary or DES). The check box at the bottom of the dialog box, **Show Audit Info**, allows you to keep track of attempts to access your data. The audit list will show all attempts, successful and unsuccessful, to open the NDisk.

Figure 13.4 NDisk Creation dialog box

Once you have set all the configuration options for your NDisk to your satisfaction, press **Enter** or select **OK**. A new dialog box will appear where you select a drive letter for the NDisk and enter your password (Figure 13.5). As with encryption of individual files, you must type the password twice in the identical form for it to be accepted. Note that the number of drive letters initially reserved for NDisks is one. If you want to create more than one NDisk and have them open at the same time, you will need to reserve more drive letters. (The assignment of drive letters to NDisks is not permanent; you can have several NDisks share the same drive letter, as long as only one is open at a time.) Use the **Driver** option on the Options menu (see later) to change the number of reserved drive letters. Changes made in the driver configuration will not take effect until you reboot your system. When you have selected your drive letter and entered your password, press **Enter** or select **OK**. The NDisk will be created, and if you have selected **Show Audit Info**, an audit box such as that in Figure 13.6 will be displayed.

Chapter Thirteen: Protecting Confidential Files with Diskreet ■ 169

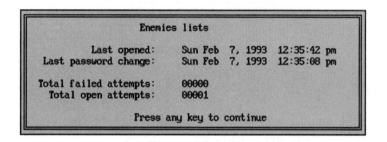

Figure 13.5 NDisk Drive and Password Selection dialog box

Figure 13.6 Audit Info box

Edit—change certain aspects of the configuration of an existing NDisk. The NDisk that you want to edit must be closed; if it is not, you will be prompted to close it before proceeding. You will be required to supply the correct password before you can edit the NDisk. When it has been accepted, a dialog box like that in Figure 13.7 will appear. The first option, **Auto Drive**, can be used to open the selected NDisk automatically, either at boot time or when you first try to access it. **Auto Drive** is off by default. To activate it, open the list box and select a drive letter under which the NDisk will be opened. (Auto Drive does not work under Windows. Windows users must manually open all NDisks.)

The next two options, **Prompt** and **Prompt At**, will be available only if Auto Drive has been activated. **Prompt** selects the type of prompt the program will

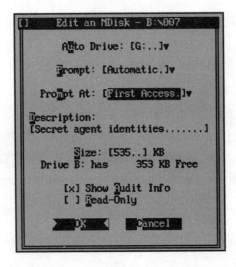

Figure 13.7 *Edit NDisk dialog box*

use to ask you to enter the password when the drive is opened. The choices are **Pop-up** (a dialog box such as that in Figure 13.8), **Automatic** (Diskreet decides which prompt to use, depending on the circumstances), and **Beep** (an audio-only prompt). To begin with, it's best to select **Automatic**. Diskreet should respond by using the dialog box on text-mode screens and the audio prompt in graphics screens. If this doesn't work properly, try one of the other options. **Prompt At** selects *when* the drive will be opened, either on boot-up or when you first try to access the drive.

Figure 13.8 *Auto Drive prompt box*

Description—modify the description you entered when you created the NDisk. The **Size** option lets you increase or decrease the size of the NDisk. You can increase the size up to the available free space on the disk (maximum 32Mb on a hard disk) or decrease it to the total size of the files currently stored in the NDisk. You can turn the **Show Audit Info** feature on or off, and you can make the

Chapter Thirteen: Protecting Confidential Files with Diskreet ■ 171

NDisk read–only. When an NDisk is set to read-only, the files in it can be read but cannot be overwritten, deleted or modified. This gives your protected files an extra level of protection. (They cannot, for example, be damaged by a virus.)

NOTE If power is interrupted when an NDisk is being resized, its contents may be irrevocably lost. Hence, it is a good idea always to back up NDisks before resizing them. Also, resizing even a small NDisk is a *very slow* process, so you shouldn't try this when you're in a hurry.

Password—change the password on an existing NDisk. If you think that someone has discovered your password, you will need to change it. Or you may want to change it periodically as a matter of routine to diminish the likelihood of its being discovered. When you select the **Password** option, a dialog box such as that in Figure 13.9 appears. (The NDisk for which you are changing the password must be closed. If it is not, the program will inform you and prompt you to close the NDisk before the dialog box appears.) Type the old password to confirm your right to access the NDisk; then type the new password twice in exactly the same form. Press **Enter** or select **OK** to activate the new password.

Figure 13.9 Change Password dialog box

Delete—delete a whole NDisk (not the individual files stored in the NDisk). Depending on the data-clearing option you have selected on the Options menu (see later), the NDisk may be simply deleted, allowing it to be recovered by the Norton UnErase or similar tools, or it may be wiped out irrevocably by overwriting it with other data. Obviously, overwriting is preferable for security purposes, but if you select this option, you need to be doubly careful about accidentally deleting an NDisk, as it will be impossible to recover.

Search—when you load Diskreet, it searches for NDisks on local hard drives and displays them. It does not, however, look for NDisks on floppy drives or other removable storage devices such as Bernoulli drives. You must use the **Search** option to find NDisks on these drives. When you select **Search**, a dialog box such as that in Figure 13.10 appears. You can either select individual drives to search or search all the drives of a particular type (i.e., all floppy drives, all hard drives, or all other drives). All the NDisks found on the selected drives will be added to the list in the main Diskreet dialog box.

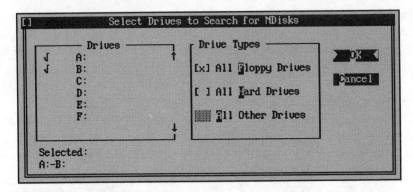

Figure 13.10 Search Drives dialog box

The Options Menu

The Options menu contains several selections for configuring the DISKREET.SYS driver and operations involving both the encryption of individual files and NDisks.

Driver

The options under the Driver menu item affect the operation of the DISKREET.SYS driver. Changes here will not take effect until you reboot your system.

Drive Letters to Reserve—select the number of drive letters to reserve for use by NDisks. You can have only as many NDisks open at one time as there are drive letters reserved. The default is one.

Chapter Thirteen: Protecting Confidential Files with Diskreet ■ 173

Auto-Close Timeout—configure Diskreet to automatically close all the NDisks that are open if they are not accessed for a specified period of time. This is desirable in case you leave your system unattended and neglect to close your active NDisks. After the specified time, all the NDisks will be closed automatically, so passersby will not be able to examine them. The drives are only closed temporarily; accessing any of the closed drives will reopen them all. Check the check box to enable Auto-Closing, then enter the time (the default is five minutes).

Auto-Close Timeout does not work under Windows. If you are working in Windows, you must close your NDisks manually.

Hot Keys—Quick Close All—configure Diskreet so that pressing a specified hot-key combination will immediately close all open NDisks and optionally blank the screen and lock the keyboard. The default hot-key combination is both **Shift** keys, but you can select from several other combinations by opening the list box. Be sure to select a combination that doesn't conflict with any other TSRs you may have installed. When you press your selected hot-key combination, all the open NDisks will be closed immediately, regardless of what is currently on the screen. As with the Auto-Close Timeout, this is a temporary closure. Accessing any of the closed drives will reopen them all.

The Hot Key Quick Close does not work under Windows. If you are working in Windows, you must manually close your NDisks.

To use the Keyboard/Screen lock option in conjunction with the hot-key combination, you must also have selected a Master Password using the option of that name (the last item on the Options menu, described later). Check the check box to activate this feature. When you press the hot-key combination with this feature active, the screen will be blanked and the keyboard locked. To free the keyboard and reenable the screen, you must type the master password. If you type anything else, the program will beep, indicating that the correct password was not entered. Hence, no one without the correct password will be able to examine your system.

NOTE Blanking the screen and locking the keyboard adds little extra security, because it does not prevent anyone from cycling power on your system or doing a hardware reset to gain access to it.

Files

The Files option sets the configuration for encrypting and decrypting single files.

Encryption Method—select the encryption method (Fast Proprietary or DES) for all single-file encryptions.

Delete Original Files After Encryption—delete original files after encryption automatically without asking permission.

Ask Whether to Delete Original Files—ask permission before deleting original files after encryption.

Hide Encrypted File—give encrypted files the hidden attribute so that they cannot be viewed or accessed via DOS.

Make Encrypted File Read-Only—give encrypted files the read-only attribute so that they cannot be deleted or overwritten.

Use Same Password for Entire Session—use one password for all the files encrypted in a given work session. You will be prompted for the password for the first file to be encrypted, and it will be used automatically for subsequent files.

Confirm Successful Encryption/Decryption—display a message indicating that a file has been successfully encrypted or decrypted.

Global

The following options appear on the Global menu:

Data Clearing Method—selects one of three methods to use when deleting original versions of encrypted files or NDisks:

- **None**—files are not cleared (a normal file deletion is done).
- **Overwrite Once**—data is overwritten once with zeros.
- **Government Wipe (DOD Spec)**—data is overwritten several times with different characters.

Warn If Driver Not Loaded—display the error message shown in Figure 13.11 when Diskreet is loaded if the DISKREET.SYS driver is not installed.

Figure 13.11 *Driver Not Loaded message box*

Master Password—guard access to certain global features of Diskreet, such as unlocking the screen and keyboard or changing the program's configuration; distinct from the individual password, which controls access to files or NDisks.

Working with NDisks

Once an NDisk has been created and opened, it behaves just like any other disk drive. Copy files to and from the NDisk using the DOS COPY command and/or any of the Norton file manipulation utilities. Load or save files from your applications. As long as the NDisk is open, the files are *not encrypted*, and anyone who has access to the system can copy or read them. For this reason, it is a good idea to use the Auto-Close Timeout feature so that you don't inadvertently leave your system running with NDisks open and accessible to unauthorized personnel.

Once an NDisk is closed, it is hidden from casual viewers, and all the files in it are protected from unauthorized access. Any attempt to access the NDisk will cause a "Drive not ready" error message. A knowledgeable person could find the NDisks on your system using the DISKREET /SHOW option, copy them to floppy disks (if they were small enough), and move them to another system, but he or she could not open the NDisks without the correct password.

Working with an Entire NDisk

You can also manipulate an entire NDisk just as you would any other file. Before you do this, you must make the NDisk visible to DOS. You could use the

Norton FA utility (see Chapter 20) to clear the hidden, read-only, and system attributes, but a quicker way is to use the DISKREET /SHOW:drive command-line option to make all the NDisks on a given drive visible at once. After you have done this, the NDisks are visible in a directory listing as files with the .@#! extension, and you can perform any operation on them that you would on any other file. However, any attempt to view the file (e.g., by using the DOS TYPE command or by copying the file to the printer), will simply show unintelligible garbage. Once you have finished working with the NDisks, hide them again using the DISKREET /HIDE:drive command-line option.

NOTE When moving or copying an NDisk for use, be sure to put it in the root directory of the new drive. An NDisk must be located in the root directory of its parent drive to be accessible. Of course, if you are just copying the NDisk for backup or storage, you can put it anywhere.

RUNNING DISKREET FROM THE DOS PROMPT

Some features of Diskreet can be activated from the command-line, bypassing the full-screen operating mode. You cannot, however, create or edit NDisks from the command line.

Command-Line Options

The following are the command-line options:

/E: filespec /P:password /T:target
Encrypt the specified file using the specified password; the target is the filespec for the encrypted file.

/D:filespec /P:password
Decrypt the specified file using the specified password.

/SHOW:drive
Show all NDisks on the specified drive—([drive] is the actual disk on which the NDisks are stored, *not* the drive letter assigned to an NDisk.) Showing the NDisks allows them to be moved, copied, and otherwise manipulated by DOS commands and other programs.

Chapter Thirteen: Protecting Confidential Files with Diskreet ■ 177

/HIDE:drive

Hide all NDisks on the specified drive. The hidden NDisks are not accessible to DOS.

/CLOSE

Close all open NDisks.

/ON

Enable the Diskreet device driver.

/OFF

Disable the Diskreet device driver.

/STATUS

Display a report of the current Diskreet status, such as the following.

```
DISKREET.SYS is loaded.
3 drive letters are reserved, G: - I:
  B:\MILHOUSE is Open, assigned to G:
  B:\007 is Open, assigned to H:
```

To see a list of possible options at the DOS prompt, type `DISKREET /?`

Examples:

`DISKREET/E:C:\PLANS\SECRET.DOC/P:MOONRISE`
      `/T:C:\PLANS\SECRET.SEC`
encrypts the file SECRET.DOC in the C:\PLANS directory using the password MOONRISE and names the encrypted file SECRET.SEC.

`DISKREET/D:C:\PLANS\SECRET.SEC /P:MOONRISE`
decrypts the file SECRET.SEC in the C:\PLANS using the password MOONRISE.

`DISKREET /SHOW:C`
shows (unhides) all the NDisks on drive C.

SUMMARY

Norton Diskreet provides security for your files by giving you a choice of two types of encryption. You can encrypt individual files, or you can create a password-protected virtual disk called an NDisk, where you can store many encrypted files.

14

PERMANENTLY ERASING FILES AND DISKS WITH WIPE INFO

The previous chapter described how the Norton Diskreet program can be used to protect confidential files while they are in use, but what about such files that you want to dispose of? If you've read Chapter 8, you know that when you erase or delete a file using DOS commands, the data belonging to the file is not removed from the disk. The first letter of the file name in the directory entry is changed to a σ (sigma), and the file allocation table entries are set to zero, indicating that the clusters belonging to the file are available for reuse, but the file data remains in the clusters where it was stored until it is overwritten by new data. Reformatting a hard disk doesn't remove the old data either, it just clears the directory entries and file allocation tables and leaves that data area of the disk unchanged.

It is quite simple for anyone equipped with readily available tools—such as Norton UnErase, Norton UnFormat, or the Norton Disk Editor—to recover your erased files if they can gain access to your disks. Even when the data is overwritten by new files, it is quite unlikely that *all* the clusters belonging to the file will be overwritten at once. A cluster or two containing your old data could

179

180 ■ *Power Of...Norton Utilities*

remain on the disk for weeks or months, and anyone who knew what to look for could easily retrieve those clusters and reconstruct part of your file—maybe just the part they need to confirm their suspicions about the project that you're working on. Old data may also be found in "slack" space, the part of the last cluster in any file that is not fully occupied by the current data.

Even if a new file does occupy all the clusters belonging to the old one, the old data may still exist in electronic "cracks." The size of the magnetized area written on the disk varies with the head current. Small differences in current can make a significant difference in the size of the magnetized area. This can leave "fringes" of the old data outside the areas occupied by the new data. Also, it is impossible to position the heads in exactly the same place each time a track is written. Differences in head position may also leave fringes. Data remaining in such fringes cannot be recovered by ordinary data recovery tools such as UnErase or the Disk Editor, but it may be recoverable by experts with specialized equipment (a good thing if your disk has been damaged and you're paying an expert to recover your data, but a bad thing if your disk has been stolen and the expert is in the employ of your competitors or a foreign government).

To make old data truly unrecoverable requires a program that systematically overwrites *all* the clusters in a file or on a whole disk. This is what the Norton Wipe Information program (Wipe Info) does. The Wipe Info program offers two levels of information wiping:

◆ *Fast Wipe* overwrites all the clusters in the specified area with zeros. This is sufficient to make the data permanently inaccessible to ordinary recovery methods such as Norton UnErase or the Disk Editor. It may, however, be possible to recover some of the data using specialized hardware and software.

◆ *Government Wipe* (DoD standard 5220.22M) is designed to defeat even sophisticated data recovery methods using specialized hardware and software. The data is overwritten first by zeros, then by ones, three times in succession, to produce the maximum disruption of the magnetic patterns on the disk. Then the character F6h or 246 decimal (÷) is written to the clusters and read back for verification. If the verification is not successful (the ÷ character is not read back from every byte in every cluster), an error message indicates that the wipe may not have been successful. When files are wiped (rather than whole disks), the file names in the directory entries are reset to a σ followed by a string of ÷'s. Use this method if you think that professional data recovery experts will attempt to recover your data or if you're working on government-related projects that require this level of security.

Network Usage

Wipe Info can be used to wipe files on network drives on which you have write privileges, but you cannot wipe entire network drives.

Where Data May Lurk

In situations demanding high security, it would be foolish merely to wipe the most recent version of a file from your disk while ignoring all the other places where your confidential data might be lurking:

- If you copied the file from another drive or directory, it may still exist in the original location.
- Earlier versions of the file that have been deleted may have left a residue in unallocated clusters or in the slack areas of current files.
- Your software may have automatically made backup copies of the file. Many word processors and other programs have automatic backup features. These are of two kinds: those that save the last copy of the file under a different name whenever a new copy is saved (usually the original file name with an extension such as .BAK or .BK!) and those that periodically save temporary backup files while you are working, so that you can recover your work in the event of a power failure or system crash.
- Some programs create and later delete temporary (or scratchpad) copies of a file as you work on it. These files only exist while the program is running, so you may not even be aware of them. Nevertheless, your data may remain accessible in the deleted copies of these files. And don't forget print spoolers and the Windows Print Manager. These too save copies of your data in temporary files that they use to feed the printer and then delete.

NOTE
To find out which of your applications save and delete temporary files and what file names and extensions they use, run SmartCan on all your drives (as described in Chapter 4) for a couple of workdays, with no restrictions on the types of files to save.

The data from all these sources can be systematically destroyed by the following combination of actions:

1. Wipe all versions of confidential files, including backups.
2. Wipe slack areas of *all files* on drives where confidential files have been stored.
3. Periodically wipe unused areas on all drives where confidential files are stored.

Obviously, you would only go to such lengths if your data was of such value to others that they would be likely to go to comparable lengths to retrieve it.

RUNNING THE NORTON WIPE INFO PROGRAM

You can run the Wipe Info program by selecting it from the Norton menu or by typing `WIPEINFO` **Enter** at the DOS prompt. The program responds with a dialog box (Figure 14.1) with four buttons: **Files**, **Drives**, **Configure**, and **Quit**. If you have not used the Wipe Info program before, select Configure to specify the type of Wipe operation you want to perform.

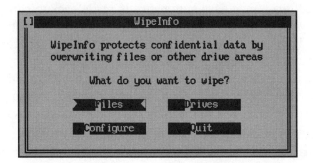

Figure 14.1 Wipe Info introductory dialog box

Configure

Selecting the **Configure** button opens the Wipe Configuration dialog box, shown in Figure 14.2. You can select either the Fast Wipe or the Government Wipe (described earlier). For the Fast Wipe, you can change the character used for the wipe (the default is zero). For the Government Wipe, you can change the number of times the clusters are overwritten with alternate zeros and ones (the default is three) and the character that is used for the final write and verification (the default is F6h/decimal 246). Note, however, that if you change the specifications of the government wipe, it will no longer conform to DoD specification 5220.22M. Use Repeat Count to change the number of times the selected wipe is repeated (the default is one). Repeating the Fast Wipe may be useful, but repeating the Government Wipe more than once probably won't accomplish much. You can specify a repeat value of 0–999 for either method.

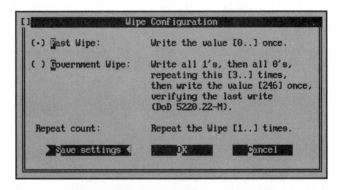

Figure 14.2 Configuration dialog box

If you want to make your settings permanent, select the **Save Settings** button at the bottom of the dialog box. If you want to use them only for the current session, select **OK**. To cancel your changes, select **Cancel**. Either choice returns you to the main Wipe Info dialog box. Having set your configuration, you have the choice of wiping either selected files or an entire disk.

NOTE A Government Wipe on a 1.44Mb diskette takes about two hours. To complete this type of wipe on a hard disk takes overnight at least. (Imagine how long 10 repeats on a hard disk would take—probably long enough for a short vacation, assuming that the disk survived that many hours of continuous activity.)

Files

Selecting **Files** from the main Wipe Info dialog box opens the Wipe Files dialog box (Figure 14.3). The dialog box initially shows the current drive/directory with a file spec of *.* (all files). You can type a new path and file spec on the file name line at the top of the dialog box, or you can use the directory button at the bottom of the dialog box to change to a different drive and/or directory. Under the File Name line are four check boxes for controlling how the program operates on the selected files.

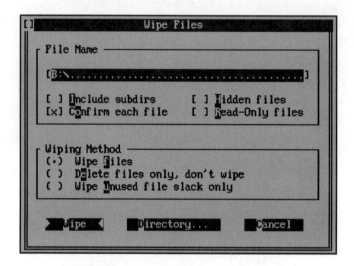

Figure 14.3 The Wipe Files dialog box

Include Subdirs—perform the selected wipe on files matching the spec in the selected directory and all of its subdirectories.

Confirm Each File—ask your permission before wiping each file that meets the spec.

Hidden Files—wipe hidden files that match the spec. By default, hidden files are *not* wiped.

Read-Only Files—wipe read-only files that match the spec. By default, read-only files are not wiped.

You can also select one of three wiping methods (not to be confused with the selection of the Fast or Government Wipe in the Configuration section):

Wipe Files—wipe the clusters allocated to the selected files, using the wipe selected in the Configuration section.

Delete Files Only, Don't Wipe—perform a standard DOS delete on the selected files. This doesn't destroy confidential data, but it can be used in conjunction with the **Include Subdirs** option to delete quickly a specified group of files from all the branches of a directory tree.

Wipe Unused File Slack Only—wipe the unused portion of the last cluster in each of the selected files, using the specified wipe.

When you have set all the parameters in the dialog box to your satisfaction, select the **Wipe** button at the bottom of the dialog box to initiate the Wipe. A warning box such as that in Figure 14.4 appears, warning you that you are about to wipe all the files matching the spec and that data in the wiped files will be permanently lost. Select the **Wipe** button to go ahead with the wipe, or select the **Cancel** button to return to the main dialog box.

Figure 14.4 Wipe Files warning box

If you have selected **Confirm Each File**, a new dialog box will appear (Figure 14.5) showing the files that match the spec and asking you to confirm the action to be performed on each file. Use the buttons at the bottom of the dialog box to select the action:

Skip—leave the current file alone and go to the next file in the list.

Wipe—wipe the current file.

Auto—wipe the current file and all the remaining files in the list.

Stop—exit the dialog box and return to the main Wipe Info dialog box.

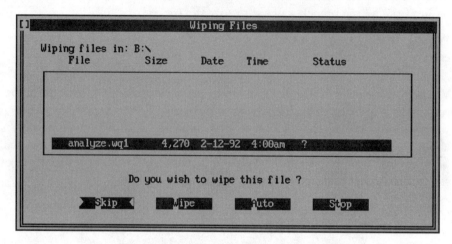

Figure 14.5 Wipe Confirmation dialog box

If you have not selected **Confirm Each File**, a similar dialog box appears, but only the **Stop** button is present. The dialog box displays the progress of the wiping process for each selected file, and when the wipe is completed a final message appears indicating the number of files wiped.

> **NOTE** When Wipe Info is running, SmartCan and the Disk Monitor are automatically disabled. This means that no areas are protected, and files that are deleted using Wipe Info (even if you do not wipe them) will not be saved in the SmartCan directory.

Drives

Select the **Drives** option from the main Wipe Info dialog box if you want to wipe an entire disk or the unallocated areas on a disk. When you select **Drives**, the Wipe Drives dialog box, shown in Figure 14.6, appears.

Chapter Fourteen: Wipe Info ■ 187

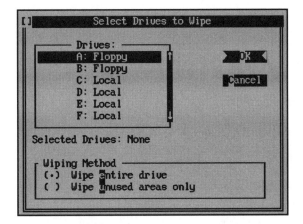

Figure 14.6 *The Wipe Drives dialog box*

 The **Files** option of the Wipe Info program will work under Windows, but the **Drives** option will not. If you select the latter option while running Windows (or DESQview), a message will appear indicating (somewhat misleadingly) that Wipe Info will not run in multitasking environments and instructing you to switch to a single-tasking environment (i.e., DOS).

NOTE

Select the drives you want to wipe by checking them with the spacebar. You can select one or more drives to wipe. Those that you selected will be listed below the drive box.

Next, select one of two areas to wipe (misleadingly called wiping methods):

Wipe Entire Drive—overwrite everything on the selected drive, including both the system areas and the data area. To use the disk again, you will have to format it first. This is the most secure method of wiping a disk.

Wipe Unused Areas Only—overwrite all data in clusters marked zero in the FAT, including files that were deleted using the DOS DELETE or ERASE commands, and all the empty clusters on the disk, which may contain left-over data from before the most recent format.

NOTE

Wiping unused areas only does not wipe slack areas at the end of files. You can wipe these areas using the **Files** option.

When you have selected the option(s) you want, select the **Wipe** button. You will see a warning message telling you that the wipe is about to be performed. You now can choose either **Wipe** or **Cancel**. Selecting **Wipe** again begins the operation. You can interrupt the wipe process at any time by selecting **Stop**.

NOTE

When wiping an entire drive, the wipe begins with the least important areas on the disk (clusters that are never used). Hence, if you start a wipe by mistake, pressing **Stop** in a timely manner may save some or all of your data.

RUNNING WIPE INFO FROM THE DOS PROMPT

You can access most of Wipe Info's features from the DOS prompt, bypassing the dialog boxes, by using appropriate command-line options. The command-line syntax for Wipe Info has two forms:

```
WIPEINFO [drive:] [options]
```

to wipe a drive, or

```
WIPEINFO [file spec] [options]
```

to wipe a file.

Option for Disk Wipes

The following option exists for disk wipes:

/E   Wipe the erased and unused data areas of the disk. If this option is not specified, the entire drive will be wiped.

Options for File Wipes

The following are options for file wipes:

/N Delete only, do not wipe. This is equivalent to the DOS ERASE or DELETE commands; files can be recovered with Norton UnErase.

/K Wipe only the slack areas of files.

/S Include files in subdirectories under the current or selected directory in the wipe.

Options for Both Wipes

/GOVn Use the Government Wipe; *n* specifies the number of times to overwrite the file with alternate ones and zeros (the default is three repeats). If this option is not specified, a fast wipe will be performed.

/Rn Repeat the specified wipe *n* times (the default is one).

/Vn Use character *n* (decimal) to overwrite the wipe area. You can enter any value from 0 to 255. In Government Wipes, the value will be used in the final write/verify. In Fast Wipes, it is the value used in the wipe. If you do not use this option, the default values (described earlier in this chapter) will be used.

/BATCH Skip all prompts and exit to DOS when finished (for use in batch files).

WARNING Be very careful in using the /BATCH option with Wipe Info. An incorrectly written batch file could irrevocably destroy the specified files without giving you any warning. For example, the command Wipe Info [drive] /BATCH will wipe *all* the data on the specified drive without any prompts or warning messages.

To view a list of available options at the DOS prompt, type **WIPEINFO /?**

Examples:

```
WIPEINFO C: /E /GOV
```
wipes the unused or erased areas of drive C, using the Government Wipe.

```
WIPEINFO C:\PLANS\SECRET.DOC /R3 /V42
```
wipes the file SECRET.DOC in the C:\PLANS directory three times using the Fast Wipe and the * character (ASCII 42 decimal). (No command-line option is required to use the Fast Wipe; it is used by default unless the Government Wipe is specified.)

```
WIPEINFO C:\PLANS\*.DOC /S /K
```
wipes the slack space in all the files with the .DOC extension in the C:\PLANS directory and all its subdirectories.

SUMMARY

Wipe Info provides another measure of security for your files. It provides a safe way to dispose of confidential files when you no longer need them. You can choose from two wipe methods and can wipe individual files, groups of files, or entire disks.

SECTION V

ENHANCING HARD-DISK PERFORMANCE

Over the last few years, microprocessor speeds have increased by leaps and bounds. Hard-disk access speeds and disk controller throughput, however, have lagged behind, making disk access and data transfer one of the leading bottlenecks in PC performance. No software can increase your basic disk access time or the data transfer rate of your controller, but the three Norton Utilities described in this section can ensure that you're getting the best performance your disk and controller can deliver.

192 ■ *Power Of...Norton Utilities*

◆ Calibrate (Chapter 15) can perform a nondestructive low-level format, restoring faded data and optionally changing your disk's interleave factor. If you have an older system and your disk's interleave factor is not optimal, this change can yield a substantial improvement in disk performance.

◆ Norton Cache (Chapter 16) is used to set up a disk cache in expanded or extended memory, reducing the number of disk reads your system has to perform. This option substantially improves the performance of "disk-intensive" applications.

◆ Speedisk (Chapter 17) optimizes hard disks by unfragmenting files and placing the most frequently accessed files in locations where they are more quickly accessed. If your disk has seen a lot of use and it has not been optimized or unfragmented previously, you can expect a substantial boost in performance from this utility.

THE NORTON UTILITIES™

15

USING CALIBRATE TO IMPROVE HARD-DISK PERFORMANCE

Calibrate is the first of a trio of Norton Utilities designed to improve disk subsystem performance. (The other two are the Norton Cache and Speedisk.) Calibrate is particularly useful with older drives and controllers. If you have an older system and the hard disk interleave factor (explained later) hasn't been optimized, Calibrate can improve your disk performance dramatically. It can also help to restore data that is beginning to "fade." On newer systems, Calibrate may not be able to change interleave factors or renew fading data, but it can still perform extensive tests to confirm that all the components of the disk subsystem are operating correctly.

What Calibrate Does

Interleave Testing/Modification

Hard disk performance (read/write speed) is directly dependent on an aspect of disk geometry known as the interleave factor. (For a more detailed discussion of disk geometry, consult Chapter 23.) The concentric tracks on a disk (hard or floppy) are divided radially into wedge-shaped sectors. Wherever possible, DOS tries to write a file to a series of contiguous sectors on the same track. This does not present a problem for most current systems with fast CPUs and disk controllers. On many older systems, however, the CPU and/or the disk controller are not fast enough to perform this operation efficiently.

When a disk write is requested by a program, DOS signals the hard-disk controller to perform a write, then sends the data. The disk head moves to the desired track, waits for the appropriate sector to rotate into position, then writes to the sector. Then it informs DOS that the write was completed and waits to see if DOS wants it to write another sector (which it usually does). While the controller is reporting the write to DOS and waiting for more information, the disk keeps rotating at about 3600 RPM. Unless the disk controller and CPU are fast, by the time these operations are completed and the controller is ready to write again, the beginning of the next sector may have already passed under the disk heads. If this happens, there is nothing that the controller can do but wait for the disk to make a complete rotation to bring the desired sector around again. A disk sector holds 512 bytes of data. Hence, a hard disk that can read or write only one sector per rotation can read or write only 30Kb per second, a rate that is inferior to the data transfer rate of floppy disks.

The solution to this problem is to place consecutively numbered disk sectors in noncontiguous locations on the disk surface. This gives the controller and CPU time to communicate, pass data, and perform housekeeping chores before the next sector comes around and still allows it to read or write several sectors per rotation, instead of just one. The way the consecutively numbered sectors are spaced on the disk is called the *interleave factor*. Disk performance can be improved significantly by selecting the interleave factor that optimally matches the speeds of the controller and the CPU. Calibrate tests interleave and determines the optimal interleave factor for the system. It can then perform a nondestructive low-level format and change the interleave factor if necessary.

Chapter Fifteen: Using Calibrate to Improve Hard-Disk Performance ■ 195

(This is a concern mainly with older systems; the drive/controller subsystems in most current PCs are set up to use 1:1 interleave—consecutively numbered sectors in contiguous locations on the disk surface—and are fast enough to achieve optimal performance with this configuration.)

Track/Sector ID and Data "Refreshment"

Data stored on magnetic media can deteriorate over time. This is the case because the magnetic particles on the disk or tape are really only temporarily magnetized by the write process. It may take a long time, but eventually the recorded data will begin to "fade." On analog recordings (audio and video tapes) the gradual fading of magnetic patterns is manifested in the gradual deterioration of the sound or image. On digital media, however, the early stages of the fading data are usually undetectable. Remember that the data recorded on a disk only represents ones and zeros; as long as the data is strong enough that the controller can distinguish correctly between them, it doesn't really matter whether they are as strong as the day that they were written. Eventually, however, the data may fade to the point where this distinction can no longer be made reliably. Then there is trouble.

The most serious problems result from the fading of track and sector IDs. These ID markers are created when a disk is low-level formatted, and they serve as the "road signs" to tell the disk controller how to find particular track/sector locations on the disk. The IDs are the oldest data on the disk (they were there before any files were saved); they don't get refreshed by resaving, copying, moving, and so on, the way data files do; and they can't be restored from a backup. Hence, they are more vulnerable to deterioration over long periods than are normal files. The only way to restore track and sector IDs is to perform a new low-level format. If you were to do this without the help of a program like Calibrate, you would have to back up all your data first (ideally twice, for increased security), then perform the low-level format, then restore your data. If you have a large hard disk and back up your data on floppies, this process can take about half a workday. Calibrate automates the process by performing a nondestructive low-level format sector by sector. It moves the data from the sector to a safe location, refreshes the IDs, then restores the data. Hence, both the IDs and the data are refreshed. At the same time, it can perform extensive pattern testing to determine the reliability of the read/write operations.

Head Alignment Problems

As a drive ages, the read/write head alignment may change slightly. If this happens, the ability of the drive to read data that was written before the head position changed may be reduced. When Calibrate performs a nondestructive low-level format, as described earlier, the track and sector IDs and the data are restored at locations that match the current head alignment.

Testing

Even if Calibrate can't or doesn't need to change your interleave factor and is unable to perform a nondestructive low-level format (which is the case, alas, with most current drives and controllers), it can perform extensive tests on your hard disk and controller to verify that they are operating correctly. These include system integrity tests, seek tests, data-encoding tests, interleave tests, and pattern read/write tests. All these tests are described in greater detail later.

CALIBRATION PROGRAM LIMITATIONS

The Calibrate program is designed to perform its tests and low-level formatting on 100% IBM-compatible hard disks only. It cannot perform low-level formatting or pattern testing on floppy drives, network drives, RAM drives, ASSIGNed drives (drives redirected with the DOS ASSIGN command), or SUBSTITUTed drives ("virtual disks" created with the DOS SUBSTITUTE command).

In addition, Calibrate will not perform low-level formatting or change the interleave factor on drives with translating controllers (controllers, such as ESDI models, that make it appear that there are 17 sectors per track when there are actually 26 or more). Calibrate cannot change the interleave on drives with controllers that do not allow low-level formatting, such as IDE or SCSI drives, although it will do pattern testing on these drives. Finally, Calibrate will not work on hard-disk controllers with on-board disk caching (although it is usually possible to disable an on-board cache).

Chapter Fifteen: Using Calibrate to Improve Hard-Disk Performance ■ 197

To summarize, Calibrate does not perform low-level formatting on

- drives that are not 100% IBM compatible;
- hard-disk controllers with an on-board disk cache;
- drives with SCSI or IDE controllers;
- controllers that perform sector translation.

Calibrate does not work at all with

- Iomega Bernoulli Boxes;
- network drives;
- hard disks with a sector size greater than 512 bytes.

NOTE

Since IDE and SCSI controllers predominate in newer systems, the Calibrate utility is of limited use on these systems. One aspect of Calibrate's operation is, in any case, unnecessary with these drives. Virtually all IDE or SCSI drives and controllers in current use are designed for optimal performance with 1:1 interleave, and the drives are formatted for this interleave factor at the factory. Hence, there would be nothing to gain by adjusting the interleave on these drives even if it were possible. The other principal reason for using Calibrate, refreshing track and sector IDs, raises some questions. Some experts recommend renewing track and sector IDs with a utility such as Calibrate at least annually to avoid deterioration and eventual data loss. Since a low-level format cannot be performed on IDE or SCSI drives, this is an option that is not available on most current systems. Although it is true that the magnetism of any magnetized substance will deteriorate over time, it is far from self-evident that the track and sector IDs on hard disks deteriorate rapidly enough that the ability of the disk subsystem to read and write data will decline to the point of unreliability within the expected lifetime of the disk. I have yet to hear any reports of an epidemic of data loss on IDE or SCSI drives.

Whether you believe deteriorating sector IDs are a real problem or not, if you have an IDE or SCSI drive, you'll just have to live with the possibility, at least until some software wizard discovers a way to trick the hardware into performing a nondestructive low-level format on these drives.

PRELIMINARIES

Before you run Calibrate for the first time, you should fully back up your hard disk. Symantec/Norton have attempted to make Calibrate compatible with all IBM-compatible hard disks, but it is impossible to test the program in every possible disk/controller/system combination, so it is best not to take chances. After running the program successfully for the first time, it will not be necessary to back up your hard disk before each subsequent use of Calibrate (although you should, of course, back up your hard disk regularly).

Copying the Diagnostic Cylinder

Calibrate uses the diagnostic cylinder of your hard disk (if it has one) to store information about its state of progress. If Calibrate is interrupted, either deliberately or accidentally (say, by a power failure), it uses this information to resume operation where it left off the next time you run the program. Running Calibrate overwrites any information that was previously stored on the diagnostic cylinder. Few programs use the diagnostic cylinder, but some diagnostic programs and other utilities similar to Calibrate may do so. As a precaution, before running Calibrate for the first time, use the Disk Editor (Chapter 24) to check, and, if necessary, back up the diagnostic cylinder. To access the diagnostic cylinder, you must run the Disk Editor in maintenance mode (type DISKEDIT /M). The diagnostic cylinder is last (innermost) cylinder on the disk. To view it, choose **Physical Sector** from the Object menu, type the highest legal cylinder number in the cylinder position, and press **Enter**. This should take you to the beginning of the diagnostic cylinder if one exists. The area may be blank, it may be filled with a repeating pattern of one or two characters, or it may have something that resembles meaningful data.

To make a copy of the cylinder, press **F2** to select hex view, move the cursor to the upper-right corner of the display (if it is not already there), then press **Ctrl+B** to begin to mark the block for copying. Next, press **End** to mark the whole cylinder for copying. Press **Alt+W** to write the cylinder to a file. Write to file to another location on your hard disk or save it on a floppy and store it in a safe place. (For a more thorough explanation of the preceding commands, consult Chapter 24.)

Chapter Fifteen: Using Calibrate to Improve Hard-Disk Performance ■ 199

NOTE

This whole procedure is primarily a precaution. You probably shouldn't restore the diagnostic cylinder after running Calibrate unless you run into a specific problem with another program that can be traced to the diagnostic cylinder. You *definitely shouldn't* restore the diagnostic cylinder if you interrupted Calibrate while it was performing tests or a low-level format and you want to resume where you left off.

Setting a Minimal Configuration

Before you attempt to run Calibrate, you should reboot your system to set up a minimal configuration with no unnecessary TSRs or device drivers. This gives Calibrate the maximum available memory to work with and minimizes the possibility of software conflicts.

Although you could reboot your system with a DOS floppy disk, I find it preferable to use special versions of my AUTOEXEC.BAT and CONFIG.SYS files to create a "plain vanilla" configuration for use with utilities such as Calibrate and for troubleshooting software conflicts, and to use batch files to select the proper versions. Create versions of your AUTOEXEC.BAT and CONFIG.SYS files with the minimum necessary commands to start your system and save them as AUTOEXEC.VAN and CONFIG.VAN, and make copies of your normal AUTOEXEC.BAT and CONFIG.SYS files with the names AUTOEXEC.NRM and CONFIG.NRM. Then create the following two batch files:

1. VANILLA.BAT (sets up a "plain vanilla" configuration)

   ```
   COPY AUTOEXEC.VAN AUTOEXEC.BAT
   COPY CONFIG.VAN CONFIG.SYS
   BE REBOOT
   ```

2. NORMAL.BAT (restores the normal configuration)

   ```
   COPY AUTOEXEC.NRM AUTOEXEC.BAT
   COPY CONFIG.NRM CONFIG.SYS
   BE REBOOT
   ```

200 ■ *Power Of...Norton Utilities*

NOTE Both of these batch files use the REBOOT subcommand from the Norton Batch Enhancer (Chapter 28). The preceding syntax assumes that the BE.EXE file is in the current directory or that the Norton Utilities directory is in the DOS PATH. If neither of these is the case, the batch files would have to include the path for the BE.EXE command.

Running Calibrate

You can run Calibrate by selecting it on the Norton menu or by typing **CALI-BRAT Enter** at the DOS prompt. You can specify a drive for analysis by typing the drive letter on the command line. However you start Calibrate, the program responds by displaying the information screen in Figure 15.1.

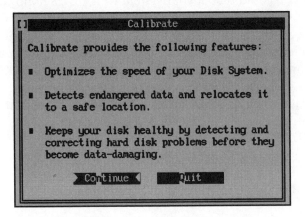

Figure 15.1 *The first Calibrate information screen*

NOTE If you attempt to start Calibrate while running a multitasking environment such as Windows or DESQview, a message will appear warning you that Calibrate will not you run under these environments and suggesting that you switch to a single-task environment (i.e., DOS) to run Calibrate.

Chapter Fifteen: Using Calibrate to Improve Hard-Disk Performance ■ 201

After reading this information screen select **Continue** to proceed. (Selecting **Quit** terminates the program.)

If you did not specify a drive on the command line, a drive selection dialog box appears. Select the drive to test and optimize from the list in the dialog box. After you select the drive, a second information screen appears (Figure 15.2). This screen shows a summary of the preliminary tests to be performed on the selected drive.

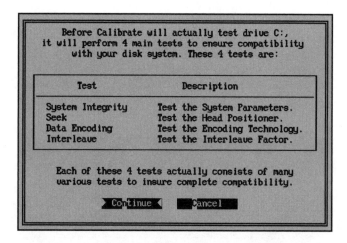

Figure 15.2 The second Calibrate information screen

After reading this screen, select **Continue**. Selecting **Cancel** returns you to the Select Drive dialog box. A screen appears listing the system integrity tests for the selected drive. These tests determine that the important components needed for low-level formatting are operating properly. Figure 15.3 shows the system integrity test on Drive C in progress.

Check marks indicate tests that have been completed and the asterisk (*) indicates the test currently being conducted. The percentage of the tests completed is shown in the Test Status box in the upper-right corner of the screen. The System Integrity tests are followed without pause by the Seek tests. The Seek tests measure the speed at which your disk read/write heads can be moved to various locations on the disk. After the Seek tests are finished, the test results are displayed. Figure 15.4 shows a Seek test results screen.

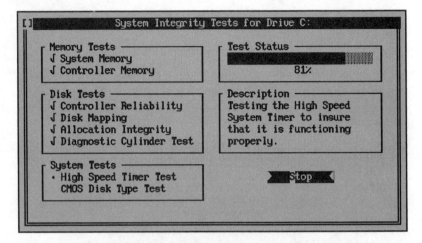

Figure 15.3 *System Integrity Tests*

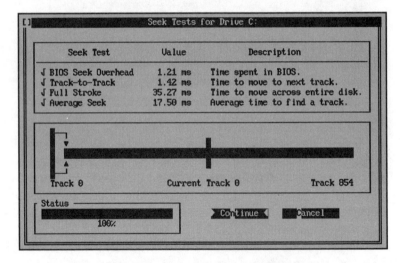

Figure 15.4 *Seek Test results screen*

The meanings of the terms used in the figure follow:

- *BIOS Seek Overhead* is the time spent preparing to read the next sector from the disk.
- *Track-to-Track* is the time it takes to move the head to the next track and be ready to read or write.

Chapter Fifteen: Using Calibrate to Improve Hard-Disk Performance ■ 203

- *Full Stroke* is the time it takes to move the head all the way across the disk.
- *Average Seek* is the average time required to find a requested track—usually equivalent to moving the head one-third of the way across the disk.

Generally, a fast disk is one with an average seek time of 20 ms or less, whereas a slow disk has a seek time of 60 ms or longer. If you use applications that require frequent disk operations, disk seek time will play a major role in overall system performance.

After viewing the results of the Seek tests, select **Continue** to proceed. This begins the Data Encoding Tests. These are designed to test the physical characteristics of the hard-disk controller and recording media. Figure 15.5 shows the data-encoding test results. The meaning of the terms used in the figure follow.

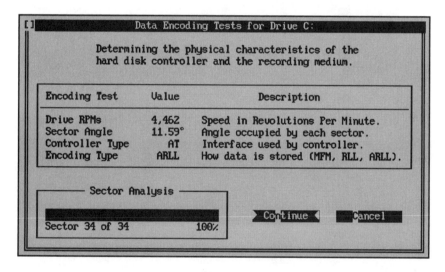

Figure 15.5 *Data Encoding Test results screen*

- *Drive RPM* is the disk rotation speed in revolutions per minute. (Most drives rotate at around 3600 RPM, but some high-performance drives rotate faster.)
- *Sector Angle* is the portion of the 360-degree platter devoted to a single sector. (The disk platter is divided into 17 or more wedge-shaped sectors.)
- *Controller Type* identifies the interface between the hard-disk controller and the system bus (either XT or AT).

◆ *Encoding Type* is the method used to record ones and zeros on the disk (MFM, RLL, or ARLL). RLL is the most common. Refer to Chapter 23 for a discussion of data-encoding techniques.

Select **Continue** to run the interleave test. Figure 15.6 shows the results of the interleave test. The bar chart displays the current interleave factor of your hard disk and the optimal setting. If the current setting is not optimal, use the arrow keys or mouse to move the box to the bar that is marked as optimal. The top of the screen shows the increase or decrease in speed that results from the selected interleave setting.

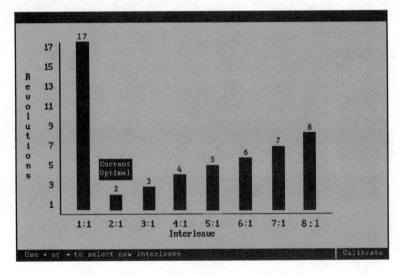

Figure 15.6 *Interleave Test results screen*

The vertical axis is labeled "revolutions." This indicates the number of disk revolutions required for the read/write head to read one entire track. For example, consider the disk shown in Figure 15.6, which has 17 sectors per track. Seventeen revolutions of the disk are required to read the 17 sectors if the interleave is 1:1, but only two revolutions are required if the interleave is 2:1.

NOTE

If Calibrate cannot perform a low-level format on your disk, a dialog box will appear to notify you of this fact and to inform you that Calibrate can perform pattern testing on your hard disk.

Chapter Fifteen: Using Calibrate to Improve Hard-Disk Performance ■ 205

Selecting **Continue** displays the Pattern Test Selection dialog box shown in Figure 15.7. Pattern testing detects disk defects before they can damage data. This test is designed to determine the read/write reliability of your disk system.

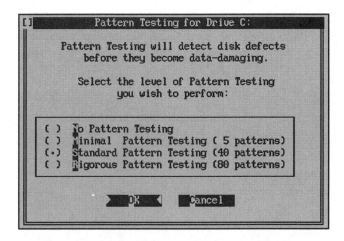

Figure 15.7 Pattern Test Selection dialog box

If it is applicable, low-level formatting is performed during the pattern tests. The pattern testing writes a series of bit patterns to every sector of the disk, one track at a time. It then reads back the patterns to verify that they were written successfully. Calibrate can use up to 80 different bit patterns. You can elect to test with all 80 patterns, 40 patterns, or only five. The more patterns you choose, the longer the tests will take. The test time is determined by the disk controller speed, CPU speed, drive (or partition) size, and number of patterns you elect to use. Testing with 80 patterns on a large-capacity disk can take several hours.

The **No Pattern Testing** option performs a nondestructive low-level format, if applicable, but does not do any pattern testing. This is the fastest option; it refreshes sector IDs but does not detect fading sectors. You might choose this option if you were just using Calibrate to adjust the interleave.

Minimal Pattern Testing writes five different bit patterns to each sector and verifies them.

Standard Pattern Testing writes 40 different bit patterns to each sector. Use this if you have any doubt as to the dependability of your disk surface.

Rigorous Pattern Testing writes all 80 bit patterns to each sector. This is a very thorough test, but it takes a long time.

A disk test map appears during pattern testing, allowing you to monitor the progress of the testing. Figure 15.8 shows pattern testing in progress. Notice that the current and finish times are shown on the screen. The finish time is updated as testing progresses.

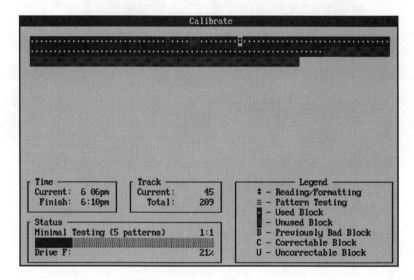

Figure 15.8 *Disk Test Map*

Screen Blanking

Pattern testing can take hours. To prevent the image of the disk map from being "burned" into your screen, you can blank the screen during pattern testing by pressing the spacebar. While the disk map screen is blanked, a moving dialog box indicating the progress of the tests is displayed. Pressing the spacebar again will restore the disk map screen.

NOTE You can safely interrupt Calibrate at any time by pressing **Esc**. Calibrate saves data about its state of operation on the diagnostic cylinder of the disk. The next time you run Calibrate, you can have it resume at the point where it left off. This allows you to break up a session of several hours into manageable units. Even if a power loss occurs during low-level reformatting, Calibrate will not lose your data. When power is restored, you can resume the Calibrate program at the point where it was interrupted.

The Calibrate Report

At the conclusion of the tests, a Test Summary screen appears, similar to that in Figure 15.9. This screen gives a short summary of the tests.

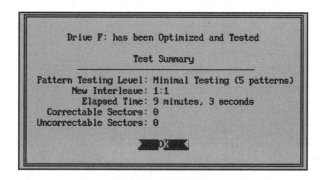

Figure 15.9 Test Summary screen

After you read the Test Summary screen, select **OK**. A report showing detailed results of all the tests performed then appears. You can scroll through the report using the **Up** and **Down** arrow keys or the **Page Up** and **Page Down** keys. Use the buttons at the bottom of the screen to print the report or save it to a file. If you opt to save the report, you will be prompted to enter a path and filename. When you exit the Report dialog box, you will be returned to the Select Drive dialog box, where you can select another drive to test, or you can terminate the program by selecting **Cancel**.

RUNNING CALIBRATE FROM THE DOS PROMPT

You can bypass most of Calibrate's information screens and prompts by running the program from the command line with appropriate options. The command-line syntax for Calibrate is as follows:

CALIBRAT [drive:] [options]

where [drive:] is the drive letter of the disk you want to optimize, and the options are as follows:

208 ■ *Power Of...Norton Utilities*

/BATCH	Skip all prompts and exit to DOS when done. Use this option when running Calibrate from a batch file.
/BLANK	Blank the screen during pattern testing.
/NOCOPY	Do not make a copy of the track currently being tested.
/NOSEEK	Do not perform seek tests. After the Calibrate program determines that the head-positioning mechanism is reliable, you can use this option for subsequent calibrations.
/NOFORMAT	Perform only pattern testing; do not perform a low-level format.
/PATTERN:*n*	Perform pattern testing using n patterns, where n can be 0, 5, 40, or 80.
/R:[A] filespec	Send a report to the specified file; use [A] to append the report to an existing file.
/X: drives	Do not test the listed drives; for example, use /X:def to exclude drives D, E, and F from testing.

To view a list of the available options at the DOS prompt, type **CALIBRAT /?**

SUMMARY

You can use Calibrate to optimize the speed and read/write reliability of your hard disk. The program performs a variety of nondestructive tests on your hard disk. It also provides a report on the tests and recommends an optimal interleave ratio. On some disks, it can perform a nondestructive low-level format to change the interleave factor and refresh track/sector IDs and file data.

16

THE NORTON UTILITIES™

USING THE NORTON CACHE (NCACHE2) TO IMPROVE DISK-ACCESS SPEED

WHAT IS A CACHE AND WHY IS IT USEFUL?

The American Heritage Dictionary defines *cache* (pronounced "cash") as "1. A hiding place used for storage. 2. A place for concealing and safekeeping valuables." In computer jargon, a disk cache is a program that sets aside a portion of your computer's memory to store the contents of the most recently accessed disk files. Why should you want to do this? Only one reason—to improve disk performance significantly. At the time of this writing, hard-disk access times range from around 15 to 80 *milliseconds* (ms) (1 ms = $^{1}/_{1000}$ of a second). In contrast, the dynamic RAM chips used for main memory in today's PCs have access times in the neighborhood of 70–100 *nanoseconds* (ns) (1 ns = 1 *billionth* of a second). Obviously, it is much faster to access data that is stored in RAM than it is to read it from even the fastest hard disk. Unfortunately, it is not practical to load enough RAM into a PC to store the entire contents of even a small hard disk. However, because of the way most programs access disk files, it is not necessary to do this, and you can achieve a considerable improvement in performance by dedicating a relatively modest amount of RAM for disk caching.

The basic premise of disk caching is that when a program reads from a disk file, it will probably want to read from it again in the near future. Another equally important premise is that when a program reads one sector of the disk, it will most likely want to read several more consecutive sectors. These premises are sufficiently true that a well-written disk-caching program can store the files or portions of files that a program will need most frequently in memory and serve them up on request without having to read from the disk. This will substantially improve the operating speed of disk-intensive programs.

NOTE

The "consecutive sectors" premise will be particularly likely to be true if you regularly "unfragment" your hard disk using the Norton SPEEDISK utility (see Chapter 17).

Disk caches are usually installed in expanded or extended memory (the difference is explained later), which reside outside the 640Kb of "conventional" memory or "DOS" memory used by DOS and application programs. If you have a computer equipped with only the 640Kb of conventional memory, you should probably not use the Norton Cache or any other disk-caching program. The reason is that many of today's applications want at least 512Kb of conventional memory, and memory is also needed for the resident portion of DOS (the amount varies with different DOS versions), TSRs, and device drivers. This leaves little room for a cache. The minimum *practical* allocation for the Norton Cache is 64Kb. Even if your applications will let you steal this much memory for cache use, they will probably perform better if you let them have all the conventional memory they want. If this is your situation and you want to gain the advantages of disk caching, you will need to add more memory to your system. If you have a relatively recent '386 or '486 PC, you can probably add the necessary memory on the motherboard. An expanded/extended memory manager program, such as 386MAX, QEMM, or HIMEM.SYS, can configure the memory so as to be most useful for disk caching and other purposes.

Chapter Sixteen: The Norton Cache (NCACHE2) ■ 211

Obviously, the more memory you set aside for cache use, the greater the likelihood that the cache will contain the data you need at any given instant. On the other hand, some of your applications may want to use this RAM for other purposes, so it may be that by setting aside too much RAM for cache use, you will improve disk performance at the expense of some other aspect of program operation. The goal is to find the balance between cache and other memory uses that yields the best overall system performance. The Norton Configuration program will make a recommendation, depending on the type and amount of memory available in your system, and this is usually a good starting point for experimentation.

NOTE Some hard-disk controller cards are equipped with built-in cache memory. These can be divided into two types, decorative and useful. The decorative type has a tiny amount of memory (say 8–32Kb), which helps the drive perform well in certain benchmark tests and allows the manufacturer to describe the controller as a caching controller in its advertising but really doesn't substantially improve disk performance under real operating conditions. If you have one of these controllers, you will probably get better results if you disable the on-board cache (consult the controller's documentation for information) and use the Norton Cache, provided that you have sufficient expanded or extended memory. Useful caching controllers are equipped with a megabyte or more of RAM. (Some can be equipped with as much as 64Mb!) If you have one of these, use the cache on your controller and save your RAM for applications, Windows, and so on.

PRELIMINARIES

System Requirements

According to the Norton Utilities documentation, you can run the Norton Disk Cache on any system equipped with DOS 3.0 or higher and 256Kb of conventional memory. Although, strictly speaking, this may be true, a system equipped with only 256Kb of conventional memory, if such a system still exists, is really not *practical* for running current applications, much less setting aside memory

212 ■ *Power Of...Norton Utilities*

for a disk cache. The smallest size for an effective disk cache is about 64Kb, which is an appreciable percentage of the 640Kb memory available to DOS. In any case, the Norton documentation doesn't recommend using conventional DOS memory for caching. (It can be done, but it's not the way to make the best use of the available resources.) For efficient caching, a minimum of 384Kb of extended and/or expanded memory is recommended. For all practical purposes, then, the minimum requirement for a system in which the Norton Cache will perform *usefully* is one with at least 1Mb of expanded or extended memory. Double that, at least, if you plan to run the cache under Windows.

DOS Buffers

DOS sets aside a certain amount of space in conventional memory for use as disk buffers, each of which is big enough to store one disk sector (512 bytes, or 0.5Kb). DOS stores the most recently accessed disk sectors in the buffers and searches these first when a program requests a disk read. It also uses the buffers to hold data to be written to disk while waiting to see if more data is coming that can go into the same sector. In other words, it tries, on a very small scale, to do the same thing that the Norton Cache does. DOS frees up space in a buffer by simply removing the least recently used sector. This is not always the smartest or most efficient way to free up buffer space. The Norton Cache uses a combination of least recently used and least frequently used data to determine which sectors to eliminate from the cache area. This results in a much higher probability that the data you need will be in the cache.

The number of buffers DOS reserves by default depends on the DOS version you are using and the number and type of disks in your system. Most likely, however, you have a larger number of buffers than the default, because the installation process for some application has increased the number to 20, 30, or even 40 by adding the line "BUFFERS=*nn*" to your CONFIG.SYS file or has instructed you to do so manually.

The Norton Cache can store much more data than the DOS buffers and can manage it more efficiently, so you will get better performance by reducing the number of buffers allocated by DOS. An appropriate number of buffers for use in conjunction with the Norton Cache is somewhere between three and 10. You might try five for a start, then adjust the number up or down to see how it affects the "hits" ratio shown in the Norton Cache Report (explained later). Adjust the number of buffers allocated by DOS by modifying the number in the

Chapter Sixteen: The Norton Cache (NCACHE2) ■ **213**

BUFFERS= line in your CONFIG.SYS file (or by adding the line if it is not already present).

Fastopen

FASTOPEN is another DOS utility that does some minor disk buffering. It buffers the file allocation table (FAT) and directory structure of a hard disk. The FASTOPEN command can be installed in either your AUTOEXEC.BAT or CONFIG.SYS file. The Norton Cache does a more efficient job of buffering the FAT and directory structure than does FASTOPEN, so check your AUTOEXEC.BAT and CONFIG.SYS files, and delete FASTOPEN if it is present.

Compatibility

Only one disk cache program can be loaded into the computer at one time. If you want to use the Norton Disk Cache, you must remove any other cache programs. Be aware that when you install Windows 3.x, it automatically installs the Microsoft SMARTDrive disk cache program in your CONFIG.SYS or AUTOEXEC.BAT file. You must remove this line when you install the Norton Cache.

The Norton Cache is compatible with essentially all versions of DOS, including IBM PC-DOS (versions 3.0 and later), Microsoft MS-DOS (versions 3.0 and later), Zenith DOS 3.3+ and later, Compaq DOS 3.31 and later, and Digital Research DR-DOS 5.0 and later. The Norton Cache is also compatible with Microsoft Windows 3.x and DESQview 2.25 and later.

Although the Norton Cache will run on a system with 640Kb or less of conventional memory, to be of much practical use the cache needs 1Mb or more of expanded or extended memory. If you plan to use the cache with Windows, figure on 2Mb or more of extended memory.

The Norton Cache operates at the DOS level, so it will work with any drive that is supported by the installed DOS. This means that it works with removable-media drives such as the Iomega Bernoulli Box and the Syquest removable-cartridge drive. Some other disk caches operate at the BIOS level and, as a result, do not support drives that use device drivers installed via the CONFIG.SYS file.

If you are using a removable-media drive that supports locking, the Norton Cache will automatically lock the drive when it defers a disk write to that drive.

214 ■ *Power Of...Norton Utilities*

When the write operation is finished, it will unlock the drive. This ensures that the media is not accidentally removed from the drive before the write is completed. To prevent repeated locking and unlocking of the drive, the cache waits approximately 2.5 seconds after the last deferred disk write before unlocking the drive. The Norton Disk Cache currently supports automatic drive-locking for Bernoulli and Syquest drives.

Certain Norton Utilities automatically disable the Norton Cache. These include the Disk Doctor, Speed Disk, Norton Diagnostics, and Calibrate. The Norton Backup (a separate Symantec/Norton product) also disables the Norton Cache.

TYPES OF PC MEMORY AND HOW THE NORTON CACHE CAN USE THEM

To configure the Norton Cache appropriately for your system, it is helpful to know about the variety of different memory types that may be installed in your PC and how the cache can use them. If you already have a thorough understanding of this material, you can skip this section and go to the next major topic, "Installing the Norton Disk Cache."

Conventional (DOS) Memory

The 8088 microprocessor used in the original IBM PC back in 1982 could address a maximum of 1Mb of memory. In designing the original PC, IBM reserved various areas of the potential 1Mb address space for other purposes, such as the video display buffer, the BIOS ROMs, the ROM BASIC interpreter, and undefined "future expansion." As a result, DOS was designed to address program code and data in only the lower 640Kb of the 1Mb 8088 address space. (In 1982, 640Kb seemed like more memory than anyone would ever need. Remember, most personal computers up to that time had addressed, at most, 64Kb, and the first IBM PCs shipped had 64Kb on the motherboard, expandable to 256Kb.) This 640Kb is accessible by DOS and all DOS-compatible programs. It is commonly referred to as conventional memory, or DOS memory.

Chapter Sixteen: The Norton Cache (NCACHE2) ■ 215

Installing the Norton Cache in conventional memory is not recommended, although it is possible. In most cases you will get better overall performance by allowing your applications to use all the available conventional memory. The Norton Cache *will* normally use some conventional memory for the cache management software, although it will load some of the management software in high DOS memory or the high memory area (explained later).

Expanded Memory

It wasn't long before people began wondering how to get more useful memory into their PCs. Various manufacturers came up with proprietary schemes, but the first practical system for this purpose to achieve wide acceptance was the Expanded Memory Specification (EMS). The Expanded Memory Specification was developed through a joint effort of Lotus, Intel, and Microsoft and is therefore called the LIM EMS. The latest version, LIM EMS 4.0, can add up to 32Mb of RAM to a PC (enough to melt your power supply!). Expanded memory is located outside of the PC's memory map (see Figure 16.1). The EMS uses a 64Kb "window," known as a page frame, located in one of the unused areas in the PC address space between 640Kb and 1Mb, to pass data back and forth to application programs designed to make use of EMS. Data is moved to and from expanded memory in 16Kb pages, and up to four such active pages can be stored in the page frame at any given time. Multiple page frames are allowed under LIM EMS version 4.0, although there may be some difficulty in many systems in finding a free location for a second 64Kb page frame. The process of moving data to and from the page frame is controlled by a program called an expanded memory manager (EMM).

To use EMS with 8086, 8088, or 80286 computers, you must add an Expanded Memory board. An EMS driver comes with the board and is loaded from your CONFIG.SYS file. To use EMS with the Norton Cache, the EMM must implement LIM EMS version 4.0. If you have an older EMS board with a driver that doesn't support EMS 4.0, you can probably obtain a new driver from the board manufacturer. In 80386 and higher PCs, extended memory (see later) can be used to simulate expanded memory by running an expanded/extended memory manager such as EMM386.EXE, 386MAX, or QEMM386.

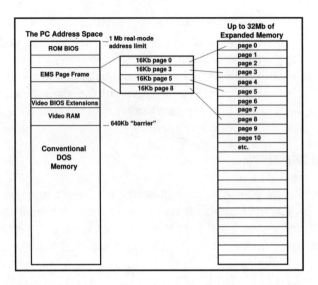

Figure 16.1 *The PC memory map, showing the EMS page frame*

Installing the Norton Cache in expanded memory is recommended if you have a substantial block available (384Kb or more) and you are not planning to use the cache under Windows. For the cache to be compatible with Windows, it should be installed in *extended* memory (see later).

Extended Memory

Extended memory is any memory located above 1Mb in the PC address space (see Figure 16.2). Extended memory is available in 80286, 80386, and 80486 PCs. With most of these machines, extended memory can be added on the motherboard, so that no expansion board is required. The 80286 can address as much as 16Mb, and the '386 and '486 can address up to 4 gigabytes (Gb) (over 4 billion bytes).

Even though '286, '386, and '486 processors can address extended memory, DOS cannot, because it was designed to operate within the 1Mb address space of the 8088. When '286, '386, and '486 processors run DOS, they normally run in what is known as real mode. In real mode, these more powerful processors emulate the humble 8088. Hence, they can run all existing DOS software but cannot use the large amounts of memory that they were designed to address. To access more memory, these microprocessors must be switched into *protected mode*. In protected mode, they can address large amounts of memory and can run multiple DOS applications in their own memory areas.

Chapter Sixteen: The Norton Cache (NCACHE2) ■ 217

Switching in and out of protected mode requires some tricky programming, particularly on the 80286 (because of a design flaw), so it was a while before a generally agreed-upon method for running DOS-type applications in protected mode and managing extended memory was developed. Although there are still competing standards, the most popular method is the Extended Memory Specification (XMS), developed by Microsoft, Lotus, AST, and Intel. In addition to extended memory proper, the XMS allows the management of high DOS memory (reserved memory or upper memory blocks) and the high memory area, both described later. To use extended memory, you must install an extended memory manager (XMM), such as DOS 5.0's HIMEM.SYS, or a combined expanded/extended memory manager, such as QEMM386 or 386MAX.

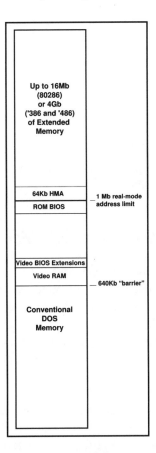

Figure 16.2 The PC memory map, showing the location of extended memory

218 ■ *Power Of...Norton Utilities*

You should install the Norton Cache in extended memory if you have a substantial block available (384Kb or more). If you want to use the cache with Windows, you *must* use extended rather than expanded memory. For a cache of a reasonable size and Windows to coexist, you should have at least 2Mb of extended memory available.

The High Memory Area (HMA)

In computers using the 80286 and higher chips, DOS can directly access the first 64Kb of extended memory. This is possible because of a quirk in the way the 80x86 processors perform memory address arithmetic. Some programs can use this area of memory, thus freeing some conventional memory. In setting up your system, you want to load the largest program that will fit into the HMA, because only one program can be loaded there at a time. An extended memory manager or expanded/extended manager must be used to manage this area (since it is part of extended memory).

The Norton Cache can install part of its cache management software in the high memory area if the /USEHMA installation option is set to ON (the default) and the area is not being used by another program. If you have DOS 5.0 or later and use the DOS=HIGH option, part of DOS will occupy the HMA and the cache will not be able to use it.

Upper Memory Blocks or High DOS Memory

Yet another potentially useful memory area is that located between 640Kb and 1Mb in the PC address space. As mentioned earlier, this area was originally reserved for a variety of purposes, including video display buffer memory, the ROM BIOS, EGA or VGA BIOS extensions, the EMS page frame (if present), and so on. However, in most cases significant parts of this address space remain unoccupied and can be filled in with memory, usually in relatively small non-contiguous blocks that fit in the cracks between the other occupants (Figure 16.3). How much useful memory you can access here depends on what kind of display adapter you have, whether you have a network adapter installed, and so on. However, as with memory above the 1Mb limit, DOS was not designed to address memory in this area directly, and an extended or extended/expanded memory manager is required to access it.

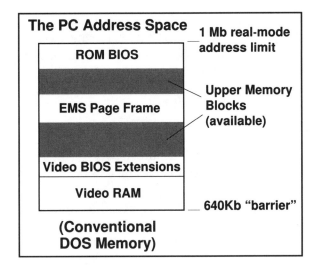

Figure 16.3 *The location of upper memory blocks*

The Norton Cache can install part of its cache management software in high DOS memory if the /USEHIGH installation option is set to ON (the default) and sufficient free memory is available.

INSTALLING THE NORTON DISK CACHE

Unlike most of the Norton Utilities, the real task with the Disk Cache is deciding how to install and configure the program. There are a great many installation and configuration options; the one you choose will depend on how you use your system, how much and what kind of memory you have installed, and whether you use Microsoft Windows, among other factors. The variety of options may prove confusing to many users, but take heart. If you don't want to be bothered with all these details, you can get a substantial boost in performance using the basic installation procedure outlined later. If, on the other hand, you are the type who takes pleasure in "tweaking" your system, you can spend hours playing with the various command options to try to squeeze out the last bit of performance from the cache. Once you have installed the Norton Cache, its operation is essentially transparent; you use your system just as you always have, except that you get noticeably faster disk operations.

You can install the Norton Cache when you initially install the Norton Utilities on your system, or you can add it later using the **Startup Programs** option on the Configuration menu of the Norton shell menu, or through the same option under the Configuration program (NUCONFIG). You can also install the cache manually, by placing the appropriate line in either your AUTOEXEC.BAT or CONFIG.SYS file.

I recommend that you use the Configuration menu or Configuration utility, rather than install the program manually, because these methods give you some useful assistance in deciding among the many available configuration options. Installing the cache in this way does not allow you to select every possible combination of start-up options, but it is probably best to begin using the cache with a basic setup created by the configuration program, then modify the options with a text editor later, if necessary.

To install the Norton Cache from either the Configuration menu or the Configuration Utility, select **Startup Programs** from the menu or dialog box. The Startup Programs dialog box (Figure 16.4) will appear. Move the highlight to the **Start Norton Cache** line and press the spacebar to select it. The program will display a message indicating that it is checking the available memory, after which it will open the Norton Cache dialog box, shown in Figure 16.5. This dialog box will also be shown if you install the Norton Cache when you first install Norton Utilities.

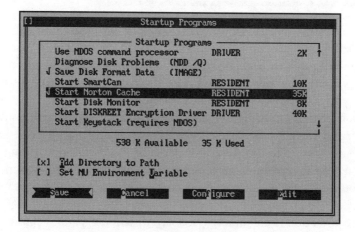

Figure 16.4 The Startup Programs dialog box

Chapter Sixteen: The Norton Cache (NCACHE2) ■ 221

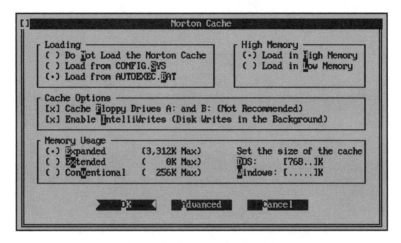

Figure 16.5 *The Norton Disk Cache dialog box*

This dialog box offers you several choices for the configuration of the Norton Cache:

- where to install the Norton Cache—in your CONFIG.SYS or AUTOEXEC.BAT file
- whether to load the cache management software into high memory or conventional memory
- whether to cache floppy disk drives
- whether to enable IntelliWrites (disk writes in the background while your program runs in the foreground)
- what type and amount of memory to be allocated for the cache buffers

The **Advanced** button at the bottom of the dialog box gives you access to a second dialog box with advanced configuration options, which will be described later in this chapter.

Where to Install the Cache

The Norton Cache can be installed in either your AUTOEXEC.BAT file or your CONFIG.SYS file. (You can also load the cache from the DOS command line at any time, but since you presumably want the cache installed at all times if you want it at all, there is really no point in doing so, except perhaps to experiment with different cache configurations.) Each installation method offers significant advantages and disadvantages.

CONFIG.SYS

If you chose to load the Norton Cache from CONFIG.SYS, the program adds the cache as a device driver in the CONFIG.SYS file. This automatically loads the cache when you boot the computer. Because the CONFIG.SYS file loads before the AUTOEXEC.BAT, the Norton Cache can help speed up the remainder of the startup process (a minor consideration in my opinion). The principal disadvantage of loading the cache from the CONFIG.SYS file is that programs loaded in this way cannot be removed from memory except by editing the CONFIG.SYS file and then rebooting the system.

The line added to the CONFIG.SYS file has the following form:

`DEVICE=[path]NCACHE2.EXE /INSTALL /INI=[path]NCACHE.INI`

where [path] is the drive and directory where the Norton Utilities are installed. The various options you specify in the configuration dialog box do not appear in the DEVICE line. Rather, they are saved in the NCACHE.INI configuration file, which is created by the configuration process. This line is placed at the end of the CONFIG.SYS file. You can change the position of the line by using the **Edit** button in the Startup Programs dialog box after you finish your configuration and exit the Norton Cache dialog box, but you should probably leave the line in the last position for maximum compatibility.

WARNING

If you are using the Norton Cache with device drivers that create a "disk-within-a-disk" (such as some compression and encryption programs), you must have the cache loaded from the CONFIG.SYS file before most such programs. This is not necessary with Norton Diskreet or Stacker, however; the Norton Cache can be loaded from CONFIG.SYS either before or after these programs.

AUTOEXEC.BAT

Choosing AUTOEXEC.BAT tells the program to place the Norton Cache command line in the AUTOEXEC.BAT file. The program will place the command line at the end of the file, which allows you to unload the cache from memory by typing **NCACHE2 /UNINSTALL** at the prompt. This is the primary advantage of loading the cache from the AUTOEXEC.BAT file. However, you lose whatever speed the cache may contribute to the start-up process. The line added to the AUTOEXEC.BAT file has the form

`[path]NCACHE2 /INSTALL /INI=[path]NCACHE.INI`

If you have added your Norton Utilities directory to the PATH statement in your AUTOEXEC.BAT file (you can do this using the Startup Programs dialog box) and if you place the NCACHE2 line *after* (below) the path statement, you can omit [path] from the line.

If you place the NCACHE2 /INSTALL command at the beginning of your AUTOEXEC.BAT file, it will speed up the execution of the remainder of the AUTOEXEC.BAT. If you do this, however, you must include [path] in the NCACHE command line. If you place the NCACHE2 /INSTALL command at the beginning of the AUTOEXEC.BAT file and then load other drivers or TSRs, you will not be able to uninstall the cache unless you first uninstall the other drivers. Given that you probably only boot up your computer once or twice per day, it is best to place the cache after the other drivers and TSRs in the AUTOEXEC.BAT file, thus preserving the ability to uninstall the cache and sacrificing the few seconds that would be saved by placing it at the beginning of the file.

NOTE You should not make the NCACHE2 /INSTALL command the *very last* item in the AUTOEXEC.BAT file if you also use the file to load Windows or a shell such as DOSSHELL or the Norton Commander. If you place the NCACHE2 line *after* the line that starts Windows or a shell, Windows or the shell takes over the system and suspends the execution of the AUTOEXEC.BAT; the cache doesn't get loaded until after you exit Windows or the shell—presumably not what you want.

Using High Memory

Select the **Load in High Memory** option (on by default) to allow a portion of the cache management software to be installed in high memory. If you have high memory, you should leave this option on under normal circumstances, in order to conserve conventional memory for applications. You might, however, choose to select the **Use Conventional Memory** option instead if putting some other combination of drivers and TSRs in high memory makes more efficient use of your available memory, or when you need to troubleshoot a possible conflict where you think that the installation of the cache in high memory might be a contributing factor.

NOTE: There are two parts to the cache: the software that manages the cache (which occupies about 36Kb) and the buffers where the cache stores disk data (which can be as big as the space will allow). The **Load in High Memory** option is concerned only with the cache management software. Memory options for the buffers are controlled by the Memory Usage item discussed later.

Cache Options

You can elect to enable or disable caching of floppy disks (off by default) and to enable or disable IntelliWrites (deferred, background disk writes—on by default). Although floppy disks are much slower than hard disks and can therefore benefit from caching, this is probably not worth bothering with because of the way most contemporary PC users work. If you're a typical computer user, you keep your program files and data files on your hard disk and use your floppy drives mostly for installing new software, moving data files between systems ("sneaker net"), and performing backups. None of these operations really benefit from caching, as they involve reading or writing a particular file only once. If you have caching of floppy drives enabled when you perform one of these operations, you will simply be loading data into the cache that will never be needed again. However, if you work in a way that involves repeatedly reading or writing the same files on a floppy, you may want to try enabling floppy caching.

IntelliWrites will be explained in more detail later. IntelliWrites considerably increase the speed of disk writes, which is a significant advantage. There is no obvious reason for not using IntelliWrites, so you should probably leave this feature on.

Memory Usage

This section specifies the amount and type of memory used for the cache buffers. You can install the buffers in expanded memory, extended memory, or conventional memory. (These three options are mutually exclusive when you configure the cache via the dialog box; however, you can select a combination of expanded *and* extended memory using command-line options, as described later in this chapter.) If you are unclear about the distinctions between these types of memory, consult the discussion of memory types earlier in this chapter. The Configuration program tests the amount and type(s) of memory installed in your system and displays the amount, along with a recommendation of how much memory to allocate to the cache for use with DOS, or, if appropriate, with Windows. If you select expanded memory, you will see only a single recommendation, for DOS. This is because Windows turns all the available memory above 1Mb into extended memory and will not work with a cache that uses expanded memory buffers. If you select extended memory, you will be given *two* figures for the cache size, a larger one for DOS and a smaller one for Windows. The cache will use the larger memory size when running under DOS and will shrink to the smaller size under Windows.

It may take some trial and error to determine how much memory to allocate for the cache to maximize disk performance without interfering with other aspects of your system's operation. By default, the Configuration program will allocate all but 16–24Kb of the available expanded or extended memory for the cache. If you don't have any applications that use expanded or extended memory, this is acceptable, but if you multitask large applications under Windows or if you have older applications, such as WordPerfect 5.x for DOS or the GEM edition of Ventura Publisher, that can take advantage of expanded memory, you may need to allocate less memory to the cache than the program recommends.

N O T E   If you have a computer equipped with only the 640Kb or less of conventional memory, you should probably not use the Norton Cache or any other disk-caching program. The reason is that many of today's applications want at least 512Kb of conventional memory, and memory is also required for DOS, TSRs, device drivers, and so on. This leaves little memory for cache use. The minimum *practical* allocation for the Norton Cache is 64Kb. Even if your applications will run with this much memory set aside for cache use, they will probably perform better if you let them have all the conventional memory they want. If this is your situation and you want to gain the advantages of disk caching, you will need to add more memory to your system. If you have a relatively recent '386 or '486 PC, you can probably add the necessary memory on the motherboard. An expanded/extended memory manager program, such as 386MAXX, QEMM, or HIMEM.SYS, can configure the memory so as to be most useful for disk caching as well as for other purposes.

Advanced Options

Selecting the **Advanced** option button enables you to set options to fine-tune the operation of the cache. (In most cases it is not necessary to do this, the defaults selected by the program will work satisfactorily in most situations.) Selecting **Advanced** will display the Advanced Options dialog box shown in Figure 16.6.

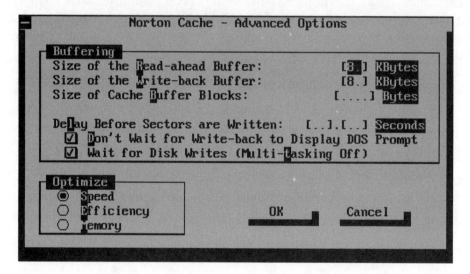

Figure 16.6 *The Advanced Options dialog box.*

NOTE

The advanced options, along with the options from the main Norton Cache configuration dialog box, are stored in the NCACHE.INI file. However, many of the advanced options can also be changed on the fly with command-line options (explained below under the heading "Reconfigure Options."

Read-Ahead Buffer—when the cache reads data from a disk, it assumes that additional data from contiguous sectors will probably be called for soon, so it reads ahead and stores the data from those sectors in anticipation of the need. This option determines how much memory will be reserved for this purpose, and hence, how far ahead the cache will read. The size of the read-ahead buffer can be any multiple of 1Kb in the range 8–64Kb or 0Kb. The default is 8Kb. If you select a buffer size of 0Kb, the read-ahead feature is disabled. Setting

Chapter Sixteen: The Norton Cache (NCACHE2) ■ 227

Optimize = Speed or Efficiency sets the buffer to 8Kb; setting the Optimization option to Memory sets the buffer to 0Kb and disables read-aheads.

Write-Back Buffer—specifies the size of the IntelliWrite write-back buffer. This value determines the largest block of data that will be written to the disk in the background in one operation. The size of the write-back buffer can be any multiple of 1Kb in the range 8–64Kb or 0Kb. The default is 8Kb. If you select a buffer size of 0Kb, IntelliWrites are disabled. The default size for the write-back buffer depends on the optimization setting. If Optimize = Speed, the buffer is set to match the largest track size in Kilobytes on the disks that are being cached. If Optimize = Efficiency, the buffer is set to 8Kb. If Optimize = Memory, the buffer is set to 0Kb, and IntelliWrites are disabled.

Size of Cache Buffer Blocks—a cache buffer block is a group of contiguous disk sectors that is stored in the cache. Larger cache blocks take less memory to manage and allow faster access to cached data, whereas smaller cache blocks result in more efficient caching. The cache block size can be can be 0.5Kb, 1Kb, 2Kb, 4Kb, or 8Kb. The default cache block size is also determined by the Optimize setting, among other factors. If Optimize = Speed or Memory, the cache block size is always set to 8Kb. If Optimize = Efficiency, the cache block size depends on the amount of memory available for the cache and on whether an upper memory block or high memory area is available for cache management. Usually, this results in a cache block size of 0.5Kb or 1Kb.

Delay Before Sectors Are Written—specifies the maximum time the program will wait before performing a disk write on a drive that has IntelliWrites enabled. The value is specified in seconds and hundredths of a second, with a range of 0.0–59.99. If Optimize = Speed or Optimize = Efficiency, the delay is set to 1.0 seconds. If Optimize is set to memory, the default delay is set to 0.0 seconds.

Don't Wait for Write-Back to Display the DOS Prompt—when IntelliWrites are enabled and a disk operation is executed from the DOS prompt, the program can display the new prompt immediately, while performing the disk write in the background, or it can wait until the new operation is finished to display the prompt. The default is on (don't wait).

Wait for Disk Writes (Multitasking Off)—if this option is on, the cache performs disk writes in the background while continuing to run applications in the foreground. If it is off, the cache suspends the foreground application while writing to the disk.

Optimization—has three settings—Speed, Efficiency, and Memory. The default optimization is for Speed. This makes sense, as increased speed is the reason for using a cache in the first place. However, if you're short on memory and still want to get at least some of the advantages of a cache, try using one of the other optimization options. Each optimization setting affects a number of different cache parameters, as summarized in Table 16.1.

Table 16.1 Optimization Parameters

Optimization	Speed	Efficiency	Memory
Read-ahead buffer	8Kb	8Kb	0Kb
Write-back buffer	8Kb	8Kb	0Kb
Block size	8Kb	0.5Kb or 1Kb (typical)	8Kb
Delay	1.0 sec	1.0 sec	0.0 sec

NOTE Changing the Optimize setting is a good way to select a group of settings that have been chosen to work effectively together. For most users, this will lead to more satisfactory results with less effort than playing with the different parameters in the Advanced Options dialog box on a trial-and-error basis. (With lots of additional adjusting and testing, you might shave an additional couple of milliseconds off the average disk access, but spending hours to save milliseconds is a questionable practice. Don't forget that your PC is a tool that you are supposed to be using to accomplish something practical.)

DISK CACHE OPTIONS

The options described later allow you to control all aspects of cache operation. There are three categories of options: Install options (used when installing the program from the AUTOEXEC.BAT or CONFIG.SYS file, or from the DOS or Norton command line), Reconfigure options (used to alter the operation of the cache when it has already been installed), and Drive options (used to change the operation of the cache for a single drive, either at installation or when the cache is already installed).

Chapter Sixteen: The Norton Cache (NCACHE2) ■ **229**

In the following discussion, optional parameters for the options are shown enclosed in square brackets [ ]. Required parameters are shown without brackets. For some options, entire groups of parameters are enclosed in brackets. This means that you can leave out all the parameters and the default setting will take effect. For example, in the entry

/EXT [=[-]n[m]]

the outer square brackets contain the expression =[-]n[m]. This means that the entire expression =[-]n[m] is optional (you could just enter **/EXT** and the default amount of memory would be allocated). However, if you specify a number, the value n must be used, because it is not in brackets. The minus sign (-) is optional, as is the parameter m, because both of these parameters are enclosed in brackets. If there is a choice of only one parameter from a group, the parameters are shown separated by a vertical bar (|), representing "or" (e.g., on|off).

Installation Options

For most users, the easiest and most efficient way to install and configure the Norton Cache is to use the dialog boxes provided by the **Startup Programs** option of the Configuration program, as described earlier in this chapter. When you use this method to configure the cache, your settings are stored in an NCACHE.INI file that is used to configure the cache when it is loaded from your AUTOEXEC.BAT or CONFIG.SYS file. However, you can, if you wish, configure the program manually by adding appropriate options to the NCACHE2 command line in your AUTOEXEC.BAT or CONFIG.SYS file. In many cases, these command-line options are direct equivalents to the various radio buttons and check boxes in the configuration dialog boxes. There are, however, certain command-line options that can be applied to individual cached drives (see "Drive Options" later). The configuration set with the dialog boxes applies to *all* cached drives.

/INSTALL loads the Norton Cache into memory. When no cache size is specified, /INSTALL tells the program to use the default size. If you do not want to specify a cache size, you must use this option to install the cache.

The default size will be determined by your system configuration. If you are running under DOS, the /INSTALL option will leave 16Kb of expanded and/or extended memory free and allocate the rest to the Norton Cache. When running Windows, the amount of memory allocated for the cache is reduced to

25% of the amount allocated under DOS. For example, if your cache was allotted 2048Kb under DOS, it would be reduced to 512Kb when running under Windows.

NOTE If this reduction results in the cache being smaller than 256Kb, the cache will be disabled temporarily while you are in Windows. When you return to DOS, the cache will automatically resume operation. If neither expanded nor extended memory is available, the default is 128Kb of conventional memory. Using conventional DOS memory for the cache is not recommended.

Memory Allocation Options

The following three options allow you to specify whether the cache will use conventional memory (not recommended), expanded memory, or extended memory and how much of the specified memory type should be used. If no unit of measure is specified, the program assumes kilobytes. For example, entering **/EXT=512** would allocate 512Kb of extended memory to the cache. If you do not specify a number, the default setting is used (refer to /INSTALL for the defaults).

The syntax for these options is as follows:

NCACHE2 Memory_option=Size

Entering a negative number reserves that amount of memory for other programs.

NOTE The memory allocation options cannot be used once the cache has been installed. They can be used only when installing the cache.

/DOS[=[-]*n*]   Use conventional DOS memory for the cache buffer; *n* is the amount of conventional memory to be used by the cache. You can specify from 24Kb to all but 128Kb of the available conventional memory. If it is preceded by the minus sign, *n* specifies the amount of conventional memory to reserve for other programs; the remaining memory is used for the cache. If you do not specify a value for *n* with the /DOS option, the cache will use

Chapter Sixteen: The Norton Cache (NCACHE2) ∎ 231

128Kb of conventional memory. The /DOS option cannot be used in combination with either /EXP or /EXT.

NOTE

Using conventional memory for the cache is not recommended.

/EXP[=[-]n] Use expanded memory for the cache buffer; n specifies the amount of expanded memory to be set aside for the cache. If it is preceded by the minus sign, n specifies the amount of expanded memory to reserve for other programs; the remaining expanded memory is used for the cache. For example, if you enter

`NCACHE2/EXP=-1024K`

1024Kb of expanded memory would be reserved for other programs and the Norton Cache would use the remaining expanded memory. If you do not set a value for n when using the /EXP option, the cache will use all but 16Kb of the available expanded memory.

/EXT[=[-]n[,m]] Use extended memory or the cache buffers. The n parameter indicates the amount of extended memory to use for the cache buffers, or, if preceded by the minus sign, the amount of extended memory to reserve for other programs. The m parameter specifies the smallest amount of extended memory to reserve for the cache when running under Windows 3.x. For example:

`NCACHE2/EXT=2M,1M`

indicates that when running outside Windows, the cache uses 2Mb of extended memory. When running under Windows 3.x in the enhanced mode, the cache will keep a minimum of 1Mb of extended memory. It will lend the difference between n and m to Windows on demand. In this example, the cache will lend a maximum of 1Mb of extended memory to Windows.

If you do not set a value for n when using the /EXT option, it will reserve all but 16Kb of the remaining extended memory for the cache. The default value for *m* is 25% of *n*, where *n* is positive.

/READ=*n*   Specifies the size of the read-ahead buffer, where n is the maximum value, in kilobytes, that can be read-ahead on the drive being cached. The acceptable range is 8–64Kb, or 0Kb (no read-ahead). The default depends on the Optimize setting. The read-ahead option cannot be used after the cache has been installed; it can only used at the time of installation.

NOTE   Do not confuse the /READ option with the /R option (discussed in the Drive Option section later) which sets the amount of data to be read-ahead.

/WRITE=*n*   Specifies the size of the write-back buffer for IntelliWrites, where *n* represents the maximum size (in kilobytes) of the data block that will be written to the disk at one time, while another program operates in the foreground. The value of *n* must be a multiple of 1Kb in the range 8Kb–64Kb, or 0Kb (IntelliWrites disabled). The default value for *n* depends on the Optimize setting.

/DELAY=*ss.hh*   Specifies the maximum delay before a deferred disk write takes place. The *ss.hh* parameter indicates the write delay, in seconds and hundredths of a second. The delay time ranges from 0.00 to 59.99 seconds. If no time is specified, default delay depends on the Optimize setting.

NOTE   If floppy disk caching and IntelliWrites are enabled, and a delay greater than zero has been selected, be careful not to remove a diskette before the disk writes are finished.

/OPTIMIZE=[S|E|M]   Specifies an optimization strategy. The three options are Speed (the default), Efficiency, and Memory. Selecting

Chapter Sixteen: The Norton Cache (NCACHE2) ■ 233

one of these options automatically sets a number of cache parameters (see Table 16.1) to optimize cache performance for the specified criterion.

/BLOCK=*n* Specifies the size of cache blocks, in bytes or kilobytes, where *n* must be one of the following values: 512, 1024, 2048, 4096, or 8192 bytes. A larger block size results in a smaller cache table (basically a table of contents for the cache). This is useful if you have large unfragmented files. On the other hand, small or highly fragmented files make better use of a small block size. When no value is specified for *n*, the default block size depends on the Optimize setting.

/USEHIGH=on|off Determines whether part of the cache management program will be loaded into high DOS memory (reserved memory between 640Kb and 1Mb). This option is on by default.

/USEHMA=on|off Determines whether part of the cache management software will be loaded into the high memory area (the first 64Kb of extended memory) to minimize the use of the 640Kb conventional memory. The high memory area is only available on 80286 and higher computers, and you must have an extended memory manager such as HIMEM.SYS or QEMM386 installed. This option is on by default.

/INI=[path]filename Specifies the location of an initialization file containing configuration options for the cache. The initialization file is created by the Norton Cache when you use the /SAVE option (discussed in the "Reconfigure" section) or when you install the cache using the Startup Programs dialog box.

If you do not specify a path and file name, the program will look for a file called NCACHE.INI in the directory where the Norton Cache is installed.

/QUICK=on|off If this option is set to ON and a disk write is performed by a DOS command or other command-line utility, the cache returns the DOS prompt while information is still being written to disk. The default setting is ON. If the option is set to OFF, the cache finishes all deferred writes before returning to the DOS prompt.

NOTE

If the /QUICK options is on, floppy disk caching is enabled, and IntelliWrites are enabled, be careful not to remove a floppy diskette before the disk writes are finished.

/REPORT[=on|off] When this option is on, the Norton Cache will display a status report whenever it loads. The report displays the current status of the cache. The Report option is off by default.

You can also display the report by typing **NCACHE2 /REPORT** at the DOS prompt, or on the command line of the Norton menu. A sample Norton Cache report is shown in Figure 16.7.

```
Conventional memory:      0K cache      0K management    583K free
High DOS memory:          0K cache     21K management     62K free
Expanded (EMS) memory:  752K cache     16K management    960K free
Extended (XMS) memory:    0K cache      0K management      0K free

        Total cache size is 752.0K - Currently using 609.0K  (80.9%)

DOS = 0K                BLOCK = 8192      USEHIGH = ON      DELAY = 1.00
EXP = 768K, 0K          READ  = 8K        USEHMA  = ON      QUICK = ON
EXT = 0K, 0K            WRITE = 8K        OPTIMIZE= SPEED   MULTI = ON

     A   C   I   W   P     R     G     Cache Hits / Disk Reads
A:   -   +   -   +   -     D8   128         0 /    0           (0.0%)
B:   -   +   -   +   -     D8   128         0 /    0           (0.0%)
C:   +   +   +   +   -     D8   128      2111 / 4905          (43.0%)
D:   +   +   +   +   -     D8   128       150 /  608          (24.6%)
E:   +   +   +   +   -     D8   128         6 /  384           (1.5%)
F:   +   +   +   +   -     D8   128         0 /    0           (0.0%)
```

Figure 16.7 The Norton Disk Cache Status Report

The first four lines of the report show the current memory allocation for the cache. They show the amount of memory used for the cache buffers, the amount used by the cache management software, and the amount remaining,

Chapter Sixteen: The Norton Cache (NCACHE2) ■ 235

for four types of memory: conventional memory, high DOS memory, expanded memory (EMS), and extended memory (XMS). The fifth line indicates how much total memory is allocated for the cache and how much of that memory is currently being used.

The next four lines show the status of 12 of the installation options described earlier. Note that you cannot change the settings for most of these items once you have installed the cache. The only settings you can change after installation are Optimize, Delay, and Quick.

Below these, on the left, is a matrix showing the caching status for each of the drives in your system. For the first five of these items, a + or - sign for each drive indicates whether the feature is currently enabled or disabled:

A   Cache active?

C   Cache accepting new sectors?

I   IntelliWrites enabled?

W   Write-through enabled?

P   Write-protection enabled?

For the remaining two items, a number indicates the size of the item in sectors (one sector = 0.5Kb).

R   Size of the read-ahead buffer

G   Group sector size

These seven items are described later in greater detail under the heading "Drive Options."

To the right of these is possibly the most important information in the report concerning improved disk performance: the hits-to-reads ratios. The left column shows the total number of cache hits (when the data a program wanted was found in the cache, eliminating the need for a disk read) versus the number of reads from the physical disk. In the right column, the same information is expressed as a percentage (e.g., if the listing for drive C is 45%, this means that 45% of the requests for file reads from drive C were successfully supplied by the cache). The higher the hits percentage, the more effective your cache settings are. When you first install the cache and have not yet read many files, the percentages will necessarily be low. As you work, the cache will gradually fill up with the data in greatest demand, increasing the likelihood of a hit and improving the hits ratio.

After you install the cache, check the report periodically to see what percentage of hits you are achieving. You may be able to improve your hits ratio by changing the number of buffers allocated in your CONFIG.SYS file and/or by changing the amount of memory allocated to the cache, among other factors. Your hits ratio will also be affected by the number of different programs you use in a given work session and what their file read/write habits are. Note that it is impossible to achieve a 100% hits ratio. Every file that is used must be first read into the cache from a physical disk before it can be reread from the cache. If you're getting hits ratios in the 75%+ range, you're doing very well.

N O T E

Although it is designed for display on the screen, you can redirect the Norton Cache report to your printer or to a file, using the DOS redirection character (>). For example, to send the report to your printer, type

```
NCACHE2 /REPORT >PRN
```

Depending on your printer and its configuration, the borders of the report may or may not print satisfactorily, but in any case, you will be able to keep a record of cache performance.

/STATUS=on|off   Displays a shorter status report, consisting of the first five lines of the full report. This option is on by default.

Reconfigure Options

The Reconfigure options are used to modify the cache after it has been installed. They allow you to uninstall the cache, to clear the data and statistical information from the cache (flush it), and to reconfigure some settings. Some of the installation options (described earlier) can also be used to reconfigure the cache, as can all the drive options, described in the following section.

/RESET   Reset the cache; performs any deferred disk writes, flushes all data from the cache, and clears the cache management tables. This is a global option that flushes data

Chapter Sixteen: The Norton Cache (NCACHE2) ■ 237

	for all cached drives. The /F option (see later) can be used to flush the data from an individual cached drive.
/UNINSTALL	Remove the cache from memory. This frees the memory used by the cache for other uses. You can only use this option if the cache was loaded from your AUTOEXEC.BAT file and was the last TSR loaded. You cannot uninstall the cache if it was loaded from the CONFIG.SYS file.

N O T E

You can disable the cache for one or more drives using the /-A option described later in the section "Drive Options." This, however, does not free the memory used by the cache.

/SAVE	Save the current Norton Cache configuration settings to the file named by the /INI option (described earlier). These settings become the default configuration settings. If you did not specify an /INI file name during installation, the information is saved to a file called NCACHE.INI, located in the directory from which the cache was loaded (usually the directory where you installed the Norton Utilities).
/DUMP	Write to disk any deferred writes not yet completed.
/MULTI=[on|off]	Enable or disable background disk writes. With /MULTI=on, the cache performs disk writes in the background while applications execute in the foreground. With /MULTI=off, foreground applications are suspended while the cache writes to the disk. Multitasking is off by default.
/QUIET	Prevent the Norton Cache from displaying any messages except error messages.
/DISKRESET=on|off	Specifies that the Norton Cache will write all cached data to disk when an application makes a disk reset request. The requesting program is suspended until the write is completed. (Most programs seldom or never make disk reset requests and are therefore not affected by this option.)
/QUICK	(See "Installation Options," earlier.)

238 ■ *Power Of...Norton Utilities*

/REPORT   (See "Installation Options," earlier.)

/DELAY   (See "Installation Options," earlier.)

Drive Options

Use drive options to configure cache operation for each drive. With the exception of the /F option for flushing the cache for individual drives, all these options can be used during installation or for reconfiguring the cache after it is installed.

Many of the options in this section can be used to disable or enable some cache function. When used with a minus sign (-), they disable the function. When used with a plus sign (+) or no parameter, they enable or reactivate the function. If any of these options is used without specifying a drive, it applies to all drives.

[drive]/-|+A   Disables or enables caching for the specified drive. Use this option to disable caching temporarily for one or more drives without uninstalling the cache. For example:

NCACHE2 C:/-A B:/-A

disables caching for drives C and B, leaving the cache enabled for all other drives. The default setting for all drives except floppy drives is /+A. Hence, it is unnecessary to use this option to enable caching for local hard disks.

[drive]/-|+C   Disables or enables the caching of additional data from the specified drive. Data from the drive that is already stored in the cache will continue to be available, but no new data will be loaded into the cache from that drive. You can use this option to "lock" important data into the cache. For example:

NCACHE2 C:/-C D:/-C

prohibits caching of additional data sectors for drives C and D. The default setting for this option is on (/+C) for all drives.

Chapter Sixteen: The Norton Cache (NCACHE2) ■ 239

[drive]/-|+W   Determines whether the cache will perform as a write-through cache for the specified drive. In a write-through cache, any sectors that are written to the disk are also saved in the cache. This is particularly useful in applications that repeatedly read and write the same sectors, such as a database sort or directory sort. The disadvantage of a write-through cache is that it fills up with data more quickly than a read-only cache. By default, the Norton Cache is a write-through cache for all drives.

NOTE

You cannot disable the write-through option for any drive that has IntelliWrites enabled (/+I).

[drive]/-|+I   Disables or enables IntelliWrites. When enabled, IntelliWrites reduce the amount of head movement needed to complete a series of disk writes and increase the amount of data written to the disk during each disk rotation. IntelliWrites also permit the application program to run in the foreground while the cache performs disk writes in the background. By default, IntelliWrites are enabled for all drives except floppy drives.

NOTE

IntelliWrites are automatically disabled when the write-back buffer has been set to 0Kb, either directly, at installation, or indirectly, by setting the /OPTIMIZE option for Memory.

[drive]/-|+P   Disables or enables write protection for the specified drive. Enabling this option has the same effect as putting a write-protect tab on a diskette. By default, write-protection is disabled for all drives.

NOTE

Enabling write protection prevents both DOS-level and BIOS-level disk writes. However, programs that access the hardware directly can still write to the disk.

240 ■ *Power Of...Norton Utilities*

/G=n   Specifies group sector size, where *n* is the maximum number of sectors to cache in one read. DOS reads and writes sectors in groups rather than individually. The maximum number of sectors it can read at once is 128 (64Kb with the standard sector size of 512 bytes). Normally, DOS loads programs in 64Kb increments. If a file is larger than 64Kb, DOS will have to make multiple reads. If you are working with a program that deals with files in small units, such as a database, in which you load and save individual records, you may make caching more efficient by specifying a much smaller group sector size (e.g., 16). By default, a group sector size of 128 is used for all drives.

[drive]/R[=[D][n]]   Specifies the amount of data to be cached during read-aheads. When the cache reads data from a disk, it assumes that additional data from contiguous sectors will probably be called for soon, so it reads ahead and stores the data from those sectors in anticipation of the need. This option determines under what conditions these reads occur and how much data is read. It should not be confused with the /READ option (described earlier), which specifies the size of the buffer that holds the data. The optional *D* parameter specifies that dynamic read-aheads should be performed. If this option is selected, data is read ahead only in sequential disk reads, *not* in random disk reads. The *n* indicates how much data to read. The value of n must be a whole number of kilobytes, and can range from zero (0) to a maximum equal to the size of the read-ahead buffer, set by the /READ option. For example, if /READ=8Kb, the maximum value for *n* would also be 8Kb. If you use zero (0) as the value for *n*, the read-ahead feature is disabled for the drives indicated. The default for all drives is /R=Dmax; that is, dynamic read-aheads are selected and the amount of data to read is equal to the size of the read-ahead buffer.

/F   Flush the cache for the specified drive. Both the data in the buffers and the cache management tables are flushed. All deferred writes are completed before the cache is flushed.

Chapter Sixteen: The Norton Cache (NCACHE2) ■ **241**

Installing the Norton Cache from the DOS Prompt

You can install and run the cache from the DOS prompt by using the options discussed earlier. It makes little sense to do this, however, except perhaps when experimenting with different cache configurations. Because one normally wants the cache installed whenever the computer is turned on, the proper way to install the cache is from the AUTOEXEC.BAT or CONFIG.SYS file, as described earlier in this chapter.

The command-line syntax for installation and for reconfiguration are as follows:

```
NCACHE2 [Install Options] [[drive:][Drive Options]]
NCACHE2 [Reconfigure Options] [[drive:][Drive Options]]
```

Summary

The Norton Disk Cache improves the speed of disk operations by providing memory storage for frequently used data. This allows DOS to access information directly from memory rather than performing slower disk read/write operations. You can load the cache automatically by including it in either your CONFIG.SYS or AUTOEXEC.BAT file. You can also install it from the command line of the Norton Menu or the DOS prompt if you only want to use it in the current session. You can change many aspects of the cache's operation from the command-line with the Reconfigure options, and you can view the current condition of the cache at any time with the Report option.

17

UNFRAGMENTING DISKS WITH SPEED DISK (SPEEDISK)

When you first begin writing or copying files to a new (or newly formatted) disk, DOS places all the data for each file in a group of contiguous clusters. (For a detailed explanation of clusters and disk organization in general, consult Chapter 23.) A file that is so placed can be read or written with the minimum amount of disk head movement, resulting in the shortest read and write times. DOS will always place files in contiguous clusters if it can, but on an active disk, where files are frequently created, edited, moved, and deleted, this soon becomes difficult. When old files are deleted, gaps are left on the disk. New files that are saved may be too large to fit entirely in the gaps, and hence may be split into two or more parts and stored in noncontiguous locations. Similarly, when an existing file is modified and increased in size, it may be too big to be saved in its original location. Part of the file may be stored in the original location and the rest placed elsewhere on the disk. After weeks or months of this kind of

244 ■ *Power Of...Norton Utilities*

activity, the disk resembles a jigsaw puzzle, with parts of large files scattered in noncontiguous clusters all over the disk. Such files are said to be fragmented.

DOS has the facilities to manage fragmented files, and under normal circumstances there's no chance of any of the clusters belonging to a fragmented file getting lost. However, fragmentation degrades disk performance: Disk read/write operations are slower as a result of the disk head having to move around the disk to find the various noncontiguous clusters. Performance of disk-intensive programs suffers as a result.

Another potential problem involves accidentally erased files and/or accidentally formatted disks. It is much more difficult for recovery programs such as Norton UnErase and Norton UnFormat to do their jobs properly on disks containing severely fragmented files. If files and disks are not protected by the Norton SmartCan and Image programs (see Chapter 4), it may be impossible to recover fragmented files in the event of an accident.

The solution to the disk fragmentation problem is to use an "unfragment" utility regularly to rearrange the data on your disks so that all the data for any given file is stored in contiguous clusters. Norton Speed Disk (SPEEDISK) is such a utility. In addition to placing the data for a given file in contiguous clusters, Speed Disk can consolidate the free space on a disk in a single contiguous block, so that large files can subsequently be saved without being fragmented. It can also reorganize the files on your hard disk by physically repositioning them. For example, it can place the most frequently accessed files near the beginning (outside tracks) of the disk, where they can be accessed more quickly.

Network Usage

Norton Speed Disk will not unfragment network drives. (Your network software probably has this capability.)

Precautions

Because of the many different computer configurations and copy-protection techniques currently in use, it is impossible to determine whether Speed Disk will work properly on every system. Therefore, you should fully back up your hard disk before running Speed Disk for the first time. Once you verify that Speed Disk is compatible with your system, you will not have to do this. (Of course, you should back up your hard disk regularly in any case.)

Chapter Seventeen: Unfragmenting Disks with Speed Disk (Speedisk) ■ 245

WARNING

Before you run Speed Disk, you should remove any memory resident programs (TSRs) that might access the disk or interrupt the optimization. You should also disable or uninstall any disk-caching programs, such as the DOS SMARTDrive program. You do not need to remove the Norton Disk Cache program or other Symantec/Norton TSRs and drivers; Speed Disk knows how to manage these programs.

The quickest way to clear your system of unwanted drivers and TSRs is to create "plain vanilla" versions of your AUTOEXEC.BAT and CONFIG.SYS files, containing only the minimum device drivers needed to operate your system (e.g., your mouse driver and extended/expanded memory manager). Give these files names, such as AUTOEXEC.VAN and CONFIG.VAN. When you want to clear your system of drivers and TSRs, copy these two files to your AUTOEXEC.BAT and CONFIG.SYS files, then reboot your system. You will also need to save your normal AUTOEXEC.BAT and CONFIG.SYS files under different names, such as AUTOEXEC.NRM and CONFIG.NRM, so that you can restore them and return to your normal configuration after the optimization is completed.

N O T E

Speed Disk will not run in multitasking environments such as Windows or DESQview. If you attempt to start Speed Disk in one of these environments, a message will appear to inform you of this fact and to advise you to change to a single-task environment (i.e., DOS).

Copy-Protection Issues

Some copy-protection schemes use position-sensitive files (files that are installed at specific physical locations on a disk). These position-sensitive files also typically have hidden and/or system attribute set. Copy-protection schemes are based on the fact that the application knows the physical location of the copy-protection file(s). If the program fails to find the file(s) at the expected location, it may conclude that an illegal copy of the program has been made and refuse to load. (Fortunately, copy-protection schemes of all kinds are much less common today then they were in the earlier days of the PC.)

Speed Disk examines each file on the hard disk before moving it. It never moves any hidden file or hidden subdirectory. Speed Disk also recognizes copy-protection techniques that do not hide the copy-protection files, such as Vault and SoftGuard Systems, and does not move these files either. Speed Disk creates a list of all unmovable files it finds on a disk. You can view this list by accessing the **Show Static Files** option on the Information menu (described later). You can also add files to the list if necessary with the **Unmovable Files** option on the Configure menu.

RUNNING SPEED DISK

Load Speed Disk by highlighting the program on the Norton menu or by typing `SPEEDISK` **Enter** at the DOS prompt. You can optionally specify a drive letter on the command line. The program briefly displays the message "Testing system memory" (if you blink, you'll probably miss it), before opening the main screen. Speed Disk writes to and reads from memory to ensure that your data won't be corrupted by its memory operations. After the memory testing is complete, if you did not specify a drive on the command line, the drive-selection box pops up in front of the main screen so that you can select the drive to optimize. (Only one drive can be selected; you cannot tag multiple drives.) After you select a drive (or immediately, if you specified a drive on the command line), Speed Disk begins its analysis of the specified drive. A message box shows the progress of the analysis.

When the analysis is complete, the program displays a Recommendation dialog box like that shown in Figure 17–1. The dialog box displays the percentage of fragmentation on the drive and recommends the appropriate optimization method, if one is needed. You can start the recommended optimization immediately by selecting the **Optimize** button, use the radio buttons to select a different optimization method, or select **Cancel** to close the dialog box and go to the main screen, where you can use the pulldown menus to configure various aspects of the program's operation.

Figure 17.1 A Recommendation dialog box

Chapter Seventeen: Unfragmenting Disks with Speed Disk (Speedisk) ■ 247

For most users in most situations, it is best to accept the optimization that Speed Disk recommends. If you have not used Speed Disk (or another unfragment program) recently, Speed Disk will probably recommend a full optimization. (See later for a description of the various types of optimizations.) Once this has been done, if you run Speed Disk regularly, once or twice per week, you will probably only need to unfragment files.

When you start the optimization process, the Recommendation dialog box is removed and the map display (Figure 17.2) is activated. You can see the progress of the optimization process as data is moved to different clusters on the disk and the disordered pattern of filled and free spaces is replaced with a more regular pattern in which the filled blocks are moved to the front (outside tracks) of the disk and empty ones are consolidated at the end (inside tracks). The status box in the lower left corner of the screen displays the current action, including which cluster is being read, written, or verified (although this information is updated so quickly that you will probably not be able to make anything of it), and the percentage of the process completed. The legend box at the lower right explains the meaning of the various symbols on the map. (A more detailed legend can be found on the Information menu.)

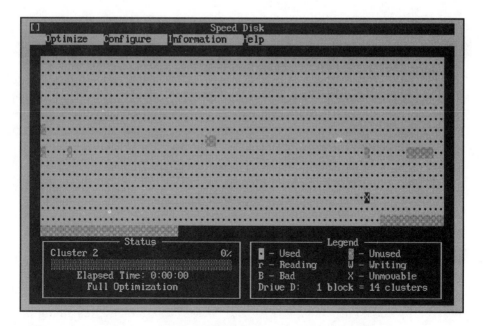

Figure 17.2 Disk map display

248 ■ *Power Of...Norton Utilities*

WARNING

Do not turn off your computer while Speed Disk is optimizing a disk. If the operation of Speed Disk is interrupted, your files may be damaged. Speed Disk takes precautions to prevent it from damaging your disk in the event of a power failure or system crash, but it is better not to challenge fate. You can safely interrupt Speed Disk while it is performing an optimization by pressing **Esc**.

NOTE

When it relocates files Speed Disk updates the IMAGE.DAT file (see Chapter 4) if one is present on the disk. This gives your data some additional protection against accidental formatting.

Optimization Methods

An optimization method can be selected either from the Recommendation dialog box that appears when the program analyzes a disk or from the Optimization menu. Speed Disk offers five different optimization methods:

Full Optimization—fully optimizes the disk and unfragments all files; places directories first, in order of their physical locations on the disk, followed by files, also in order of physical location. No gaps are left between the files. This is the fastest optimization method and is adequate in most cases.

Full with Directories First—uses the Directory Order and Files to Place First information specified under the Configure menu (see later) to determine the order in which directories and file types (not individual files) are placed on the disk. Specified directories are placed first (just the directories, not their contents), then the other directories, then specified files (e.g., *.COM and *.EXE files), then the remaining files are placed according to their physical locations on the disk. All files are unfragmented, and no gaps are left on the disk. This method offers higher gains in performance but takes longer to run than Full Optimization.

Full with File Reorder—also uses the Directory Order and Files to Place First information to determine the order in which directories and file types are placed on the disk. Specified directories are placed first, then the other directories, then specified files (e.g., *.COM and *.EXE files), then the remaining files are placed according to their directory locations, rather than by their physical locations on the disk. All files are unfragmented and no gaps are left on the disk. This is the most thorough optimization, but it does not offer substantial increases in performance over the previous method.

Unfragment Files Only—unfragments as many files as possible, but does not consolidate free space or fill gaps between files. Some large files may not be unfragmented. You should use this method regularly (once or twice weekly) to maintain order on your disks after initially running one of the more thorough methods described earlier.

Unfragment Free Space—moves data to fill in gaps between files and consolidates free space at the end (inside tracks) of the disk. It does not unfragment files. This method does not significantly improve performance, but it may be useful when you need to create a large contiguous free space (e.g., to install a new program without fragmenting its files or to create a Windows permanent swap file).

NOTE

Whether your system performance is noticeably enhanced by disk optimization will depend to a large degree on the access time of your hard disk. On older, slower drives, the improvement will probably be quite noticeable if files were severely fragmented before optimization. On faster drives, the improvement will be less significant and may or may not be observable.

Menus

The menu bar at the top of the screen has three pull-down menus—Optimize, Configure, and Information. To access the menus, press **F10** or **Alt**.

The Optimize Menu

The Optimize menu allows you to specify how the Speed Disk is to optimize the selected drive.

Begin Optimization—starts the optimization process. The default optimization is full optimization. The shortcut key for this option is **Alt+B**.

Drive—selects the drive to optimize. This option opens the same drive-selection dialog box that appears when you start Speed Disk without specifying a drive on the command line.

Optimization Method—displays the Optimization Method dialog box shown in Figure 17.3. The options offered are the same as those presented in the Recommendation dialog box when you start the program as described earlier.

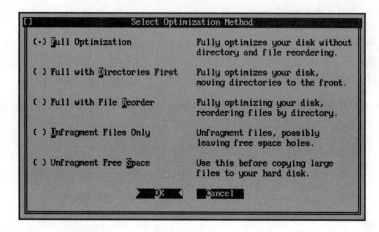

Figure 17.3 *The Optimization Method dialog box*

The Configure Menu

The Configure menu allows you to specify how Speed Disk operates.

NOTE

The selections you make from this menu affect how fast Speed Disk works.

Directory Order—specifies the order in which directories will be placed on the disk. (This will affect only Full Optimizations with Directories First or Full Optimizations with File Reorder.) When you select this item, the Directory Order dialog box (Figure 17.4) appears. A directory tree of the selected drive is displayed in a scrolling box on the left. Selected directories can be placed in the scrolling box on the right. These directories will be placed at the front of the disk, in the order in which they are listed in the box. This reduces the time required to access these directories. The default order is the path you specified in your AUTOEXEC.BAT file.

Chapter Seventeen: Unfragmenting Disks with Speed Disk (Speedisk) ■ 251

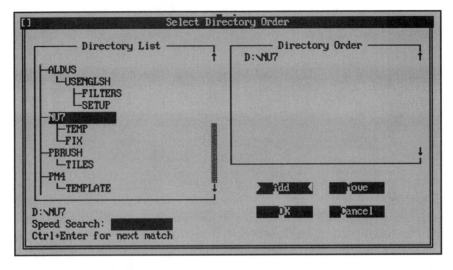

Figure 17.4 Directory Order dialog box

Use the **Left/Right** arrow keys to move the highlight from one box to the other. To add a directory to the list in the Directory Order box, highlight it in the directory tree, then select the **Add** button. The new directory appears for the Directory List box. To change the order of the files in the list, move the highlight to the file that you want to move, then press the spacebar to select it. (Inward-pointing arrowheads appear to indicate that the file is selected, and the **Move** button is highlighted automatically.) Use the **Up/Down** arrow keys to move the file to the desired location in the list, then press **Enter** to drop it. To delete a directory from the Directory Order list, highlight the directory and press **Enter**. (The **Add** button changes to **Delete** and becomes the default button when you highlight a directory in the list.) When you have finished sorting the directory list, select **OK** to save your changes and return to the Speed Disk main dialog box. Selecting **Cancel** returns you to the main dialog box with no changes made.

File Sort—displays a dialog box where you can select the sort criteria for files in directories. (This affects only Full Optimizations with File Reorder.) The options are **Unsorted** (the default), **Sort by Name**, **Sort by Extension**, **Sort by Date and Time**, and **Sort by Size**. In addition, you can specify whether the selected sort is performed in ascending or descending order.

252 ■ *Power Of...Norton Utilities*

Files to Place First—selects the file types that are to be placed nearest the front (outside tracks) of the disk, where they can be accessed quickly. (This affects only Full Optimizations with Directories First or Full Optimizations with File Reorder.) Initially, the scrolling list box in the dialog box contains the file specs *.COM and *.EXE. Because files with the .COM and .EXE extensions are frequently read and seldom written to (unless you're a programmer), they make good choices for this location. You can add more file specs to the list, and you can rearrange the order of the list using the **Move** and **Delete** keys in the same manner as described earlier for the **Directory Order** option. Use the **Insert** button to add a blank line in the list at the cursor position in order to type a new spec.

Unmovable Files—Speed Disk considers all hidden files and directories and copy-protected files unmovable. If you want to designate files or classes of files as unmovable, you can add them to this list, but in most cases you can depend on Speed Disk to identify the appropriate files. See the **Show Static Files** option under the Information menu for a list of the files on the selected disk that Speed Disk has identified as unmovable.

Other Options—displays a dialog box with three options:

◆ **Read After Write**—the default setting is ON. Data is read back from the disk immediately after it is written to verify that it was written correctly.

◆ **Clear Unused Space**—wipes (writes zeros) to all unused clusters of the disk after optimization. This is done for security purposes, to prevent confidential data from being read from unused clusters on the disk. For more information on wiping and disk security, consult Chapter 14.

◆ **Beep When Done**—sounds an audio prompt when the selected optimization is completed. This can be useful because some of the optimizations can take a long time on a large disk, and you may wish to do something else while waiting for the optimization to be finished.

◆ **Save Options to Disk**—use this item to save the settings you have created with the options on the Optimization and Configuration menus so that you can use them in future work sessions. The settings are stored in the file SD.INI in the Norton Utilities directory.

The Information Menu

The items on this menu give you a detailed account of the current state of the disk selected for optimization. You can use these options, for example, to view

Chapter Seventeen: Unfragmenting Disks with Speed Disk (Speedisk) ■ 253

the state of the disk before optimization and then view it again afterward to see precisely what changes the optimization has made.

Disk Statistics—shows a detailed description of the current condition of the selected disk, such as that shown in Figure 17.5.

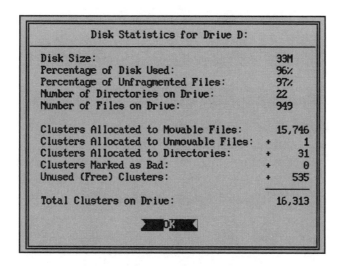

Figure 17.5 The Disk Statistics display

Map Legend—displays a more detailed version of the map legend shown in the lower right corner of the main display, explaining the symbols used on the disk map display.

Show Static Files—displays a list of files that Speed Disk has determined to be unmovable. For example, if you have selected a bootable disk, the IBMBIO.COM and IBMDOS.COM (or MSDOS.SYS and IO.SYS) files will be listed.

Walk Map—allows you to determine which files occupy specific clusters. When you select this item, a flashing cursor appears on the disk map. Move the cursor to any block on the disk map and press **Enter**. A list box (such as that in Figure 17.6) appears showing the clusters occupying the selected block, what files they belong to, and their current state vis-a-vis optimization, fragmentation, and so on. (A block is an arbitrary unit of disk space use by Speed Disk in setting up the disk map display. The number of clusters in a block depends on the size of the disk being optimized and the resolution of your display. This figure is shown at the bottom of the legend box on the right side of the main screen.)

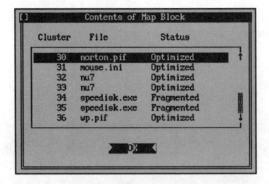

Figure 17.6 A Walk Map cluster list

Fragmentation Report—provides a detailed report indicating which files are fragmented and how many fragments each file occupies. The Recommendation dialog box displayed when you first run Speed Disk shows a percentage of fragmented files, as does the **Disk Statistics** option on the Information menu.

Figure 17.7 is a typical File Fragmentation Report. The left scroll box shows a directory tree of the selected drive, and the right scroll box shows a list of the files in the highlighted directory, with their sizes in clusters and their fragmentation status. Speed Disk describes as moderately fragmented those files that are 90% contiguous or better. Highly fragmented files are less that 90% contiguous. In addition, the fragmented files are color coded to make them stand out in the list (on monochrome displays the fragmented files are bulleted).

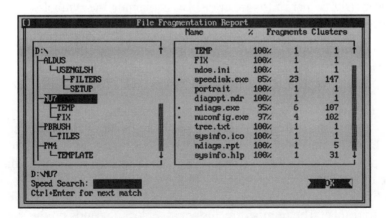

Figure 17.7 A File Fragmentation report

Chapter Seventeen: Unfragmenting Disks with Speed Disk (Speedisk) ■ 255

RUNNING SPEED DISK FROM THE DOS PROMPT

Most of Speed Disk's features can be accessed from the command line, bypassing the dialog boxes and menus, by using the appropriate command-line options. The command-line syntax for Speed Disk is

SPEEDISK [drive:] [options]

For the program to operate without user intervention, you must, at a minimum, specify the drive to optimize and the optimization method. The program will run the specified optimization, displaying the disk map, and will return to the DOS prompt on completion.

The following are the optimization methods:

/F	Full optimization
/FD	Full optimization with directories first
/FF	Full optimization with file reordering
/U	Unfragment files only
/Q	Unfragment free space (fill gaps)

Other options include

/V	Use read-after-write verification
/B	Reboot after optimization
/S[order]	Sort files by specified order:

       N Name

       D Date and Time

       E Extension

       S Size
       (A minus sign [-] following any of these options reverses the order.)

/SKIPHIGH Do not use high memory

To see a list of the available options at the command line, type **SPEEDISK /?**

It is useful to create a batch file to perform a weekly or biweekly unfragmentation of all your logical disks. Simply include the line

```
SPEEDISK [drive:] /U
```

for each drive that you want to unfragment.

NOTE When you run Speed Disk for the first time, use the full-screen mode to set a configuration, then save the configuration to disk using the **Save Options to Disk** selection on the Options menu. When you run Speed Disk from the command line, the saved configuration will be used, except where command-line options conflict with the saved configuration. In this case, the command-line options take precedence.

SUMMARY

Speed Disk is a disk optimization program that unfragments files, consolidates free space, and moves directories and frequently accessed files to the front of the disk. All these actions can improve file access times and thereby enhance the performance of disk-bound programs.

RECOMMENDATIONS

If you have not previously optimized your hard disk, you should run Speed Disk on all your logical drives using one of the Full Optimization options at your earliest convenience. (This is what the program will recommend if your files are highly fragmented.) Once your disks have been fully optimized, keep them in good condition by running the program with the Unfragment Files option once or twice per week, depending on the amount of activity on your disks.

NOTE Although you can run Speed Disk on floppy disks, there is probably little point in doing so, except perhaps when preparing a master disk for duplication.

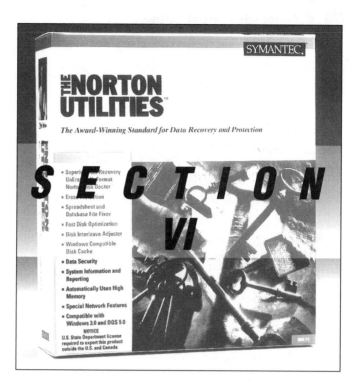

GENERAL HARD-DISK MANAGEMENT TOOLS

Hard disks keep getting bigger and program and data files keep proliferating, but the disk management tools provided by DOS have been slow to meet the challenge. If you're used to using DIR to view your directories and CD to get around your directory tree, the Norton Utilities includes a number of tools to help you manage your files and directories more efficiently.

◆ Norton CD (Chapter 18) lets you navigate through your directory structure by visually moving around the directory tree or by typing "shorthand" directory names at the prompt.

258 ■ *Power Of...Norton Utilities*

◆ Directory Sort (Chapter 19) allows you to sort the files in your directories by a variety of criteria.

◆ The File Attribute utility (Chapter 20) allows you to view and change the attributes of any file.

◆ The File Find and File Locate utilities (Chapter 21) can find files matching a particular specification or containing a particular search string anywhere on your disks.

◆ File Size (Chapter 22) computes the size of a group of files and determines whether they can be copied to a specified disk.

◆ File Date (Chapter 22) changes the date/time stamps on one or more files.

◆ Text Search (Chapter 22) searches for a specified text string anywhere on your disk, even in erased files.

18

MANAGING YOUR DIRECTORY STRUCTURE WITH NORTON CHANGE DIRECTORY (NCD)

As hard disks grow ever larger, it becomes more and more difficult to find your way around. You can't, one might say, tell the subdirectories without a program. If you've been navigating an increasingly complex directory tree using only the DOS Change Directory (CD) command and are growing tired of typing long strings of subdirectory names to get to your files, the Norton Change Directory utility (NCD) will greatly simplify and speed up your work. Even if you are accustomed to getting around in your directory structure by means of a shell program, such as the DOSShell program supplied with DOS versions 4.0 or later or the Norton Commander, or are using Windows or another GUI, NCD will give you powerful new commands for viewing and modifying your directory structure.

NCD provides a quick way to navigate through your directory structure, no matter how complex it may be. When you select **Norton CD** from the Norton

260 ■ *Power Of...Norton Utilities*

menu or type **NCD** at the DOS command line, the screen displays the directories for the current drive as a tree (see Figure 18.1). You can move about the tree using the cursor keys or the scroll bar, and change directories by pressing **Enter** on the highlighted directory. This makes it easy for you to go from one directory to another. NCD allows you to

- ◆ move quickly to another directory without having to type the path name on the DOS command line;
- ◆ make or rename a directory;
- ◆ delete a directory (including its subdirectories);
- ◆ print a directory tree;
- ◆ modify, add, or delete a volume label for a given disk;
- ◆ move a directory.

You will find it easy to manage your directories with NCD because you can make, delete, or rename directories while you view the directory tree. If the directory tree is too large to be seen in its entirety, you can conduct a speed search to find the directory you want by entering the beginning letter(s) of the directory name. If there is a directory name that matches the letters you entered, it will be found and highlighted. If there is no match, highlight stays where it is and the letters are not shown in the search box. Pressing **Ctrl+Enter** causes the highlight to cycle among all the directories on the current drive that match the letters in the search box.

If you have an EGA or VGA display, you can select a display with more than 25 text lines (via the View menu) to see more of the tree on the screen at one time.

Network Usage

NCD can be run on networks. When it is run for the first time on a given drive, it creates a file called TREEINFO.NCD. On non-network drives, the TREEINFO.NCD file is stored in the root directory. However, most networks do not give users rights to the root directory. For this reason the supervisor should create a directory named NCDTREE under the root directory and give all network users all rights to this directory. NCD will store the TREEINFO file in this directory.

Running Norton Change Directory

You can run NCD from the Norton menu or from the DOS command line. When you start the program, the Norton Change Directory main screen appears, displaying the directory tree for the current drive. Figure 18.1 shows the NCD main screen with a typical directory tree. The current drive and directory are shown in the lower left corner of the screen.

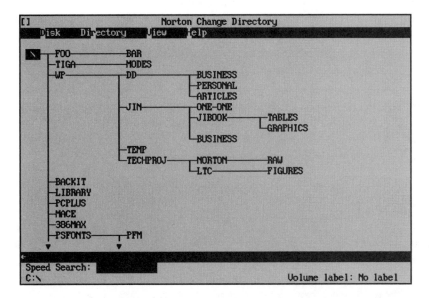

Figure 18.1 *NCD main screen, showing directory tree*

The first time you run NCD, it will scan the current drive and create a file called TREEINFO.NCD, where the directory data is stored. This file is always stored in the root directory of the drive and should not be moved. When you run NCD again, this information is used to create the directory tree instantly, saving the time needed to rescan the disk.

If you always rely on NCD to create, rename, or delete your directories, the TREEINFO.NCD file will always contain current directory information. If you use the DOS commands MD (make directory) or RD (remove directory) your TREEINFO file will not contain this new information and you will need to update the file by running the **Rescan Disk** command on the Disk menu.

NOTE A TREEINFO.NCD file will not be created for disks that have fewer than three directories. NCD can rescan the tree faster than it can rebuild the TREEINFO.NCD file.

You can navigate through the directory tree on the Norton CD screen by using the arrow keys to move the highlight to the directory or subdirectory you want to access. Press **Enter** to make it the current directory. You are taken back to the Norton menu (if you started the program from the menu) or to the DOS prompt, and the highlighted directory is now the current directory. If you exit the Change Directory screen by pressing **Alt+F4** or **Esc**, you will also return to the Norton menu or to the prompt, but when you exit the program you will be in the Norton directory, *not* in the directory that was highlighted on the directory tree.

NOTE If you run NCD strictly for the purpose of changing to a new directory, it is more efficient to run the program from the DOS command line with a partial directory specification, as described later (and efficiency is what this operation is about).

The Menu Bar

There are four selections on the menu bar: **Disk**, **Directory**, **View**, and **Help**. To access the menu bar, press **F10** or **Alt** + the highlighted letter in the menu title. Highlight the menu item you want and press **Enter**. Selecting **Help** (or pressing **F1**) displays help screens related to the NCD program. The remaining three selections—**Disk**, **Directory**, and **View**—contain commands for changing disks, managing the directory tree, and changing the way the tree is displayed on the screen. All the menu commands except those on the View menu have keyboard shortcuts, which are shown to the right of the commands on the menus.

The Disk Menu

The Disk menu, shown in Figure 18.2, has six options, which are described next.

Change Disk—allows you to change to a different drive. When you select this option, a list of the available drives is displayed. Highlight the one you want and press **Enter**. The directory tree is displayed for that drive. The shortcut for this option is **F3**.

Chapter Eighteen: Norton Change Directory (NCD) ■ 263

Figure 18.2 *The Disk menu*

Rescan Disk—rescans the current disk and updates the TREEINFO.NCD file. Use this menu item if you have used DOS to add or delete directories since you last used NCD. The shortcut for this option is **F2**.

Volume Label—allows you to place a volume label on a disk or to change the current volume label. You can use both uppercase and lowercase letters. When you enter a volume label, it is displayed at the lower right of the screen. The keyboard shortcut is **Ctrl+V**.

NOTE
The DOS LABEL command can only create volume labels with uppercase text characters and other characters that are acceptable for use in a file name, although it will recognize volume labels, including upper- and lower-case characters and most other characters from the extended ASCII set. The **Volume Label** option allows almost any 11-character name to be entered as a volume label.

Free Space—tells you how much total space is available on the current drive, how much space is currently occupied, and how much space is free. The keyboard shortcut is **Ctrl+F**.

Print Tree—prints a copy of the directory tree on your printer or saves it to a file. This is useful if the tree is too large to fit on the screen. The shortcut for this option is **Alt+P**. Selecting this command displays the Print Tree dialog box shown in Figure 18.3. Use this dialog box to specify the output device and the print style. The output device can be either a DOS logical device name, such as PRN, LPT1, or COM1, or a file name. If you enter a file name without a path, the file will be written in the current directory. There are three print styles: **Graphic Characters**, **Nongraphic Characters**, and **List**. **Graphic Characters** produces a printout similar to the tree display on the screen. Use this option if your printer prints the PC line-drawing characters. **Nongraphic**

Characters prints the tree using +, -, and | instead of the PC line-drawing characters. Use this option if your printer does not support the PC line-drawing characters. The **List** option prints a list of directories indicating the number of files and number of bytes occupied in each directory.

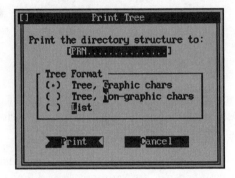

Figure 18.3 The Print Tree dialog box

Exit—terminates the NCD program with the Norton directory selected.

The Directory Menu

The Directory Menu, shown in Figure 18.4, contains nine options, three of which (**Copy Tree**, **Remove Tree**, and **Prune and Graft**) are unavailable unless you have used the **Configure** option to enable them. Each of the options on the Directory menu is described next.

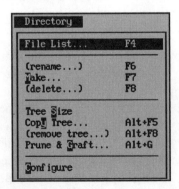

Figure 18.4 The Directory menu

Chapter Eighteen: Norton Change Directory (NCD) ■ 265

File List—displays a list of the files in the highlighted directory (see Figure 18.5). The list can be sorted by a number of criteria, including **Name**, **Extension**, **Date**, **Time**, and **Size**. Select the sorting criteria via the check boxes on the right side of the dialog box. You can create a sort "key" with two or more criteria and with different orders of priority among the criteria. For example, if you checked **Name** first and then checked **Extension**, the files would be listed in alphabetical order by name, but if two files had the same name but different extensions (e.g., DISKMON.EXE and DISKMON.INI), they would appear in alphabetical order by extension. After selecting a new sort key, select the **Re-sort** button to see the files in the new sort order. (I tried to come up with some sort of pun about the "last Re-sort" but couldn't manage it.) The keyboard shortcut for **File List** is **F4**.

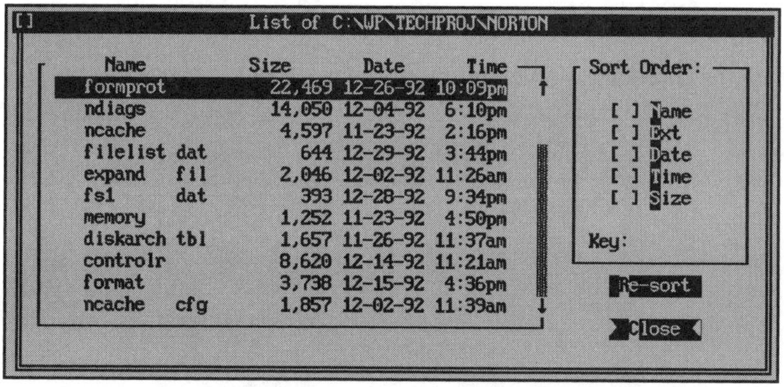

Figure 18.5 File List dialog box

Rename—allows you to rename a directory. Highlight the directory you want to rename and select this command or press the shortcut key, **F6**. Enter the new name in the dialog box and select **OK**. The new name appears in the directory tree.

NOTE

The **Rename** command is especially useful because DOS has no command for renaming directories. You will need it if you have used the Norton Disk Tools to recover from the DOS RECOVER command or if you have run the Norton UnFormat program without an IMAGE.DAT file. In these cases, you will need to rename the recovered directories because they have been given sequential numbers instead of their previous names, making it hard to identify them. You must be using DOS version 3.0 or later to use the **Rename** option.

Make—allows you to create a new directory. Highlight the parent directory to which the new subdirectory is to be added, then select **Make** on the menu or press the shortcut key, **F7**. A dialog box appears, showing the path and prompting you to enter the name of the directory to be added. Enter the name of the new directory and select **OK**. The new directory is added and is highlighted on the tree.

Delete—removes a directory. With DOS commands, a directory cannot be deleted unless all its files have been deleted first (i.e., a directory cannot be removed unless it is empty). **Delete** allows you to delete a directory and its contents in one operation. To use it, highlight the directory to be deleted, then select **Delete** on the menu or press the shortcut key, **F8**. If the highlighted directory is empty, it will be deleted immediately. If the directory is not empty, a dialog box similar to Figure 18.6 appears, advising you of the files in the selected directory and asking you to confirm that you want to delete it. If you select **Yes**, the directory along with all of its files will be deleted.

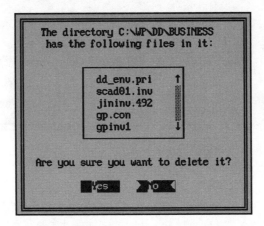

Figure 18.6 Delete-Directory prompt box

Tree Size—allows you to display the total size of all the files in the current directory. There is no keyboard shortcut for this command.

Copy Tree—unavailable unless you first enable it using the **Configure** command. **Copy Tree** allows you to copy a directory tree to a new location. When you select it, the Select Directory dialog box is displayed (see Figure 18.7). Select a destination for the Tree. The new location can be on the same or another drive. You can delete the directory and its contents from the original location if you wish. Deleting the original directory after moving a copy to another drive makes this, in effect, a "move" to the new drive. The shortcut for this command is **Alt+F5**.

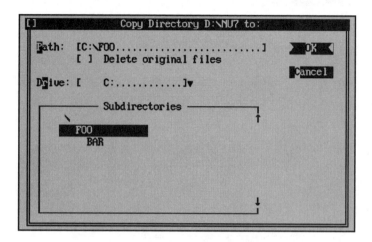

Figure 18.7 Select Directory dialog box

Remove Tree—allows you to delete a directory and any subdirectories under it, with all their contents. It is not available unless you first use the **Configure** option to enable it. Move the highlight to the highest node on the branch that you want to remove, then choose **Remove Tree** from the Directory menu. A prompt box will warn you that you are about to remove all the files in the directory tree, starting at the location you have highlighted. If you elect to proceed, you will be shown another dialog box with a list of all the files contained in the directory to be deleted. If you select **Yes**, the directory, and all its files are deleted. The shortcut for this option is **Alt+F8**.

 Use extreme caution with this command, because it completely removes all files in the selected subdirectories. Once removed, the directory, its files, and any subdirectories under it are permanently gone (unless you immediately use Norton UnErase to restore them).

Prune and Graft—allows you to move a directory and all its subdirectories to another location. You must first enable this command using the **Configure**

option. The shortcut for this command is **Alt+G**. Highlight the directory you want to move and select **Prune and Graft** from the Directory menu. The Prune and Graft screen is displayed (see Figure 18.8).

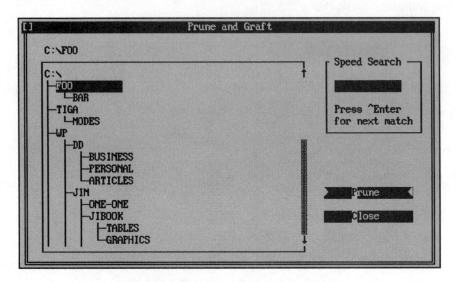

Figure 18.8 *Prune and Graft screen*

The top line of the screen displays the currently highlighted directory. Below this is a box showing the directory tree structure. At the right is a box where you can enter characters for a speed search. As soon as you type a character, it appears in this box and the first match found in the tree will be highlighted. At the lower right side are two buttons. When you first enter the Prune and Graft screen, they are labeled **Prune** and **Close**.

Move the highlight to the directory or subdirectory you want to prune, then use the **Tab** key to move to the **Prune** button and press **Enter** to activate it. Note that the two buttons now say **Graft** and **Cancel** and the highlighted directory now has a blinking (or bold) cursor next to it. Use the arrow keys to relocate the highlighted item to its new location. Use **Tab** to move to the **Graft** button and press **Enter** to activate it. The item is now moved to the new location. Selecting **Cancel** would have returned you to the directory tree with the old configuration restored.

Once you select **Graft** and the item is moved, the buttons say **Prune** and **Close** again. You can now move another directory if you wish. When you have finished, select **Close** to write the changes to disk. The new directory structure is now in effect and is displayed on the NCD main screen.

Prune and Graft cannot be used when running a multitasking environment such as Windows or DESQview.

NOTE

Configure—allows you to enable or disable, on the Directory menu, three menu items: **Copy Tree**, **Remove Tree**, and **Prune and Graft**. By default these three commands are disabled because they can be dangerous if not used carefully. Select the items you want to enable by checking their respective check boxes. Select **OK** to activate your choices. Selecting **Cancel** returns you to the main NCD screen with no changes made.

The View Menu

The View menu allows you to set the number of lines in the display if you have an EGA or VGA display. If you have an MDA or CGA display, you can only show 25 lines. The choices are 25 (all displays), 35 (EGA only), 40 (VGA only), 43 (EGA only), and 50 (VGA only). Only the choices that are available on your system will be displayed on the menu.

The Help Menu

The Help menu allows you to select from an index of help topics and to view information about your version of Norton Utilities, registration, and system configuration.

RUNNING NCD FROM THE DOS PROMPT

There are several different formats for running the NCD command from the DOS prompt:

1. NCD [drive:] [pathname] [options]—where

[drive:] is the drive letter containing the directory

270 ■ *Power Of...Norton Utilities*

[pathname] is the directory you want the command to affect

[options] are one or both of the following:

/R   Rescan the disk directory and update the TREEINFO.NCD file.

/N   Do not write or update the TREEINFO.NCD file.

2. NCD [drive:] /V:label—place a volume label on the specified drive; the label must be 11 or fewer characters long.

3. NCD [drive:] /L[:output] [options]—is the syntax for printing the directory tree, where [options] are one or more of the following:

/L:output   Print the directory tree on the specified drive to the specified output; this can be either a printer port or a file name.

/A   Display the tree for all drives (except floppies).

/G   Print the tree graphically.

/NG   Print the tree using nongraphic characters instead of line-drawing characters.

/T   Print the total number and total size of all files.

/P   Pause after each screen.

4. NCD command [source] [destination] [options]—copy a directory, remove (prune) branches of a directory tree, and graft (move) branches of directories to other locations, where

[command] is one of the following commands:

[source] is the name of the directory to be moved or grafted

[destination] is the name of the directory to move or graft to

The following commands are available:

COPY   Copy a directory tree to a new location. Has the option to delete the source files after copying.

GRAFT   Move a branch of the source directory tree to another location (destination).

Chapter Eighteen: Norton Change Directory (NCD) ■ 271

RMTREE Remove (prune) a branch of a directory tree.

/NET Use the network method (copy and then delete) to move directories. This works just like the command NCD COPY /DELETE.

NOTE

You will not usually need to use the /NET option because Norton Change Directory automatically recognizes network drives. But in some cases the /NET option may avoid certain network errors.

/BATCH Skip all prompts and exit to DOS when finished.

WARNING

The /BATCH option is designed for use in batch files. It applies to the RMTREE option only. This option prevents NCD from prompting you before removing the directory tree. /BATCH is a dangerous option because the command NCD RMTREE \ /BATCH will delete all the files on the disk without prompting you. Be very careful to check (and recheck) your entries if you use this option. Better still, don't use it at all. Its not worth the risk to save a few seconds.

5. NCD [command] [pathname]—make a new directory, remove a directory, or display the size of a directory, where [command] is one of the following:

MD Make a directory with the name and path of [pathname].

RD Remove the directory with the name of [pathname].

SIZE Display the total size of the files in the directory named and the space allocated for the directory.

NOTE

If you always use the NCD MD (make directory) and RD (remove directory) commands instead of the equivalent DOS commands, the TREEINFO.NCD file will be automatically updated. You won't have to wait for NCD to rescan the disk the next time you run the program.

The following are examples:

NCD View the directory tree for the current disk. You are placed in the directory tree where you can use the

272 ■ *Power Of...Norton Utilities*

NCD PAYDUES cursor keys to move about the tree. You can access the menu bar as described earlier.

Make the subdirectory PAYDUES on the current disk the current directory. If the directory name is unique, you need only specify is the end-point directory. You do not have to give the entire path, but the directory must be on the current disk.

NCD MD TPD Create a new directory called TPD and update the TREEINFO.NCD file to include the name.

NCD RD TPD Delete the directory TPD and update the TREE-INFO.NCD file to reflect this change.

NCD /R Rescan the directory tree. Use this command if you have made or deleted directories using DOS commands or have been working in NCD with the /N options set.

NOTE If you are using NCD to change directories on a write-protected diskette, you should include the /N option to turn off the automatic update of the TREEINFO.NCD file. Otherwise, you will get a write error message. (The write error will not, however, prevent you from viewing the directory of the protected disk.)

NCD B: /L:LPT1 /G /T Print the directory tree of drive B. Send it to the printer connected to LPT1. Print the tree graphically, and list the number and size of all files.

To view a list of the available options and the correct syntax for each, from the DOS prompt, type **NCD /?**

SUMMARY

Norton Change Directory allows you to view and print your directory structure. The directory tree can be printed graphically as a tree or as a text list. You can create new directories, delete directories, move complete directories or branches of a directory, rename directories, or add or change the volume label of a disk.

19

SORTING YOUR FILES WITH DIRECTORY SORT (DS)

When you create a new directory and add files to it, DOS places the files in the directory structure in the order in which they are created. Then, as old files are deleted, new ones are added to the structure wherever there are gaps. As a result, when you list a much-used directory with the DOS DIR command, what you see is a hodgepodge—old files and new files, files of different types, and subdirectories all mixed together with no intelligible order. If you typically manage your files with a shell program, such as the Norton Commander or the DOSShell program supplied with DOS versions 4.0 or later, or if you use a GUI such as Windows or DESQview, you are probably used to seeing your directories sorted in alphabetical order or in some other sensible manner. Many current applications also have built-in file management facilities that display the directories belonging to the application sorted meaningfully.

However, if you don't use a shell or GUI or if you use applications that don't have good file management facilities, the Norton Directory Sort utility can help you transform chaos into order. If you just want to sort the files in a directory by name, extension, date, time, or size, you can run Directory Sort from the command line or from a batch file. If you want to perform more complex tasks, such as moving the files in a directory or arranging a directory in ways that the sort keys cannot manage, you should run Directory Sort in the full-screen mode.

When you sort a directory, all its subdirectories are grouped first, followed by the files. The order depends on the sort criteria you have selected. Subdirectories and files are placed in two separate groups so you can easily distinguish between them, and so that DOS can move quickly through directory listings. To move the subdirectories to another location in the directory you must use the full-screen mode.

NOTE Files with the Hidden and/or System attributes cannot be moved with Directory Sort. This means Directory Sort will not interfere with copy-protection schemes that rely on finding a file at a specific physical disk location.

NETWORK USAGE

Directory Sort can read directories of network drives, ASSIGNed drives, and SUBSTituted drives. It cannot, however, write any changes to these disks. A warning message will be displayed when any of these drives is selected or when the **Write** button is pressed for one of these drives.

Subdirectory sorting always involves writing to disk, therefore, a separate message is displayed if the subdirectory box (full-screen mode) is checked and you press the **Re-sort** button.

FULL-SCREEN MODE

The full-screen mode allows you to work interactively with files and subdirectories in a scrolling list box. You can enter the full-screen mode in three ways.

1. Enter the command with a path name but with no sort keys; for example:

    DS A:\MARKETS

Chapter Nineteen: Sorting Your Files with Directory Sort (DS) ■ **275**

2. Enter the command with no path name or sort keys:

DS

3. Choose **Directory Sort** from the Norton menu.

When you load the program in full-screen mode, the Directory Sort dialog box (Figure 19.1), is displayed.

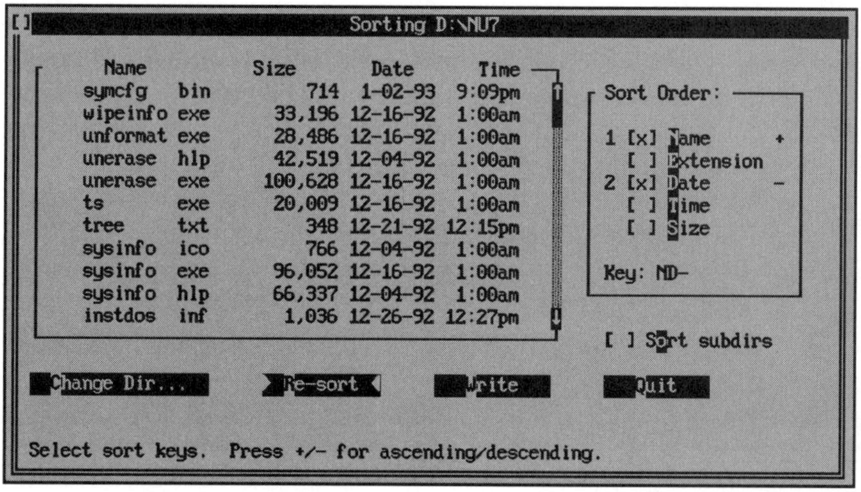

```
[ ]                         Sorting D:\NU?
   ┌ Name        Size      Date      Time ┐      ┌ Sort Order: ─────────
     symcfg  bin      714  1-02-93   9:09pm              ┌
     wipeinfo exe  33,196 12-16-92   1:00am
     unformat exe  28,486 12-16-92   1:00am      1 [x] Name          +
     unerase hlp   42,519 12-04-92   1:00am        [ ] Extension
     unerase exe  100,628 12-16-92   1:00am      2 [x] Date          −
     ts      exe   20,009 12-16-92   1:00am        [ ] Time
     tree    txt      348 12-21-92  12:15pm        [ ] Size
     sysinfo ico      766 12-04-92   1:00am
     sysinfo exe   96,052 12-16-92   1:00am      Key: ND−
     sysinfo hlp   66,337 12-04-92   1:00am
     instdos inf    1,036 12-26-92  12:27pm
                                                 [ ] Sort subdirs

  ▶Change Dir...   ▶ Re-sort ◀    ▶Write     ▶ Quit ◀

  Select sort keys.  Press +/- for ascending/descending.
```

Figure 19.1 *Directory Sort dialog box*

At the top of the box is the name of the directory to be sorted. Below that is a listing of all the files in the directory (except hidden and system files). Files are listed in the same format as that used by the DOS DIRectory command.

You can move files or subdirectories around in this list by moving the highlight to the file you want to move and tagging it by pressing the spacebar. (Arrowheads appear to the left and right of the file listing.) Use the **Up** and **Down** arrow keys to move the file to a new location in the list or drag it with the mouse. Pressing **Esc** cancels the move and returns the file to its original location.

At the right of the file list is the Sort Order box. Move the cursor to the sort key you want and check its check box. A number is displayed indicating its order of precedence (whether it is to be done first, second, and so on). This order depends on the order in which you selected the items. At the right of a

276 ■ *Power Of...Norton Utilities*

selected item is a + indicating a normal sort. Use the **Tab** key or **Right** arrow key to move to this sign. If you want a reverse sort order, you can toggle the + to a - by pressing the spacebar. Pressing the spacebar again toggles the sign back to a +.

Below the Sort Order box is a line labeled "Key:". The sort criteria you have selected are shown on this line in command-line notation. For example, if you select an ascending sort by size followed by a descending sort according to extension, the Key: line displays SE-. (An ascending sort does not require the + sign to be included.)

There is also a check box for specifying a sort of the subdirectories. Press the spacebar to place a check by this item. Selecting this item sorts all subdirectories below the displayed directory. When you initiate a sort with this option checked, a prompt box indicates that when subdirectories are sorted, changes are always written to disk. If you select **Proceed**, the sorting begins. **Cancel** stops the procedure.

At the bottom of the screen are four buttons: **Change Dir**, **Re-sort**, **Write**, and **Quit**. If you want to sort a different directory, select the **Change Dir** button. If you have moved a file or sorted the list but have not written the changes to disk, selecting **Change Dir** will display a dialog box asking if you want to write the changes to disk before changing directories. Select **Yes** to do this. Selecting **No** takes you to the Change Directory box without writing the changes (the changes are lost), and **Cancel** takes you back to the main Directory Sort dialog box.

If you have made sort order selections but have not yet executed the sort when you select **Change Dir**, a prompt box will appear asking if you want to apply the sort order before changing directories. If you answer **Yes**, the sort is performed and the changes are written to disk.

When all the required operations have been completed, the Change Directory dialog box is displayed (see Figure 19.2).

On the top line is the current drive and directory. Beneath this is a list box for selecting among the available drives. Below this is the subdirectory box, where a list of subdirectories below the current directory is displayed. Highlighting a directory name from this list and pressing **Enter** places it in the path statement on the top line. The directories below the selected directory are now displayed in the subdirectory box. Select **OK** to return to the main Directory Sort screen.

Chapter Nineteen: Sorting Your Files with Directory Sort (DS) ■ 277

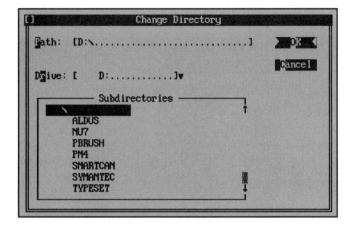

Figure 19.2 *Change Directory dialog box*

When you have selected the directory you want and have specified the sort keys, select **Re-sort**. If you have checked sorting of subdirectories, you will see the notice about automatically writing to disk. The sort is done according to the specifications you have given.

Select **Write** to write a sorted directory to disk. (If you have specified the subdirectory item, the sort is automatically written to disk.) This does not work for networks. You cannot write a resorted network directory back to a network disk.

Pressing **Esc** or selecting **Quit** exits Directory Sort and takes you back to the DOS prompt or the Norton menu. If you choose **Quit** and changes have been made but not saved, you are notified of this. If you want to save the changes, select **Yes**.

COMMAND-LINE USAGE

The command-line syntax for the Disk Sort command is:

```
DS [sortkeys] [path name] [/S]
```

where [sortkeys] = one or more of the following sortkeys. If you specify more than one sortkey, files that are the same under one sortkey are arranged by the

278 ■ *Power Of...Norton Utilities*

next sortkey specified. You must specify at least one sortkey or you will enter the full-screen mode.

N   By name in ascending alphabetic order

E   By extension in ascending alphabetic order

T   By time, earliest to latest

D   By date, earliest to latest

S   By size, smallest to largest

Any of these sort orders can be reversed by putting a minus sign (-) immediately after the sort key you want reversed. For example:

DS NS   Sorts first by name, in ascending alphabetic order, then by size, from smallest to largest.

DS NS-   Sorts first by name, in ascending alphabetic order, then by size, from largest to smallest.

[Path name] is the path to the directory you want to sort. If you enter sort keys but do not specify a path name, the current directory is sorted according to the specified keys. For example, if you are currently in the C:\WORD directory, typing

DS ED

would sort the C:\WORD (current) directory by extension, then by date.

If you want to sort a particular subdirectory, include it in the path name. For example,

DS NE C:\MARKETS\BEAR

sorts the BEAR subdirectory of the MARKET directory by name, then by extension.

/S   sorts all subdirectories under a given directory. For example,

DS NE C:\MARKETS /S

would sort all the subdirectories of the MARKET directory by name, then by extension.

Chapter Nineteen: Sorting Your Files with Directory Sort (DS) ■ **279**

To sort an entire disk, starting at the root directory, including all subdirectories, enter the following command with your sort keys:

DS N \ /S

The N specifies a sort by name, the \ indicates the root directory is to be sorted, and the /S switch indicates all the subdirectories are to be sorted.

For a summary of command-line options, type **DS /?**

SUMMARY

The Directory Sort command gives you a convenient way to perform directory sorts from the DOS prompt. If you want to do more specialized sorting or reorder some of the files or directories manually, you can use the full-screen mode, which allows you to fine-tune your results.

Viewing and Changing File Attributes

Whenever you create a file, DOS creates a directory entry in the directory of the disk where the file is stored. The directory entry includes important information about the file. Information about the size of the file and the date and time of its creation or last modification can be viewed by using the DOS DIR command. There is more information in this directory entry, however, than can be seen with the DIR command.

One of the things you don't see with DIR is the attribute byte. This byte consists of eight attribute bits, six of which are used to describe the type of file and control operations that can be performed on it by programs or DOS commands. Two of these bits have special functions: one specifies a directory (which, from DOS's point of view, is just a special class of file); the other specifies a volume label, of which there can be but one on any disk. The remaining four can be assigned to any file:

282 ■ *Power Of...Norton Utilities*

◆ **Archive**—indicates that the file has been created or changed since your last backup. Any time a file is created or changed, DOS sets the Archive attribute. As soon as the file is backed up (using the DOS BACKUP or XCOPY command or a backup utility such as Norton Backup), this attribute is cleared (to zero).

◆ **System**—indicates that the file is part of the operating system or other control program. File names with this attribute are not shown when you use the DIR command.

◆ **Read-Only**—indicates that the file cannot be written to; it is protected from being changed or deleted, either accidentally or deliberately. (However, programs such as Norton Commander or other DOS shells can delete Read-only files.) You can assign this attribute to files you want to protect, but be aware that it may interfere with some of the programs that must work with the file. (A detailed discussion of this file protection method is found in Chapter 4, Protecting Files from Accidental Erasure.)

◆ **Hidden**—also prevents files from being shown in a DIRectory listing. Any files that are of critical importance (such as program files that are part of the system software) may be protected with the Hidden attribute. If they cannot be found, they cannot be changed or deleted. The DOS files IBMBIO.COM and IBMDOS.COM (or MSDOS.SYS and IO.SYS) are hidden files. The user can also set this attribute to protect important files from unauthorized access.

The File Attributes utility allows you to view and/or change the settings of your files' attributes quickly. The command works on both files and directories. If you wish, you can assign new attributes to a file or clear attributes previously assigned to a file.

Sometimes you may want to see Hidden/Systems files or directories. For example, you may want to delete files left over from programs you have deleted, so that you can remove their directories, or you may want to set the Read-Only attribute on some of your important files to prevent accidental modification or erasure. Another possible use is to set the Archive attribute for valuable files after you perform a backup (which automatically clears the Archive attribute). That way you can make multiple backup copies of these files.

Chapter Twenty: Viewing and Changing File Attributes ■ 283

COMMAND-LINE USAGE

File Attributes is a command-line utility; it can be run from either the DOS command line or the Norton menu command line, but it doesn't have any menus, dialog boxes, and so on. It is controlled strictly by the options you type on the command line. The command-line syntax for the File Attribute command is:

`FA [filespec] [options]`

where

1. [filespec] is the name and path to the directory or file you want to view or set attributes on. If no filespec is included, the command acts on all files in the current directory.
2. [options] refers to one or more of the following 10 options. Six of the options are attribute related; the others are concerned with the way the command operates. An option used alone will display all the files containing the specified attributes. An option followed by a + sets the attribute (to a one). An option followed by a - clears the attribute (to a zero).

/A[+|-]	View, set, or clear files with the Archive attribute.
/SYS[+|-]	View, set, or clear files with the System attribute.
/R[+|-]	View, set, or clear files with the Read-Only attribute.
/HID[+|-]	View, set, or clear files with the Hidden attribute.
/DIR[+|-]	Displays a list of directories. (DOS treats directories as files with the directory attribute set.) With the + or - option, /DIR sets or clears the Hidden option for directories.

NOTE A hidden directory is invisible when you do a DIR listing of its parent directory, but it can still be accessed with the CD (change directory) command if you know that it exists and know its name. The files *in* the directory may or may not be hidden; this is independent of the status of the directory.

284 ■ *Power Of...Norton Utilities*

/CLEAR	Removes all file attributes.
/P	Pause after each screen.
/S	Include subdirectories in the operation.
/T	Display the totals of attributes changed for files or directories only. Do not list individual file names.
/U	Display files with any attribute set (unusual files, since the most common case with a well-backed-up disk is to have no attributes set).

When you use multiple attribute options, they are logically ANDed. For example:

```
FA /R /H
```

means that only those files that are both Read-Only and Hidden will be displayed.

If you want to view information about this command from the DOS prompt, type **FA /?**

Examples:

```
FA /A
```
This displays all files in the current directory with the Archive attribute set.

```
FA /A+
```
This option sets the Archive attribute for all files in the current directory.

```
FA /A-
```
This clears the Archive attribute for all files in the current directory.

A command that includes an option to display a group of files with one attribute, and a second option that changes a different attribute, will only change the second attribute on those files that have the first displayed attribute set.

```
FA /A /R+
```
This displays all the files in the current directory with the Archive attribute set. Only these files will have the Read-Only attribute set; all other files in the current directory will not be changed.

Chapter Twenty: Viewing and Changing File Attributes ■ 285

`FA C:\WORD /P /S /U`
This displays all the files in the Word directory and its subdirectories that have any attribute set. The display pauses after each screen.

`FA C:\WORD /U /S /CLEAR`
This lists all the files in the Word directory and its subdirectories that have any attribute set. All attributes for these files are cleared.

`FA /SYS- /HID-`
This removes both the System and Hidden attributes from all files in the current directory. This is useful for removing hidden and system files from programs you have deleted. After removing the attributes, you can delete the files.

WARNING Be careful about changing the attributes of files that have Hidden and/or System attributes. These files may be essential components of your operating system. The best-known case is that of the two DOS files IBMBIO.COM and IBMDOS.COM (or MSDOS.SYS and IO.SYS). *If you delete these files, your system will not boot.* Other hidden files may be part of copy-protection schemes for application programs. If you delete these files, copy-protected programs may refuse to load. In short, unless you are certain about what you are doing, it's best to leave hidden and system files alone. (If there are hidden files left in a directory where you have deleted all the visible files from a program, it's probably safe to delete them.)

SUMMARY

File Attributes is a command-line utility that you can use to view and change the attributes of files, directories, and subdirectories.

SEARCHING FOR MISSING FILES WITH FILE FIND (FILEFIND) AND FILE LOCATE (FL)

The similarity of their names might lead you to expect File Find and File Locate to be very similar programs, but they're not. Whereas File Find is a full-screen program with a long list of file manipulation features, File Locate is a simple, straightforward command-line utility that essentially does just one thing: locates missing files or directories. To find files containing a particular text string, perform search-and-replace operations, create and save or print file catalogs, or create batch files that work on a group of files, use File Find. Use File Locate when you know the name or approximate name of the file or directory that you want but can't remember where you put it.

288 ■ *Power Of...Norton Utilities*

FILE FIND

File Find helps you locate work you have lost or misplaced, whether it is data, a file, or a whole directory. It is a real time saver. Instead of laboriously searching through directory after directory, you can use File Find to do the job. File Find can search all physical and logical drives. In addition, it duplicates many of the features of other Norton file management utilities: It can view, set, or clear file attributes, like FA; it can test whether a file or files can be copied to a specified target drive, like File Size; it can drop you at the prompt in a directory where the file you are searching for is found, like Norton Change Directory; and it can change time and date stamps, like File Date.

Network Usage

File Find can search network drives. An added feature is its ability to search network files by "owner."

Running File Find

You can run File Find from the Norton Utilities Main menu or from the DOS prompt. The main File Find dialog box is displayed (see Figure 21.1).

Full-Screen Operation

At the top of the main dialog box is the **File Name** line. Use this line to specify either a complete file name to search for, if, for example, you know the name of the file you want but can't remember the directory you saved it in, or a filespec, using the standard DOS wild-card characters * and ?, to search for all the files of a particular type. The second line, **Containing**, allows you to narrow the search further by specifying a text string to be searched for in all the files meeting the specification in the **File Name** line. The third line, **Replace With**, allows you to replace the search string in the files where it is found with another text string that you specify. The check box to the left of the line must be checked for this feature to operate. (It is off by default.)

Chapter Twenty-one: File Find (FILEFIND) and File Locate (FL) ■ 289

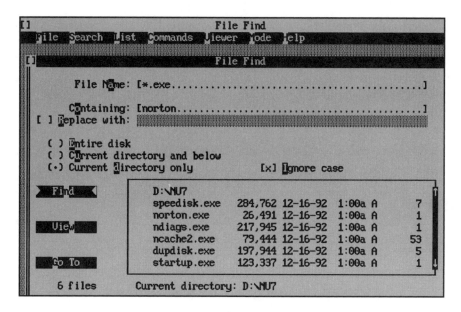

Figure 21.1 File Find main dialog box

When you have completed a search with the replace feature activated, a prompt will appear on the screen indicating that you should press the **Replace** button to select the matching text to replace. (The **Replace** button appears in the location previously occupied by the **View** button when the search is completed.) Move the highlight in the file list to the name of the file in which you want to replace the text string and press **Enter**. (The **Replace** button will automatically be selected when you highlight a file in the list.) A new screen will be displayed showing the contents of the selected file with the first occurrence of the search string highlighted. At the bottom of the screen are two groups of buttons: The upper group of five buttons consists of **No Change**, **Replace**, **Close**, **Next File**, **Undo**. Pressing **No Change** causes the highlight to move to the next occurrence of the search string without replacing the previous occurrence. Selecting **Replace** replaces the highlighted occurrence of the string and moves the highlight to the next. Selecting **Close** returns you the File Find main dialog box. Selecting **Next File** takes you to the next file in the list. If you have replaced any instances of the search string in the current file, you will be prompted to indicate whether you want to save your changes before moving to the next file. Selecting **Undo** restores the most recently replaced instance of the search string to its original state. You can step backwards through all of the instances of the replaced string and restore them all by pressing **Undo** several times in succession. The lower group of buttons, labeled "Continue w/o Pause," contains two buttons: **This File** and **All Files**. Selecting **This File** replaces all occurrences of the search string in the file currently on view. Selecting **All Files** replaces the string in all files in the list.

Below the **Replace With** line, on the left side of the dialog box, are three radio buttons for selecting the area of the disk to be searched. The available options are the whole disk, the current directory and its subdirectories, and the current directory alone.

NOTE

It is not always intuitive what drives File Find will search, as this is affected by the interaction of a number of different menu options and radio buttons. The **Drive** and **Directory** commands on the File menu (see later) allow you to select the current drive and directory, and these will be searched if the **Current Directory and Below** or the **Current Directory Only** radio button is selected. However, if **Entire Disk** is specified, the drives to be searched will be affected by the settings in the **Search Drives** option on the Search menu. If **Default Drive** is selected, then the search will be limited to the default drive. If **All Drives** or **The Following Drives** is selected, then all drives or the specified drives will be searched, regardless of the settings for the current drive and directory.

To the right of the radio buttons is a check box labeled **Ignore Case**. This is checked by default, but if you want a case-sensitive search (e.g., files that include the string "File Find" but not those that include "file find," or vice versa), you should uncheck this box. For many simple file searches, these controls will be all that you need. (More complex operations may require the use of the pull-down menus, described later.)

When you have set up the conditions for your search, select the **Find** button at the left side of the screen to begin the search. As soon as the search begins, the label on this button changes from "Find" to "Stop." You can stop the search in progress at any time by selecting this button. This can be useful if, for example, you are searching the whole disk for one particular file. Once the file has been found, you can stop the search to save the time of searching the remainder of the disk. You can also stop a search by pressing **Esc**, in which case you will be prompted to indicate whether you want to **Cancel** or **Resume** the search.

Chapter Twenty-one: File Find (FILEFIND) and File Locate (FL) ■ 291

When the file (or files) you are searching for has been found, it will be displayed, with its size, date, and time, in the scrolling window that occupies most of the lower half of the box. The list of files will be organized by the directories in which they are found, with a directory heading above the list of files from a given directory. To the right of the time stamp for each file will be a number indicating how many occurrences of the search string were found, if one was specified. You can view the contents of the found files by moving the highlight to the file of interest and pressing **Enter**. (The **View** button, on the left side of the box, is automatically selected when the highlight is on a file name.)

When you enter the View box (Figure 21.2), you will be positioned at the first occurrence of the search string, if one was specified. You can navigate through the selected file in the View box using the cursor keys, the scroll bars and mouse, and the four buttons at the bottom of the screen. **Prev. Match** moves to a previous occurrence of the search string. **Next Match** moves to the next occurrence of the search string. **Next File** moves to the next file in the list, and **Close** exits the View box.

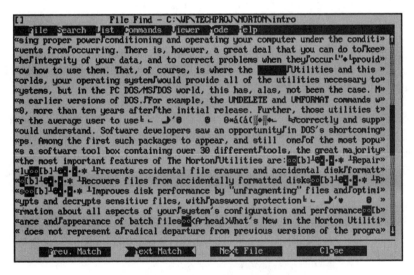

Figure 21.2 *The View box*

Back at the main dialog box, you can exit File Find to the directory where your files were found by highlighting a directory name in the list box and pressing **Enter**. (The **Go To** button is automatically selected when you highlight a directory name.)

The Menu Bar

Above the main File Find dialog box is a menu bar with seven pull-down menus: File, Search, Lists, Commands, Viewer, Modes, and Help. Press **Alt** or **F10** to access the menu bar. Move the cursor to highlight the menu you want and press **Enter** or the **Down** arrow key to open a menu. Many of the options on these menus have keyboard shortcuts and/or hot keys.

The File Menu

The File menu has three options: **Drive**, **Directory**, and **Exit**.

Drive—allows you to change the current drive. The shortcut for this option is **Ctrl+D**.

Directory—allows you to change the current directory. The shortcut for this option is **Ctrl+R**.

Exit—terminates the program. The shortcut is **Alt+X**.

The Search Menu

The Search menu has four options: **Search Drives**, **Advanced Search**, **Hex Strings**, and **Make Backup Files**.

Search Drives—allows you to select the drives to search. Move the cursor to one of the three radio buttons in the Search Drives dialog box (Figure 21.3) and press the spacebar to select it. The three options are **Default** (the current drive), **All Drives**, or **All the Following Drives** (use the check boxes to select from among the available drives). The shortcut for this option is **F2**.

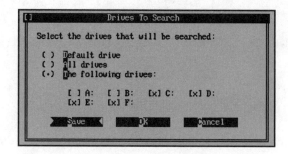

Figure 21.3 Search Drives dialog box

Chapter Twenty-one: File Find (FILEFIND) and File Locate (FL) ■ 293

If you always want to search the same drives, you can save your choices by selecting **Save**. Select **OK** to activate your selections. **Cancel** returns you to the File Find screen. If you select a different drive(s) than the default, a line appears in the main File Find dialog box indicating which drives will be searched. Notice that the current drive remains the same.

Advanced Search—allows you to specify multiple search criteria, including the following:

- **Date**—before and/or after a specific date
- **Size**—greater and/or less than a specific size
- **File Owner**—networks only
- **Find As**—how the search string is to be used
- **File Attributes**—Hidden, System, Read-Only, and Archive
- **Include directories**

The Advanced Search dialog box is shown in Figure 21.4. The shortcut for this option is **F4**.

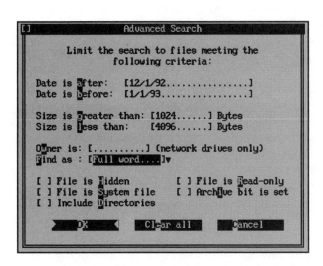

Figure 21.4 Advanced Search dialog box

The **Find As** option is particularly useful for narrowing your searches for text strings. There are four options under this heading: **Any Match**, **Full Word**, **Prefix**, and **Suffix**. If you select **Any Match**, your search string will be found,

294 ■ *Power Of...Norton Utilities*

regardless of whether it is a free-standing word or embedded in larger strings. For example, if your search string was "form," this option would find files including "form," but also those including "per*form*," "uni*form*," "in*form*ation," "*form*at," and so on. If you selected **Full Word**, the search would find only files with "form" as a free-standing word. Selecting **Prefix** would find files including "*form*at," "*form*ative," and so on; and selecting **Suffix** would find files including "per*form*," "uni*form*," and so on.

After you have set your search criteria, select **OK** to activate them. You are returned to the main File Find dialog box. Selecting **Clear All** in the Advanced Search dialog box clears all previous search criteria. **Cancel** takes you back to the main File Find dialog box without making any changes.

Hex Strings—allows you to specify and view search-and-replace strings in both ASCII and hexadecimal formats. This is useful if you want to search for a string that includes nonprintable characters, such as "carriage return," "line feed," "escape," "tab," and so on. You cannot enter these characters on the **Containing** or **Replace With** lines in the main File Find dialog box, but you can enter their hex codes in the appropriate locations in the Hex strings dialog box (Figure 21.5). An advanced programmer might use this feature to patch the executable file of a buggy program (although there are more effective tools for this purpose). Most users should scrupulously avoid modifying executable files, using this or any other tool.

The List Menu

The List menu contains three items: **Set List Display**, **Print List**, and **Create Batch**.

Set List Display—allows you to select how File Find displays the files it finds. The list can display file names with sizes, dates, and attributes; file names and sizes; file names and dates; file names and attributes; or file names alone. You can also specify whether the files are to be sorted and, if so, what the sort criterion should be. Files can be sorted by name, extension, date and time, or size. The sort can be in ascending or descending order. The List display dialog box is shown in Figure 21.6. The shortcut for this option is **Ctrl+F**.

Chapter Twenty-one: File Find (FILEFIND) and File Locate (FL) ■ 295

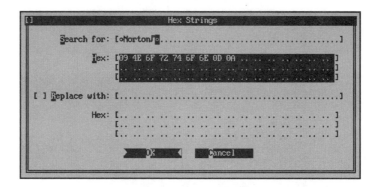

Figure 21.5 *Hex strings dialog box*

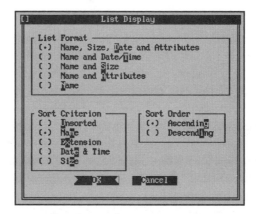

Figure 21.6 *List Display dialog box*

Print List—cannot be accessed until a search has been completed. Printing is controlled from the Print List dialog box (Figure 21.7). You can print the list to your printer or to a file. To print to a file, enter a file name. You can also specify the format in which the list will be printed; the choices are the same as those given for the **Set List Display** command. Other options include printing the number of occurrences of the search string in each file, the total file size and number of files per directory, and the total file size, number of files, and number of occurrences of the search string for the complete search. The shortcut for this option is **Ctrl+P**.

296 ■ *Power Of...Norton Utilities*

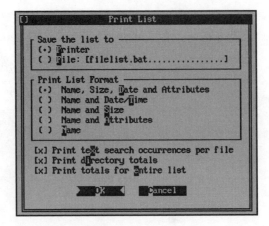

Figure 21.7 *Print List dialog box*

Create Batch—cannot be used until a file search has been completed. This command allows you to create easily a batch file that acts on the files found by the search. Use the dialog box in Figure 21.8 to specify the commands to include in the batch file. Specify the filespec (path/filename) for the file to be created. The **Save Full Path** check box specifies whether the full filespec, including drive and path, will be used in the batch file or whether only the file name will be used. The **Directory Title Line** check box determines whether the name of the directory where the files were found will be added to the head of the file. If the search found files in more than one directory, a directory header is added before each group of files.

Figure 21.8 *Create Batch dialog box*

Chapter Twenty-one: File Find (FILEFIND) and File Locate (FL) ■ 297

The command to be executed by the batch file is created by adding text before and/or after the file names. Type the text in the lines indicated in the dialog box. For example, to copy the files to a different drive/directory, type **copy** on the before line and the destination drive/directory on the after line. A line is available to add text before the directory titles as well. If you have included directory titles, you might want to add "REM" or "ECHO" before them, so that you don't get a "Bad Command or File Name" message from DOS when your batch file runs. When you have entered all your text and settings, select **OK** to save your batch file to disk.

Each execution of the Create Batch command creates a simple batch file that performs only one operation, and the same operation is performed on each of the files (e.g., you can copy all the files to the same drive or directory, or delete them all). You can make a batch file that performs two or more successive operations on all the files, such as copying them to another drive or directory and then deleting them from the source drive/directory, by making a second batch file with the second command and then attempting to save it with the same name as the first file. The program will warn you that a file by that name exists and will ask whether you want to overwrite it or append to it. Select **Append** and the commands of the second file will be added to the end of the first. You cannot, however, create a file that performs one operation on one group of files and a different operation on others except by modifying the file with a text editor. The shortcut for **Create Batch** is **Ctrl+B**.

The Commands Menu

The three options on the Commands menu—**Set Attributes**, **Set Date/Time**, and **Target Fit**—duplicate features available in other Norton file management utilities. None of the options on this menu can be accessed until a file search has been completed. There are no shortcuts for these items.

Set Attributes—allows you to specify (Figure 21.9) if the attributes are to be set for the highlighted file or for the entire file list. You can set (or clear) one or more of the following attributes: Archive, Read-Only, Hidden, and System. Unlike those used in most of the Norton Utilities, the check boxes for these attributes have three possible settings. A check means "set the attribute," a blank box means "clear the attribute," and a rectangular block means "leave the attribute as it is." Use the spacebar to cycle through the options for the check boxes.

After you have selected the attributes you want, press **Enter**. A box will display a summary of the changes you have made. The changed attributes are not displayed on the list of files in the main File Find dialog box. Use the File Attributes utility (FA) to view them.

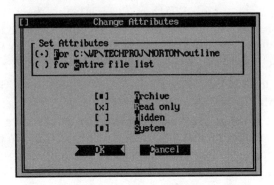

Figure 21.9 Set Attributes dialog box

Set Date/Time—use the radio buttons at the top of the Set Date/Time dialog box (Figure 21.10) to indicate whether the date/time stamp should be changed for the highlighted file or the entire file list. Use the check boxes on the left side of the dialog box to indicate whether the time and/or date should be changed. If you do not enter a new date and/or time, the current system-clock time will be used. Select **OK** to activate your changes (a box will display a summary of the changes you have made), or select **Cancel** to exit the dialog box without making changes.

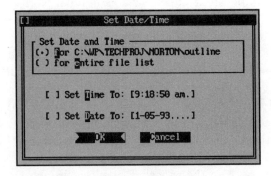

Figure 21.10 Set Date/Time dialog box

Chapter Twenty-one: File Find (FILEFIND) and File Locate (FL) ■ **299**

Target fit—like the File Size utility, determines whether the files in the list will fit on the specified target drive. Select the target drive from the dialog box that appears when you select the command. The program checks the specified drive, displays a summary of space use, and indicates whether there is enough space for the files.

The Viewer Menu

You must have selected **View** from the File Find dialog box to display a file before you can use the options on this menu. In addition, the first two options are only available if you have conducted a search for a text string. Three of the four options on this menu—**Previous Match**, **Next Match**, and **Next File**—duplicate the functions of the buttons at the bottom of the Viewer box, as described earlier. The fourth option, **Previous File**, is self-explanatory.

The Mode Menu

The Mode menu has three commands that switch you between the main File Find dialog box ("Search") and the Viewer box. You can select one of two views, ASCII and hexadecimal.

The Help Menu

The final menu on the menu bar, Help, gives you an index of help topics and a summary of version, registration, and system information.

Running File Find from the DOS Prompt

You can also run the File Find program from the command-line. (File Find is *not* a command-line utility. Running File Find from the DOS prompt loads the program in full-screen mode and executes the options specified on the command line.) At the prompt, type

```
FILEFIND [filespec] [search text] [replace text] [options]
```

where

[filespec] is the file name and path to be searched.

[search text] (optional) is the text string to search for. (If the text contains spaces and/or commas, you must enclose the entire text string in quotes.)

[replace text] (optional) is a text string with which to replace the search text.

[options] specify what is to be done during and after the search. The following options are available:

/S	Include files in subdirectories.
/C	Search only the current directory.
/CS	Case-sensitive search.
/O:filespec	Save the list of files to the specified file.
/BATCH	Exit the program automatically when the specified options are completed (for use in batch files).
/TARGET:d	Test whether the files will fit on the specified target drive.
/D[:][mm-dd-yy]	Set the date to [month-day-year].
/T[:][hh:mm:ss]	Set the time to [hour:minute:second].
/NOW	Set the date and time to the current system-clock values.

NOTE If /D or /T is used and no date or time is specified, the file date is set to 0-0-80 and the time stamp is blanked.

/A[+/-]	Search for archived files or set/clear the Archive bit.
/R[+/-]	Search for Read-Only files or set/clear the Read-Only attribute bit.
/HID[+/-]	Search for hidden files or set/clear the hidden attribute bit.
/SYS[+/-]	Search for system files or set/clear the system attribute bit.
/CLEAR	Clear (remove) all file attributes.

NOTE If any of the four attribute options is used by itself (no + or - is included), it searches only for files with specified attribute bit set.

Chapter Twenty-one: File Find (FILEFIND) and File Locate (FL) ◼ 301

You can view a list of available options at the DOS prompt by typing
FILEFIND /?

Examples:

`FILEFIND /C /A /R+`
This searches the current directory for all files that have the Archive attribute
(/A). The files meeting this criterion will have their Read-Only attribute set
(/R+). They will then be Archive, Read-Only files.

`FILEFIND C:\PROJECTS "Norton Utilities" /S /O:NORTON.LST`
This searches the directory C:\PROJECTS and all its subdirectories for files that
have the text string "Norton Utilities" and saves a list of those files in a file
named NORTON.LST in the current directory.

`FILEFIND C:\PROJECTS\*.TXT switches options /BATCH`
This searches the C:\PROJECTS directory for files with the text string "switches"
and substitutes the text string "options," then exits the program.

File Find Summary

File Find makes it easy to search for a file or group of files that have some specified set of characteristics, such as containing a specified text string, having
been created within a specified range of dates, and so on. You can search the
current directory, specified drives and directories, or all the drives connected to
your system, including network drives. You can also perform search-and-
replace operations on the files that you specify.

FILE LOCATE

File Locate is a command-line utility, it can be run from either the DOS command line or the Norton Menu command line, but it has no menus, dialog
boxes, or full-screen operating modes. Its actions are controlled entirely by the
options you type on the command line when starting the program, and they
begin executing immediately when you press **Enter** after typing the command.

Command-Line Usage

The syntax of the File Locate command is

FL [drive:] [filename] [options]

where

[drive:] is the drive to search (if no drive is specified, the current drive is searched).

[filename] is the name (or partial name) of the file or directory to search for. The wild-card characters * and ? can be used. If no name is specified, all files are listed (the same as entering *.*). You do not need to include a path to the file because File Locate automatically searches the entire drive that is specified.

[options] refers to the six options you can use with the File Locate command:

/A	Search all drives.
/P	Pause after each screen.
/W	List files in a wide format (no file lengths or date/time stamps are displayed).
/F[*n*]	Find the first *n* files that match the specification. (The default number of matches to list is 1.)
/E:[name]	Search only the path specified by the [name] environment variable.
/T	Search only the directories included in the DOS PATH statement.

To view information about this command, at the prompt type **FL /?**

NOTE If you want to view the contents of your PATH statement and/or your environment variables, type the DOS SET command (with no parameters) at the prompt. This command will display the PATH, any active environment variables, and other values stored in the DOS environment space.

When you run the File Locate command, it responds by displaying a list of the files that match the specification that you have given. By default, the

Chapter Twenty-one: File Find (FILEFIND) and File Locate (FL) ■ 303

list is output to the screen, in a one-column format, with file lengths and date and time stamps. As the list scrolls on the screen, you can pause it by pressing any key and you can cause it to resume scrolling again by pressing any key *except* **Esc**. Pressing **Esc** when the list is paused will terminate the listing.

You can redirect the output of File Locate to a file or to your printer using the DOS redirection character (>). For example, to direct the output to a file, you would type

```
FL [drive:] [filename] [options] >[filespec]
```

where [filespec] is the path and file name where you want the list to be saved. To send a list of all the files on all your drives to your printer, type

```
FL /A >PRN
```

or

```
FL /A >LPT1
```

(Substitute COM1 if your printer is connected to a serial port, or any other DOS logical device name that is appropriate for your system configuration.)

Examples:

```
FL B: notes /P /W /F5
```
This searches drive B for the first five files or directories matching the spec "notes"; pauses after each screen, and displays the file list in the wide format.

```
FL B: > PRN
```
This prints a list of all files on drive B.

```
FL *.EXE /T
```
This lists all the .EXE files in directories in the DOS PATH.

```
FL *.INI /E:WINDIR
```
This lists all the files with the .INI extension in the directory pointed to by the WINDIR environment variable.

304 ■ *Power Of...Norton Utilities*

File Locate Summary

File Locate is a command-line utility that can find files or directories on any disk in your system and display or print a list of the files it has found.

THE NORTON UTILITIES

22

MISCELLANEOUS FILE MANAGEMENT UTILITIES

Norton Utilities includes a number of small utilities that perform fairly simple operations on files or groups of files (directories, trees, or even whole drives). Three of these utilities are gathered together in this chapter: File Size, which determines the size of a specified group of files and checks whether they can be copied to a specified target disk; File Date, which changes the date/time stamp on specified files; and Text Search, which can search for a specified text string anywhere on a disk, even in erased files. These three are command-line utilities; that is, they can be run from either the DOS command line or the Norton menu command line, but they have no menus, dialog boxes, or full-screen operating modes. Their actions are determined entirely by the options you type on the command line when starting the program, and they begin executing immediately when you press **Enter** after typing the command. There is considerable overlap among the features of these utilities and between them and some of the larger file management utilities discussed previously, and often there will be several ways of accomplishing a given task.

305

FILE SIZE

If you want to know the size of a file or a group of files, File Size provides a quick way to find out. It lists the sizes of the specified files as well as the amount of slack space (the unused space at the end of the last cluster in each file; see later) used by the files. File Size can also determine the amount of space that will be required to copy a file or group of files to a target disk; it takes into account the different disks' cluster sizes when calculating the space required for the files.

Cluster Sizes

A cluster is the smallest unit of disk space DOS can allocate. It is made up of one or more sectors, each of which contains 512 bytes. (See Chapter 23 for a detailed examination of how DOS manages and organizes disk space.) Depending on the type of disk and the DOS version you are using, a cluster consists of between one and 16 sectors and thus contains from 512 bytes (0.5Kb) to 8192 bytes (8Kb) of data. Since a cluster is the smallest unit DOS allocates, even a one-byte file will be assigned the exclusive use of an entire cluster. The rest of the space in that cluster will be unused (slack) and wasted.

The amount of wasted space depends on the type of disk being used. For example, a high-density, 1.2Mb diskette uses one sector per cluster, so each cluster contains 512 bytes. If you write a 40-byte file to a 1.2Mb floppy disk, that 40-byte file occupies 512 bytes, of which 502 bytes are slack space. On a 30Mb AT hard disk, however, there are four sectors, or 2048 bytes per cluster. If you copy that 40-byte file from the 1.2Mb floppy to this hard disk, it will require 2048 bytes, of which 2008 bytes would be slack (98% of the cluster space required is wasted).

In most cases, nothing can be done about slack; each disk type has its characteristic cluster size, and that's that. (See Chapter 23 for information about partitioning large hard disks to obtain the most advantageous cluster size.) However, the difference in cluster sizes between disk formats may make a difference when you try to copy a group of files from one disk to another with a different format. Depending on whether the target disk has a larger or smaller cluster size than the source, the amount of space required for the files may increase or decrease when they are copied. (The size of the files as reported by the DIR command will not change. DOS reports the actual size of the files, *not* the size of the clusters they occupy.) If the total size of the files is close to the

Chapter Twenty-two: Miscellaneous File Management Utilities ■ **307**

amount of space on the target disk, they may not fit, even though the combined length of the files in bytes is smaller than the available space on the target disk. Use the File Size utility to determine how much space the files you want to copy will occupy on the target disk and whether there is enough space to accommodate them.

Command-Line Usage

File Size is a command-line utility; it can be run from either the DOS command line or the Norton menu command line, but it doesn't have any menus, dialog boxes, and so on; it is controlled strictly by the options you type on the command line. The command-line syntax for the File Size command is

```
FS [filespec] [target-drive:] [options]
```

where

[filespec] is the file and/or directory name that you want the command to work on. The filespec can include the DOS wild-card characters, * and ?. If no file name is specified, all the files in the specified directory are included (the same as using *.*). If no drive is included in the filespec, the current drive is assumed.

[target-drive] is the drive to test for sufficient space to copy the specified file(s).

[options] refers to the following choices for this command:

/P   Pause after each screen.

/S   Include subdirectories.

/T   Display totals only (don't include file names).

To see a list of available options, at the prompt type **FS /?**

Examples:

1. To display the size of all files contained in the current directory, type **FS** at the DOS prompt and press **Enter**. The names and sizes of all files in the current directory are listed. At the end of the list is a summary of the total

308 ■ *Power Of...Norton Utilities*

size of the files listed, the disk space occupied by the files (i.e., the total cluster size occupied) in bytes, and the percentage of slack. The drive usage is also listed: the total bytes available on the drive and the amount of unused space on the drive (in bytes and as a percentage of the available space).

2. To list the space occupied by all the files in the root directory of drive A and determine the amount of space required to copy them to drive B, type

```
FS A: B: /T
```

This command gives results similar to the following:

```
A:\
   154,407 total bytes in eight files
   156,160 bytes disk space occupied, 1% slack

   157,696 bytes disk space needed to copy to B:
   730,112 bytes available on B:, enough disk space

Drive usage
   1,213,952 bytes available on drive A:
   468,480 bytes unused on drive A:, 39% unused
```

Note that the same files that require 156,160 bytes on drive A would require 157,696 bytes on drive B. This is the case because drive A is a 5.25" 1.2Mb floppy, which uses 512-byte clusters, whereas the disk in drive B is a 720Kb formatted 3.5" disk, which uses 1024-byte (1Kb) clusters. The larger cluster size results in increased slack.

The similar command

```
FS A: D: /T
```

gives this result:

```
A:\
   154,407 total bytes in eight files
   156,160 bytes disk space occupied, 1% slack
   161,792 bytes disk space needed to copy to D:
```

Chapter Twenty-two: Miscellaneous File Management Utilities ■ **309**

```
    5,242,880 bytes available on D:, enough disk space
Drive usage
    1,213,952 bytes available on drive A:
      468,480 bytes unused on drive A:, 39% unused
```

Because drive D is a 32Mb hard-disk partition, which uses 2048-byte (2Kb) clusters, the same group of files would occupy 161,792 bytes if copied to that disk.

3. To list all the files in the Adobe Illustrator directory on drive C, including its subdirectories, and the amount of space the files occupy, while pausing after each screen, type

```
FS C:\AI4 /P /S
```

at the DOS prompt and press **Enter**.

4. To perform a total File Size disk analysis, type

```
FS \ /S /T
```

and press **Enter**. In this example the filespec \ indicates the root directory. The /S option indicates that subdirectories are to be included. Since no drive is given, the command acts on the current drive. No file name is specified, so all files are included (the same as entering *.*).

File Size searches the root directory and all its subdirectories. It lists the total bytes in the files, the number of files, the total bytes used and percentage of slack for each directory and subdirectory. It also lists the total disk space, the amount of disk space still unused, and the percentage of the total space that is unused.

FILE SIZE SUMMARY

Use File Size to determine quickly the size of files and the total size and slack space used. File Size displays the amount of disk space needed to copy files to a different drive.

FILE DATE

File Date is used to change the date and time stamp for a file or a group of files. This may be useful if you have software that backs up files based on their date and time. If you use a MAKE program (a programming utility that compiles and links the many files required to build a large program), this command may also be useful.

You can set, remove, or update the settings for any file (and path) you specify. If you do not include a date or time option, the files are updated to the current DOS (system clock) date and time.

NOTE

The date format depends on the country where the command is used.

Command-Line Usage

File Date is a command-line utility; it can be run from either the DOS command line or the Norton Menu command line, but it doesn't have any menus, dialog boxes, and so on. It is controlled strictly by the options you type on the command line and begins executing immediately when you press **Enter**. The command-line syntax for the File Size command is

FD [filespec] [options]

where

[filespec] is the file name and path on which the command is to operate. If no path or file name is included, the current directory is used, and *.* is assumed for the file name (all files are included).

[options] refers to the four options for this command:

    /D[:][date]   Sets the specified date as month-day-year. The colon (:) is optional. You should always use hyphen delimiters for your

Chapter Twenty-two: Miscellaneous File Management Utilities ■ **311**

date entries to avoid confusion. Remember that a forward slash (/) indicates an option character, so it should never be used in a date entry.

/T[:][time]   Sets the specified time (hour:minute:second). Only the hour is required. The colon (:) is optional. Time is entered in a 24-hour format; for example 10:05 P.M. is entered as 22:05.

/P   Pause after each display screen.

/S   Include all subdirectories.

Examples:

```
FD C:\WP51 /D:3-5-93
```
This changes the date stamp for files in the WP51 directory on drive C to 3-5-93.

```
FD C:\QUATTRO /T:16:45 /S
```
This sets the time stamp for files in the QUATTRO directory on drive C and all its subdirectories to 4:45 P.M.

```
FD /D:3-5-93 /T:4:45
```
Sets the date and time stamp for all files in the current directory to 3-5-93 and 4:45 A.M.

```
FD D:\RECORDS\DUES.DBF /T:0:00
```
Sets the time stamp for the file DUES.DBF in the RECORDS directory on drive D to 12:00 A.M. (midnight).

```
FD D:\RECORDS
```
Since neither a date nor a time option was used, this sets the date and time to the current DOS system clock date and time for all files in the RECORDS directory of drive D.

To view information about the File Date command and to get a list of available options from the DOS prompt, type **FD /?**

You should be careful when using this command to be sure you understand which files and directories you are working on. Although it cannot damage files or cause data loss, it can be a bit of a nuisance to set the dates of the files in all your directories accidentally to the current system date and then try to determine which files are old and which are current. If you do this there's no way to restore the correct file dates except to restore the files from a backup. (Or, if your backup program will print a catalog of the backed-up files with dates, you could correct all the dates individually with FD, which is still a considerable nuisance.)

File Date Summary

The File Date utility operates from the DOS prompt or from the Norton command line to change the date and time stamp quickly on the files you specify.

TEXT SEARCH

Text Search is a command-line utility; it can be run from either the DOS command line or the Norton menu command line, but it has no menus, dialog boxes, or full-screen operating modes. Its actions are controlled entirely by the options you type on the command line when starting the program, and they begin executing immediately when you press **Enter** after typing the command. Unlike most Norton command-line utilities, Text Search is interactive; if you type **TS Enter** on the command line without including a sufficient string of options, the program will prompt you to enter the information it needs to conduct a search.

Use Text Search to locate specific text in one or more files on a disk, including erased files. If the search text contains spaces, enclose it in quotes. The search is more likely to succeed if you keep the search string short. Longer strings are more likely to contain hidden word-processor formatting codes that will cause them to fail to match the search string. (Of course, you can include formatting codes in a string if you know the codes that your word processor or other applications use and if they are relevant to the search.)

Chapter Twenty-two: Miscellaneous File Management Utilities ■ **313**

The DOS wild-card characters (* and ?) can be used in the filespec to restrict the files reported (for the first form listed under syntax).

Command-Line Usage

The command-line syntax for the Text Search command has two forms:

```
TS [filespec] [string] [/S] [/T] [/A] [/CS] [/EBCDIC]
[/LOG] [/WS]
```

or

```
TS [string] /D|/E [/Cn] [/A] [/CS] [/EBCDIC] [/LOG] [/WS]
[/F:filename]
```

where

[filespec] (first form) is the path and file name for the file(s) to search.

[string] (both forms) is the text string to search for. If spaces are contained in the search string, they must be enclosed in quotes (e.g., "look for this").

/S (first form)	Include subdirectories in the search.
/T (first form)	List only the names of files that contain text matching the search text (does not display the text following the matching text, as with the /A option).
/D (second form)	Search the entire disk, including erased files.
/E (second form)	Search only erased files.
/Cn (second form)	Start searching at cluster *n*.
/A (both forms)	Automatic search, answers **Yes** to all prompts. (The /A option defaults to ON when /LOG is used. Displays text following the matched text.)
/CS (both forms)	Search is case sensitive.
/EBCDIC (both forms)	The search string is translated to EBCDIC format and the translated string is used in comparisons.

314 ■ *Power Of...Norton Utilities*

/LOG (both forms)   The output is formatted as a LOG, suitable for output to the printer or to a file.

/WS (both forms)   The eighth (most-significant) bit in each character is ignored in the search.

To view information about this command when you are at the DOS prompt, type **TS /?**.

NOTE   EBCDIC (Extended Binary Coded Decimal Interchange Code) is a text-encoding format used on IBM mainframes. It is rarely used in PC files. The /WS option is designed for use with WordStar text files or files from other applications that use the WordStar format. In this format only seven bits are used to encode characters, and the eighth bit is used for formatting purposes. When searching with the /WS option, only seven bits per character are used in making comparisons. Characters in the IBM extended ASCII set (characters with ASCII codes 128–255) cannot be found when searching with this option.

SEARCHING FOR TEXT ON A DISK

Either form of the Text Search syntax given earlier can be used, regardless of whether you start from the Norton Menu or the DOS prompt. The following examples use both forms, in combination with various options.

1. To search the current directory of any drive, use the first form of the command. Use the drive letter in place of the filespec (e.g., A: to indicate the root directory of drive A):

   TS A:

   If you press **Enter** at this point, you will be prompted for the text to search for. Enter a text string and press **Enter**. The text search is initiated. If matching text is found, a portion of the text around it will be displayed and the program will ask if you want to continue the search. Only the root directory of drive A is searched.

Chapter Twenty-two: Miscellaneous File Management Utilities ■ 315

2. If you know the specific path you want to search, specifying it will speed things up. For example,

```
TS C:\PROJECTS
```

will only search the PROJECTS directory on drive C. You will be prompted for the search text. If a matching string is found, a portion of the surrounding text will be displayed and the program will ask if you want to continue the search. Only the specified directory is searched.

3. If you need to search a specific path and all its subdirectories, use the /S option:

```
TS C:\PROJECTS /S
```

You will be prompted for the search text. Type the text string and press **Enter**. The C:\PROJECTS directory and all its subdirectories are searched. When a match is found, the path and file name of the file containing the match are displayed, along with the text following the match.

4. If you don't need to see the text surrounding the search text, use the /T option:

```
TS C:\PROJECTS /S /T
```

You will be prompted for the search text. The C:\PROJECTS directory and all its subdirectories will be searched. When a match is found, the path and file name of the file(s) containing the matching text will be displayed, but not the text or the context in which it was found.

5. To use the syntax in Example 4 to search for the word "RAIN", type

```
TS C:\PROJECTS RAIN /S /T
```

The C:\PROJECTS directory and all its subdirectories are searched for the word "RAIN". When a match is found, the path and file name of the file(s) containing the matching text will be displayed, but not the text or the context in which it was found.

6. If you need a permanent record of the results of your search, use the /LOG option, along with the DOS redirection symbol, to store your search results in a file. For example,

```
TS C:\PROJECTS RAIN /S /T /LOG >C:\RAIN_LOG
```

will search the C:\PROJECTS directory and all its subdirectories for the word "RAIN". If matches are found, the path and file name(s) of the file(s) containing the matching text will be saved to the file RAIN_LOG on drive C.

7. To restrict the search to those files in the PROJECTS directory on drive C, with a .DOC extension, change Example 6 to

```
TS C:\PROJECTS\*.DOC RAIN /S /T /LOG >C:\RAIN_LOG
```

NOTE In Examples 6 and 7, if the file (C:\RAIN_LOG) does not exist, the command creates it. If it does exist, the command overwrites it. Use double greater-than characters (>>) if you want to append text search reports to an existing file.

8. To search all of drive C for the word "RAIN", use the second form of Text Search. At the DOS prompt, type

```
TS C: RAIN /D
```

and press **Enter**. You will be prompted for a filespec to which to save the matching information. This is not a file to save a log of *where* the information was found (use the /LOG option, described earlier, for this purpose); rather, it is a file of the actual clusters in which the search text was found. You would do this if you were trying to reconstruct an erased and partially overwritten file by finding and saving all the clusters containing the specified text. If you want to save the clusters in a file, type an appropriate path and file name and press **Enter**. You must specify a drive other than the drive you are searching. If you do not want to save the clusters in a file, just press **Enter**, and any text match (and the text following it) will be displayed on the screen along with the cluster and sector number(s) where it was found.

If you have specified a file, you will be prompted when a match is found to indicate whether you want the cluster saved to the file. Answer by pressing **Yes** or **No**. The program will then ask whether you want to continue the search. Again answer **Yes** or **No**. You can eliminate the prompting and cause all the clusters to be saved to the specified file by adding the /A

Chapter Twenty-two: Miscellaneous File Management Utilities ■ 317

option to the command line.

9. To search the entire C drive (including erased files) for files containing the word "RAIN" and save the clusters where the text was found in the D:\RAIN_DAT file, use the second syntax form, as follows:

   `TS C: RAIN /D /F:D:\RAIN_DAT`

   The clusters where the search text is found are saved in the RAIN_DAT file, in the root directory of drive D.

NOTE

The /F option works only in conjunction with the /D or /E option.

Text Search Summary

Text Search allows you to search for text anywhere on a disk, even in erased files. You can store a list of the locations where the search text was found in a log file or you can capture the complete clusters containing the search text in a file for use in reconstructing a lost or damaged file.

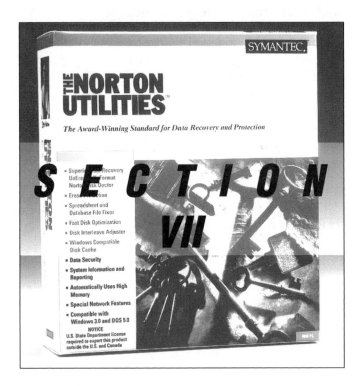

ADVANCED DISK REPAIR TECHNIQUES

Most common disk problems can be solved using the built-in intelligence of the tools described in Section II. This is especially true if you faithfully follow the preventive procedures outlined in Section I. Occasionally, however, you may encounter a problem that is beyond the ability of these tools. At that point you can do one of two things: get professional assistance or use the Norton Disk Editor. The Disk Editor is the most powerful of the Norton Utilities' many tools, but it is also the most difficult and potentially the most dangerous to use. This is so because the Disk Editor allows you to examine and modify any portion of a disk, including those areas used by DOS to keep track of files or boot the system. This power may be just what is needed if one of these vital areas is acci-

320 ■ *Power Of...Norton Utilities*

dentally damaged, but by the same token, it is possible to damage these vital areas, making a disk unreadable or unbootable, if you use the Disk Editor carelessly or unskillfully.

Unlike most of the other Norton Utilities tools, successful use of the Disk Editor requires detailed knowledge of how disks store and organize data. Hence, we will devote Chapter 23 to this important topic before we go on to examine the Disk Editor and its uses in Chapter 24.

THE NORTON UTILITIES

23

HOW YOUR DISK
SUBSYSTEMS WORK

There's a lot of information packed into this chapter, some of which is fairly abstruse, so you shouldn't be too disturbed if you don't get it all on the first reading, especially if you are new to these topics. Feel free to go on to the next chapter and explore your disks using the Disk Editor (in Read-Only mode, of course) and to refer back to this chapter to clarify the phenomena you observe there, or to jump back and forth between the two chapters, reading about disk concepts here and examining the corresponding structures with the Disk Editor.

DISK ARCHITECTURE

Magnetic Recording Media

Computer disks, whether floppy (diskettes) or hard disks, use a magnetic medium to store information. This medium consists of a thin coating of a

322 ■ *Power Of...Norton Utilities*

metallic oxide, usually iron oxide or a combination iron oxide and other compounds, on a circular disk. On a blank disk, the particles of magnetic oxide are randomly oriented. Disk subsystems record data by magnetizing selected portions of the medium so that all the particles have a common orientation. This is not unlike the process used to record on audio tape or video tape, except that these media record *analog* information, where many different levels of magnetic intensity are used to represent signals of varying strengths, whereas computer disks need to record only two levels, representing ON or OFF, one or zero. (Yes, audio and video can be converted to digital formats and stored on computer disks and other digital media, such as DATs, CDs, laser disks, and so on, but that is beyond the scope of the current discussion.) *How* ones and zeros are represented on computer disks will be described later in this chapter.

Computer disks also differ from audio tapes, video tapes, and the like, in that they are *random access* media. That is, whereas you normally play an audio tape or video tape from the beginning to the end (or if you don't, you have to fast-forward past the parts you don't want), with computer disks you can go right to the area where the data you want is stored, without having to start at the beginning and read through everything until you find it. The various organizational structures described next exist for the sole purpose of allowing you to find a particular file anywhere on a disk, without having to start at the beginning and read through everything until you find what you're looking for.

Tracks and Sectors

Computer disks are divided into concentric *tracks*, and they are further subdivided radially into wedge-shaped *sectors* (see Figure 23.1). These tracks and sectors are established on the disk by a *low-level format* (more about this topic follows). They are not physical divisions on the disk surface (you couldn't see them if you inspected the disk surface with a magnifying glass), they are simply magnetic markers on the disk that instruct the disk drive and controller mechanism where to store data on the disk. As a disk rotates on its spindle, the *head* that writes to or reads from it can be moved in and out over the surface of the disk (see Figure 23.2). The combination of these two motions allows the head to be positioned over any sector on any track. The head is simply moved to the desired track, where it waits until the desired sector rotates into place, at which time a read or write operation can be performed.

Chapter Twenty-three: How Your Disk Subsystems Work ■ 323

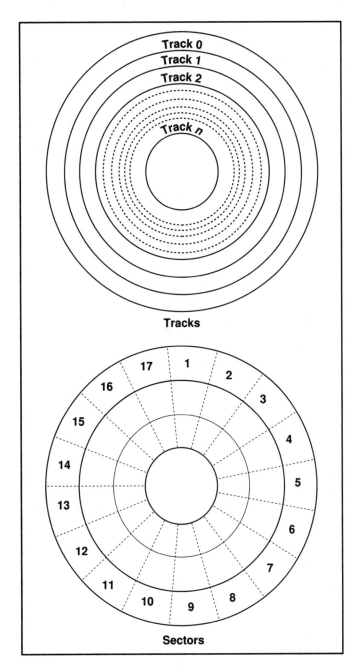

Figure 23.1 *A Disk divided into tracks and sectors*

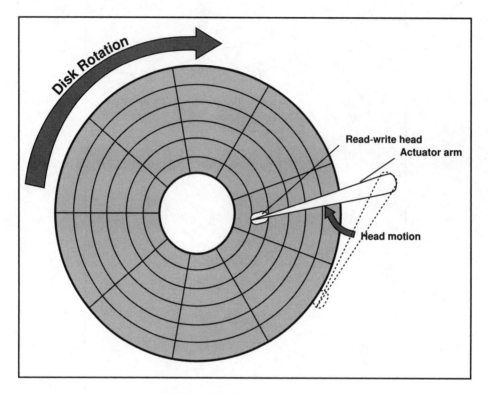

Figure 23.2 *Disk head motion*

Unlike audio and video tapes, computer disks are coated with oxide on both sides. Therefore, floppy disk drives are equipped with two heads, one for each side of the disk. The two heads always move in parallel, so that they are always positioned over the same track and sector on opposite sides of the disk. Hard disks use the same system, except that they typically comprise multiple platters, with a pair of heads for each one, as shown in Figure 23.3. Under all DOS versions released thus far, a sector stores 512 bytes of data. Hence, the amount of data a disk can store depends solely on the number of tracks and sectors it holds. The track/sector formats and storage capacities for the various floppy disk types supported by DOS through version 5.0 are given in Table 23.1.

Chapter Twenty-three: How Your Disk Subsystems Work ■ 325

Table 23.1 Common Track/Sector Formats

Size	Capacity	Tracks per Side	Sectors per Track	Supported by DOS Versions
5.25"	360Kb	40	9	2.0 and later
3.5"	720Kb	80	9	3.2 and later
5.25"	1.2Mb	80	15	3.0 and later
3.5"	1.44Mb	80	18	3.3 and later
3.5"	2.88Mb	80	36	5.0 and later

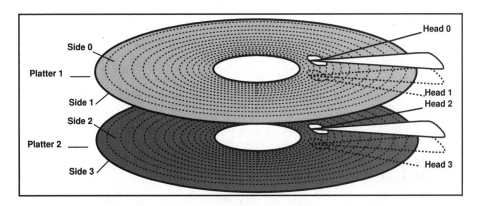

Figure 23.3 A two-platter hard disk

How Hard Disks and Floppy Disks Differ

Hard disks (or *fixed disks*, in IBM-speak) are not radically different in principle from floppy disks. Both storage devices use a rotating disk coated with a magnetic medium, and a movable read/write head mechanism, and both divide the disk surface for organizational purposes into concentric tracks and radial sectors. However, the similarity ends there. Whereas in a floppy disk, the magnetic coating is on a sheet of flexible mylar, hard disks apply the coating to rigid metal platters. This difference is necessary because hard disks rotate at much higher speeds than floppy disks. Typically, hard disks rotate at 3600 rpm, whereas floppy disks rotate at only 360 rpm. The higher speed of rotation is one of the

326 ■ *Power Of...Norton Utilities*

factors that make hard-disk read/write operations much faster than those of floppies. If a flexible mylar disk was rotated as fast as the metal platters of a hard disk, the forces acting on it would deform the disk surface, making it impossible to read or write reliably. Also, hard disks spin as long as the computer is turned on, whereas floppy disks turn only when they receive a read or write command. This is another factor in the relative speeds of the two disk types—a floppy disk must first come up to the correct speed from a dead start before a read or write can occur. Hard and floppy disks also differ in the precise methods of head operation. Floppy disk drive heads actually touch the disk surfaces, which is another reason that their speed of rotation must be limited. (If the disk rotated faster, the friction created by the head rubbing on the disk surface would be more likely to wear away the oxide. Even at the relatively slow speed of 360 rpm, this no doubt contributes to wear and tear on floppies.) Hard-disk heads never touch the disk surface (or at least they're not *meant* to touch the surface; when they do, it's called a head crash, one of the major causes of data loss); instead they ride on a very thin cushion of air. Typically, hard-disk heads are separated from the disk surface by about 0.3–0.6 microns, or less than 1/200 the thickness of a human hair. For this reason, hard disks are built into sealed enclosures, to protect them from dust and other contaminants that could become trapped between the head and disk surface and cause damage. A third way that hard disks differ from floppy disks is that, as mentioned, they consist of multiple platters attached to a common spindle. Hence, a hard disk is also equipped with multiple pairs of read/write heads, one pair per platter.

Hard disks store more data than floppies for two primary reasons. First, they consist of multiple platters. Obviously, all else being equal, a disk with more surfaces can store more data. Second, the data on the hard-disk surface is much more densely packed than that on floppy disks; that is, there are many more tracks and sectors on a hard-disk platter than on a floppy disk of comparable size. Typical hard disks have 305 or more tracks, with 17 or more sectors per track. Other common sectoring schemes use 26, 34, or 54 sectors per track. The 100Mb disk on the machine I'm using to write this book has 855 tracks with 34 sectors per track, and there are seven sides. (When you see an odd number of sides in the specification of a hard disk, it means that the drive and controller have reserved one side of one platter for house-keeping.) As the amount of data stored in a sector is a constant 512 bytes, more tracks and sectors can store more data. To find the capacity of a hard disk in megabytes, multiply the number of tracks by the number of sectors per track, and multiply that by the number of sides. This will give the number of sectors; then divide by 2048.

Cylinders and Clusters

In addition to tracks and sectors, there are two other terms you will commonly encounter that are used to specify portions of a disk: *cylinders* and *clusters*. A cylinder refers to all the tracks with the same track number on the different surfaces of a disk. For example, on a hard disk with three platters (see Figure 23.4), there are six occurrences of a given track number—that is, side 0, track, 0; side 1, track 0; side 2, track 0; ... side 5, track 0. All these occurrences of track 0, taken together constitute cylinder 0. Similarly, all the occurrences of track 1 on the six different surfaces constitute cylinder 1, and so forth for as many tracks as this disk supports. Cylinders are a useful concept because of the way that disk heads move in parallel over the disk surface. When a large file is being written and it uses up all the available sectors in a track on a given surface, it is logical to continue writing that file on the same track on the next available surface if sectors in that track are free, because this can be done without moving the head. Similarly, a file that has been written in the manner described earlier can be read more quickly, because a minimum of head movement is required. Therefore, provided that you keep your hard disk unfragmented, all or most of a file will frequently reside in a given cylinder. Remember that cylinders are an abstraction. If you disassembled your hard disk (*Don't;* you'll void the warranty and probably destroy the poor thing in the process), you wouldn't see any physical structures corresponding to cylinders.

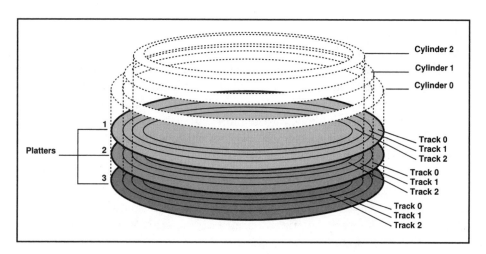

Figure 23.4 Cylinders on a three-platter hard disk

328 ■ *Power Of...Norton Utilities*

Clusters are the minimum units of disk space allocated by DOS for file storage. A cluster consists of from one to 16 sectors, depending on the size and format of the disk. The cluster sizes used by DOS for various disk types are summarized in Table 23.2. Unlike tracks and sectors, clusters are not part of the low-level format of the disk. They are simply an organizational concept used by DOS in managing disk space.

Table **23.2** *Cluster Sizes for Common Disk Formats*

Disk Type	Cluster Size	Sectors/Cluster
5.25", 360Kb floppy	1024	2
3.5", 720Kb floppy	1024	2
5.25", 1.2Mb floppy	512	1
3.5", 1.44Mb floppy	512	1
3.5", 2.88Mb floppy	512	1
0–15Mb hard disk	4096	8
16–128Mb hard disk	2048	4
128–256Mb hard disk	4096	8
256–512Mb hard disk	8192	16

The choice of cluster size is a compromise between conservation of disk real estate and simplicity of organization and speed of access. The smaller the cluster size, the less disk space will be wasted in file allocation. For example, if you have a cluster size of one sector (512 bytes), any file from one byte to 512 bytes will occupy one cluster. There is no way to allocate one-half or three-fourths of a cluster, so a very small file will waste most of the cluster it occupies. Similarly, a file of 513–1024 bytes will require two full clusters, one of 1025–1536 bytes will require three full clusters, and so on. Analogous situations exist for disks with larger cluster sizes. On a disk with eight sectors per cluster (4096 bytes), it is possible to waste as much as 4095 bytes if one has a file with a length of n full clusters plus one byte. With disk space always at such a premium, does it make sense to waste so much potentially useful disk space? Why not organize the disk so that every sector can be used?

Chapter Twenty-three: How Your Disk Subsystems Work ■ 329

It does make sense, because the smaller the minimum unit of storage space that can be allocated, the larger the disk space that must be devoted to keeping track of what all those units of space are currently being used for. At the extreme limit, if one tried to design a system in which single bytes were allocatable, one might end up with as much or more space devoted to record keeping as for actual file storage. And if one could tolerate that situation, the time required to search through these records to find a given file would probably prove unsatisfactory.

DOS Sector Numbering

So far we have referred to sectors in a three-dimensional format (i.e., side *x*, track *y*, sector *z*). This format, known as *absolute* or *physical* sector numbering, is how the hard-disk controller and the ROM BIOS refer to sectors. This system begins numbering with side 0, track 0, sector 1. DOS uses a different, one-dimensional numbering scheme, known as *relative* or *logical* sector numbering, which assigns consecutive numbers to all the sectors on a disk. This system begins with sector 0. (The Norton Disk Editor can use either numbering scheme.) The DOS relative sector numbering system works like this: head 0, track 0; sector 1 is off-limits to DOS and is not included in the DOS numbering scheme. This is the location of the master boot record (MBR), which includes the partition table (explained later). Most hard disks reserve the remainder of track 0 and begin the logical sector numbering at the physical address side 1, track 0, sector 1, where the DOS boot record for the primary DOS partition is located. This sector is designated DOS sector 0. Consecutive sectors on side 1, track 0 receive consecutive sector numbers. So, for example, on a hard disk with 17 sectors per track (spt) the sectors on side 1, track 0, are numbered 0–16. DOS then goes on to assign consecutive numbers to the sectors on the next track in the same *cylinder*. Thus, side 2, track 0, sector 1 on our 17-spt disk would be sector 17, and the last sector on this track would be sector 33. This process continues through all the tracks that comprise cylinder 0, before moving on to the first sector of the first track in cylinder 1. All the sectors of all tracks on consecutive cylinders receive consecutive numbers in this fashion, to the limits of the *primary DOS partition*. If there is an extended DOS partition, the numbering system skips over the extended partition table—and, in most cases, the remainder of the track that it resides on—and begins anew with track

330 ■ *Power Of...Norton Utilities*

0 of the first volume of the extended partition, where the boot record for that volume is located.

FORMATTING

Before any disk can be used for data storage, the magnetic surface of the disk must be set up to receive information. DOS cannot use a disk until it has been divided into tracks and sectors and until information about these divisions has been recorded on the disk. This process is called *formatting*. The formatting operation is essentially a three-part procedure, consisting of low-level formatting, partitioning (hard disks only), and high-level formatting.

The initial, low-level (physical) formatting operation places magnetic tracks on the previously unmagnetized surface of the disk. Each of the magnetic tracks is then subdivided into sectors. The low-level format writes the track and sector ID numbers in spaces between the sectors so that the disk controller hardware can determine the locations of the sectors on the disk surface. Track and sector ID numbers consume significant disk space, accounting, at least in part, for the discrepancies between unformatted and formatted disk capacities that one sees in disk specifications.

For hard disks, the low-level formatting is usually done at the factory or, in the case of some disks with ST506-type controllers, by firmware that resides on the controller. If you are adding a new hard drive, or changing your hard-drive controller, you will find low-level formatting instructions in the documentation for your controller. (The end user cannot low-level-format drives with IDE controllers or many drives with ESDI or SCSI controllers. If you are in doubt, contact the manufacturer of the drive and/or controller, or the dealer you purchased them from.)

High-level formatting establishes the system area, which contains the DOS boot record, the FATs, and the root directory. High-level formatting is performed with the DOS FORMAT command, or, preferably, with the NORTON Safe Format utility (see Chapter 4). If you purchase a new system from a dealer with a hard disk already installed, the partitioning and high-level-format will most likely have been done as well. If you are configuring your own system or replacing an older hard disk with a new one, you may need to partition and high-level-format the drive yourself.

Chapter Twenty-three: How Your Disk Subsystems Work ■ 331

For a hard disk, the DOS FDISK command is used to partition the disk. (For more about partitioning, see later.) After partitioning, the DOS FORMAT command is used to high-level-format each of the logical drives created in the partitioning process. For example, the command

```
FORMAT C: /S
```

is used to format the C drive and install the files necessary to make it bootable. The same process, without the /S option, must be performed for any other logical drives residing on the physical hard disk.

On floppy disks, the DOS FORMAT command performs both the low-level and high-level format (floppy disks cannot be partitioned). The Norton Safe Format (see Chapter 4) can perform a high-level format on a floppy disk that has been formatted already, while storing information that allows the disk to be unformatted. (This is where the safety comes in.)

Interleave Factors

We have been speaking thus far as though the consecutively numbered sectors on a hard-disk track were always located adjacent to one another. This is sometimes true, but not always, especially on older machines with slower CPUs and disk controllers. To understand why consecutive clusters might not be placed next to one another, consider the steps involved in a hard-disk read or write operation. When a program wants to read from or write to the disk, it normally calls a DOS function that performs the desired operation. The DOS function, in turn, sends the necessary commands to the disk controller, telling it what sector to read. The controller sends the necessary signals to the disk, which responds by moving the heads to the desired track, waiting for the requested sector to appear, and then performing the read or write. The disk then must inform the controller, which in turn reports back to the DOS function that the operation was successful (or not), and, if the operation was a read, transfer the data. So far, so good. Now the DOS function will probably tell the disk controller that it wants to read or write the next consecutive sector. But while the data transfer, reporting back, and requesting the next read/write were taking place, the disk kept spinning at 3600 rpm. Hence, unless the CPU and the disk controller are very fast, it is likely that the beginning of the next sector has already passed under the disk heads. If this is the case, there is nothing the controller can do but wait for a full rotation of the disk until the desired sector comes around again. Since one sector contains 512 bytes and since a hard disk rotates at 3600 rpm (= 60 revolutions per second), a disk that could read or write only one sector per rotation could transfer only 30Kb per second, a rate that is inferior to that of a floppy disk.

Fortunately, there is a simple solution to this problem: Don't place consecutively numbered sectors adjacent to one another on the physical disk; leave enough space between them so that the controller and CPU can complete a read or write and be ready for the next sector by the time it comes around. This process of laying out consecutive sectors in nonconsecutive order on the physical disk is known as *interleaving*. The way the consecutive sectors are spaced on a disk is called its *interleave factor* and is expressed as a ratio. When the consecutive sectors are adjacent to one another, the interleave factor is said to be 1:1. Most current '386 and '486 PCs have disk controllers that are fast enough to operate at a 1:1 interleave factor, and you will often see the specification "1:1 hard-disk controller" in advertising. Older PCs, however, need increased interleave factors for the best disk performance.

For example, the original IBM XT used an interleave factor of 1:6, as illustrated in Figure 23.5. The XT controller is not fast enough to handle a 1:1 interleave. The 1:6 interleave allows the XT to read or write three sectors on a single rotation (90Kb/second), a threefold improvement over its performance with a 1:1 interleave. The original IBM AT used a 1:3 interleave, which allowed it to make six reads or writes on a rotation, for a throughput of 180Kb/second. Most contemporary AT-compatible machines, especially those with IDE, ESDI, or SCSI disk controllers, use 1:1 interleave factors. The resulting throughput depends on the number of sectors per track on the disk and the speed at which the controller can transfer data to the bus.

NOTE You don't have to know the interleave factor of your hard disk to use the Disk Editor. Your disk controller knows the interleave factor and finds the consecutively numbered sectors and presents them to the Disk Editor (or any other program) in the proper order. You can check your disk's interleave factor with the Norton Calibrate utility (CALIBRAT), and, depending on the type of disk controller you have, you may be able to change your interleave if necessary to improve disk performance. (See Chapter 15 for details.)

Chapter Twenty-three: How Your Disk Subsystems Work ■ 333

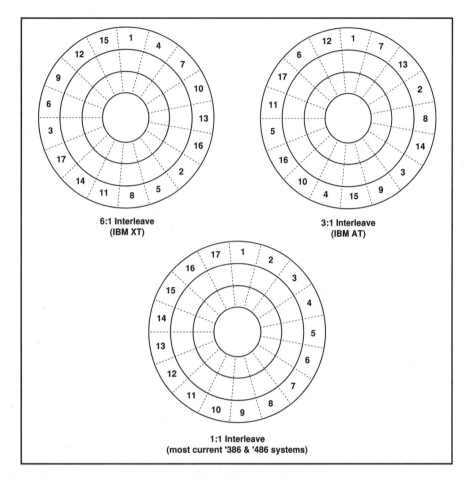

Figure 23.5 Hard-disk interleave factors

How DOS Organizes and Manages Files

DOS uses two data structures to keep track of your files: the directory structure and the file allocation table (hereinafter abbreviated FAT). For safety's sake, DOS maintains two copies of the FAT, which immediately follow the DOS boot record. These copies are immediately followed by the root directory of the disk.

334 ■ *Power Of...Norton Utilities*

The Root Directory

The amount of space allotted for the root directory is fixed. On a hard disk, the root directory can contain a maximum of 512 entries. The root directories of floppy disks hold a smaller number of files. The complete structure of a root-directory entry is displayed in Table 23.3. Some parts of this structure are familiar to every PC user (you see them whenever you type **DIR** at the DOS prompt), but others are normally hidden from view unless you use a tool like the Norton Disk Editor to make them visible.

Table 23.3 Root-Directory Entry

Bytes	Assignment
1–8	File name
9–11	File extension
12	File attributes
13–22	Reserved for future use
23–24	Time stamp
25–26	Date stamp
27–28	Starting cluster
29–32	File size, in bytes

Each root-directory entry begins with the familiar eight-character file name and three-character extension (in terms of storage, one character = one byte). The "." between the name and extension is not stored; it is assumed by DOS and other programs and is inserted between the name and extension when directory information is displayed. Next is the attribute byte. It consists of eight attribute bits, only six of which are used. The settings of these bits (1 = set; 0 = cleared) represent information about the type of file and the operations that can be performed on it:

◆ The Archive bit, if set, indicates that the file has been backed up since it was last modified.

◆ The Hidden bit, if set, makes the file invisible to most DOS functions and other programs (but not to the Disk Editor).

- The Read-Only bit, if set, tells DOS not to allow the file to be modified or erased.
- The System bit, if set, tells DOS that the file is "position-sensitive" (must be at a particular location on the disk) and should not be moved.
- The Label bit, if set, indicates that the entry is not a normal file, but the volume label. Only one volume label per disk is allowed; it can be up to 11 characters long, as it is stored in the location in the directory entry normally used for the file name and attribute.
- The Directory bit, if set, indicates that the entry points not to a normal file but to a subdirectory, which is a special type of file with a structure similar to that of the root directory (more about subdirectories shortly).

You can modify the settings of the attribute bits with the Norton FA utility (see Chapter 20), as well as with the Disk Editor.

NOTE

You should probably not modify the attributes of files that have the system bit set. These files are essential for the operation of your computer, or in some cases, may be part of copy protection schemes. If they are relocated, erased, or modified, you might be unable to boot your system, or you might find that copy-protected programs would no longer load.

WARNING

After the attribute byte are 10 unused bytes that are reserved for future expansion. They are followed by the date and time the file was created or last modified (two bytes each), the cluster number where the file begins (two bytes), and the length of the file (four bytes).

Subdirectories

As mentioned earlier, the root directory of a hard disk can hold a maximum of 512 entries. A typical hard disk has space for many thousands of files, so DOS must use another structure to keep track of them. This is the function of subdirectories. (Subdirectories can be used on floppy disks too, although they're less common.) DOS organizes files in what is known as a *tree-structured* directory system, a concept that was borrowed from Unix and added to DOS as of version 2.0.

The tree that is used to represent the DOS file system is a little strange, because it is normally pictured as growing *downward* from its root (Figure 23.6). In addition to allowing you to store far more files than will fit in the root directory, subdirectories perform the important task of organizing your files into logical categories so that you can quickly find any particular file that you need. How many subdirectories you create and what you call them will depend on the programs you use and your work style, but it is normal practice to keep each of your major application programs in a separate subdirectory and to have one or more subdirectories *under* each of those directories to hold the data files created by those applications. Many, if not most, contemporary application programs automatically create subdirectories for themselves when you install them on your system.

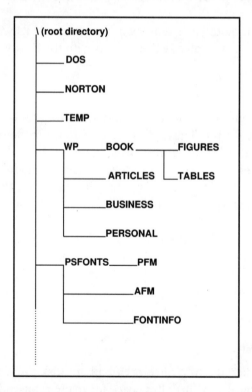

Figure 23.6 *A typical hard-disk directory tree*

Subdirectories appear as files in the root directory (or in other subdirectories) that have the "directory" bit in their attribute bytes set and a file length of zero. The data structure of a subdirectory entry is exactly the same as that described earlier

Chapter Twenty-three: How Your Disk Subsystems Work ■ **337**

for the root directory. The only real differences between subdirectories and the root directory is that the number of entries in a subdirectory is unlimited (except for the limit imposed by the capacity of the disk) and that the first two entries in a subdirectory are always called "." and "..". You have probably observed these two cryptic file names when listing a subdirectory in DOS. The "." entry refers to the subdirectory itself, and the ".." entry refers to the parent directory (the directory one step higher in the hierarchy, where the subdirectory resides).

The FAT

If every file was always stored in a series of consecutive clusters, then the information in the root directory (and in the subdirectories) would be sufficient to locate any file. Unfortunately, this is often not the case. Files very often are fragmented; that is, they are written to nonconsecutive clusters or groups of clusters. On a disk that has not been unfragmented recently, it is not unusual to find pieces of a large file scattered all over the disk. (See Chapter 17 for information on "unfragmenting" disks.)

To understand why this is so, consider the following example: You have just set up a new system with a pristine new hard disk and installed your favorite word processor. Inspired by the speed and power of your new machine (and by the fact that your boss is on vacation this week), you sit down and start the first chapter of the Great American PC Novel. Time passes and you save your file, under the name of CHAPTER.1. It happens that your file is 3968 bytes long, which amounts to two clusters, assuming that the cluster size on this disk is four sectors (2048 bytes or 2Kb, the most common size on hard disks). The first sector of your file is stored in cluster 129 (which was the first free cluster after those occupied by DOS and your word processor) and, because there is plenty of free space, the remainder of the file is stored in the next cluster (130). Your boss faxes from the Caribbean and reminds you that she expects the Consolidated Wombat report on her desk when she returns from vacation on Monday. So you reluctantly put aside your literary efforts and get to work on the report. When you finish and save the report, it is four clusters long and is saved in the next four free clusters, 131–134. It is still an hour before quitting time, so you decide to work on your novel again. By quitting time, you've written enough to fill nearly three more clusters. When you go to resave your CHAPTER.1 file, it no longer fits in the two clusters that it was originally allocated (129–130), nor can it spread out into the adjacent clusters, because 131–134 are occupied by the Con Wombat report.

338 ■ *Power Of...Norton Utilities*

What's DOS to do? It could move the report over three clusters to make room for the rest of your chapter file, but this is impractical. Although in this case the file that would need to be moved is only four clusters long, it could just as easily be 400 clusters. This would take some time to move, assuming that there was another space on the disk large enough to move it to. Then the records of where that file was stored would have to be changed to reflect its new location before the new file could be saved. It is far simpler just to write the new clusters for the chapter file in the next free space(s) available on the disk and keep a record of their locations, which is exactly what DOS does. This is where the FAT comes in. Every cluster on the disk has a FAT entry, which must contain one of the following items:

◆ a zero, indicating that the cluster is unallocated; that is, it is not currently being used by any file

◆ a "bad" marker (FFF7 hex), indicating that the cluster contains bad sectors and should not be used

◆ an end-of-file marker (any value from hex FFF8 through FFFF), indicating that this is the last cluster in a particular file

◆ a nonzero cluster number, pointing to the next cluster that belongs to the same file as the current entry

FAT Arithmetic

Two types of FATs are in current use, 12-bit FATs and 16-bit FATs.

Twelve-bit FATs are limited to 4096 clusters and are used by hard disks (or disk partitions) of up to 15Mb (rare creatures these days) and by floppy disks. Sixteen-bit FATs can contain up to 65,636 clusters and are used for hard disks or partitions larger than 15Mb (meaning just about any hard disk you're likely to encounter). Sixteen-bit FATs use a variety of cluster sizes, depending on disk capacity. Disks between 16 and 128Mb use clusters of 2Kb (four sectors); disks between 128 and 256Mb use clusters of 4Kb (eight sectors); and those between 256 and 512Mb use clusters of 8Kb (16 sectors).

How DOS Locates the Clusters Belonging to a File

The procedure for finding all the clusters in a given file is as follows: Let's use the CHAPTER.1 file from the previous example (see Figure 23.7), and let's assume that it's saved in the root directory of the disk (not likely, but it simplifies the example). We look up the entry in the root directory and see that the starting cluster is 129 and the file is 8559 bytes long (Figure 23.7). Let us again assume that the cluster size on this disk is four sectors. We see, therefore, that the file occupies five clusters. (Remember that DOS can only allocate whole clusters—8559 bytes = about 4.2 clusters, but we round up to the nearest whole cluster.) We know from the directory entry that the file begins at cluster 129, but where are the remaining clusters? To find out, we look up cluster 129 in the FAT, where we see the value 130, indicating that the file continues in the following cluster. The FAT entry for cluster 130, however, holds the number 135, indicating that the file is fragmented. Clusters 131–134 are skipped over. (Remember, those contain the Con Wombat report.) So we skip to the FAT entry for cluster 135, where we see that the file continues in cluster 136. The FAT entry for cluster 136 indicates that the file continues in 137. Finally, the entry for cluster 137 contains an <EOF> marker, indicating that this is the last cluster of the file. Thus, the CHAPTER.1 file is located in the clusters 129, 130, and 135–137. This is exactly the method that DOS uses when it reads or performs other operations on a file.

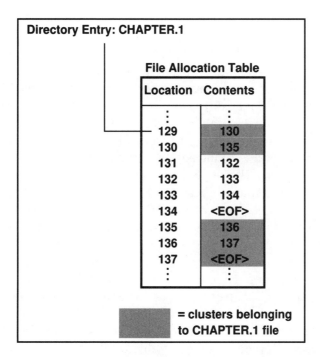

Figure 23.7 The FAT chain for the CHAPTER.1 file

340 ■ *Power Of...Norton Utilities*

The FAT is a data structure of the type that programmers call a *one-way linked list*. Starting from the directory entry, we can read down the list and find every cluster that belongs to the file. However, if we were to start at the last entry in the list, or somewhere in the middle, there is no way to work back up through the list to the beginning. The only way to find the rest of the file going backward would be to read through every item in the FAT until we find the pointer to the previous cluster (possible but extremely tedious). We can also see how important the integrity of the FAT and the directory system is. If any link in the chain leading from the first cluster to the last is damaged, DOS has no way of locating the remaining clusters belonging to the file. If the whole FAT were be wiped out, although all your data would remain on the disk, there would be no practical way to determine what clusters belonged to which file. You can see, then, why DOS maintains two copies of the FAT (it ought to maintain one of them in a bank vault) and why it is so important that you perform the preventive procedures described in Chapters 4–7 to help keep your FAT in good order (and out of the fire!) at all times.

Partitions and Logical Disks

Hard disks are often divided, or *partitioned*, into two or more logical disks that DOS treats as if they were independent, physical disks. (Floppy disks cannot be partitioned.) Hard-disk partitions exist for a couple of reasons. The one most commonly cited in the literature is to allow DOS and another operating system, such as Unix, Xenix, OS/2, or the now obsolete CPM/86, to coexist on the same physical disk. Although this is theoretically possible, it is seldom done. Personally, I have never encountered a system that was set up to run two different operating systems. (It's more than enough trouble for most of us to cope with one!) The more common reason for partitioning a hard disk into two or more logical disks is because earlier DOS versions were limited to logical disks of 32Mb or less. In fact, in DOS versions 2.0–3.2, only one DOS partition of 32Mb or less was allowed, along with optional partitions for other operating systems. (Remember, this was several years ago, when hard disks larger than 32Mb were still fairly uncommon and expensive.) PC DOS 3.3/MS DOS 3.2 allowed one primary DOS partition of up to 32Mb and one *extended* DOS partition that could be any size but that, if larger than 32Mb, had to be divided into two or more *logical drives* or *volumes* of 32Mb or less. Each partition has its own DOS boot record. If there is a second physical drive in a system, it need not have a primary DOS partition; it can be occupied entirely by an extended partition or partitions. With DOS 4.0 or later (Compaq DOS 3.31 or later) the 32Mb limit for DOS partitions and/or logical drives was lifted. Now DOS supports drives of up to 512Mb.

Partitions and logical drives are created by the DOS FDISK utility or, in some cases, by software provided by the disk manufacturer. Every hard disk must be partitioned before it is high-level-formatted for the first time, even if it is to have only a primary DOS partition. Hence, every DOS hard disk has a partition table. When you buy a new system, the hard disk probably has been partitioned and formatted already by the dealer or manufacturer, but if you configure your own system or install a new hard disk in an older system, you may have to perform this operation yourself. Consult your DOS manual and/or the hard-disk manufacturer for information on partitioning and formatting. (You can also use the Norton Safe Format utility to high-level-format a hard disk.)

NOTE

Some third-party disk management programs, such as SpeedStor, EDISK, and Disk Manager, also permit you to use partitions larger than 32Mb with earlier versions of DOS.

NOTE

It is conventional to use the term "partition" as though it were synonymous with "logical drive" or "volume." Hence, you will often hear someone speak of a hard disk with three or more DOS *partitions*. Although this usage is not strictly accurate, it does no real harm, provided that you understand the difference when you run a partitioning program.

The Partition Table

The data structure responsible for keeping track of disk partitions is the *partition table*. It resides in the first sector of the disk and is part of the master boot record (MBR). The partition table contains pointers to the beginning of the primary DOS partition (where the DOS boot record resides) and to the beginnings of partitions dedicated to other operating systems and/or to the extended DOS partition, if they exist. Figure 23.8 shows how the primary and extended partitions are connected through primary and extended partition tables. The extended DOS partition, although not bootable, also includes a DOS boot record. If the extended DOS partition is divided into two or more logical disks, the first sector of the extended partition will include a partition table that points to the beginning of the second volume of the extended partition. Each volume on the extended partition includes an extended partition table that (except, of course, for the last) includes a pointer to the beginning of the following volume.

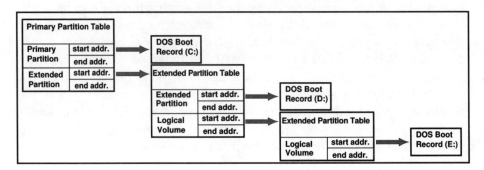

Figure 23.8 The linkage between primary and extended partition tables

DOS still cannot cope with disks with more than 1024 cylinders. These large disks require special controllers that remap the tracks and sectors into a format that DOS can cope with, or special software drivers that are available from the disks' manufacturers.

If you have a hard disk that was formatted with DOS 3.3 and partitioned into several logical drives of 32Mb or less, you might want to consider repartitioning and reformatting your drive with the most recent DOS version as a single volume. This will eliminate the annoying problem of running out of room on one logical disk while there is ample free space on another. It will also make it easier to manage your files, as you will only have to search a single directory tree to find any file on your disk. However, if you have a physical drive that is larger than 128Mb, you might still want to use partitions to limit your logical drives to 128Mb or less because of the effect this has on cluster size. You will recall from the preceding discussion of FAT arithmetic that with the 16-bit FATs now used with all drives larger than 15Mb, disks between 16Mb and 128Mb use clusters of 2Kb, disks between 128Mb and 256Mb use clusters of 4Kb, and disks between 256Mb and 512Mb use clusters of 8Kb. By using logical drives of 128Kb or less, you will use a cluster size of 2Kb, thereby minimizing the amount of wasted space ("slack") on your hard disk. (If you're about to order a new system with a hard disk already installed, these same considerations apply. If you don't intend to partition and format the drive yourself, it would be a good idea to inform your dealer how you want the drive partitioned. Regrettably, you cannot assume that the dealer will partition the drive in the most efficient manner.)

WARNING It is essential to back up all the data on your drive before reformatting or repartitioning it. When you reformat and/or repartition a drive, all the data on it will be lost. In fact, if you are going to do something as drastic as reformatting a drive, it is a good idea to make two backups, in case one proves faulty.

PHYSICAL LAYOUT OF A HARD DISK

The first sector of a hard disk is occupied by the master boot record (MBR), which contains, among other things, the partition table. The partition table is the only element of the MBR that we can examine with the Norton Disk Editor. The MBR is followed directly by DOS boot record for the first partition, which is normally the primary DOS partition. The DOS boot record resides in DOS sector 0 and contains the code that is used to begin booting the system. This code tells the system to find and load the two hidden system files (IBMBIO.COM and IBMDOS.COM in PC-DOS or MSDOS.SYS and IO.SYS in MS-DOS) that comprise most of DOS. Immediately following the DOS boot record are the two copies of the FAT. The FATs are followed by the root directory. After the root directory comes the data area. The first two files, occupying consecutive clusters, are the two DOS hidden system files. After that come program and data files, in whatever order you and DOS have organized them. The data area occupies the remainder of the primary DOS partition. The extended DOS partition, if present, begins with its own partition table, which is followed by the DOS boot record, two FATs, the root directory, and the data area, replicating the structure of the primary partition exactly, except for the absence of the two DOS hidden system files. Additional volumes in the extended partition, if present, also replicate this structure.

Disk Controllers

Every hard disk is connected to a *controller*, which is a circuit board connected to your PC's bus that receives signals from the CPU and translates them into a format that can be understood by the disk hardware. The controller is also responsible for moving blocks of data between the disk and the CPU. Disk controllers have a number of important characteristics, including what *encoding format* and what *interface* standard they use.

NOTE
You don't really have to understand what kind of disk controller you have in order to use the Disk Editor or other Norton programs, so if you are in a hurry to use the editor to solve a problem, you can skip over this material. If you want to gain a more detailed understanding of how your hard-disk subsystem works, read on. This information will be helpful if you ever need to upgrade or replace your hard disk.

Interface Types

Currently, four different hard-disk *interface standards* are in common use in IBM-compatible PCs. An interface standard specifies what types of signals a hard-disk controller will send and receive and what kind of cabling and connectors the controller will use to connect to the disk.

ST506

The earliest of these standards, and the one most likely to be found in older systems, is known as the ST506, after a product produced by the now defunct Shugart Company. ST506-type controllers use a 20-wire cable for data and a 34-wire cable for control signals. The ST506 interface must be installed on both the drive and the controller card (i.e., an ST506 drive must have an ST506 controller, and vice versa). ST506 drives are normally limited to 17 sectors per track. ST506 is a low-level, hardware-oriented interface; that is, it sends commands that relate to the specific operations that the drive has to perform to read or write to the disk. You will rarely see ST506 drives or controllers offered for sale these days. Almost all new drives and controllers belong to one of the three types described next.

ESDI

ESDI stands for "Enhanced Small Device Interface." It is a sort of souped-up version of the ST506 interface. Like the ST506, it is a low-level interface. ESDI supports larger drives and faster data transfer than ST506. ESDI drives can report their geometry (number of heads, cylinders, tracks, sectors, and so on) to the controller, although not many systems take advantage of this capability. It appeared at one time that ESDI would succeed ST506 as the primary hard-disk interface standard for AT-compatible systems, but it has been eclipsed by two more recent standards, IDE and SCSI (described later).

IDE

The IDE interface was originated by Compaq in 1984 and is now widely used in AT-compatible machines. Depending on who you ask, "IDE" stands for either "Integrated Drive Electronics" or "Intelligent Drive Electronics." Either term makes sense, because the characteristic that distinguishes IDE is that the controller electronics are on the drive itself (in the form of a circuit board mounted on the outside of the drive case) rather than on a separate controller board. An IDE drive still needs a circuit board to connect it to the bus, but this board doesn't do much except transfer signals between the bus and the drive. Often an IDE adapter is combined with a floppy drive controller card or is built into the motherboard of newer systems. IDE controllers cause the system to assume that their drives are ST506 types, which allows them to be used with the drive specification tables that are part of a typical AT-compatible BIOS, without the need for special software drivers. Actually the drive may be quite different—in terms of its number of tracks, sectors, and cylinders—from anything supported by the BIOS, but the IDE controller conceals this from the system and translates between the two formats. IDE currently seems to be the most common interface standard for small to moderate-sized disks (up to about 250Mb) in AT-compatible systems, though IDE disks as large as 500Mb are available. Larger disks more commonly use the SCSI interface (described later), although large ESDI drives are still found occasionally.

Because the IDE controller hides the physical structure of the disk from the system, certain utilities that work on ST506 drives don't work properly on IDE drives. These include programs that perform nondestructive low-level formats or change the interleave factor, such as the Norton Calibrate utility (see Chapter 15). (Calibrate can be used safely on IDE drives, but it won't do a low-level for-

346 ■ *Power Of...Norton Utilities*

mat or change the interleave factor.) IDE drives receive their low-level format and interleave at the factory and cannot normally be reformatted by the user. (This refers to low-level or physical formatting only; the high-level or logical format is performed with the DOS FORMAT command or Norton Safe Format, as with any other type of hard disk.) The inability to change the interleave doesn't really cause a problem; virtually all IDE controllers use a 1:1 interleave factor and operate optimally at it, so there would be no reason to change it even if it were possible to do so. The inability to perform a low-level format is potentially more serious. Some experts believe that it is necessary to perform periodic, nondestructive low-level formats to refresh sector IDs in order to ensure reliable long-term disk operation. Whether this is really a problem remains to be seen.

SCSI

SCSI (pronounced "scuzzy") stands for "Small Computer Systems Interface." SCSI is the standard hard-disk interface in the Macintosh environment and is gaining popularity in the IBM-compatible environment, especially for larger drives. SCSI is also commonly used for other types of mass storage devices, including CD ROMs, WORM (write once/read many) drives, magneto-optical drives, and some tape backup systems. Like IDE, and unlike ST506 or ESDI, SCSI is an intelligent, logic-level interface. The intelligence resides in the hardware on the drive, and the host adapter does not need to know details about the drive hardware. Unlike any of the other interface standards discussed here, a single SCSI adapter can support up to eight SCSI devices connected together in a "daisy chain" configuration. Each device in the chain has a unique ID number that can be selected by the user, usually by means of switches or jumpers, so there is no confusion about the device for which a command is intended. This means that if you have a server with, for example, three large SCSI drives and a SCSI tape backup unit, you would not need to take up four expansion slots in the system with separate controllers for each device. All four could share a single SCSI adapter.

Despite its obvious advantages and despite the fact that SCSI has been the Mac hard-disk standard for several years, SCSI has been slow to catch on in the IBM-compatible environment. At least one reason for this is that the SCSI standard has been slow in solidifying. As a result, one could not safely assume that a SCSI drive or other I/O device from one manufacturer would necessarily interface successfully with a SCSI adapter from another manufacturer. Now, however, these problems seem to have been largely worked out, and SCSI has become the dominant interface for large drives (500Mb+) in the PC environment, surpassing ESDI. As with IDE drives, SCSI drives do not allow resetting of the interleave factor by means of the Norton Calibrate utility or similar programs. However, virtually all SCSI drives use a 1:1 interleave, so there is nothing to gain by changing their interleave factors. Nevertheless, the same concerns about refreshing the sector IDs via nondestructive low-level format expressed in regard to IDE drives also apply here.

Encoding Techniques

The storage capacity of a disk is limited by the number of tracks and the density of the data recorded on each track. The number of tracks is determined by the head width and head-positioning mechanism. The density of the recorded data depends on the controller clock speed and the recording technique used. The disk-controller clock speed is the basic internal speed of the disk controller. A series of pulses generated by the internal oscillator (clock) on the controller is used to synchronize disk read and write operations.

FM Recording

With early floppies, data was recorded using a simple frequency modulation (FM) encoding technique. The top line of Figure 23.9 shows the electronic data to be recorded on the disk. In this example, the byte 10110001 is to be recorded. The second line shows the disk-controller clock pulses.

The FM (single-density) system records a clock pulse with each recorded data bit (recorded between clock pulses). If the data bit is a one, a magnetic pulse is recorded between two clock pulses. If it is a zero, no pulse is recorded between the clock pulses. This technique, therefore, requires eight clock pulses, plus eight information pulses, for a total of 16 pulses, to record eight bits of binary information.

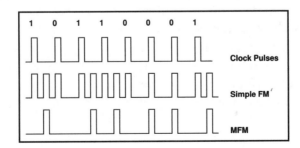

Figure 23.9 Common disk data recording techniques

MFM Recording

Current PC-compatible floppy disks and some hard disks use a recording system called modified frequency modulation (MFM). This does not automatically place a clock pulse at the start of each information bit, as is in FM recording. Nevertheless, the controller clock keeps running even when its pulses are not being recorded on the disk, so the spacing of the data pulses is still governed by the clock.

As before, a one bit is represented by a pulse and a zero bit is represented by the absence of a pulse. However, if a zero data bit follows another zero data bit, a clock pulse is recorded at the beginning of the second data bit, and at the beginning of each of the rest of the zero bits in the sequence, until a one bit is recorded. This is shown on the MFM line in Figure 23.9.

MFM requires a maximum of eight pulses to record eight bits of information—only half the number of pulses required by simple FM recording. If the space between the data bits is reduced by half, then only half the track length is required and more information can be placed in a track. Hence, the name "double-density disk." Note that the minimum spacing between pulses of MFM and FM is the same. The same recording media used for FM (single-density) recording can be used for MFM (double-density) recordings.

High Density

Originally, double-density floppies divided each track into eight sectors. As technology improved, the number of sectors per track was increased to nine. Additional improvements made it possible to divide a track into more sectors. Thus, the tracks on a high-density 5-1/4" disk are divided into 15 sectors, and 18 sectors are used on high-density 3-1/2" disks. The controller clock speed is increased to compress the data to fit the smaller sector sizes. Each sector still holds 512 bytes of data, but this information is recorded using physically shorter sectors, allowing more sectors to be placed on a disk of a given size.

The MFM technique is also used for some hard disks, particularly older ones using the ST506 interface. Hard-disk controllers raise the clock speeds still higher, and pack even more sectors into ever narrower tracks. MFM-encoded hard disks typically use 305 or more tracks, with 17 sectors per track.

Run Length Limited (RLL) Recording

Run Length Limited (RLL) recording is yet another technique used to encode data on hard disks. It packs even more bits into the same space than the older MFM technique. Almost any drive with more than 17 sectors per track and/or almost any drive that uses the IDE, SCSI, or ESDI interface probably uses RLL encoding. RLL converts, or translates, each byte into a unique 16-bit pattern, or code. The codes are selected for their numerical properties, especially for the number of zeros that occur in the byte. The logic used to determine these codes is quite complicated. Currently, two types of RLL encoding are used: 2,7 RLL and 3,9 RLL.

In 2,7 RLL the codes are chosen so that the sequence of consecutive zeros without a timing pulse is always in the range from 2 to 7. In other words, the "run length" of zeros between timing pulses is limited to between 2 and 7. 3,9 RLL (Advanced RLL, or ARLL) limits the range of zeros between timing pulses to between 3 and 9.

The RLL technique increases the number of sectors per track (26, 34, and 54 sectors per track are common formats). This results in a faster data transfer rate and reduced head movement.

24

THE NORTON UTILITIES™

RUNNING THE NORTON DISK EDITOR (DISKEDIT)

The Norton Disk Editor is a powerful tool for correcting a wide variety of disk problems. Using the various options available on the Disk Editor's menus, you can view any object on any disk: files, directories, empty spaces, the data structures that make up the system area, partition tables, even areas that are off-limits to DOS. You can copy the data from any of these areas to a file, print it on your printer, edit it, or change it in just about any way imaginable.

Most Norton Utilities rely on intelligence built into the program to prevent or solve disk problems. The Disk Editor, however, relies mostly on *your* intelligence. The power to cure is also the power to destroy, and you can use the Disk Editor to do both. It is up to you to understand how data is structured on your disks and how modifying the essential data structures will affect your ability to access your files. Unless you're very familiar with the architecture of your disks, you should read the previous chapter, if you have not already done so, before attempting to use the Disk Editor. If you're still uncertain about what's going on, *go slowly and tread softly*. Keep the Disk Editor in Read-Only mode (the

351

default) so that you can examine various options in the Disk Editor with no risk of damaging your disks. Skip back to the previous chapter whenever necessary to refresh your memory about how the various data structures are organized and what they do.

If you have a serious disk problem, try the other, more automatic utilities before resorting to the Disk Editor. If you're not sure what tool to try first, check the Norton Advisor on the Norton menu for suggestions. Whatever you do, don't succumb to "computer machismo" and get in over your head by trying to use a tool that you don't understand fully to solve a problem that is beyond your ability. And don't be afraid to ask for help.

WARNING
Before you attempt to edit a disk using the Disk Editor, you should take the precaution of backing it up. You should also make a rescue disk, as described in Chapter 7, so that you can undo any damage done to the system area of the disk. It is possible to make a file or even a complete disk unusable through careless use of the Disk Editor.

RUNNING THE DISK EDITOR IN EMERGENCIES

If you have just purchased Norton Utilities to solve a disk problem, such as accidentally erased files, an accidentally formatted disk, or any other problem that makes some of your files inaccessible, *do not install Norton Utilities on your hard disk!* Doing so could overwrite the data that you are trying to save. Instead, you should run the appropriate Norton program from the Norton emergency disk. Depending on the nature of your problem, you should try UnErase (see Chapter 8), UnFormat (see Chapter 9), or the Norton Disk Doctor (see Chapter 10) before trying the Disk Editor. Each of these programs has the intelligence to solve particular problems without much user intervention and usually does so. The Disk Editor, on the other hand, puts almost unlimited power in your hands, but you must have the knowledge to use it.

If the other tools on the emergency disk fail to solve your problem and you want to try the Disk Editor, put the emergency disk in the appropriate drive, log onto that drive, and type DISKEDIT **Enter**.

Then proceed as set forth in the following discussion.

STARTING THE DISK EDITOR

You can load the Disk Editor by selecting it from the Norton menu or by typing DISKEDIT **Enter** at the DOS prompt. You may specify a drive, directory, and/or file to be examined on the command line. Before the Disk Editor finishes loading, it will display a message indicating that the Disk Editor is configured for Read-Only mode and will ask for your permission to proceed. This is normal. The Disk Editor is configured for Read-Only mode by default, and you should leave it that way until you understand the editor and the disk data structures. If you do not specify a drive, the Disk Editor will initially display the current directory of the current drive (normally your Norton Utilities directory; see Figure 24.1).

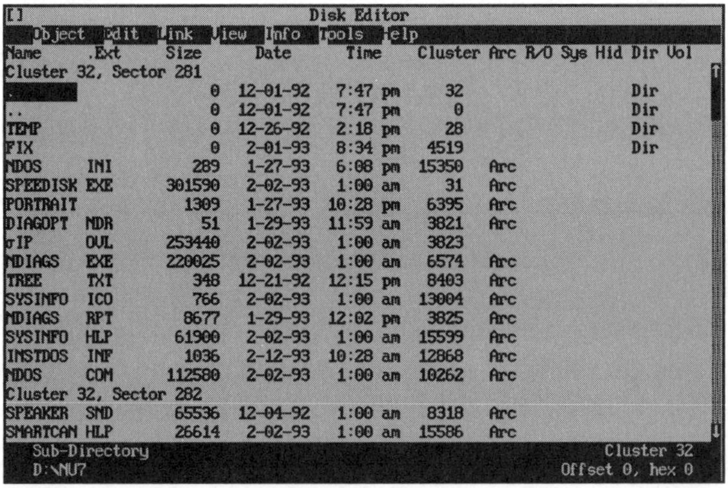

Figure 24.1 Disk Editor initial display, showing contents of Norton Utilities directory

NOTE If you attempt to start the Disk Editor while running a multitasking environment such as Windows or DESQview, you will be warned that it is dangerous to run the editor in these environments because they keep many files open and write to them unpredictably in order to manage the environment. You can work on floppy disks in the Disk Editor without danger, but you should definitely exit to DOS before working on your hard disk.

Configuring the Disk Editor

Once you are in the Disk Editor, the first thing to check is its current configuration. To do this, open the Tools menu and select **Configuration**. The Configuration dialog box will appear, as shown in Figure 24.2.

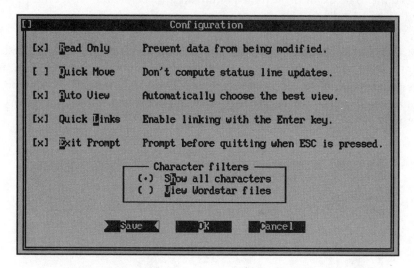

Figure 24.2 *The Configuration dialog box*

The settings in the Configuration dialog box determine how the Disk Editor behaves. The options in the Configuration dialog box can be turned on or off by checking or unchecking their check boxes. They are as follows:

Read-Only—you can view any object but you cannot change it. Selecting this item disables all selections on the Edit menu except **Mark**. When the Disk Editor is in Read-Only mode, you can mark a block of information and copy it to the clipboard (see later). The information then can be edited on the clipboard or saved to another disk.

N O T E

Read-Only is the default mode when you first load the Disk Editor. You are strongly advised to leave the Disk Editor in this mode until you have mastered the program and need to make serious repairs. As long as the editor is in Read-Only mode, you can examine any part of the disk without getting into trouble.

Chapter Twenty-four: Running the Norton Disk Editor (DISKEDIT) ■ **355**

Quick Move—the default setting (Quick Move off) displays the selected file names on the status line as you move the cursor in an object. Generating this information takes the Disk Editor additional time. Suppressing it may enable you to move around the screen more quickly, particularly in FAT view, which suppresses both the file name on the status line and the highlighting of the current cluster chain.

Auto View—with this option on (the default) the Disk Editor selects the most appropriate view for the selected object. For example, when you select a directory as the object, the Disk Editor automatically uses the directory viewer. When a text file is selected, the editor selects text view. The hex view is used when Auto View is off or when hex is the most appropriate view (i.e., when viewing program code or other binary files).

Quick Links—when this option is on (the default), you can link to a related object by pressing **Enter**, or by double-clicking the mouse. You can quickly and easily switch between related items (e.g., between a FAT entry and a file).

If you change an object and then link to a related object without saving your changes, the program will prompt you to save, discard, or review the changes.

Exit Prompt—if this item is on (the default), you will be prompted to confirm that you want to terminate the program when you press **Esc** to exit the Disk Editor.

Character Filters—this item provides two mutually exclusive options for the Disk Editor to interpret character data.

Show All Characters—this is the default setting; it uses all eight bits of a byte in interpreting characters. The most-significant (eighth) bit defines the special characters in the IBM extended ASCII set (characters 128–255). Some eight-bit characters that cannot be displayed are shown as dots. Some programs, such as WordStar, use the eighth bit for formatting information and do not display correctly using this setting.

View WordStar Files—this setting causes the editor to ignore the eighth bit of characters to produce readable WordStar file displays. In other types of files, however, it will prevent graphic characters from being displayed correctly.

Configuration Settings Selections

There are three buttons at the bottom of the Configuration dialog box:

356 ■ *Power Of...Norton Utilities*

Save—saves the current configuration settings in the file NORTON.INI. This makes these settings the default. A message appears indicating the drive and directory where the configuration information is saved.

OK—use the current configuration settings for the current work session, but do not save them in the NORTON.INI file.

Cancel—exit the Configuration dialog box without accepting any changes (restores the default configuration).

THE MENU BAR

At the top of the Disk Editor screen is a menu bar with six pull-down menus that control most of the editor's operations: Object, Edit, Link, View, Info, and Tools, plus a Help option.

The Object Menu

The Norton Disk Editor uses the term "object" to refer to the various types of data structures that can be viewed and edited, such as directories, files, boot records, and file allocation tables. The object menu allows you to select the type of object you want to work with. To edit an item, you must first choose an appropriate object from this menu. In many cases, this will take you directly to the desired object without your having to know its physical location on the disk. When a menu item is "grayed out" (enclosed in parentheses on monochrome displays), this indicates that it is not currently available. This generally means that you have to perform some other operation or change the configuration before you can use that menu option.

Drive

Use the **Drive** option to select the drive to view and/or edit. The default is the current drive. All objects on the Object menu (other than **File**) assume the default drive. Selecting **Drive** displays a dialog box showing a list of available drives. The radio buttons on the right side of the screen allow you to select a list of physical drives or logical drives. The selection you make here will determine how you can access the selected drive. **Logical Drives** is the default; this is the appropriate

Chapter Twenty-four: Running the Norton Disk Editor (DISKEDIT) ■ 357

option for most situations. When you select a drive from the logical drive list, you will be able to use all the other options on the Object menu, described later to access the various data structures on the selected disk. If you select **Physical Drives**, you will be limited to the **Drive, File, Physical Sector**, and **Partition Table** objects. This doesn't mean that you won't be able to view the other objects, but you will have to find them by manually entering the appropriate physical sector, paging through the sectors in hex mode, or searching for an appropriate byte string. The **Physical Drive** option is intended primarily for use on disks that have been formatted by systems other than DOS or for disks that have been damaged and cannot be accessed by DOS. If you have one physical hard disk in your system and it is partitioned into several logical volumes, it will appear as a single drive if you have selected **Physical Drives**, but all the volumes will appear as separate drives if you select **Logical Drives**. The shortcut for this option is **Alt+D**.

Directory

The **Directory** option displays a dialog box showing the directory tree for the current drive (see Figure 24.3). The shortcut for this item is **Alt+R**.

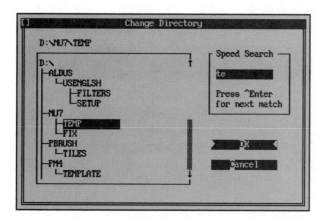

Figure 24.3 The Change Directory dialog box

You can select a new directory by highlighting it on the tree and pressing **Enter**. Directory has a speed search capability that allows you to move quickly to a directory item, even if it is not shown in the display box. Type one or more initial letters of the directory name that you want to find and the highlight will move to the first matching directory. The letters you type are displayed in the Speed Search box in the upper right corner of the dialog box; only letters that match a directory name are displayed. If several directories start with the same letters, you can view each of them by using **Ctrl+Enter**.

File

Use the **File** option to view a particular file. When you select this option, the Select File dialog box appears (see Figure 24.4). The files in the current directory are displayed in a scroll box on the right side of the dialog box. You can type a filespec, including wild cards, or a specific file name, on the File line at the top of the dialog box, or you can select a file by highlighting it in the scroll box. You can also select a different drive from the Drive list box, immediately below the File line, and select a new directory from the directory box on the left side of the dialog box. Select **OK** to choose the file. **Cancel** returns you to the Disk Editor screen. The shortcut for this item is **Alt+F**.

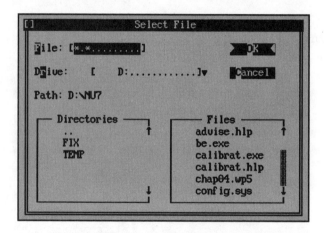

Figure 24.4 The Select File dialog box

Cluster

Selecting the **Cluster** option opens a dialog box showing the valid clusters for the selected drive. (Remember that DOS cluster numbers start at 2.) Enter starting and ending cluster numbers to view the specified clusters. To view just one, use the same cluster number as both the starting and ending cluster. Use the **Tab** or arrow keys to move between Starting and Ending Cluster boxes. The shortcut for this item is **Alt+C**.

Chapter Twenty-four: Running the Norton Disk Editor (DISKEDIT) ■ 359

Figure 24.5 *The Select Cluster dialog box*

If you press **Enter** after specifying only a beginning cluster, you will select the entire range of clusters, from the specified beginning cluster to the end of the selected disk. Once you have specified the cluster(s) you want, press **Enter** to accept the choices and view the clusters.

For speed, select only those clusters you want to investigate. A smaller object is faster and easier to handle, especially if you want to make a backup copy before you start editing.

Sector

The **Sector** option displays the dialog box shown in Figure 24.6. The display uses logical sector numbering; the sectors are sequentially numbered starting from zero. (Physical numbering uses a three-coordinate system, and the first sector number is 1.) The shortcut for this item is **Alt+S**.

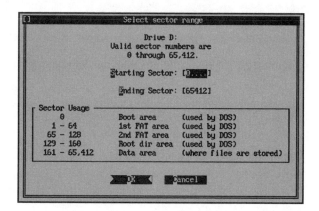

Figure 24.6 *The Select Sector Range dialog box*

360 ■ *Power Of...Norton Utilities*

You can select a range of sectors by using the **Tab** or **Up** and **Down** keys to move to Starting Sector and Ending Sector boxes and typing appropriate values.

The text box occupying the lower portion of the Select Sector Range dialog box displays the sectors occupied by a number of important data structures. Use this information to narrow your search for a particular range of sectors to work on.

Physical Sector

Norton Utilities sometimes reports the physical sector coordinates of a problem area. The **Physical Sector** option allows you to select a sector by its physical coordinates. This option ignores disk formatting or partitioning and allows you access to any location on the hard disk except the diagnostic cylinder. The shortcut for this item is **Alt+P**. When you select this option, the Physical Sector Range dialog box is displayed, as shown in Figure 24.7.

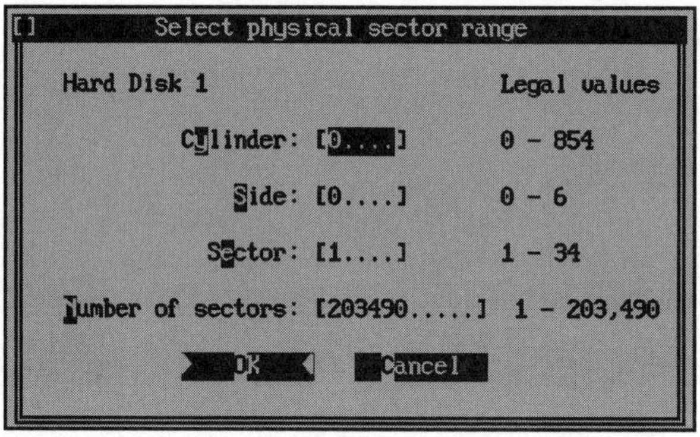

```
[]            Select physical sector range

    Hard Disk 1                              Legal values

             Cylinder: [0....]              0 - 854

                 Side: [0....]              0 - 6

               Sector: [1....]              1 - 34

     Number of sectors: [203490.....]   1 - 203,490

              ▶ OK ◀          Cancel
```

Figure 24.7 *The Select Physical Sector Range dialog box*

This option uses the three-coordinate, physical sector numbering system discussed in Chapter 23. Physical sector numbering always starts with 1 at the beginning of each track.

The number of sectors on a track varies according to the disk type. The dialog box shown in Figure 24.7 lists the legal values for the selected drive. There are spaces for entering the cylinder, side, and sector numbers and for indicating the number of sectors you want to view.

Partition Table

The first sector of track 0 on a hard disk is always reserved for the partition table. (Floppy disks cannot be partitioned and hence do not have partition tables.) The DOS FDISK command creates the partition table. The partition table is created after low-level (physical) formatting and before high-level (logical) formatting. Figure 24.8 shows a typical partition table display. The shortcut for this item is **Alt+A**.

System	Boot	Starting Location			Ending Location			Relative	Number of
		Side	Cylinder	Sector	Side	Cylinder	Sector	Sectors	Sectors
DOS-16	Yes	1	0	1	6	274	34	34	65416
EXTEND	No	0	275	1	6	854	34	65450	138040
unused	No	0	0	0	0	0	0	0	0
unused	No	0	0	0	0	0	0	0	0

Figure 24.8 A Partition Table display

The partition table shown when you select this item from the object menu is the primary partition table, on the primary DOS partition. The primary partition table is part of a data structure called the master boot record (MBR). The MBR contains the first code loaded from the disk on boot-up, which instructs the system to find the DOS boot record and load the DOS boot code. If you have an extended DOS partition comprising one or more logical volumes and you want to examine their extended partition tables, you must use the **Physical Sector** option to move to the location indicated in the primary partition table as the beginning of the extended partition, then select **Partition Table** as the view. (This procedure is described in more detail later in this chapter.) If there are additional logical volumes in the extended DOS partition, you can use the same method to find the extended partition table for the next volume, and this process can be continued down the chain of extended volumes. (Refer to the preceding chapter for an explanation of primary and extended partitions and partition tables.)

The Partition Table view uses the physical numbering system. Although Partition Table uses only the first sector of track 0 (on side 0), the remaining sectors on the track are left empty. Therefore, the DOS boot record of a partitioned disk is located in sector 1 of track 1, instead of sector 1 of track 0, where it is located on a floppy disk. Since the FAT follows the DOS boot record, the FAT on a hard disk starts at sector 2, track 1.

WARNING The partition table is critical to the operation of a hard disk. Making changes to it can be extremely dangerous. Before editing the partition table, it is important to back up your hard disk. (This assumes your hard disk is accessible. Of course, if your partition table or some other vital area is trashed, you may be unable to back up your hard disk or to do anything else with it. That's why you need to make full backups of your hard disk *regularly*.

A Rescue disk created with the Rescue utility (see Chapter 7) contains a copy of the partition table. You should try to restore the partition table from a rescue disk (if you had the foresight to make one) before manually editing the table with the Disk Editor.

Boot Record

Selecting **Boot Record** from the Object menu displays the boot record for the current drive, as shown in Figure 24.9. The shortcut for this item is **Alt+B**. The Boot Record includes important disk information, such as the bytes per sector, sectors per cluster, and sectors per track.

WARNING Be especially careful when editing the boot record on a hard disk. If you make a mistake, you can easily make your hard disk unbootable. Back up your boot record before making any changes. If you included the Image utility in your AUTOEXEC.BAT file (see Chapter 4), you can restore the boot record from the IMAGE.DAT file. If you created a Rescue disk (see Chapter 7) you can restore the boot record from that disk. Try either of these methods before attempting to edit the boot record manually.

1st Copy of FAT

Selecting **1st copy of FAT** from the Object menu displays the first copy of the FAT. The shortcut for this item is **Alt+F1**. The FAT (file allocation table) is so vital that DOS stores two copies of it. Each field in the FAT display (Figure 24.10) represents an entry (one cluster) in the FAT. It can contain one of the following entries:

Chapter Twenty-four: Running the Norton Disk Editor (DISKEDIT) ■ 363

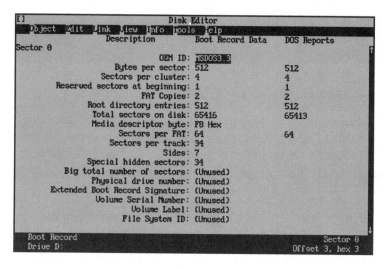

Figure 24.9 *A Hard-Disk Boot Record*

0—an unused cluster

NN (any nonzero value)—the number of the next cluster belonging to the same file

<EOF> (end-of-file)—the last cluster in the cluster chain for a given file

<Bad>—a bad cluster

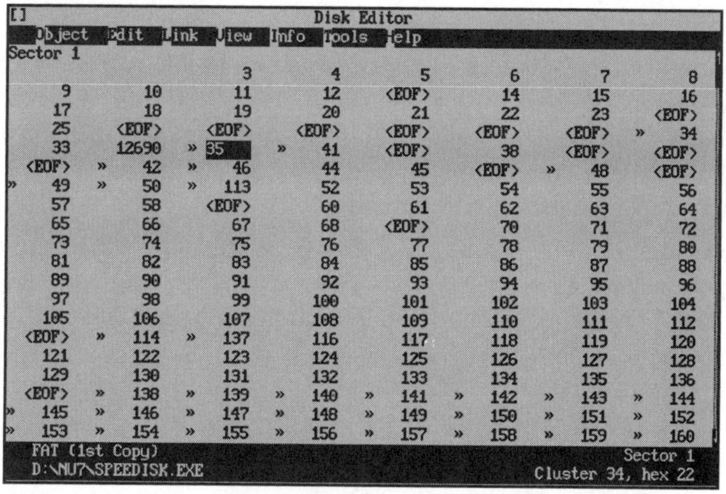

Figure 24.10 *A FAT display*

364 ■ *Power Of...Norton Utilities*

In the FAT view, with the **Quick View** option off, two chevron (») symbols point to all the clusters that belong to the same file as the cluster that is highlighted in the display.

2nd Copy of FAT

Selecting **2nd copy of FAT** from the Object menu displays the second copy of the FAT. The shortcut for this item is **Alt+F2**. The second copy of the FAT should look exactly the same as the first. If there is any difference between the two copies, this is a sign of a potentially serious disk problem.

Clipboard

The Clipboard is a 4096-byte memory buffer you can use to copy blocks of data from one location to another. Use the **Mark** and **Copy** commands on the Edit menu (see later) to copy a block to the clipboard, and use the **Paste Over** command to copy the data from the clipboard to a new location. The clipboard can be used to copy from any of the screen views.

You can only access the **Clipboard** option if it contains data. Selecting **Clipboard** from the menu allows you to review and edit the clipboard contents just like any other object. After you finish editing, you can paste the edited version using the **Paste Over** command.

Data remains in the clipboard until it is overwritten or until you exit the Disk Editor. The same data can be pasted to several locations if you wish. When data is copied to the clipboard, it completely overwrites whatever is there (e.g., if you had a 4096-byte block on the clipboard and then copied one byte of data to the clipboard, the one-byte block would completely replace the 4096 bytes). You cannot append data to the clipboard.

If you attempt to copy a block of data larger than 4096 bytes to the clipboard, you will see an error message. You must select an area no larger than 4096 bytes. (This is equivalent to 256 lines in the hex viewer.)

The following steps outline the general procedure for using the clipboard:

1. Place the cursor at the beginning of the block to be marked and select **Mark** from the Edit menu. The shortcut for this item is **Ctrl+B**. Use the arrow keys or **Page Up** and **Page Down**, or drag with the mouse to highlight the block you want.

Chapter Twenty-four: Running the Norton Disk Editor (DISKEDIT) ■ 365

2. To unmark a block, select **Mark** again from the Edit menu and press an arrow key or click with the mouse.

3. To copy a marked block to the clipboard, select **Copy** from the Edit menu. The shortcut for this item is **Ctrl+C**. The marked block is copied to the clipboard. The **Clipboard** option on the Object menu is now available.

4. If you want to view or edit the block of data, select **Clipboard** from the Object menu.

5. To move this block of data from the clipboard to another location, position the cursor at the desired location. Select **Paste Over** from the Edit menu. The shortcut for this item is **Ctrl+V**.

Memory Dump

Use the **Memory Dump** option to view, search, and copy data from memory below the 1Mb limit. The shortcut for this option is **Alt+M**. When you select **Memory Dump**, the Memory Dump dialog box shown in Figure 24.11 appears.

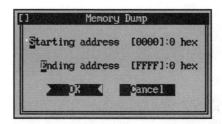

Figure 24.11 The Memory Dump dialog box

The box has spaces where you can enter starting and ending addresses (in hex) for the block of memory you want to view. The addresses use the PC's standard segment:offset format, but you can specify only the segment address; the offset portion of the address is fixed at zero. To have full access to the address space, press **Alt+M** and then press **Enter** to accept the default address range of 0000–FFFF. (If you know a specific address that you want to view, enter a different address range.) Memory Dump displays the contents of the selected memory area in hex view; no other views are available. You can use Memory Dump to browse through a large block of memory until you locate an area of interest. Once you have located the data you need, you can copy it to the clip-

366 ■ *Power Of...Norton Utilities*

board using the procedure described earlier. You can also use the **Write To** option on the Tools menu to copy the data to disk.

Because the memory dump is not restricted to the lower 640Kb, you can view areas such as the video display adapter memory, the EMS page frame (if present), buffers on hardware devices such as network adapters, and ROM BIOS code. Of course, making sense of what you see in these areas requires a sophisticated understanding of the low-level details of PC hardware and software that is beyond the scope of this book.

It's hard to predict what you will see with a memory dump; it depends on how your system is configured and what device drivers, TSRs, and so on, are loaded. Two things are more or less universal: DOS and BIOS data areas and the resident portion of DOS are at the bottom of the address space, and the ROM BIOS is at the top. You can search for specific strings in memory using the **Find** command on the Tools menu. For example, in the display in Figure 24.12, I used the search string "Bad Command or" to find the part of DOS that includes the error messages used for the internal DOS commands. To find the beginning of the ROM BIOS, try searching for "BIOS" or for (c) (in the copyright notice).

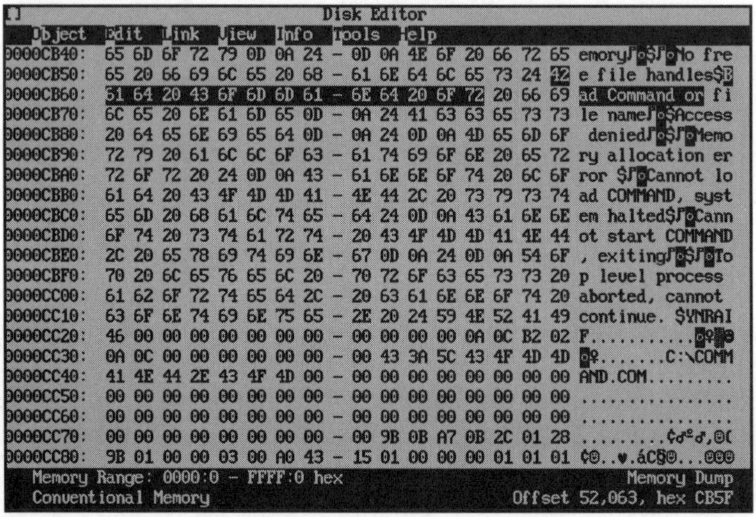

Figure 24.12 Memory Dump from the resident portion of DOS

Chapter Twenty-four: Running the Norton Disk Editor (DISKEDIT) ■ 367

WARNING

Viewing certain areas of memory may cause the computer to lock up (especially on PS/2 models).

Edit Menu

The Edit menu includes various options for use in editing objects. When you first open the Edit menu, all the options except **Mark** are "grayed out" (or shown in parentheses on monochrome displays) to indicate that they are not currently available. If the **Read-Only** option is on, only the **Mark** and **Copy** options will be available. Even if **Read-Only** is not on, you must use **Mark** to select a block of data before you can use any of the other options.

You can edit any object when it is displayed in the hex, directory, FAT, Partition Table, or Boot Record view. The Text view cannot be edited. If you need to edit text, you must switch to the hex view. You can change the view at any time via the options on the View menu (see later) but usually only one view makes a given object intelligible. If you have selected **Auto View** as part of your configuration (described earlier in this chapter), the program will select the appropriate view.

WARNING

Be extremely careful when editing any of the system records (FATs, partition tables, and boot records). You can damage your files or even make your system unbootable.

In addition to using the commands on the Edit menu, you can edit an object by typing over the existing data with the new information. You cannot insert data. (Each change is highlighted on the screen and stays highlighted until you either save it, discard it, or undo it. You can copy, move, or paste data using the **Clipboard** option on the Object menu.)

Undo

Each time you make a change in a sector, the Disk Editor saves a copy of the original data. You can undo any changes you've made within a sector by select-

368 ■ *Power Of...Norton Utilities*

ing **Undo** from the Edit menu or pressing the shortcut, **Ctrl+U**. The undo process works backward, restoring the data in the opposite order to that in which you made the changes (i.e., the last change is restored first, then the next to last, and so on, down to the first change you made).

Undo stores up to 512 bytes of data (the number of bytes in one sector). If you add a 513th byte, the earlier data is lost. If you cross a sector boundary after editing some data, you will be warned and asked whether you want to write, discard, or review your changes. You cannot undo changes that have been written to disk.

Mark

The **Mark** option selects a block of data. The shortcut for this option is **Ctrl+B**. Place the cursor at the beginning of the block you want to mark, then select **Mark** from the menu. Use the cursor keys or drag the mouse pointer to highlight the desired block.

To remove the highlight from a block of data, click anywhere on the block or select **Mark** again and press one of the arrow keys.

Copy

The **Copy** option copies the selected block to the clipboard. The menu disappears after the block has been copied. The block that is copied to the clipboard replaces any previous clipboard contents. The data remains in the clipboard until it is overwritten or you exit Disk Editor. The shortcut for this option is **Ctrl+C**.

Paste Over

The clipboard contents are written into the object starting at the cursor position. Place the cursor at the position where you want the clipboard contents to be written and select **Paste Over** from the Edit menu. The shortcut for this item is **Ctrl+V**. The current contents of the object are overwritten and the bytes that have been changed are highlighted. You can paste data across a sector boundary, but you will be warned that these changes will not be undoable. However, you can select **Discard** to cancel the changes.

Fill

The **Fill** option is used to fill a marked block of any size with a specified character. If you attempt to write across a sector boundary, you will be warned that the changes will be permanent (there is no undo). There is no shortcut for this option. To use the **Fill** option, mark the block to be filled (see the "Mark" section earlier), then select **Fill** from the Edit menu. The dialog box shown in Figure 24.13 will display a list of the characters you can use to fill the block. Scroll through the list and highlight the character you want to use. Selecting **OK** places the selected character in every byte of the selected block.

Figure 24.13 The Fill Characters dialog box

If you attempt to fill a FAT table, the Mark Selected FAT Regions As dialog box appears. The available selections are **Unused**, **Bad**, **End of File**, **Decimal**, and **Hex**. These are the possible legal values for a FAT entry. (The **Decimal** and **Hex** options allow you to enter a "next cluster" number in either hex or decimal format.)

 WARNING Generally, you should avoid filling a block of a FAT with any single value, unless your object is to render all the files on the disk unreadable. However, you could use this option to mark a group of bad clusters as good (mark them "unused" or give them an arbitrary number) so that you can attempt to recover data from them.

Write Changes

Use the **Write** option to save changes made to the sector without leaving the sector. The shortcut for this item is **Ctrl+W**. The changes made to the sector are permanently written to the disk in the same location as the original data. (The original data is overwritten.)

 Any time you cross a sector boundary after making changes, a message will appear indicating that you have made changes to the sector. You will be given a choice of saving the changes, discarding them, or going back to review them.

If you have selected an object for viewing and you want to write it to a different location, you must use the **Write To** option on the Tools menu. The **Write Changes** option cannot be used to do this.

Discard Changes

Select **Discard Changes** to undo all unsaved changes made in the sector. This option will only work within a sector, not across sector boundaries.

The Link Menu

Various objects that can be viewed and edited with the Disk Editor (files, directory entries, and FAT entries) are closely related. Often, when you are viewing one object, you may want to look at one of the others. The Link menu allows you to switch quickly between related objects, without using the Object menu. If Auto View is on (see the Configuration dialog box), the appropriate viewer for the linked object will automatically be selected. If it is off, the view will remain the same until you select another from the View menu (described later).

File

The **File** option links to a file from its FAT entry or directory entry. The shortcut for this item is **Ctrl+F**.

Chapter Twenty-four: Running the Norton Disk Editor (DISKEDIT) ■ 371

Directory

The **Directory** option links to a directory from its FAT entry or a file in the directory. The shortcut for this item is **Ctrl+D**.

Cluster Chain (FAT)

The **Cluster Chain** option links to a FAT entry in the first copy of the FAT to from a directory entry or file. The first cluster belonging to the related item (the directory or file you were viewing) is highlighted (if Quick Move is off). The shortcut for this item is **Ctrl+T**.

Partition

The **Partition** option links the partition table to the boot record for the partition. This menu item is available only when viewing a partition table. There is no shortcut.

NOTE

You cannot go from the boot record to the partition table or anywhere else by using the Links menu. You must go back to the Object menu to select a different object.

Window

The **Window** option creates a dynamic link between two windows, one of which must contain a directory or FAT. Moving the cursor in one window causes the related file to be displayed in the other window. This option is available only if you are working with two windows (see the View menu) and the active window contains either a directory or a FAT object. There is no shortcut.

The View Menu

The View menu allows you to select the type of view in which the current object will be displayed. Six views are possible: hex, text, directory, FAT, partition table, and boot record.

372 ■ *Power Of…Norton Utilities*

Each of these options has a single function key as a shortcut. This makes it easy to switch back and forth among views. The View menu also controls window splitting. If the Disk Editor shows a chaotic display or one in which the data makes no sense in the context in which it is presented, you are probably looking at the wrong view.

Hex

With the **Hex** option the current object is displayed in hexadecimal format. The shortcut is **F2**. The hex view is appropriate for program files and other binary data.

The hex display (Figure 24.14) is divided into four columns: On the left is a column of addresses, expressed as offsets (in hex) from the beginning of the object being viewed. Next are two columns of eight bytes each (two hex digits per byte) showing the contents of the object. At the right is an ASCII "translation" of the printable characters in the preceding two columns. (An explanation of hex numbering can be found later in this chapter.)

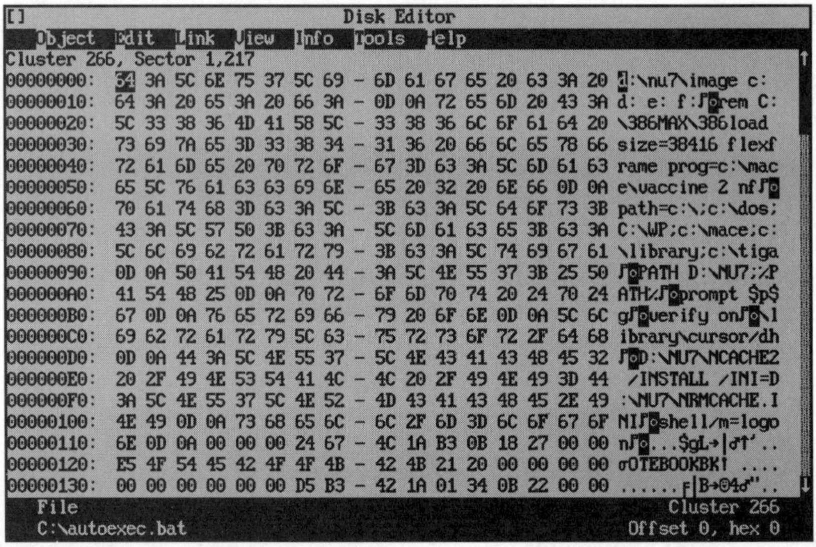

```
[]                           Disk Editor
   Object  Edit  Link  View  Info  Tools  Help
Cluster 266, Sector 1,217
00000000: 34 3A 5C 6E 75 37 5C 69 - 6D 61 67 65 20 63 3A 20  d:\nu7\image c:
00000010: 64 3A 20 65 3A 20 66 3A - 0D 0A 72 65 6D 20 43 3A  d: e: f:♪rem C:
00000020: 5C 33 38 36 4D 41 58 5C - 33 38 36 6C 6F 61 64 20  \386MAX\386load
00000030: 73 69 7A 65 3D 33 38 34 - 31 36 20 66 6C 65 78 66  size=38416 flexf
00000040: 72 61 6D 65 20 70 72 6F - 67 3D 63 3A 5C 6D 61 63  rame prog=c:\mac
00000050: 65 5C 76 61 63 63 69 6E - 65 20 32 20 6E 66 0D 0A  e\vaccine 2 nf♪
00000060: 70 61 74 68 3D 63 3A 5C - 3B 63 3A 5C 64 6F 73 3B  path=c:\;c:\dos;
00000070: 43 3A 5C 57 50 3B 63 3A - 5C 6D 61 63 65 3B 63 3A  C:\WP;c:\mace;c:
00000080: 5C 6C 69 62 72 61 72 79 - 3B 63 3A 5C 74 69 67 61  \library;c:\tiga
00000090: 0D 0A 50 41 54 48 20 44 - 3A 5C 4E 55 37 3B 25 50  ♪PATH D:\NU7;%P
000000A0: 41 54 48 25 0D 0A 70 72 - 6F 6D 70 74 20 24 70 24  ATH%♪prompt $p$
000000B0: 67 0D 0A 76 65 72 69 66 - 79 20 6F 6E 0D 0A 5C 6C  g♪verify on♪\l
000000C0: 69 62 72 61 72 79 5C 63 - 75 72 73 6F 72 2F 64 68  ibrary\cursor/dh
000000D0: 0D 0A 44 3A 5C 4E 55 37 - 5C 4E 43 41 43 48 45 32  ♪D:\NU7\NCACHE2
000000E0: 20 2F 49 4E 53 54 41 4C - 4C 20 2F 49 4E 49 3D 44  /INSTALL /INI=D
000000F0: 3A 5C 4E 55 37 5C 4E 52 - 4D 43 41 43 48 45 2E 49  :\NU7\NRMCACHE.I
00000100: 4E 49 0D 0A 73 68 65 6C - 6C 2F 6D 3D 6C 6F 67 6F  NI♪shell/m=logo
00000110: 6E 0D 0A 00 00 00 24 67 - 4C 1A B3 0B 18 27 00 00  n♪...$gL►...'..
00000120: E5 4F 54 45 42 4F 4F 4B - 42 4B 21 20 00 00 00 00  σOTEBOOKBK! ....
00000130: 00 00 00 00 00 00 D5 B3 - 42 1A 01 34 0B 22 00 00  ......╒B►..4..
  File                                          Cluster 266
  C:\autoexec.bat                               Offset 0, hex 0
```

Figure 24.14 Disk Editor hex display

Chapter Twenty-four: Running the Norton Disk Editor (DISKEDIT) ■ **373**

Text

The **Text** option displays the current object as text. The shortcut for this option is **F3**. You cannot edit this view; use the hex view to edit text.

Directory

The **Directory** option displays the current object using the directory viewer. The shortcut for this option is **F4**.

FAT

The **FAT** option displays the current object using the FAT viewer. The shortcut for this option is **F5**.

Partition Table

The **Partition Table** option displays the current object using the partition table viewer. The shortcut for this option is **F6**.

Boot Record

The **Boot Record** option displays the current object using the boot record viewer. The shortcut for this option is **F7**.

Split (Unsplit) Window

The **Split (Unsplit) Window** option splits the display into two windows. If the display is already split, this item changes to Unsplit; selecting it eliminates the inactive window. The shortcut for this option is **Shift+F5**. You can move back and forth between windows by moving the mouse to the other window and clicking on it or pressing **Shift+F8** (the shortcut for the **Switch Window** option).

You can also split the screen into two windows with the mouse. Use the mouse to drag the status bar up to display the second window. The second window appears at the bottom of the screen; initially it contains the same object and view as the upper window. To unsplit the windows, click on the small square at the upper left of the status bar in either window.

You can change the contents of either window by activating the window (placing the cursor in that window) and using the Object and View menus. The active window will change as you make your selections. (The other window will remain unchanged.)

NOTE To compare the contents of two windows byte for byte, select the **Compare Windows** option on the Tools menu.

Grow Window

The **Grow Window** option is available only when the screen is split into two windows. It adds one line to the active window if the inactive window has not reached its minimum size. The shortcut is **Shift+F6**. You can also change the relative size of the windows by dragging the dividing bar with the mouse.

Shrink Window

The **Shrink Window** option is available only when the screen is split into two windows. It removes one line from the active window if the active window has not reached its minimum size. The shortcut for this option is **Shift+F7**. You can also change the relative size of the windows by dragging the dividing bar with the mouse.

Switch Windows

The **Switch Windows** option switches the active window. You can also change windows by clicking in the inactive window with the mouse. The shortcut for this option is **Shift+F8**.

The Info Menu

The commands on the Info menu display information concerning the currently selected object or disk.

Object Info

The **Object Info** option displays information on the selected object. The format and contents of the display are determined by the type object.

Drive Info

The **Drive Info** option displays detailed information about the current drive.

Map of Object

The **Map of Object** option displays a disk map showing the clusters occupied by the selected object. Figure 24.15 shows the clusters occupied by the NORTON.EXE file on drive D.

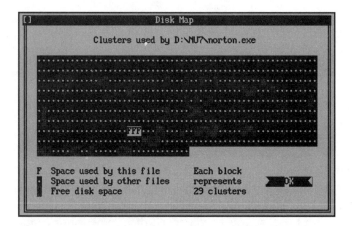

Figure 24.15 A Disk Map display

NOTE This option is not available when the root directory of a disk is being displayed.

The Tools Menu

The Tools menu contains a variety of options for searching for data and objects, modifying data structures, changing file entries, and configuring the Disk Editor.

Find

Use the **Find** option to search for a specified string (a sequence of bytes) in the selected object. The shortcut for this option is **Ctrl+S**. When you select this item, the dialog box in Figure 24.16 appears. You can enter the search string in hex or ASCII. The search starts at the current cursor position and stops at a matching string, if one exists, or at the boundary of the selected object.

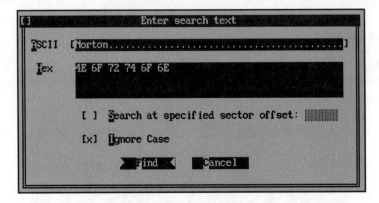

Figure 24.16 *The Find Search Text dialog box*

Find Object

Use the **Find Object** option to locate a particular data structure that you cannot find using the commands on the Object menu. The objects you can search for are partition table/boot record, FAT, and subdirectory. This option is used primarily to find these objects on damaged disks when they cannot be located by ordinary means.

Find Again

With the **Find Again** option the previous search is repeated from the current cursor position, using the same search string. This option is only available if Find was previously used. The shortcut for this option is **Ctrl+G**.

Write To

Use the **Write To** option to copy the current object (as edited) to disk. The shortcut for this option is **Ctrl+W**. When this option is selected, the Write dialog box

Chapter Twenty-four: Running the Norton Disk Editor (DISKEDIT) ■ 377

in Figure 24.17 prompts you to select a destination for the data. Depending on your choice, you are then prompted for a file name and path or a target drive and a starting cluster number, starting (logical) sector number, or starting physical sector number. When you press **OK**, the program warns you that you may be destroying information by writing the object in the cluster or sector mode.

Figure 24.17 The Write dialog box

Print As

Use the **Print As** option to print the selected object. The shortcut for this option is **Ctrl+P**. When you choose **Print As**, the dialog box shown in Figure 24.18 appears. You can send the data from the current object to the printer or to a file. If you choose to send it to a file, you must enter a filespec. By default, the object is printed using the current view, but you can use the radio buttons to select a different view if you wish. You cannot print a text view, but you can use the **Write As** option to write a text view to disk.

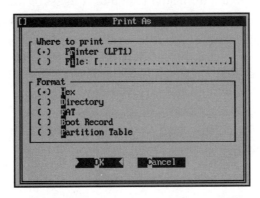

Figure 24.18 The Print As dialog box

A useful feature of the **Print As** option is its ability to append output to a file. If you specify a file name that already exists, the program offers you the choice of overwriting the file or appending the new data to it.

Recalculate Partition

The **Recalculate Partition** option is available only when you are in the partition table viewer, the Read-Only option is turned off, and a block is marked. This option calculates the relative sector number based on the starting sector and calculates the number of sectors based on the ending sector.

WARNING

Use this option with extreme care. Incorrect values in the partition table can make your hard disk inaccessible to DOS. Generally, changes to the partition table should be made with the DOS FDISK command. (Consult your DOS manual.) Use the Disk Editor for special cases, such as partitions created by systems other than DOS. Before you modify your partition table (by whatever means) be sure your hard disk is fully backed up.

Compare Windows

The **Compare Windows** option performs a byte-by-byte comparison of the contents of two objects. To use it, the screen must be split into two windows, and both windows must be set for the same view. Position the cursor at the byte where you want the comparison to start and select **Compare Windows** from the Tools menu. Starting at the cursor position, the Disk Editor will compare each pair of bytes until a mismatch is found. A message will appear indicating that a comparison is being made. This display contains a **Stop** option to allow you to cancel the operation.

If a mismatch is found, the cursor is placed at the mismatched byte in the active window and the comparison is stopped. You can resume the comparison from this point by selecting **Compare Windows** again.

A common use for this option is to compare the first copy and the second copy of the FAT. To do this, load the first copy of FAT into the top window and the second copy into the bottom window. Place the cursor on the first cluster in either window and select **Compare Windows**. The two copies match if no clusters are highlighted. If a cluster is highlighted, this means that

Chapter Twenty-four: Running the Norton Disk Editor (DISKEDIT) ■ 379

a mismatch was found. There may be other mismatches, so you should select **Compare Windows** again to continue. Normally, no mismatches will be found. The presence of a mismatch between the two FATs indicates that one of the FATs is in error, a bad situation. If this happens to you, run the Norton Disk Doctor (see Chapter 10) to attempt to correct the problem automatically, or restore the FAT from an IMAGE.DAT file (see Chapter 9) before resorting to the Disk Editor.

Set Attributes

Use the **Set Attributes** option to change the attributes of one or more files. To use it you must first select a directory view from the View menu and mark one or more entries. After you mark the desired files, the **Set Attributes** option becomes available. When you choose this option, a dialog box will appear in which you can set or clear the following attributes: Archive, Read-Only, Hidden, and System. The check boxes in this dialog box have three states rather that the usual two: a rectangular box means "leave the attribute in its current state"; a check means "set the attribute"; and a blank box means "clear the attribute." Use the spacebar to cycle through the choices for the check boxes; then select **OK** to change the attributes.

N O T E

The attributes of individual files can be changed more conveniently from the root directory display. Use the **Tab** to move the cursor to the desired item. Then use the spacebar to toggle the attribute on or off. If you just want to change the attributes of one or more files, it's better to use the FA utility (see Chapter 20) than to mess about in the Disk Editor with Read-Only turned off.

Set Date/Time

Use the **Set Date/Time** option to change the date and time stamps for one or more files. To use this option you must first select a directory view from the View menu and mark one or more entries. When you have done this, the **Set Date/Time** option becomes available. Select it and a dialog box appears in which you can choose to set the date and/or time by checking their respective check boxes. The current system date and time are the default settings, but you can change them if you wish. Select **OK** to activate the changes.

NOTE: You can also change the dates and times of individual files by typing over that data in the directory entries. If you just want to change the date and/or time of one or more files, it is quicker and safer to use the File Date utility (see Chapter 22) than to use the Disk Editor.

Calculator

A new feature of the Disk Editor in Norton Utilities 7.0 is that the calculator replaces a simple hex/decimal/ASCII converter in previous versions. The calculator performs normal four-function arithmetic in either hex, decimal, or binary notation and calculates two's complements and swaps low- and high-order bytes in a 16-bit word.

Advanced Recovery Mode

The **Advanced Recovery Mode** option, another new feature of version 7.0 of the Disk Editor, displays a dialog box, such as that in Figure 24.19, in which you can modify the vital parameters of the disk. This feature is intended for use with disks that are so badly damaged that the basic parameters cannot be read from the master boot record. It may be possible to access such a disk as a physical disk but not as a logical disk. If this is the case, you will only be able to navigate through the disk using physical sector numbers. You will not be able to use clusters or logical sectors, or directly access such structures as FATs or boot records via the Object menu. This can make it difficult to find and recover important data. With the **Advanced Recovery** option, you can create a set parameters and use them to access the disk as a logical disk.

When you first open the Advanced Recovery dialog box, it displays the parameters that the program has calculated for the disk. If you are trying out this feature on a good disk, all the parameters will be valid, but on a damaged disk, they may not be. To find out, select the **Test** button at the bottom of the screen. This will open a second dialog box, like that in Figure 24.20, showing the test results. If there are errors, the message "Invalid" will appear in one or more locations. If the dialog box displays this message for the BIOS parameter block (the master boot record), you can view the difference between the parameters read from the disk and those calculated by the program by selecting the **BPB Differences** button. You can also write back the calculated parameters to the disk (if the editor is not in Read-Only mode) by selecting the **Write** button. You should not do this, however, *unless you are certain that the parameters are correct.* Select **Done** to return to the main Advanced Recovery dialog box.

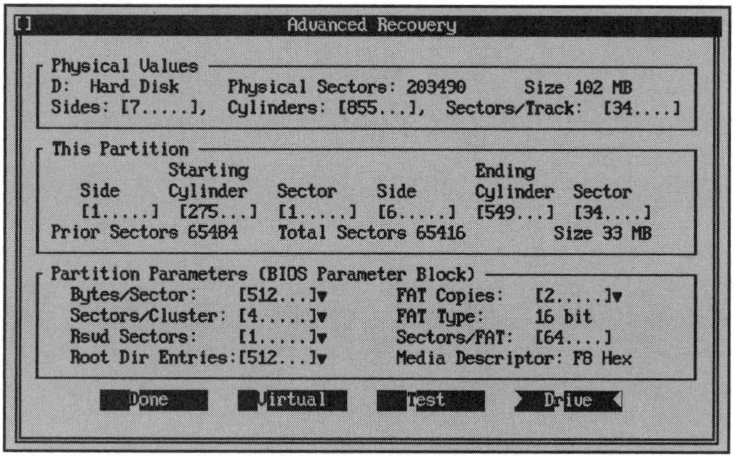

Chapter Twenty-four: Running the Norton Disk Editor (DISKEDIT) ■ 381

Figure 24.19 Advanced Recovery dialog box

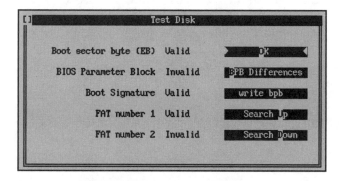

Figure 24.20 Test results dialog box

If the test indicated that some of the parameters were invalid, you may want to edit some of them and test again. Most of the parameters have pull-down list boxes that contain likely values, so you won't be totally in the dark in selecting possible parameters. (Obviously, it is a good idea to be familiar with the architecture of your disk *before* you run into problems that require you to use the Disk Editor.) Test your new parameters again, and when you've got them right, select the **Virtual** button at the bottom of the dialog box to apply them to the disk. This does not write the new parameters to the disk, but allows you to navigate around the disk using the parameters. When you select the **Virtual** button, you exit the Advanced Recovery dialog box and are placed back at the main Disk Editor screen, where you can use any of the options to examine or modify the virtualized disk.

382 ■ *Power Of...Norton Utilities*

ASCII Table

Selecting the **ASCII Table** option allows you to scroll through a table of the IBM extended ASCII character set, showing the characters and their hex and decimal equivalents.

Quitting the Disk Editor

You can quit the Disk Editor by pressing **Esc**, by selecting **Exit** from the Object menu, or by pressing **Alt+X** (the shortcut for **Exit**). If you try to quit the Disk Editor after making changes to a sector/cluster, you are prompted either to write or to discard the changes before you can exit.

Running the Disk Editor from the DOS Prompt

The Disk Editor is basically a full-screen utility. You can control a few aspects of the Disk Editor's behavior with command-line options, but for the most part the program's features must be activated using the menus and dialog boxes, as described earlier. The command-line syntax for the Disk Editor is

```
DISKEDIT [drive:][path][filename] [options]
```

The available options are

/M	Maintenance mode (bypasses DOS and looks at the disk directly).
/X:[d][d]	Excludes the specified drive(s) from absolute sector processing.
/W	Enable disk writes (Read-Only off).
/SKIPHIGH	Don't use high memory.

To view a list of available options, at the DOS prompt type **DISKEDIT /?**

Computer Numbering

The Norton Disk Editor displays and operates on the data on your disks at a very low level. To understand the Disk Editor's displays and make reasonable

Chapter Twenty-four: Running the Norton Disk Editor (DISKEDIT) ■ 383

judgments about what needs to be done, it is helpful to understand the hexadecimal (base-16) numbering system, which is used for some of the Disk Editor's displays. Internally, computers use *binary* (base-2) numbering. This system uses only two digits, 0 and 1. Binary digits, more commonly referred to as bits, are normally grouped together as eight-bit values, known as bytes. A byte can represent a numerical value between 0 and 255, one of 256 different characters, or anything else that can be represented by 256 different values. Bytes must be grouped together to represent larger numbers (e.g., a two-byte "word" [16 bits] can represent 65,536 different values).

People normally use a *decimal* (base-10) system, using the digits 0–9. Because binary numbers of more than a few digits long are very confusing to the human eye, computer scientists and programmers developed the convention of using base-16 numbers (hexadecimal, or "hex" for short) to represent computer data of various kinds. Hex numbers are much easier to read than binary numbers, and it is relatively easy to translate between the two formats (much easier, for example, than translating between binary and decimal).

Hex digits are represented by the symbols 0–9 and A–F. (A–F are equivalent to the decimal values 10–15.) In hex notation, each hex digit represents a group of four binary digits (also called a nibble). Hence, a byte (eight bits) is represented by a pair of hex digits. The Disk Editor writes all its hex numbers as pairs (e.g., 13, 06, A1).

Table 24.1 *Decimal, Binary, and Hexadecimal Equivalent Values*

Decimal	Binary	Hexadecimal
0	0000	0
1	0001	1
2	0010	2
3	0011	3
4	0100	4
5	0101	5
6	0110	6
7	0111	7

Continued on page 384...

384 ■ *Power Of...Norton Utilities*

Table 24.1 Continued...

Decimal	Binary	Hexadecimal
8	1000	8
9	1001	9
10	1010	A
11	1011	B
12	1100	C
13	1101	D
14	1110	E
15	1111	F

To convert from binary to hex, first group the binary number into four-bit groups (starting from right to left). Then convert each group to a hex digit in accordance with Table 24.1. For example, to convert the binary number 1011111001000110 to hex, first arrange the number into four-bit groups (1011 1110 0100 0110), then convert each group to hex, then group the hex digits in pairs (BE 46). Its easy enough to do without the table; just remember that the four binary digits in a nibble represent, from right to left, the decimal values, 1, 2, 4, and 8. Substitute the appropriate decimal value for each digit in the nibble that is a 1 (zeros remain zeros); then add the values together to get the decimal value of the nibble. Substitute the appropriate hex digit for the decimal number and proceed as earlier. Do it often enough, and you'll come to recognize the hex digit that corresponds to the binary nibble without having to go through the decimal stage.

Simple so far, right? People count from right (lowest value) to left, one character at a time. People read, however, from left to right, one character at a time. The 80x86-family microprocessors count the way people read, from left to right, two bytes at a time (PCs are 16-bit machines, remember). So the PC stores each 16-bit word with the bytes reversed: low-order byte first, high-order byte second. This may be confusing, but it is an unavoidable fact of PC life. The number in our previous example, therefore, will be displayed on the Disk Editor screen as 46 BE.

A Walking Tour of Your Hard Disk

You can learn how the Disk Editor works and become more familiar with the data structures and concepts described in Chapter 23 by using the Disk Editor to examine your hard disk thoroughly. By learning how the various items on your disk look when they're in good order, you'll be better able to recognize and correct problems when they occur.

NOTE For the safety of your hard disk, perform the following exercises with the Disk Editor in Read-Only mode. The editor should come up in this mode by default, but if you don't see the message box indicating that this is the case when you start the program, open the Tools menu and select **Configuration**; then check the **Read-Only** option.

Load the Disk Editor by selecting it from the Norton menu or by typing **DISKEDIT** at the DOS prompt. In either case, add the drive letter of your boot drive (normally C:) on the command line. The Disk Editor will load, display the message indicating that the editor is in Read-Only mode, then scan the disk and display the root directory of drive C in a directory view.

Viewing the Master Boot Record and Partition Tables

We are going to examine the disk in hierarchical order, "from the top down," so we'll start with the master boot record and partition tables. To view the MBR, we'll first switch to a physical sector view (**Alt+P**) and specify the lowest legal physical sector number: cylinder 0, side 0, sector 1. This is the location of the MBR and the primary partition table. This initially displays a partition table view of the primary partition table, the only part of the MBR that the Disk Editor has a viewer for. We'll come back to this view shortly, but first we'll look at the complete MBR. To do this press **F2** for hex view, then press **Home** to go to the beginning of the MBR. When you view the MBR in hex, you will see something like the display in Figure 24.21. Note the string of error messages embedded in the boot code: "Invalid partition table.Error loading operating system.Missing operating system." The master boot record contains the code

386 ■ *Power Of...Norton Utilities*

that starts the loading of the operating system on boot-up. If the operating system or the primary partition table is missing or damaged, it will display one of these messages and suspend operation.

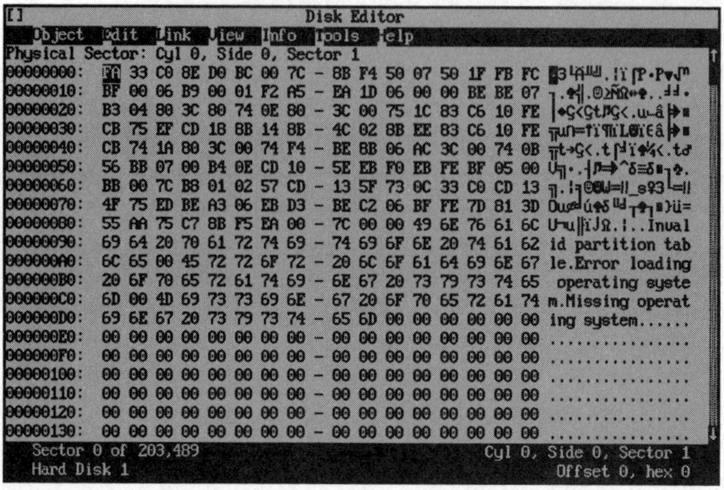

Figure 24.21 *Hex view of the Master Boot Record*

To see the primary partition table in an intelligible form, we must switch back to the partition table view (**F6**). This will result in a display similar to that in Figure 24.22A. What you see in a partition table view on your system, of course, will depend on the size of your hard disk and how it is partitioned. The system used in these examples has a 100Mb hard disk with 855 cylinders, seven sides, and 34 sectors per track. It has a primary and a secondary DOS partition and four logical volumes (C, D, E, and F). In this case, the primary partition table has two entries: the first (DOS-16) is a bootable DOS partition using a 16-bit FAT structure; this is logical drive C. The second is a non-bootable extended partition; this extended partition comprises the other three volumes on the physical disk. The partition table indicates that the bootable DOS partition starts at cylinder 0, side 1, sector 1 and ends at cylinder 274, side 6, sector 34. Observe that the partition begins on side 1, rather than on side 0 of the drive. This, as we'll see later, is the location of the drive's DOS boot record. The MBR and partition table are not part of the partition, and the rest of track 0 on side 0 is left blank. The extended partition begins at cylinder 275, side 0, sector 1, and ends at cylinder 854, side 6, sector 34. In other words, it consumes all the remaining space on the drive except the diagnostic cylinder, cylinder 855.

A.

System	Boot	Starting Location Side	Cylinder	Sector	Ending Location Side	Cylinder	Sector	Relative Sectors	Number of Sectors
DOS-16	Yes	1	0	1	6	274	34	34	65416
EXTEND	No	0	275	1	6	854	34	65450	138040
unused	No	0	0	0	0	0	0	0	0
unused	No	0	0	0	0	0	0	0	0

B.

System	Boot	Starting Location Side	Cylinder	Sector	Ending Location Side	Cylinder	Sector	Relative Sectors	Number of Sectors
DOS-16	No	1	275	1	6	549	34	34	65416
EXTEND	No	0	550	1	6	824	34	65450	65450
unused	No	0	0	0	0	0	0	0	0
unused	No	0	0	0	0	0	0	0	0

C.

System	Boot	Starting Location Side	Cylinder	Sector	Ending Location Side	Cylinder	Sector	Relative Sectors	Number of Sectors
DOS-16	No	1	550	1	6	824	34	34	65416
EXTEND	No	0	825	1	6	854	34	130900	7140
unused	No	0	0	0	0	0	0	0	0
unused	No	0	0	0	0	0	0	0	0

Figure 24.22 *Primary and extended partition tables*

If your drive has more than one partition, it also has more than one partition table, but it's a bit more difficult to view the extended partition table(s). One might think that if we used the Drive option on the Object menu, selected another logical drive, and then chose **Partition Table** as the object, we would see the extended partition table of that logical drive. This, however, is not the case. Regardless of the logical drive you've selected, selecting **Partition Table** as an object takes you back to the *primary* partition table that we just finished examining. What to do? To get to the extended partition table, go into physical sector addressing (**Alt+P**) and select the address of the starting sector of the extended partition (in the preceding example, cylinder 275, side 0, sector 1). This yields a hex view of the starting sector of the extended partition, a view that doesn't provide much useful information. Press **F6** for a partition table view and you'll see a display like that in Figure 24.22B, another partition table similar to the primary partition table we examined earlier.

388 ■ *Power Of...Norton Utilities*

The Extended Partition Table(s)

Again, we have a partition table with two entries: a 16-bit DOS partition (logical drive D) and an extended partition (logical drive E). In this case, the 16-bit DOS partition is not bootable. This is normal; only one partition per drive can be bootable. Observe that the DOS partition again begins on side 1 of the drive rather than on side 0. The extended partition begins at cylinder 550, side 0, sector 1. If we go to this address in physical sector mode and then switch to partition table view, we will find yet another extended partition table (Figure 24.22C) with two entries, a 16-bit DOS entry for logical drive E and an extended entry for drive F. We can follow the chain one step further to find the extended partition table for logical drive F, which is the last logical drive on this physical disk and hence contains no further entries. However your drive is partitioned, you should be able to follow an analogous chain of partition table entries.

DOS Boot Records

The next data structure we'll look at is the DOS boot record (DBR). Every logical drive on the physical disk has a DBR, even though only one logical drive is bootable. As indicated earlier, the DBR is normally located on side 1, sector 1 of the first cylinder of the logical drive (i.e., on the track following the partition table for the drive). This is the location where DOS (logical) sector numbering for the logical drive begins; that is, cylinder *nn*, side 1, sector 1 in physical sector numbering (where *nn* is the first cylinder allocated to the logical drive), is logical sector 0 for the drive.

Boot records are easier to find and navigate among than partition tables: Just select the logical drive you want to view using the **Drive** item on the Object menu, then press **Alt+B** to view the boot record for that drive. A typical DBR is shown in Figure 24.23. The DBR contains various pieces of essential information about the disk. How many of the fields in the boot record contain information will depend on the DOS version that formatted the disk.

File Allocation Tables (FATs)

The next structure after the boot record on any logical drive is the FAT. Two identical copies of the FAT are kept on each logical drive, in contiguous locations. Select your boot drive with the **Drive** option on the Object menu; then

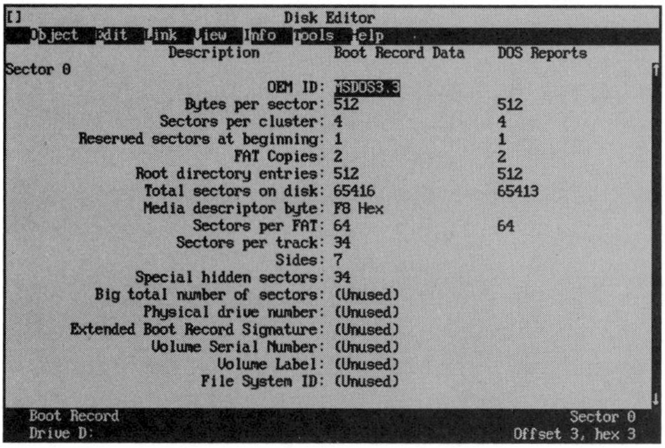

Chapter Twenty-four: Running the Norton Disk Editor (DISKEDIT) ■ **389**

Figure 24.23 *A DOS Boot Record*

press **Alt+F1** to view the first copy of the FAT. You will see a display of eight columns consisting of decimal numbers and <EOF>s (end-of-file markers), such as that in Figure 24.24. Each entry in the FAT represents one cluster on the selected drive. A decimal number points to the *next* cluster belonging to the same file as the numbered entry. An <EOF> indicates the last cluster belonging to a file, or a file that is a single cluster long. If your disk has recently been optimized with Norton Diskreet or a similar program, as is the case with the disk in the figure, then you will see mostly consecutive numbers in adjacent entries.

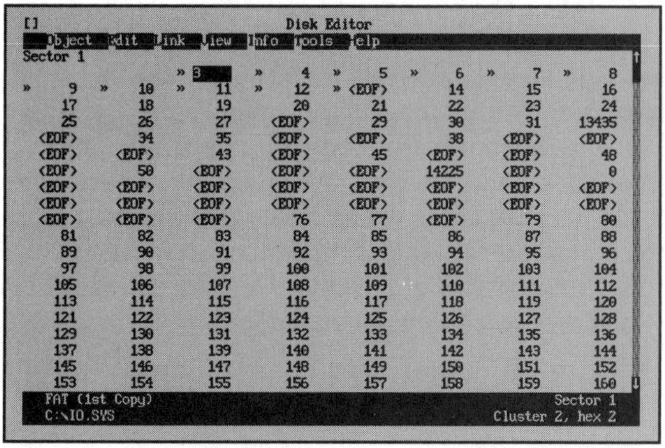

Figure 24.24 *Boot drive FAT number 1*

390 ■ *Power Of...Norton Utilities*

Use your cursor keys to move the highlight through the entries in the FAT. The name of the file that owns the highlighted cluster will be displayed on the status line at the bottom of the screen. On your boot drive, the first two files will probably be IO.SYS and MSDOS.SYS (or with IBM DOS, IBMBIO.COM and IBMDOS.COM). These are the two files that contain most of DOS. In DOS versions prior to 5.0, these files are position sensitive; they must be located in contiguous clusters at the beginning of the data area, as they are shown in the figure. Assuming that you have the **Quick Move** option turned off (the default), you will see double chevron characters (») pointing to all the entries belonging to the same file as the currently highlighted cluster. As you move the highlight through the FAT, the chevrons will move to new groups of entries. If your drive has been optimized, you will probably find directories clustered just below the DOS system files. Most directories will be only a single cluster long, so the directories will appear as a large group of consecutive <EOF>s.

To view the second copy of the FAT, press **Alt+F2**. The second copy of the FAT on a given drive should be identical to the first. There is a pair of FATs on each logical drive. You can view the FATs on each drive by switching to the drive with **Alt+D** and then selecting the first or second FAT as an object.

Linking

You can use the options on the Link menu to move quickly between the FAT and the directory where the file is located or the file itself. You can cycle among these objects quickly using their respective hot-key combinations: **Ctrl+D** for the directory, **Ctrl+F** for the file, and **Ctrl+T** for the FAT. The directory view for IO.SYS is shown in Figure 24.25. Observe that the directory display is more detailed than that produced by the DOS DIR command. It shows, in addition to the usual information, the starting cluster number and the full attribute settings. It also makes hidden files and directories visible. In addition to the options on the Link menu, you can move around the directory tree by highlighting a directory or file and pressing **Enter**. For example, if you are in the root directory in directory view, highlight a subdirectory and press **Enter**. This will take you to that directory. Highlight a file name in the subdirectory and press **Enter** again to see the file in hex view.

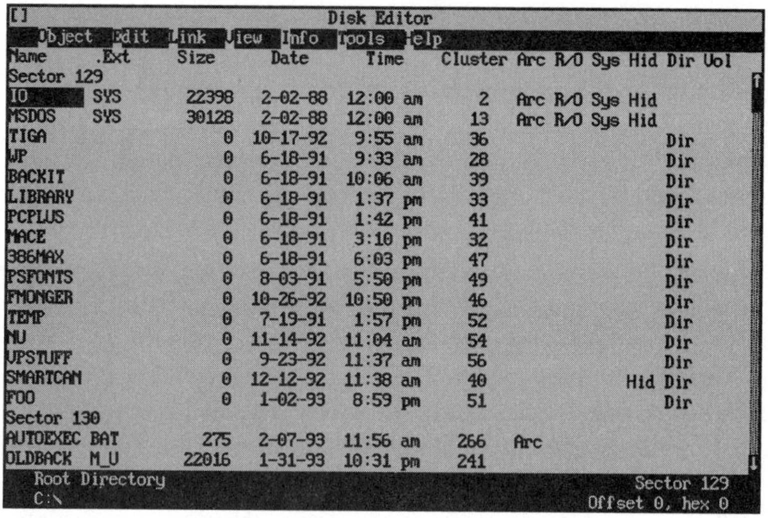

Chapter Twenty-four: Running the Norton Disk Editor (DISKEDIT) ■ **391**

```
[]                          Disk Editor
    Object  Edit  Link  View  Info  Tools  Help
Name    .Ext    Size      Date      Time    Cluster Arc R/O Sys Hid Dir Vol
Sector 129
IO        SYS    22398   2-02-88  12:00 am      2    Arc R/O Sys Hid
MSDOS     SYS    30128   2-02-88  12:00 am     13    Arc R/O Sys Hid
TIGA               0   10-17-92   9:55 am     36                    Dir
WP                 0    6-18-91   9:33 am     28                    Dir
BACKIT             0    6-18-91  10:06 am     39                    Dir
LIBRARY            0    6-18-91   1:37 pm     33                    Dir
PCPLUS             0    6-18-91   1:42 pm     41                    Dir
MACE               0    6-18-91   3:10 pm     32                    Dir
386MAX             0    6-18-91   6:03 pm     47                    Dir
PSFONTS            0    8-03-91   5:50 pm     49                    Dir
FMONGER            0   10-26-92  10:50 pm     46                    Dir
TEMP               0    7-19-91   1:57 pm     52                    Dir
NU                 0   11-14-92  11:04 am     54                    Dir
UPSTUFF            0    9-23-92  11:37 am     56                    Dir
SMARTCAN           0   12-12-92  11:38 am     40                Hid Dir
FOO                0    1-02-93   8:59 pm     51                    Dir
Sector 130
AUTOEXEC BAT     275    2-07-93  11:56 am    266    Arc
OLDBACK M_U    22016   1-31-93  10:31 pm    241
   Root Directory                                     Sector 129
   C:\                                            Offset 0, hex 0
```

Figure 24.25 *Directory view for IO.SYS*

Cluster View

There is another way to view the area on your disk allocated to or available for files: select **Cluster** view (**Alt+C**). When you select this view, a dialog box appears in which you can enter a range of clusters. By default the full range of clusters on the current drive is selected. The Cluster view is applicable *only* to the data area of the disk (i.e., you can't examine FATs, boot records, or the root directory in this mode), and it is available *only* if you accessed the disk as a logical disk, not as a physical disk. Cluster numbering begins with cluster number 2 (don't ask me why), which is the first cluster in the data area of the logical drive, immediately following the root directory. If there is more than one logical drive on the physical disk, cluster numbering stops at the end of the first logical drive, skips the system area of the second logical drive, and begins again with cluster number 2 at the first cluster in the data area of the second drive. Cluster sizes vary with disk size and format, but most logical drives in current use have a cluster size of four sectors (2048 bytes, or 2Kb).

392 ■ *Power Of...Norton Utilities*

Accessing the Diagnostic Cylinder

When you use the **Maintenance** option on the command line (DISKEDIT /M), the Disk Editor bypasses DOS and looks directly at the disk. This capability is important for two reasons: You have access to every part of the hard disk, whether it is used by DOS or not, and you can examine the diagnostic cylinder of your hard disk (if one exists) to see if any special data is stored there.

The diagnostic cylinder is an area of the hard disk that is used to store special data. A few programs rely on this data, and they may fail if it is lost. This area is also used by some diagnostic programs when testing the disk. For example, the Norton Calibrate program uses the diagnostic cylinder for storing data when it performs pattern tests on the hard disk. This will destroy any information stored on the diagnostic cylinder, but you can use Disk Editor to save this data before you use the program.

The diagnostic cylinder is the last (innermost) cylinder on the disk. To view it, choose **Physical Sector** from the Object menu, type the highest legal cylinder number in the cylinder position, and press **Enter**. This should take you to the beginning of the diagnostic cylinder if one exists. The area may be blank, it may be filled with a repeating pattern of one or two characters, or it may have something that resembles meaningful data.

SUMMARY

The Disk Editor is a powerful tool that can be used to examine and modify any file or data structure on any disk, including many disks that have been damaged so that they cannot be read by DOS or repaired by other Norton Utilities. It is the ideal tool for learning the details of how DOS organizes disks and files. Used skillfully it can repair the most arcane disk problems; used without the necessary skills, it can create or exacerbate those same problems.

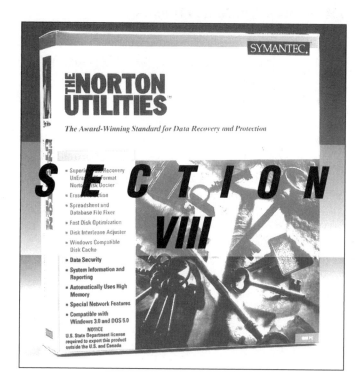

Miscellaneous Features

Unlike those described in the previous sections, the utilities collected in the following six chapters are not concerned primarily with disk protection, repair, or maintenance. Instead, they deal with just about every other aspect of PC operation that can tested, altered, tuned, or managed by software. These programs are presumably not what you bought the Norton Utilities for, and most of them will not protect or restore your data, but one or two of them might come in handy from time to time. Consider them a bonus.

- ◆ The Norton Control Center (Chapter 25) is itself a collection of 10 different utilities for tuning or configuring various aspects of your system's operation.
- ◆ The Disk Duplicator (Chapter 26) is a utility for copying diskettes (an improvement on DOS's DISKCOPY command).

394 ■ *Power Of...Norton Utilities*

◆ The Line Print utility (Chapter 27) prints ASCII files with a variety of formatting options.

◆ The Batch Enhancer (Chapter 28) provides a dozen new commands for creating interactive batch files.

◆ The System Information utility (Chapter 29) provides detailed information on system configuration and performance.

◆ The Norton Diagnostics (Chapter 30) performs detailed testing on all hardware subsystems.

25

TUNING YOUR SYSTEM WITH THE NORTON CONTROL CENTER (NCC)

The Norton Control Center (NCC) gathers together a number of utilities that you can use to configure various hardware devices other than the disk subsystems that are the subject of most Norton Utilities programs. Although these utilities will not save you from the heartache of data loss, they can help change the "look and feel" of your display and perform other minor chores. You can use the NCC to

- ◆ change cursor size;
- ◆ change DOS colors;
- ◆ change palette colors;
- ◆ change the video mode;

- set rate and speed of keyboard repeat;
- set mouse speed;
- configure serial ports;
- set up stopwatches;
- specify the time, date, currency, list, and number formats for a country;
- permanently change the system time and date (on AT-type computers).

All the settings made with the NCC can be saved in a file and loaded from the DOS prompt or from a batch file.

Many of the features of the NCC duplicate features of DOS utilities, particularly the DOS MODE command, which can also be used to set the video mode and configure serial ports. Your video display adapter may have come with a utility that allows you to modify display colors, and your mouse driver may have provisions for modifying mouse speed. However, even if you do have other utilities that duplicate most of the features of the NCC, you may find it more convenient to deal with all these operations in a single program and save the configuration in a single file.

The changes that the NCC makes operate at the DOS level, and there is no guarantee that they will remain in effect when you load an application. Most of today's applications have provisions for selecting screen colors, and they may modify the cursor size as well. You might set the screen resolution to, say, 50 text lines, with the NCC and successfully view large DOS directories or ASCII text files on the screen, but that does not mean that you will be able to load your word processor or spreadsheet and successfully display 50 lines there as well. They may reset the screen resolution, or they may simply produce a garbled display when run in a video mode that they are not designed for. Similarly, communications programs have their own facilities for setting and storing serial port parameters. Only by trial and error will you discover which applications successfully make use of changes made by the NCC.

Chapter Twenty-five: The Norton Control Center (NCC) ▪ **397**

RUNNING THE CONTROL CENTER

Like all the Norton Utilities, the NCC can be run either from the Norton menu or from the DOS prompt. In addition, you can save your settings (except time and date) in a file that can be used to load the settings from the command line. (Refer to the section on running the program from the command line for details.) NCC can also be called from a batch file.

NOTE You can automatically set all your hardware options at start-up by running NCC with the /SET option in your AUTOEXEC.BAT file. (For details see the complete description of command-line options that follows.)

To load the NCC, select **Control Center** from the list of commands on the Norton menu or type **NCC** at the DOS prompt. When you run Control Center, you will see Control Center menu with the first item (**Cursor Size**) highlighted, as shown in Figure 25.1. To leave the Control Center, press **Esc** or pull down the File menu and select **Exit**.

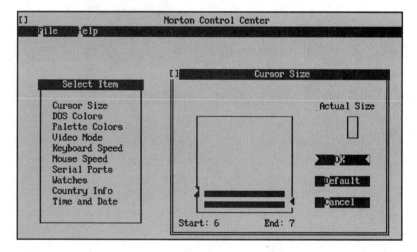

Figure 25.1 The Norton Control Center Main Screen

Use the **Up** and **Down** arrow keys to highlight the item you want on the Control Center menu. Press **Enter** or type the highlighted letter in the item name to select an item. This moves the highlight to the right side of the screen, where the choices for your selected item are displayed.

Cursor Size

The **Cursor Size** option allows you to change the size of the text-mode cursor to suit your needs. Your choices depend on your video display adapter. When you first select this item, the current cursor setting is shown in the Actual Size box in the upper right area of the dialog box. Figure 25.2 shows a cursor setting of Start:6 and End:7.

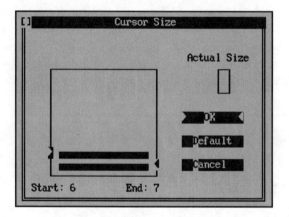

Figure 25.2 *Cursor Size dialog box*

In the box showing the start and end positions are small arrowheads on the left and right borders. These allow you to adjust the height of the cursor. The arrow on the left is highlighted when you begin. Using the **Up** and **Down** arrow keys to move the screen arrow up or down to adjust the starting point of the cursor. When you have adjusted the starting point, move to the right side of the box using the **Right** arrow or **Tab** key. The right arrowhead is now highlighted for you to adjust the end point.

Refer to the Actual Size box in the upper right of the screen to see the specified cursor size. As you change the start and end points, this cursor size will change to reflect your settings. When you have the size you want, use the arrow keys or mouse to highlight **OK** and press **Enter**. If you want to revert to the default size, select **Default**. Select **Cancel** to exit without making any changes.

NOTE Depending on your video display adapter, your cursor may disappear if you select a starting point that is higher than the ending point.

DOS Colors

The term "DOS Colors" refers to the colors displayed on your monitor when you are operating at the DOS prompt. These colors consist of a text color, a background color, and a border color. You can change the color selections using the NCC. Your choices will depend on your monitor and display adapter. Changes in colors made at this level may not last when you load an application.

When you select **DOS Colors** in the Control Center dialog box, the cursor moves to the right side of the screen, where you have two windows (Figure 25.3), one for selecting text/background color and another for selecting the border color. Use the arrow keys to select text and border colors. When you have the color combinations you want, select **OK** and press **Enter** (or click the mouse button). If you want the default colors, select **Default**. Select **Cancel** to exit without making any changes.

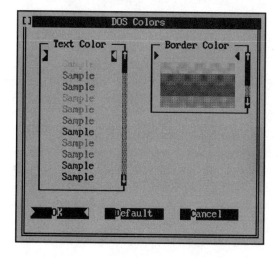

Figure 25.3 DOS Colors dialog box

Palette Colors

The **Palette Colors** option is only available for EGA or VGA displays. The DOS option allows you only 16 colors at a time, even if your monitor can display more. With the **Palette Colors** option, you can decide which 16 colors out of a larger selection will be displayed. These are the colors that programs running on your computer will have available (assuming that they do not reprogram the palette). When you select this item, the Palette Colors dialog box (Figure 25.4) appears on the right side of the screen.

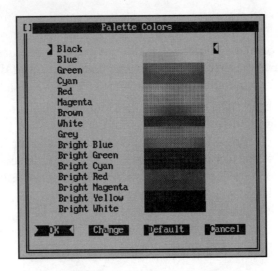

Figure 25.4 Palette Colors dialog box

Use the **Up** and **Down** arrow keys to move through the list of 16 colors and select a color to change, then select the **Change** button at the bottom of the dialog box. A new dialog box with a larger section of colors will appear (Figure 25.5). Scroll through the available colors until you find the one you want; then select the **OK** button to substitute it for the previous color. If you want to go back to the original color for this selection, select the **Default** or **Cancel** button. Continue this process until you have selected all the new colors you want. To exit the Palette dialog box with your new colors active, select the **OK** button. If you want to go back to the default settings, select **Default**. Select **Cancel** to exit without making any changes.

Chapter Twenty-five: The Norton Control Center (NCC) ■ 401

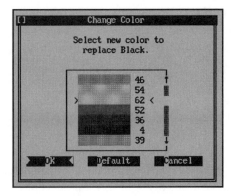

Figure 25.5 Color Selection dialog box

Video Mode

The **Video Mode** option lets you set the Video Mode of your display. If your display adapter can display more than 25 lines on the screen, you can choose to have more lines (up to 50 if you have a VGA). If it does not, you can choose between a black and white or color display.

When you highlight **Video Mode**, the Video Mode dialog box will appear on the right side of the screen, as shown in Figure 25.6.

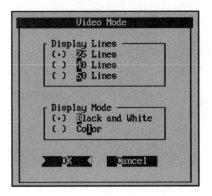

Figure 25.6 The Video Mode dialog box

Press **Enter** to move the cursor to the Display Lines box. Select one of the choices and press the spacebar. Next, you can move to the Display Mode and pick **Black** and **White** or **Color** (if you have it). Highlight **OK** and press **Enter** to activate your choices. You are returned to the Select Item menu on the left with the new video choice in effect. Select **Cancel** to exit without making any changes.

NOTE: Even if your display adapter supports more than 25 text lines, this doesn't necessarily mean that the resulting display will be useful or legible. The more text lines you display on a screen of a given size, the fewer video scan lines are used to draw each character, meaning that the characters are both smaller and more crudely rendered than on a 25-line screen. Also, the fact that you have set the screen to more than 25 lines does not mean that your applications will run at this resolution. If they do, it will be because they have configuration options of their own for selecting such a screen resolution, *not* because you have set the resolution with the NCC.

Keyboard Speed

If your computer is an AT-style or higher (80286, 80386, or 80486 processor), you can change two items relating to keyboard operation. These are the repetition rate (the number of characters the keyboard will repeat in one second when a key is held down), and the initial pause time before the key begins to repeat. When you initially select **Keyboard Speed**, the dialog box in Figure 25.7 appears with the highlight on the **Characters/Second** area. To change the repetition rate, use the **Left** and **Right** arrow keys. The slowest rate is 2.0 characters/second, and the fastest is 30 characters/second. Next, use the **Down** arrow or **Tab** to move to the delay bar. Set this the same way as the repetition rate. You can vary the delay time from 0.250 second to 1.000 second. To set both the repetition and delay rate for the highest speed (fastest repetition rate/shortest delay time), select the **Fast** button at the bottom of the dialog box. Test your keyboard settings by typing in the Keyboard Test Pad box at the bottom of the screen.

Mouse Speed

The **Mouse Speed** option only works with Microsoft-compatible mouse drivers. You can set the sensitivity of the mouse control—the amount of on-screen pointer movement for a given movement of the mouse. Use the **Left** and **Right**

Chapter Twenty-five: The Norton Control Center (NCC) ■ 403

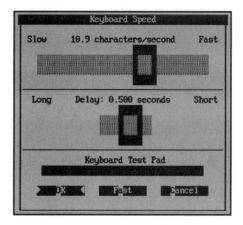

Figure 25.7 *Keyboard Speed dialog box*

arrow keys or the mouse to move the indicator on the control bar (see Figure 25.8). You have a range of sensitivity from 0 (low) to 100 (high). The default setting is 50. After you choose your setting, select the **OK** button to return to the Control Center menu. Select the **Default** button to restore mouse speed to its default value or select **Cancel** to exit without making any changes.

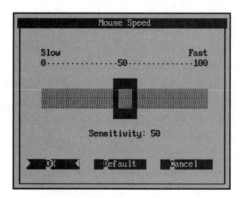

Figure 25.8 *Mouse Speed dialog box*

NOTE

If you set the speed to zero, the mouse pointer will no longer move. You will have to change the speed from the keyboard to restore mouse movement.

404 ■ *Power Of...Norton Utilities*

Serial Ports

IBM-compatible PCs are normally equipped with two types of input/output (I/O) ports, serial and parallel. Serial ports send and receive data one bit at a time over a single channel; parallel ports send and receive data eight bits (one byte) at a time over multiple lines. (Both types use additional lines for control signals.) Today's typical PC is equipped with at least one parallel port and two serial ports, which may reside on the motherboard or an I/O card. At present, serial ports are used primarily for connecting mice and other pointing devices and for modems. The vast majority of current printers use the parallel port, although you may find an older printer or a plotter that requires a serial port connection. DOS recognizes up to four serial ports, which it refers to as COM1–COM4.

For your system to communicate properly with serial peripherals, each COM port must be configured to exactly match the requirements of the connected peripheral, as specified in the peripheral's documentation. This used to be one of the more difficult and annoying aspects of PC operation, but as application software and device drivers have become more intelligent, it is much less likely that the user will have to adjust serial-port settings. Although my system is equipped with a serial mouse and a modem, the two most common serial devices, I have never had to configure a serial port at the DOS level to use them. My mouse driver software knows how to configure the port for the mouse without my intervention, and my communications software has convenient facilities for setting and storing the configurations used with regularly called numbers. If you find that you need to configure a serial port at the DOS level, you may find the facilities of the NCC easier to use than the DOS MODE command.

The NCC allows you to specify all the necessary settings for any available port, including the baud rate, data bits, parity bits, and stop bits. Figure 25.9 shows the Serial Ports dialog box.

Selecting **Serial Ports** moves the highlight bar to the list of available COM (serial) ports. Depending on your system, you can have up to four COM ports on the list. The dialog box shows the current settings for the highlighted port, as shown in the figure.

When you first open the serial port dialog box, the highlight is on the first COM port in the list. Use the arrow keys to highlight the COM port whose settings you want to change. Next, use the **Tab** key to move to the other boxes. Use the arrow keys to move to the setting you want and press the spacebar to select it. When you have selected all the settings you want, highlight **OK** and press **Enter** (or click on **OK**) to activate them. Select **Cancel** to exit without making any changes.

Chapter Twenty-five: The Norton Control Center (NCC) ■ **405**

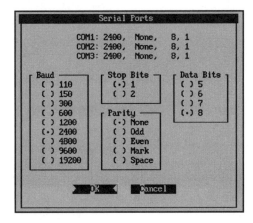

Figure 25.9 *Serial Ports dialog box*

Baud Rate

The baud rate is the rate of data transmission. For modems, common settings are 1200, 2400, and 9600. For peripheral devices such as serial printers and plotters, settings are usually 4800 or 9600. Note that the baud rate is not the same as bits per second. At low speeds they are close, but at higher rates the differences become significant.

Parity

The parity bit is an error detection technique that is used to check the accuracy of the data transmission. The bit following the data is used to check its accuracy. There are five choices for this item:

- ◆ **None**. (No parity) The parity bit is ignored. This is the most common setting.
- ◆ **Even Parity**. When a character is transmitted, the sending terminal adds up the bits in the character. If the sum of the one bits in the character is even, the terminal adds a zero as the last (parity) bit. If the sum is odd, the terminal adds a one as the last bit. This results in the character bits always summing to even.
- ◆ **Odd parity**. This works the same as even parity, except that the sending terminal adds a zero as the last bit if the sum of the one bits in the character is odd. When the sum is even, a one is added as the last bit. This results in the character bits always summing to odd.

- **Mark**. In mark parity, the last bit is always set to one.
- **Space**. In space parity, the last bit is always set to zero.

Data Bits

The **Data Bits** option lets you choose the number of data bits in each transmitted character. The most common number is seven, unless parity is set to Space (none), in which case a setting of eight is used. Other settings are very rare. Note that seven bits are needed to represent the standard ASCII character set, and eight bits are needed for the IBM extended ASCII character set.

Stop Bits

The end of each character is set off by the stop bit, which is a one bit and indicates the end of the character. More than one stop bit can be used, but inserting more than one just slows down the data flow. You can choose one or two stop bits.

NOTE

For bulletin boards and other dial-up services catering to the PC community, a configuration of eight data bits, one stop bit, and no parity has become almost universal. This makes a good starting point for accessing a service with unknown requirements.

Watches

The **Watches** option allows you to run from one to four "stopwatch" timers that continue to run in the background while you use other programs. This is useful whenever you need to time the duration of an event or activity, as when logging the time spent on a project. Although you can start and stop the watches by loading the Control Center and selecting **Watches** on the menu, it is usually more convenient to start and stop the watches from the command line, either directly or from a batch file. For example, you can keep track of how much time you spend on a particular project by starting and stopping a timer from a batch file. The command-line syntax for using the NCC Watches is

NCC /START:WATCH|/STOP:WATCH [/N|/L] [/C:COMMENT]

where

Chapter Twenty-five: The Norton Control Center (NCC) ■ 407

/START:WATCH   Start a watch. WATCH can be a number from 1 to 4 (default is 1).

/STOP:WATCH   Stop a watch. WATCH can be a number from 1 to 4 (default is 1).

NOTE

The START:WATCH and STOP:WATCH options are mutually exclusive. Only one can be used in any given NCC command.

/N   Prevents the display of the current time and date.

/L   Start the display of the current time and date on the left.

NOTE

The /N and /L options are mutually exclusive. Only one can be used in any given NCC command.

/C:COMMENT   Displays a comment (useful for batch files).

Examples:

1. If you want to keep track of how long you spend working on a particular file in your word processor, the following three-line batch file may prove useful.

```
NCC/START:3 /C:%1 >> BOOK.LOG
[WordProcessor] %2
NCC/STOP:3 >> BOOK.LOG
```

Save this file with the file name T.BAT. The first line of the batch file starts timer 3. If you did not indicate a timer, the default timer 1 would be used. The NCC Watches can be individually addressed using the respective options 1, 2, 3, or 4. The timer information placed in the BOOK.LOG file consists of the time, day, and date you started the timer.

The /C:%1 in the first line allows you to enter a note for yourself each time you start the file. Any note you enter must be one word long, but the "word" can be made up of a string of connected words. If you want to enter

408 ■ *Power Of...Norton Utilities*

a note that is more than one word long, use either an underscore (_) or a hyphen (-) to connect the words. Do not use a space. The output of the timer and the note (designated by %1) are sent to the BOOK.LOG file. If the BOOK.LOG file does not exist, it is created in the current directory.

The two greater-than signs (>>) are used to append the output of the command to the end of the specified file. This creates the log by appending new data to the file each time you run the file T.BAT. The single greater-than sign (>) sends the output to a designated file. If the file already exists, the data in the file is overwritten by the new data. If the file does not exist, the program creates it.

The second line of the batch file is used to start the word processor. Substitute the path and starting command for your word processor. The %2 indicates the file that the word processor is to open.

The third line of the batch file is used to stop timer 3 when you exit the word processor. The timer output is sent to the BOOK.LOG file. The timer output consist of the time, day, and date you stopped the timer.

To use this batch file, type the batch file name (T) followed by a space. Then type the note you want to enter. (Be sure not use any spaces in the note.) Place a space after the note, and then enter the path and file name of the data file you want your word processor to load.

2. If you want to add a closing comment to the log, you can modify the original batch file to the following:

```
NCC/START:3 /L /C:%1 >> B:\BOOK.LOG
[WordProcessor] %2
@ECHO (Type T2 and a closing comment, then press Enter.)
ECHO (Or just type T2 and press Enter if you do not want a closing comment.)
QUIT
```

and save it with the file name T1.BAT. (Remember not to wrap the @ECHO command line.) The /L option in the first line left-justifies the time and date display.

Next, create a second batch file to stop the timer after you leave your word processor:

```
NCC/STOP:3 /1 /C:%1 >> BOOK.LOG
```

Chapter Twenty-five: The Norton Control Center (NCC) ■ 409

Save it with the file name T2.BAT. Run the batch file T1.BAT. When you exit your word processor the display will prompt you to type **T2**, followed by a closing comment for the file, or just type **T2** and press **Enter** if you don't want a closing comment. Running T2.BAT stops the timer and writes the closing comment (if any) and then the time, day, and date to the BOOK.LOG file.

If you run the watches from the Control Center menu, the Watches dialog box will appear on the right side of the screen, as shown in Figure 25.10.

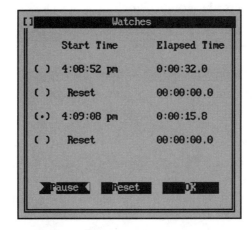

Figure 25.10 Watches dialog box

Press **Enter** to move to the Watches dialog box and use the arrow keys to move to a timer; then press the spacebar to select it. Next, select the **Start** button at the bottom of the dialog box. This starts the timer. Note that the **Start** button changes to **Pause** at this point. If you press **Enter** to select **Pause**, the timer displays the elapsed time to the nearest tenth of a second. Pressing **Enter** again allows the watch to resume timing (continuing from the original start time).

If you want to have another timer running at the same time, move the cursor to that timer and press the spacebar. Note that the **Pause** button now changes back to **Start**. Select **Start** to start the new timer. Repeat this for as many timers as you need.

When you want to stop a timer, move the cursor to it and press the spacebar, then select **Pause**. Select **Start** again to restart a timer. Selecting **Reset** sets the designated timer back to zero. You must reset each timer individually. If you exit Norton Utilities and run another program, the timers keep running.

Country Info

Different countries use different formats for the date and time, currency, and the way lists and numbers are written. Providing your DOS version allows it, the NCC **Country Info** option permits you to specify the country format for DOS to use. This affects the way the preceding items are formatted in DOS displays.

NOTE If you use your computer only to work in English, with American-style date and currency notations, you can skip this section and go to the section on the date and time feature.

Figure 25.11 displays the Country Info dialog box. The box in the lower left corner allows you to select a country. The dialog box contains a display for the time, date, currency, list, and numbers formats for the country you select.

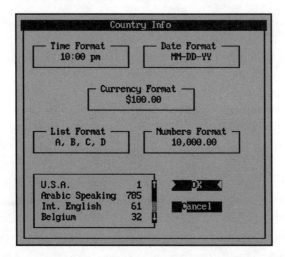

Figure 25.11 *Country Info dialog box*

To use the Country Info option, you must first do two things:

Chapter Twenty-five: The Norton Control Center (NCC) ■ **411**

1. You must load a COUNTRY configuration command from your CONFIG.SYS file to tell DOS which country's format you intend to use.

2. You must load the National Language Support Function file (NLSFUNC.EXE), either from your AUTOEXEC.BAT file or from the DOS prompt.

If these commands are not loaded, the **Country Info** option cannot be used.

To load the COUNTRY configuration file, you can use a word processor or text editor to enter a line in your CONFIG.SYS file similar to the following:

```
COUNTRY=[country-code],[code-page],[country-file]
```

where

[country-code] is a three-digit code used to specify a country (identical to the country's international telephone prefix).

[code-page] is a three-digit number that specifies the code page defining the character set DOS is to use. (See the "Code Page" section later in this chapter.)

[country-file] is the name and path of the file that contains the country-specific information. If the file name is omitted, DOS uses the default file, COUNTRY.SYS. For example, to specify the French country code, the multilingual code page and the COUNTRY.SYS file (located in the DOS directory on drive C) you would enter the following line in your CONFIG.SYS file:

```
COUNTRY=033,850,C:\DOS\COUNTRY.SYS
```

If you require national language support for every session, you should place the NLSFUNC.EXE command in your AUTOEXEC.BAT file. If you only need it occasionally, load it from the DOS prompt when you need it. If you forget to issue this command, DOS will not allow you to specify code pages or keyboard codes. This command is entered as follows:

```
NLSFUNC [country-file]
```

You will find the COUNTRY.SYS and NLSFUNC.EXE files in your DOS directory or on your DOS diskettes. Refer to the DOS manual for your particular version of DOS for details.

412 ■ *Power Of...Norton Utilities*

Code Page

A code page is a table that defines the character you use. There are 256 characters in each character set. These characters are translated from the code page and are used by your keyboard, display adapter, and printer. For example, the Nordic code page contains 256 characters that include all the specific characters used by the Norwegian and Danish languages. (The code-page parameter is only valid for DOS version 3.3 and higher.)

There are two types of code pages—hardware and prepared. A hardware code page is one that is built into a device such as a printer or keyboard; it is specific for the country where the device will be used. For example, a printer manufactured for use in Denmark would have a Nordic code page built in.

Prepared code pages are provided by DOS and are contained in code-page information (.CPI) files. DOS versions 3.3 and higher include five prepared code pages. These can be used by some devices to switch to another character set. (Not all devices can do this, some can only use their own hardware code page.) Refer to your DOS manual for details. The prepared code pages are the following:

- ◆ **437**—United States.
- ◆ **850**—Multilingual. (This includes all the characters for English and most Latin-based languages, such as French and Spanish.)
- ◆ **860**—Portuguese.
- ◆ **863**—Canadian-French.
- ◆ **865**—Nordic. (This includes all the characters required by Norwegian and Danish.)

Outside DOS

Even if you have included the required commands in your CONFIG.SYS and AUTOEXEC.BAT files, your country configuration passport is only good within the borders of DOS. If you want to create a document and print it, your word processor, spreadsheet, or other program and your printer will have their own formatting routines. The programs and the printer, rather than the settings made with NCC and DOS, will determine what you can print.

If you have DOS version 3.3 or higher and if your display adapter and printer support code-page switching, you can set up your system so you can change between country formats by typing in the appropriate code page at the DOS prompt. Refer to your DOS manual for a list of appropriate display adapters and printers and for details on setting up code-page switching.

Keyboard

Unless you change your keyboard layout with the KEYB command, you may not be able to employ all the characters required by the language of the country you select. The syntax for the keyboard command is as follows:

KEYB [country-letters],[code-page],[kbdfile]

where

[country letters] is a two-letter code specifying the country.

[code-page] is the page number containing the desired character set.

[kbdfile] is the path and file name containing the keyboard definition information. The default is KEYBOARD.SYS.

For example, to change your keyboard from its present layout to a French layout, at the DOS prompt type

KEYB FR,850,C:\DOS\KEYBOARD.SYS

where FR is the two-character country code for France, 850 is the multilingual code page number, and C:\DOS\KEYBOARD.SYS is the path to the keyboard driver file.

After you enter a keyboard command, you can switch back to the default layout (usually the United States) by pressing **Ctrl+Alt+F1**. To return to the memory-resident layout you specified, press **Ctrl+Alt+F2**.

NOTE

DOS checks to make sure the codes you specify will work together. Valid combinations are defined in the COUNTRY.SYS and KEYBOARD.SYS files. If you have entered an invalid combination, you will see a message to that effect.

If you change the keyboard layout, the labels on the keys may not match the characters displayed on your screen. You can purchase keyboard overlays to help you keep the key layout straight. For more information on this subject, consult your DOS manual.

Time and Date

If your system date and time settings are incorrect, you must reset the internal clock of your computer to correct them. For PCs and XTs this is not a problem. It is handled nicely by the DOS DATE and TIME commands. (In any case, these systems require you to enter the time manually whenever you boot the system unless you have installed an expansion card that has a clock with a battery backup.) For ATs and later systems, however, permanently changing the internal clock is a time-consuming process involving a special program on the DOS Diagnostics disk. In these computers, the DOS TIME and DATE commands only set the current session. As soon as the session ends (power off or reboot) the time and date revert to that of the internal clock.

 NOTE The prededing description applies to true IBM ATs. Many AT-compatibles based on the C&T NEAT chip set allow you to reset the date and time (or any other settings in the CMOS setup memory) from the keyboard at bootup.

The Control Center's **Time and Date** option allows you to reset the internal system clock for any computer without having to resort to the Diagnostic disk. Figure 25.12 shows the Time and Date dialog box.

Figure 25.12 *Time and Date dialog box*

The Time and Date dialog box has two controls. The top is for the date and the bottom is for the time. Use the **Tab** or arrow keys to move to the field you want to alter and use the **+** and **-** keys on the numeric keypad (gray keys) to adjust the value. When you have completed the changes, select **OK** to activate them.

Saving Your Settings

The settings you have chosen in the Norton Control Center program are not permanent. They are only active for the current session. However, you can save your new settings to disk if you wish. You can activate them directly from the DOS command line by typing **NCC** with the appropriate options and the file name. For example, suppose you have saved settings for cursor size, DOS colors, palette colors, and video mode in a file named CUSTOMIZ. If you want to activate all these settings at the DOS prompt, you would type

    NCC CUSTOMIZ /SET

If you only want to use the cursor size and DOS colors settings, type

    NCC /CURSOR /DOSCOLOR CUSTOMIZ

To create a file where you can save your new settings, do the following:

1. When you have your settings the way you want them, press **F10** or **Alt+F** to access the File menu on the menu bar and select **Save Settings** from the menu, or press **F2** to go directly to the Save dialog box (Figure 25.12), bypassing the menu.
2. Use the spacebar to check the check boxes for the items you want to include in the file. Next, enter a file name in the box below. If you do not specify a path, the file is saved to the current directory. Press **Enter**.

NOTE   You must place this file in the same directory as NCC (the NORTON directory) because NCC will not search for it. If it is not in the same directory, you will have to include the path each time you access the file. If you entered NCC from the NORTON directory, this is not a problem. But if you enter it from a different directory, you must be certain to include the path to the NORTON directory when you load the SETTINGS file.

416 ■ *Power Of...Norton Utilities*

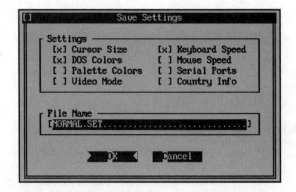

Figure 25.13 *The Save Settings dialog box*

You can also load the settings you have saved to a file from the Control Center by selecting **Load Settings** on the File menu or by pressing **F3**. Type the name of the settings file you want to use and select **OK**.

If you want to use these new settings all the time, you can load the file automatically from your AUTOEXEC.BAT file. Place a line similar to the following in your AUTOEXEC.BAT:

```
NCC \NORTON\CUSTOMIZ /SET
```

This loads all the settings in the CUSTOMIZ file located in the NORTON directory.

If you wish to use different settings for different programs, you can use a batch file to set the NCC settings before and after the application is called.

Running the Control Center from the DOS Prompt

You can run NCC from the DOS prompt in one of three ways. You may

- start the NCC program and use it in the full-screen mode;
- load your settings from a file;
- set individual NCC settings from the DOS prompt.

Chapter Twenty-five: The Norton Control Center (NCC) ■ 417

If you are in the NORTON directory or if it is in your DOS path, start the NCC program in full-screen mode by typing **NCC Enter** at the DOS prompt. If the NORTON directory is not the current directory or in your path, you will need to type [path]\NCC Enter.

If you have created a file for your NCC settings, you can load it from the command line by typing **NCC** [filespec] [options], where [filespec] is the path and file name for your NCC SETTINGS file and the available options are as follows:

/SET	Tells NCC to read the information in the named file and set all the parameters.
/CURSOR	Read the named file and set only cursor size.
/DOSCOLOR	Read the named file and set the selected DOS colors.
/PALETTE	Read the named file and set the selected palette colors.

If you do not have an NCC SETTINGS file, you can still set some of the options from the DOS prompt by entering the NCC command with the appropriate options. At the DOS prompt, type **NCC** [options].

The following are the available options. These are used to specify settings for the video display, keyboard speed, stopwatches, and date and time:

1. Video and keyboard options

/BW80	Set display mode to black and white, 25 × 80.
/CO80	Set display mode to color, 25 × 80.
/25	Set display mode to 25 lines.
/35	Set display mode to 35 lines (EGA only).
/43	Set display to 43 lines (EGA only).
/40	Set display mode to 40 lines (VGA only).
/50	Set display mode to 50 lines (VGA only).
/FAST	Set keyboard speed to the fastest rate.

2. Stop watch, date, and time options

/Start:*n*	Start watch number *n*. If no number is entered, the default is 1.

418 ■ *Power Of...Norton Utilities*

/Stop:n	Stop watch number *n*. If no number is entered, the default is 1.
/N	No display of current date and time.
/L	Prints the current date and time left-justified.
/C:comment	Displays the text of a comment you supply. If the comment contains any blank spaces, the entire comment must be enclosed in quotes. Comments are useful for keeping track of timers when you are running more than one.

To see a list of the available options at the DOS prompt, type **NCC /?**

Examples:

```
NCC /50
```
Changes your video display to 50 lines.

```
NCC /START:1 /L /C:"Start clock #1"
```
Start watch 1, display the current date and time on the left of the screen, and display the note "Start clock #1" on screen.

SUMMARY

The Norton Control Center utility allows you to select a variety of operational settings for your computer. Among the choices are video mode, mouse speed, keyboard rate, and country-specific formats. You can save these settings to a file that can be loaded automatically from the AUTOEXEC.BAT file, or you can load the entire file (or selected settings) from the command line. In addition, you can create a batch file to run the **Watches** option and keep a log of the time spent in specific activities.

26

COPYING FLOPPY DISKS WITH THE DISK DUPLICATOR (DUPDISK)

A new feature of Norton Utilities 7.0, the Disk Duplicator is essentially an improved version of the DOS DISKCOPY command. Like DISKCOPY, DUPDISK makes an exact copy of a floppy disk, called the *source disk*, on another floppy of the same size and format, called the *target disk*. That is, rather than merely copying the files from one disk to another, it makes a copy that matches the original, cluster for cluster. In the process, it also copies any hidden files, which would be missed by the DOS command COPY *.*.

Disk Duplicator can only be used to copy from one diskette to another of the same size and format; you cannot, for example, use it to copy from a 5.25", 360Kb floppy to a 5.25", 1.2Mb floppy or from a 3.5", 720Kb floppy to a 3.5", 1.44Mb floppy. Also like DISKCOPY, Disk Duplicator will format the target disk if necessary. (The program will ask you for confirmation before formatting the target disk.)

Unlike DISKCOPY, Disk Duplicator can use expanded or extended memory, if available, to hold the contents of the source diskette. This allows it to copy a diskette using a single disk drive, without requiring you to do multiple disk swaps. Given that most contemporary PCs have either a single floppy drive or one 5.25" drive and one 3.5" drive, this is a significant improvement. Because it stores a copy of the source disk in expanded or extended memory, Disk Duplicator can also make multiple copies of a single floppy disk using a single drive, without your having to return the source diskette to the drive after it is first read. This greatly simplifies the process of creating multiple distribution copies of a diskette.

USING DISK DUPLICATOR

Disk Duplicator is simple to use. Move the highlight to **Disk Duplicator** in the Norton command window, type the source and target drives, and press **Enter**, or type DUPDISK [source drive] [target drive] **Enter** on the command line. You can even omit the source and target drives and the dialog box that appears (Figure 26.1) will prompt you for the appropriate drives. (The source and target drives must be the same size and format, but DUPDISK knows what kind of drives your system has and won't let you specify an invalid combination.)

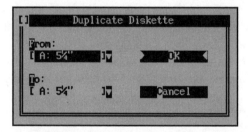

Figure 26.1 Drive Selection dialog box

Once the source and target drives are selected, the program will prompt you to place the source disk in the appropriate drive and will then begin reading the source disk into memory. While the program is reading, it displays its progress

Chapter Twenty-six: Disk Duplicator (DUPDISK) ■ 421

on screen in a dialog box like that in Figure 26.2. When it has read as much as your available memory will hold (the whole disk if you have sufficient extended or expanded memory available), it will prompt you to place the target disk in the appropriate drive and then begin copying. If there are files on the target disk, the program will show you a list of the files such as that in Figure 26.3 and will ask you to confirm that you want to copy over them. Answer **Yes** to overwrite the files or **No** to substitute a different target disk. When it has finished copying the diskette, the program will ask if you want to make additional copies of the same disk. If you answer **Yes**, it will prompt you to place another target disk in the appropriate drive and then repeat the process.

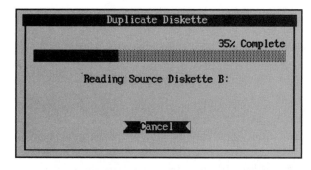

Figure 26.2 Disk Duplicator progress dialog box

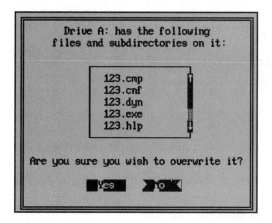

Figure 26.3 Confirm Overwrite dialog box

WARNING Making a copy with the Disk Duplicator will destroy any data on the target disk. Be absolutely certain that the target disk contains nothing of value before performing this operation, as it will be impossible to recover any files overwritten by the Disk Duplicator.

There can be some disadvantages to making an exact copy of a diskette. For example, any files that are fragmented on the source diskette will remain fragmented on the copies. If you want to make a distribution diskette and you want all the files to be unfragmented, you can make a clean master diskette by copying the files to a newly formatted diskette using the DOS COPY or XCOPY command. If you need to copy a diskette with subdirectories, use the XCOPY command with the /S option. Alternately, if you have already created a master diskette and it has fragmented files, you can use the Norton Speedisk utility (see Chapter 17) to unfragment the files on the master before making copies. When you have created a master diskette that is free of fragmented files, you can use Disk Duplicator to make copies for distribution.

NOTE There is a minor difference between copies made by recent versions of the DOS DISKCOPY command and the Norton Disk Duplicator. In DOS versions 4.0 and above, the DISKCOPY command gives copies unique volume serial numbers distinct from the serial number of the source disk. The Disk Duplicator gives each copy the same serial number as the source disk.

COMMAND-LINE OPTIONS

The following options are available:

```
DUPDISK [source_drive] [target_drive]
```

where [source_drive] is the drive where the original diskette is located and [target_drive] is the drive where the duplicate will be made. If the source drive and the target drive are the same, the program will prompt you when to swap the disk.

Chapter Twenty-six: Disk Duplicator (DUPDISK) ■ **423**

SUMMARY

DUPDISK makes an exact copy of a diskette on another diskette of the same size and format. It speeds up the copying process by using extended or expanded memory, if available, to store a copy of the source diskette.

Printing ASCII Text Files with Line Print (LP)

The Norton Line Print utility (LP) is designed for those times when you want to print an ASCII text file without loading your word processor or text editor. Use it to print batch files, program source code, README files, or any other ASCII text files. You can also use LP to print text files encoded in the EBCDIC format or WordStar-type text files.

NOTE EBCDIC is a text-formatting standard that is used on IBM mainframes; it is rarely used for PC text files, although you may encounter it if you download files from a mainframe. WordStar files use only seven bits for encoding the characters. The eighth bit is used for formatting purposes, such as distinguishing between hard and soft carriage returns.

426 ■ *Power Of...Norton Utilities*

Using Line Print is preferable to sending ASCII files to the printer with the DOS TYPE or COPY commands because it provides a number of useful options for controlling the format of the output:

- ◆ prints line numbers
- ◆ prints page numbers
- ◆ generates headers
- ◆ sets margins
- ◆ sets page width (80 or 132 columns)
- ◆ sets tabs
- ◆ generates output for a variety of printers

Printing ASCII files from a full-featured word processor can sometimes be more trouble than its worth. If you have an ASCII file in which lines have been padded out or indented with spaces rather than tabs and terminated with carriage returns, and you load that file into a word processor, unless you set the word processor margins exactly right, the lines will not wrap correctly and the resulting document will be a mess. If you print program source code from many text editors, the listing will ignore page length and print across perforations. Both of these problems can be avoided by printing text files from LP.

COMMAND-LINE OPERATION

Line Print is a command-line utility. It can be started from either the Norton menu command line or the DOS prompt, but in either case, there are no menus, dialog boxes, or full-screen operating modes. The program is controlled entirely by the options you type on the command line (or by a CONFIG file, described later), and the program begins printing immediately when you press **Enter**. The command-line syntax for Line Print is as follows:

```
LP filespec [output] [/CONFIG:description] [/Tn] [/Bn]
[/Ln] [/Rn] [/HIn] [/Wn] [/TABn] [/SPn] [/HEADERn] [/PAn]
[/N[+|-]] [/A] [/80|132] [/WS|EBCDIC] [/SET:pathname]
[/PR:xx]
```

Chapter Twenty-seven: Printing ASCII Text Files with Line Print (LP) ■ 427

where

[filespec] is the file name, with optional drive and path, to print. Wild-card characters (* & ?) can be used to print multiple files with a single command.

[output] is the device to print to. You can specify any DOS logical device name, such as PRN, LPT1, COM1, and so on, or a file name. If no output is specified, the output is sent to PRN (the default printer, normally the same as LPT1).

[/CONFIG:description] is a configuration file for a particular printer that you create with the **Printer Configuration** option in the Norton Configuration utility. It is not necessary to specify a path for the CONFIG file; LP has a method for locating the configuration file. Printing from a configuration file will be described in more detail later.

NOTE

Description is the description displayed in the **Printer Configuration** dialog box (see Chapter 3), *not* the DOS file name of the configuration file.

/Tn /Bn /Ln /Rn	Sets the top, bottom, left, and right margins. The defaults are 3, 3, 5, and 5 characters, respectively.
/HIn /Wn	Sets the page height and width. The defaults are 66 lines and 85 columns, respectively.
/TABn	Sets the tab spacing, every *n* characters. The default is every eight characters.
/SPn	Sets the line spacing. The default is 1 (single spacing).
/HEADER[0|1|2]	Specifies the type of header to print. 0 = no header; 1 = a one-line header: the page number, the file name, and the current date and time; 2 = a two-line header: header 1 plus a second line indicating the file creation date and time.
/PAn	Sets the starting page number. The default is 1.
/N[+|-]	Turns line numbering on or off. The default is off.
/A	Appends output to the specified output files. This option works only if you specify a file as the output device. If the specified file doesn't exist, LP will create it.

/80|132   Sets 80- or 132-column print width. The default is 80 columns. (These two options are mutually exclusive.)

/EBCDIC   Specifies printing EBCDIC-encoded files.

/WS   Specifies printing WordStar files.

/PR:xx   Specifies printing to a specified type of printer. The recognized options are as follows:

    TT   teletypewriter

    GE   generic

    EP   Epson dot matrix

    PR   IBM Proprinter

    QU   IBM Quietwriter

    TO   Toshiba dot matrix

    LA   HP LaserJet

    PO   PostScript

If no printer is specified, the generic option will be used.

/SET:filespec Sends the setup string in the specified file to the printer before printing the main file. Setup strings will be described in more detail later.

To see a summary of the command-line options at the DOS prompt, type **LP /?**

NOTE The preceding syntax may seem excessively complex and intimidating, but take heart. Most of the options in the preceding example can be omitted and LP will work satisfactorily with its default settings. Or you can create one or more configuration files with commonly used settings and use the /CONFIG option in place of a host of complex options.

PRINTING WITH LINE PRINT

A simple way to demonstrate how Line Print works is to print your AUTOEXEC.BAT file. The following example assumes that your AUTOEXEC.BAT

Chapter Twenty-seven: Printing ASCII Text Files with Line Print (LP) ■ 429

file is in the root directory of drive C and that your Norton Utilities directory is the current directory. To print your AUTOEXEC.BAT file with a two-line header and with line numbers, type

    LP C:\AUTOEXEC.BAT /HEADER2 /N

To print the file with a one-line header and no line numbers, type

    LP C:\AUTOEXEC.BAT /HEADER1

NOTE

This will work with most printers, but if you have a PostScript-only printer, you must add the /PR:PO option or use a configuration file (described later).

Using Wild Cards

You can use DOS wild-card characters (? and *) to print several files with a single command. For example, if you use the command LP *.DOC /HEADER2, each matching file will be printed with its own header. Each new document will begin on a new page and will restart page numbering with 1.

Using Configuration Files

A printer configuration file can take the place of all the possible command-line options for the Line Print utility except the /PA option for setting the starting page number and the /A option for appending output to an existing file. Hence, you can save yourself a great deal of unnecessary typing by just using the /CONFIG option rather than a long string of command-line options. Several configuration files are supplied with the Norton Utilities and are installed on your hard disk when you install the program. You can select one of these files as the default printer configuration and LP will use it automatically if you don't specify a configuration file on the command line. Printer configuration files can be created or modified with the **Printer Configuration** option of the Configuration utility (NUCONFIG) or with the analogous option on the pull-down Configuration menu on the Norton menu. Consult Chapter 3 for information on creating and editing printer configuration files.

You can modify the effect of a configuration by using command-line options to override options contained in the configuration file. For example, if you want to print a file using all the options in the PostScript/Portrait configuration *except* that you want to use two-line headers (assuming the configuration file specifies one-line headers), you could type

```
LP /CONFIG:postscript_portrait /HEADER2
```

Using Printer Setup Strings

Use the /SET option if your printer requires a setup string to print properly. Setup strings (sometimes called escape sequences because they usually begin with the escape character, ASCII 027 decimal) can be used to initialize a printer, to select different character sets, to select colors on a color printer, and so on. Consult the owner's manual for your printer to determine what setup strings, if any, your printer requires or accepts.

Using the format described later, you can create a setup string using any text editor that saves ASCII files and save the string in a file. Use the /SET option to cause Line Print to load the setup file and send it to the printer before printing the main text file(s).

The Line Print utility accepts setup strings in either the Lotus 1-2-3 or Norton format. In either case, the string can contain the following items:

\nnn   The ASCII code in decimal format for a character to send. Three digits are required. Use leading zeros if necessary.

\C   A control character to send.

C   Any character to send.

NOTE These distinctions may be a bit foggy for nonprogrammers. What they mean is that, in many cases, there are two different ways to represent a given character in a setup string. For example, the character "A" could be added to a setup string simply by typing **A**, or it could be represented by its ASCII code as \064. The same thing is true of nonprinting (control) characters. The escape character, which begins control sequences for many printers, can be represented in a setup string as \027 or as \[(Ctrl+[). Either representation will have the same effect on a printer. Your printer manual may represent control codes in either or both forms.

Chapter Twenty-seven: Printing ASCII Text Files with Line Print (LP) ■ **431**

In addition to representing the codes in various ways, you can type several control codes on a single line (Lotus format), or you can separate them with line breaks (Norton format), which may make them easier to read. The effect on the printer is the same. The following example, used with an Epson EX dot-matrix printer, selects near-letter-quality printing, selects the italic character set, and prints the line "This is a setup string", followed by a carriage return and line feed:

```
\027\120\001
\027\033\064
This is a setup string
\013\010
```

The next example does exactly the same thing:

```
\[x\A\[!AThis is a setup string\M\J
```

To create a setup string, use your word processor or text editor to type the appropriate characters, in whichever format you prefer. Save the result as an ASCII file (called "nondocument mode" or "DOS text" by some word processors) with an appropriate file name, such as SET01. Then run Line Print with the /SET option to print any ASCII file that you want printed with the characteristics you specified in the setup file. For example:

```
LP C:\README.TXT /SET:SET01
```

This assumes that the SET01 file is in the same directory as LP. If not, you would have to include the appropriate path.

The only restriction on setup strings is that you can only send one setup string, whether short and simple or long and elaborate, at the beginning of the file. You cannot, for example, start the print job with a string to select one font, then send another string to change fonts in the middle of the document. If you want to do something like this, use your word processor rather than LP.

SUMMARY

Use Line Print to print ASCII files conveniently from the command line without loading a word processor or text editor. Line Print can add headers and line

432 ■ *Power Of...Norton Utilities*

numbers to existing files and can otherwise configure the output in ways that are not possible with DOS commands. Use a configuration file to save yourself the trouble of typing complex command-line options. Use a setup file to activate specific features on your printer.

28

ENHANCING BATCH FILE PERFORMANCE WITH BATCH ENHANCER (BE)

A batch file is an ASCII text file containing a series of commands that can be executed in a "batch" from the DOS prompt by typing the file name and pressing **Enter**. A batch file can contain any command that you can type individually at the DOS prompt. In addition, a group of DOS commands, such as ECHO, FOR, IF, and GOTO, can be used *only* in batch files. These commands comprise a sort of crude programming language that can be used to control or modify the action of the commands contained in the file. Batch files are useful for automating fairly simple tasks, such as copying a group of files that meet a particular file spec from a hard disk to a diskette and then deleting them from the source directory on the hard disk, or loading a memory-resident driver, starting an application that requires the driver, then deinstalling the driver when the application terminates. One batch file that most readers are familiar with is the AUTOEXEC.BAT, which is used to execute a series of commands to configure the system, load TSRs, and so on, when you boot your system.

434 ■ *Power Of...Norton Utilities*

The usefulness of batch files is limited, however, by the fact that they are not *interactive;* that is, once you have typed the batch-file name on the command line and pressed **Enter**, there is no way that you can intervene and control the operation of the commands in the file. (This is what the term "batch" really means. It's a throwback to the early days of computing, when you programmed a job on punch cards and turned it over to the high priests in the white coats to run it in "batch mode" on the monster in the back room.) Batch files would be much more useful if they could ask you for input and take different actions based on your responses. That is exactly what the Norton Batch Enhancer (BE) does. It gives you a series of new commands that can be used in batch files, or in special BE "script files," to display messages and menus on the screen, accept your input from the keyboard, and execute different commands based on that input.

If you're like most Norton Utilities users, you bought the program to correct or prevent disk problems, and you probably aren't very interested in building elaborate menus using interactive batch files. In any event, with the advent of Windows and with the free DOSSHELL program provided with DOS versions 4.0 and later, there really isn't as much need for this kind of thing as there used to be, and the whole idea seems a bit outmoded. Nevertheless, it may be useful to browse through this chapter to see what the BE commands can do. You may not use them often, but once in a while you may find that one of them is just what you need to solve a troublesome problem.

Using Batch Enhancer

Batch Enhancer is not a stand-alone program with menus and dialog boxes, nor is it a command-line utility like File Locate or Text Search. Rather, BE acts like an extension to the DOS command-line interpreter (COMMAND.COM) that gives you a dozen new commands that can be typed on the command line or included in batch files to display messages and menus on the screen, produce audio prompts, accept keyboard input, and control program flow. These commands serve to make the DOS batch file language a little less crude and a little more functional.

Batch Enhancer commands can be executed individually from the command line (from either the Norton menu or the DOS prompt), from a batch file (along with DOS commands), or from a script file (a file containing *only* BE commands).

Chapter Twenty-eight: Batch Enhancer (BE) ■ **435**

Command-Line Execution

You can execute single BE commands from the Norton menu or the DOS prompt. (This is useful mostly as a way of learning how the different commands work. To really harness the power of the BE commands, you must combine them in batch file or script file.) If you select BE on the Norton menu, you will see that it is initially followed on the command line by a question mark to show you a list of BE commands. Press **Enter** to see a list of the BE commands. To execute a command, delete or backspace over the question mark; type one of the 12 BE subcommands (see later) followed by appropriate parameters and options; then press **Enter**. DOS command-line operation is exactly the same, except that you don't have a question mark to eliminate; just type the BE command plus appropriate parameters or options, then press **Enter**. For information about any of the BE commands, from either the Norton menu or the DOS prompt, type BE command-name ? **Enter**.

Batch Files

You can use BE commands in batch files along with normal DOS commands. When BE commands are used in a batch file, each command is placed on a separate line (just like DOS commands), and each consists of BE, followed by a space, then the subcommand name, then the parameters and options for the command. This assumes that the Norton directory, where the BE utility is installed, is included in the DOS PATH statement in your AUTOEXEC.BAT file. If it isn't, you must preface each BE command with the appropriate path. If you are going to use BE commands regularly, it's obviously a good idea to include your Norton directory in the path statement, to save yourself the tedium of typing the full path for every BE command that you use.

Script Files

A script file is an ASCII text file that contains *only* Batch Enhancer commands. (DOS commands, if present, are ignored.) A script file does not use a .BAT extension and cannot be run from the command line just by typing the file name. A script is *interpreted* by the BE program. You execute a script file by typing

```
BE script_file [[GOTO] label]
```

436 ■ *Power Of...Norton Utilities*

on the command line. [GOTO] and [label] are optional parameters that cause execution to begin at a specific location in the file, rather than at the beginning. BE subcommands are entered in a script file just as they are in a batch file, except that you do not need to include BE before the subcommand name, and forward slashes are not required before command options.

BE script files can be executed alone or from within batch files. If what you are trying to do can be done with BE commands alone, it is preferable to use a script file rather than a normal batch file, because BE can execute the commands more quickly this way than when they are passed through DOS from a batch file. A script file can also be used to pass a long parameter list to the BEEP subcommand (see later), to play a musical phrase, for example.

BATCH ENHANCER SUBCOMMAND REFERENCE

You must use the BE preface on each Batch Enhancer command in a DOS batch file. Within a script file, the BE preface is not required (BE ASK and ASK are equivalent). The syntax shown for each of the following commands is shown as the command would be used in a batch file or on a command line. The BE subcommands are ASK, BEEP, BOX, CLS, DELAY, MONTHDAY, PRINTCHAR, REBOOT, ROWCOL, SA, SHIFTSTATE, TRIGGER, WEEKDAY, and WINDOW.

ASK

The ASK subcommand requests an input from the keyboard and returns a DOS errorlevel code. Its syntax is as follows:

```
BE ASK "prompt" [key-list] [DEFAULT=key] [TIMEOUT=n]
[ADJUST=n] [color] [/DEBUG]
```

The available parameters are the following:

prompt   Display a text string on the screen when the command is run. The prompt must be enclosed in quotes. Use two quotes together ("") for no prompt.

Chapter Twenty-eight: Batch Enhancer (BE) ■ **437**

key-list	List the keys (characters or numbers) that are acceptable for the response. If no key-list is given, pressing any key will continue the batch file.
DEFAULT=key	Specify the key to be returned if no key is pressed within the timeout period or if **Enter** is pressed.
TIMEOUT=n	Specify the time in seconds to wait before the default key is returned. If n is zero, or if no TIMEOUT is specified, ASK will wait indefinitely.
ADJUST	Add this amount to the errorlevel value returned.
color	Set the screen colors and attributes for the prompt message in SA format (see later).
/DEBUG	Display the errorlevel code returned by the command.

Comments

ASK queries the user for a response in the form of keyboard input and then returns this input to the calling batch file or script file as an errorlevel code (a numeric value) that can be used by the next command to control program flow. The first key in the key-list returns errorlevel 1, the second key returns errorlevel 2, and so on. In combination with the DOS IF ERRORLEVEL n GOTO command, this makes interactive batch files possible.

The prompt text asks the user for a response and the key-list specifies what keys are acceptable responses. The command can wait indefinitely for a response, or it can wait for a specified period before executing a default option.

The following simple batch file illustrates the use of the ASK command. (It uses several other BE commands as well, but we need not be concerned with them at the moment.) The batch file writes a prompt on the screen asking you to choose whether to draw a magenta window, draw a green window, or quit. It accepts the input from the keyboard; draws the specified window, if appropriate; then quits, displaying the message "the END" at the bottom of the screen.

Listing 28.1

```
echo off
be cls black on white
be ask "magenta window (M) green window (G), or Quit (Q)?" mgq
```

```
if errorlevel 3 goto quit
if errorlevel 2 goto green
if errorlevel 1 goto magenta

:magenta
be window 7 19 19 59 bright white on magenta
goto quit

:green
be window 7 19 19 59 bright white on green

:quit
be delay 90
be rowcol 24 1 "The END  "
```

The first line that is of real interest is line 3, which consists of the BE ASK command with its prompt message and key-list. (The various other optional parameters of the ASK command have been omitted.) Observe that the key-list, at the right end of the line, consists of the letters "mgq," in the same order that they appear in the prompt statement. No TIMEOUT is specified, so the batch file will wait an indefinite period until an appropriate key is pressed. Any key other than those in the key-list will cause the program to beep, indicating an error. Note that the ASK command is not case sensitive; either upper-case or lower-case characters will produce the same response.

The next three lines test the errorlevel code to determine what action to take. Observe that in these lines, the errorlevel codes are tested for in an order *opposite* to that in which they are specified in the key list. This is essential for the proper operation of the batch file. The errorlevel codes *must* be tested in the order opposite to that in which they are listed in the key list.

The remainder of the file consists of the labels that are the targets of the GOTO statements: ":magenta," ":green," and ":quit," and the commands that execute their actions. Note that at the ":magenta" label, the command that draws the magenta window is followed by a GOTO QUIT command. If this command were not present, the magenta window would be overwritten immediately by a green window.

Errorlevel codes are a method used by DOS to pass information about the outcome of an operation to a batch file. In this context, the use of errorlevel codes does not indicate that any error has occurred or is expected to occur.

Chapter Twenty-eight: Batch Enhancer (BE) ■ **439**

BEEP

The BEEP command produces a tone of specified frequency and duration from the computer's speaker. Its syntax is as follows:

```
BE BEEP [/Dn] [/Fn] [/Rn] [/Wn] [/E]
```

or

```
BE BEEP script-file [/E]
```

The parameters are the following:

/Dn	The duration of the tone, *n* eighteenths of a second.
/Fn	The frequency of the tone, *n* cycles per second (Hertz).
/Rn	The number of times (*n*) the tone is repeated.
/Wn	The wait time following the tone, n eighteenths of a second.
script-file	The path and name of the script file containing a parameter list.
/E	Display the quoted text in comments.

Comments

The BE BEEP command uses the computer speaker to produce tones of a specified frequency and duration. These tones can be used to signal error conditions or the completion of a task, or, if you're feeling ambitious, you can use than to play a tune using an appropriate script file. A comment can be entered on any BE BEEP command line if you precede it by a semicolon. If you use the /E option and if you enclose the comment in quotes, the comment will be displayed on the screen when the file is executed (see Example 2).

Examples:

1. To play the A above middle C for one second and repeat it four times with a half-second pause between notes, type

```
BE BEEP /F440 /D18 /R4 /W9
```

2. The following is an example of how the BEEP command is used with a script file. Type the following script:

440 ■ *Power Of...Norton Utilities*

```
/F260 /D10 ; "The"
/F520 /D15; "rain"
/F494 /D5 ; "in"
/F520 /D10 ; "Spain"
/F554 /D10 ; "stays"
/F588 /D15 ; "main-"
/F466 /D5 ; "ly"
/F392 /D10 ; "in"
/F330 /D10 ; "the"
/F392 /D5 ; "plain.--"
/F350 /D20 /W36 ; "—"
EXIT
```

Save the preceding script in an ASCII file called "FAIR" (no extension required). At the DOS prompt, type

```
BE FAIR /E
```

The opening phrase of "The Rain in Spain" is played on the speaker, and the lyrics are displayed on the screen in sync with the notes. Omit the /E option and the notes will be played, but the lyrics will not be displayed.

BOX

The BOX command draws a rectangle at the specified location on the screen. The resulting rectangle is transparent; that is, it doesn't overwrite text that is currently on the screen, except for text that falls directly under the borders, which are one character thick. Its syntax is as follows:

```
BE BOX top left bottom right [SINGLE|DOUBLE] [color]
```

The parameters are the following:

top/left   The row/column coordinates of the upper-left corner of the box.

bottom/right   The row/column coordinates of the lower-right corner of the box.

[SINGLE|DOUBLE] A single or double outline (double is the default).

[color] The color for the box border, in SA format (described later).

To draw a blue, double-lined box on a cyan background type

```
BE BOX 5 5 20 50 DOUBLE BLUE ON CYAN
```

CLS

The CLS command clears the screen and sets an optional color specification. Its syntax is as follows:

```
BE CLS [color]
```

The parameter is the following:

[color] Set the screen colors and attributes using the SA format (see later).

Comment

Unlike the DOS CLS (clearscreen) command, BE CLS can clear the screen to a specified foreground/background color combination with optional attributes. This is useful in setting the stage for commands such as ASK, ROWCOL, and BOX, so that they can be used with the default color settings.

BE CLS produces the same results as BE SA /CLS (see later), but BE CLS doesn't require the ANSI.SYS driver, and therefore may be preferable for casual use.

DELAY

The DELAY command pauses the execution of a batch file or script file for a specified length of time, in clock ticks (one tick = $\frac{1}{18}$ second). Its syntax is as follows:

```
BE DELAY [ticks]
```

The parameter is the following:

[ticks] Set the number of clock ticks to pause.

442 ■ *Power Of...Norton Utilities*

Comments

This command is generally used to slow the progress of the batch file so that information is left on the screen long enough to be read. To pause the execution of a file for two seconds, for example, use

```
BE DELAY 36
```

EXIT

The EXIT command terminates the execution of a Batch Enhancer script file. Its syntax is as follows:

```
BE EXIT
```

Comments

The EXIT command can only be used in script files. "BE EXIT" has no meaning when used at the DOS prompt or in a batch file. (There is a DOS EXIT command, but it has an entirely different purpose.) When called, "BE EXIT" terminates the script file and returns you to the DOS prompt. This allows you to have to have several self-terminating execution sections in a single script file. Use the GOTO command to branch selectively to a self-terminating section of a script file.

GOTO label

The GOTO label command controls the starting point in a Batch Enhancer script file. Its syntax is as follows:

```
BE script-file [[GOTO] label]
```

The parameters are the following:

script-file   The path and file name of the script file containing the label.

label   A label within the script file.

Comments

This command is used when starting a script file from the command line or from a batch file. It is *not* used inside a script file to control the flow of execution. Use the JUMP command (see later) for the latter purpose. The GOTO label command, used in conjunction with the EXIT command, allows you to include several independent commands in a single script file and execute only one by specifying its label on the command line. The GOTO portion of the parameter is optional. The label parameter alone is sufficient to control the starting point in a script file. The label must be on a line by itself and must start in column 1 with a colon.

JUMP

The JUMP command allows conditional branching within script files. Its syntax is as follows:

```
JUMP label1 [, label2 [, ..., labeln]] [/DEFAULT:label]
```

The parameters are the following:

label	A label in a script file.
/DEFAULT:label	The label used if the errorlevel is zero or if it is greater than the number of labels.

Comments

The JUMP command allows conditional branching based on the errorlevel code of the previous command. It is used in script files in place of the IF ERROR-LEVEL *n* GOTO command, which is used only in batch files.

You use JUMP by specifying a series of labels. The errorlevel code resulting from a previous command is used to select one of the labels for execution. For example, if the errorlevel code is 1, the first label is selected; if the errorlevel code is 2, the second label is selected; and so on. If the errorlevel code is zero or if no label exists for the errorlevel code, the execution continues at the DEFAULT label. For example, if the errorlevel code is 8 but there are only seven labels, the execution continues at the DEFAULT label. If no default label was specified, execution continues with the next line in the script file.

444 ■ *Power Of...Norton Utilities*

MONTHDAY

The MONTHDAY command returns the day of the month (1–31) to a batch or script file. Its syntax is as follows:

```
BE MONTHDAY [/DEBUG]
```

The parameter is the following:

/DEBUG   Display the errorlevel value returned.

Comments

MONTHDAY returns a number (1–31) to a batch file as an errorlevel code. The DOS IF ERRORLEVEL command can be used in a batch file to test the errorlevel code, or the BE JUMP command can be used in a script file for the same purpose.

   To display the day of the month, type

```
BE MONTHDAY /DEBUG Enter
```

PRINTCHAR

The PRINTCHAR command prints the specified character the specified number of times beginning at the current cursor position. Its syntax is as follows:

```
BE PRINTCHAR character, count [color]
```

The parameters are the following:

character   The character to be displayed (the actual character, *not* its ASCII code).

count   The number of times to print the character (maximum 80).

color   The colors for the character and background in SA format (see later).

Comments

This command can be used to quickly draw lines separating blocks of text. For example, to print 15 green underscores beginning at the current cursor position type

BE PRINTCHAR _ 15 green **Enter**

REBOOT

The REBOOT command causes a warm reboot of the computer (equivalent to pressing **Ctrl+Alt+Del)**. Its syntax is as follows:

BE REBOOT [/V]

The Parameter is the following:

/V (for verify) Prompt for confirmation of the reboot command.

Comments

BE REBOOT gives you the ability to boot your computer from a batch file. This is useful when the batch file affects the system configuration.

The following is a batch file that I use to reconfigure my environment and reboot the system. I have three different sets of AUTOEXEC.BAT and CONFIG.SYS files: one to run a shell, one to run Windows, and a "plain vanilla" set that doesn't install any unnecessary TSRs or drivers (for troubleshooting, diagnosing conflicts, and so on). This batch file allows me to select one of the three setups from the keyboard, copies the necessary files, and then reboots the system to activate the new AUTOEXEC.BAT and CONFIG.SYS files. Note that as in listing 28.1, the if-errorlevel statements are in the opposite order to the keys in the key-list. For a full explanation, see the description of the ASK command given earlier.

Listing 28.2

```
echo off
be cls black on white
be ask "configure for Shell (S), Windows (W) or Plain
Vanilla (V), or Quit (Q) ?" swvq
if errorlevel 4 goto quit
if errorlevel 3 qoto vanilla
if errorlevel 2 goto windows
```

446 ■ *Power Of...Norton Utilities*

```
if errorlevel 1 goto shell

:shell
copy autoexec.shl autoexec.bat
copy config.shl config.sys
be reboot

:windows
copy autoexec.win autoexec.bat
copy config.win config.sys
be reboot

:vanilla
copy autoexec.van autoexec.bat
copy config.van config.sys
be reboot

:quit
```

ROWCOL

The ROWCOL command positions the cursor at the specified horizontal row and vertical column and displays an optional message. Its syntax is as follows:

```
BE ROWCOL row col ["text"] [color]
```

The parameters are the following:

row/col   The row and column coordinates of the cursor position to move to.

text   An optional line of text to be displayed (quotes are required).

color   The foreground and background colors for the text, in SA format (see later).

Comments

The ROWCOL command allows you to position the cursor anywhere on the screen. The next command will then display the text beginning at this cursor position. You can also use this command to select a color specification for the text. If you do not specify a color, the current screen colors are used.

Chapter Twenty-eight: Batch Enhancer (BE) ■ **447**

The text-mode screen is normally divided into 25 rows and 80 columns. (EGA and VGA screens, however, can use display formats with more rows and columns of text. See Chapter 25.) Hence, the row parameter is normally a number from 0 to 24 and the col parameter is normally a number from 0 to 79. The text parameter in the ROWCOL subcommand is a message you want displayed at the specified location. You must enclose the text in quotation marks. For example, to display text near the middle of the screen, type

BE ROWCOL 12 27 "CENTER SPOT" BRIGHT RED ON WHITE **Enter**

The words "CENTER SPOT" are displayed near the center of the screen with red text on a white background.

SA (Screen Attributes)

The SA command controls the colors and attributes displayed on the screen. Its syntax is as follows:

SA NORMAL|UNDERLINE|REVERSE [/N]

or

SA [BRIGHT|BLINKING] foreground [ON background] [/N] [/CLS]

The parameters are the following:

UNDERLINE	Underline subsequent text. (This only works on monochrome monitors.)
REVERSE	Reverse foreground and background colors.
NORMAL	Restore the subsequent text to the default setting after using the UNDERLINE or REVERSE attribute.
BRIGHT	Display subsequent test in high intensity. BOLD may be used in place of BRIGHT.
BLINKING	Turn the "blinking" attribute on for subsequent text.
foreground	Specify the foreground color.
background	Specify the background color.

/N   Do not set the border color (defaults to the same color as the background).

/CLS   Clear the screen after setting the attributes.

Comments

The SA command has two forms. The first form allows you to specify either underline or reverse video for subsequent text. Use NORMAL to undo the UNDERLINE or REVERSE setting.

The second form of the SA command sets text (foreground) and background colors and can select high-intensity (bright) colors or the blinking attribute. The available colors for the foreground and background are white, red, blue, cyan, black, magenta, green, and yellow. Used in combination with the bright or bold attribute, this gives eight background and 16 foreground colors, for a total of 128 possible foreground/background combinations. The SA format color settings are also used by the ASK, BOX, CLS, PRINTCHAR, ROW-COL, and WINDOW commands.

The BE SA command requires that you install the ANSI.SYS driver in your CONFIG.SYS file. The ANSI.SYS is probably in your DOS directory or on one of your DOS diskettes. To load the ANSI.SYS file, add the following line to your CONFIG.SYS file:

```
DEVICE=ANSI.SYS
```

If ANSI.SYS is not in your root directory, you will have to either copy it there or include the path in the DEVICE line (e.g., DEVICE=C:\DOS\ANSI.SYS).

NOTE   Some versions of DOS automatically install ANSI.SYS, but most do not. To test whether you have the ANSI.SYS driver installed, type the command BE SA NORMAL at the prompt. If the ANSI.SYS driver is not installed, a message appears indicating that the driver is not installed and that the specified colors may change.

NOTE   You can also use the Norton Control Center (NCC) to set the DOS colors (see Chapter 25).

The SA command is convenient for setting the color and attributes for use in DOS. (The colors you set with SA at the DOS prompt or in a batch file may not remain in effect when you load an application. Most current applications have their own facilities for setting screen colors and attributes that override settings made at the DOS level.) You can also use it to call attention to special conditions during the course of a batch file operation. The reverse and blinking attributes are useful for this purpose. The color and attribute combinations that work best will depend on the lighting conditions in your work environment and on your personal taste, but the following combinations are usually considered attractive:

```
BE SA BRIGHT WHITE ON BLUE
BE SA BRIGHT YELLOW ON BLUE
BE SA BLACK ON WHITE
```

Many programs alter screen colors and attributes and do not restore them to their previous state on termination. You can use SA in a batch file such as the following to restore your screen colors:

```
start_program
BE SA BRIGHT WHITE ON BLUE
```

The first line of this batch file starts your application (substitute your program's path and name for start_program). The second line restores your screen settings after you exit the application.

NOTE

Although several other Batch Enhancer commands use the same color format as the SA command, they do not require the ANSI.SYS driver.

The following are some examples:

1. To set the display to reverse video, type

BE SA REVERSE **Enter**

To return the screen to the usual display, type

450 ■ *Power Of...Norton Utilities*

```
BE SA NORMAL
```

2. To set the display to blinking red text on a white background, type

```
BE SA BLINKING RED ON WHITE Enter
```

3. To change the display to nonblinking white text on a black background, type

```
BE SA BRIGHT WHITE ON BLACK Enter
```

SHIFTSTATE

The SHIFTSTATE command reports the status of the **Shift**, **Alt**, and **Ctrl** keys as an errorlevel value:

Value	Key
1	**Right Shift**
2	**Left Shift**
4	**Ctrl (left or right)**
8	**Alt (left or right)**

The syntax for SHIFTSTATE is as follows:

```
BE SHIFTSTATE [/DEBUG]
```

The Parameter is the following:

/DEBUG   Displays the errorlevel value.

TRIGGER

The TRIGGER command halts the execution of a batch file until a specified time (according to the system clock). The syntax is as follows:

Chapter Twenty-eight: Batch Enhancer (BE) ▪ 451

```
BE TRIGGER hh:mm [AM|PM]
```

The parameters are the following:

hh:mm Time using 24-hour format (0:00 to 23:59).

AM|PM Optional time using 12-hour format.

Comments

The BE TRIGGER command allows a batch file to be paused until a specified time. The time can be entered in either a 24-hour or 12-hour format. With the 12-hour format, the AM and PM options are used. (12:00 AM is the same as midnight. 12:00 PM is the same as noon.)

The following provides an example of this command: Type **TIME** and press **Enter** to determine your current system time. Return to the NDOS prompt and type the BE TRIGGER command with a time about one minute later than the current system time. For example, if the current system time is 2:00 P.M., type **BE TRIGGER 2:01 PM** and press **Enter**. The system is locked for one minute. At the end of the one minute the prompt is again available for entering data.

You can type **Ctrl+Break** to cancel the trigger command (or any command in a batch file).

NOTE

WEEKDAY

The WEEKDAY command returns the day of the week to the batch file as an errorlevel code (Sunday = 1; Saturday = 7). The syntax is as follows:

```
BE WEEKDAY [/DEBUG]
```

The parameter is the following:

/DEBUG Display the errorlevel value returned.

WINDOW

The WINDOW command draws a filled rectangle of a specified size at a specified location on the screen, with an optional drop shadow and zoom effect. The syntax is as follows:

```
WINDOW top left bottom right [color] [SINGLE|DOUBLE]
[ZOOM|EXPLODE] [SHADOW]
```

The parameters are the following:

top/left	The row/column coordinates of the upper left corner of the window.
bottom/right	The row/column coordinates of the lower right corner of the window.
color	The window colors in SA format.
SINGLE|DOUBLE	The border style for the window (DOUBLE is the default).
ZOOM	The window zooms in (or expands) while it is drawn. (EXPLODE is a synonym for ZOOM.)
SHADOW	A transparent drop shadow is added to the window.

Comments

The WINDOW and BOX subcommands are similar in that they draw rectangular boxes. They differ in that WINDOW draws an opaque box that overwrites anything that was displayed on the screen within its boundaries, whereas the BOX command just draws a border around the specified area. The WINDOW command is useful for creating menus and/or highlighting messages.

For example, to draw a white window with a blue double border and a drop shadow, type

```
BE WINDOW 5 5 18 50 BLUE ON WHITE SHADOW
```

NOTE The drop shadow is always black and therefore cannot be seen if it is drawn over a black background.

Chapter Twenty-eight: Batch Enhancer (BE) ■ 453

CREATING AND EDITING BATCH OR SCRIPT FILES

A batch file is an ASCII text file containing one or more DOS or Batch Enhancer commands. A script file is an ASCII file that contains *only* BE commands. Either can be created and edited using the same tools and procedures.

The EDLIN line editor, supplied with all DOS versions since 1.0, is intended for creating batch files and other ASCII files, but it is very awkward and difficult to use. If you want to experience what computing was like 20 years ago, try to create a significant file using EDLIN. Otherwise, avoid it.

You can also use the DOS COPY CON command to create simple batch and script files. If you're not familiar with this command, the syntax is as follows:

COPY CON:file_spec Enter

This command redirects subsequent command lines typed at the DOS prompt to the file you have specified. Type each line then press **Enter** at the end of the line. After the last line, type **^Z** (**Ctrl+Z**) and press **Enter** again to save the file.

The problem with this method is that there's no way to correct an error after you've pressed **Enter** at the end of a given line. The only way to change the file is to abort the process by typing **^Z** or **^C** and then to start again at the beginning. Hence, this method is suitable for creating simple files of two or three lines, but not much more.

You can use your word processor to create a batch file, but you must remember to save the file as an ASCII file, rather than in the word processor's format. Another possible problem is line wrap; each BE command or DOS command in a batch or script file must occupy a single line. BE and DOS will accept lines up to 128 characters long, but word processors are designed to format lines so that they print properly on a standard sheet of paper within specified margins. Lines that are too long will be broken and wrapped to the next line. This is fine if you're writing a letter or a memo, but it is unacceptable in a batch or script file. If a line in a file is broken and the file is saved as ASCII, a carriage return and line feed are inserted in the file at the line break. When DOS or the BE command tries to read the file, the first half of the line is incomplete. It will probably execute but may be missing some parameters. The second half of the line will be interpreted as an illegal command and will generate an error condition. You may be able to get satisfactory results from your word processor by

454 ■ *Power Of...Norton Utilities*

setting the left and right margins as wide as possible and selecting a small font. Check your files carefully after you save them to be sure that no inappropriate line wraps have occurred.

The best way to create and edit batch and script files is to use an ASCII-only text editor, such as the Windows Notepad, the editor in the Norton Commander, or the EDIT program that comes with DOS version 5.0 or later. A great many other ASCII text editors exist that are designed for creating and editing program source code and loaded with the features that serious programmers want. If you're a programmer, you probably already have one or more and will use it for creating batch and script files. If you're not a programmer and don't intend to become one, one of the simple programs listed earlier will prove more than adequate for creating the occasional batch or script file.

A Sample Batch File

Listing 28.3 is a sample batch file that uses BE commands and DOS commands to create a menu or shell from which you can start application programs or run DOS commands. It creates a menu on the screen using the WINDOW and ROWCOL commands, then accepts keyboard input to select the application to run, using the ASK and IF ERRORLEVEL commands. It would not be possible to do this using only DOS commands, but the BE commands make it relatively simple. Obviously, to use this batch file on your system, you must substitute the names, directory locations, and start-up commands of your applications for those in the sample.

Listing 28.3

```
REM A Sample Batch File that Creates a Screen Menu
REM From which you can select Applications or a DOS Shell
PAUSE
ECHO OFF
:start
BE SA BRIGHT WHITE ON RED /CLS
BE WINDOW 1 1 23 77 BRIGHT WHITE ON BLUE ZOOM
BE WINDOW 3 9 20 69 BRIGHT WHITE ON MAGENTA SHADOW
BE ROWCOL 5 32 "Selection Menu"
```

Chapter Twenty-eight: Batch Enhancer (BE) ■ 455

```
BE ROWCOL 7 30 "1 - WordPerfect" BRIGHT WHITE
BE ROWCOL 8 30 "2 - Norton Utilities" BRIGHT WHITE
BE ROWCOL 9 30 "3 - Norton Commander" BRIGHT WHITE
BE ROWCOL 10 30 "4 - Lotus 1-2-3" BRIGHT WHITE
BE ROWCOL 11 30 "5 - Hotshot Grab" BRIGHT WHITE
BE ROWCOL 12 30 "6 - Cakewalk" BRIGHT WHITE
BE ROWCOL 13 30 "7 - DOS Shell" BRIGHT WHITE
BE ROWCOL 14 30 "8 - Quit" BRIGHT WHITE
BE ROWCOL 16 17 "Please select a number." BRIGHT WHITE
BE ROWCOL 18 17

BE ASK "Select 1, 2, 3, 4, 5, 6, 7, or 8", 12345678
   IF ERRORLEVEL 8 GOTO quit
   IF ERRORLEVEL 7 GOTO DOS shell
   IF ERRORLEVEL 6 GOTO cakewalk
   IF ERRORLEVEL 5 GOTO hotshot
   IF ERRORLEVEL 4 GOTO 123
   IF ERRORLEVEL 3 GOTO nc
   IF ERRORLEVEL 2 GOTO nu
   IF EFRRORLEVEL 1 GOTO wp


:wp
CD\WP51
WP
GOTO start

:nu
CD\NU
NORTON
GOTO start

:nc
CD\NC
NC
GOTO start

:123
D:
CD\LOTUS
123
GOTO start
```

456 ■ *Power Of...Norton Utilities*

```
:hotshotgrab
C:
CD\HSG
GRAB
HSG
GOTO start

:cakewalk
E:
CD\CAKEWALK
CAKEWALK
GOTO start

:dos shell
BE CLS
BE BOX 10 20 15 60 DOUBLE BRIGHT BLUE
BE ROWCOL 11 25 "The DOS Shell allows you to run" bright
white on blue
BE ROWCOL 12 25 "any DOS command. To Return to " bright
white on blue
BE ROWCOL 13 25 "the Selection Menu, type " bright white on
blue
BE ROWCOL 14 25 " EXIT " bright green on white
BE DELAY 180
BE SA NORMAL
C:
CD\DOS
COMMAND.COM
GOTO start

:quit

BE SA NORMAL
BE CLS
ECHO ON
```

The first command, ECHO OFF, is a DOS command that prevents the text of the batch file from being displayed on the screen while the file is being executed. This makes operation faster and prevents our menu from being cluttered with unnecessary messages.

Chapter Twenty-eight: Batch Enhancer (BE) ■ **457**

The block of lines after the ":start" label clears the screen, draws a window with the WINDOW command, then uses a series of ROWCOL commands to print the text of the menu. Next comes the ASK command, which accepts keyboard input for the menu selections, and the series of IF ERRORLEVEL statements that process the keyboard input and direct the program flow to the appropriate label to start the specified application.

Most of the labeled subroutines are fairly self-explanatory. They change to the appropriate drive and directory for the specified application and then issue the command to start the application. Each subroutine ends with the line "GOTO start"; this is necessary so that when you quit the application you will be returned to the menu so you can select another application. If this line were omitted, when you left an application the batch file would "fall through" to the next application, and so on, to the end of the list.

The DOS shell subroutine is a bit more elaborate than the others. It allows you to execute DOS commands and then return to the menu. It clears the screen, uses the BOX command to draw a frame, and then uses a series of ROWCOL commands to explain how the DOS shell works. After a delay of 10 seconds, it loads a new copy of COMMAND.COM (as all DOS shell programs do) to execute your DOS commands. When you terminate the DOS shell by typing **exit**, you are returned to the menu.

The :quit subroutine restores screen colors to normal, clears the screen, and turns echo back on.

SUMMARY

The Batch Enhancer provides 12 new commands that you can use in combination with DOS commands to create more powerful batch files. Batch Enhancer commands can also be used alone in script files for faster execution.

Examining Configuration and Analyzing Performance with Norton System Information

The Norton System Information utility (SYSINFO) lets you examine all aspects of your system. You can obtain information on hardware, disks, memory usage, network conditions, and benchmark comparisons to other computers. You can use System Information to

- ◆ examine the configuration of your system;
- ◆ view the contents of configuration files;
- ◆ get information needed for installing expansion boards or other peripheral devices;
- ◆ solve device driver and TSR conflicts;

460 ■ *Power Of...Norton Utilities*

◆ examine the configuration of the disks;

◆ get information on your network;

◆ test your CPU and hard-disk performance and compare it with other systems.

NETWORK USAGE

If your system is connected to a Novell NetWare network, SYSINFO will report on user and network information. This feature is available only with Novell NetWare networks.

Compatibility Considerations

System Information attempts to identify the make and model of computer it is running on. It recognizes and reports on all standard IBM PC-family members and many compatibles, but it cannot identify all MS-DOS-type computers. If SYSINFO is unable to identify your computer, it will attempt to show you some identifying marks, such as the copyright notice in your ROM BIOS.

In performing its tests, SYSINFO probes every part of an IBM computer's memory. On some computers, some of the memory that SYSINFO tries to test may not exist. When SYSINFO attempts to probe the nonexistent memory, the computer may report a parity error and lock up. This does not harm the computer, but you will have to reboot before you can continue. You can bypass this test by using the /N (no memory test) option.

RUNNING SYSTEM INFORMATION

Start the System Information utility by selecting it from the Norton menu or by typing SYSINFO **Enter** at the DOS prompt.

The System Summary Screen

When you first load the SYSINFO program it displays a System Summary screen such as that in Figure 29.1. The screen displays the basic information about your system configuration, most of which is self-explanatory.

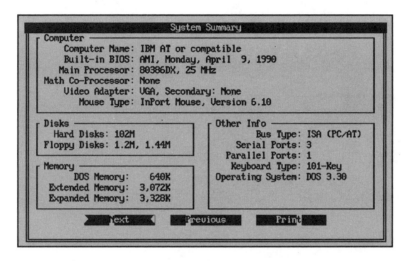

Figure 29.1 *The System Summary screen*

At the bottom of the screen are three buttons: **Next**, **Previous**, and **Print**. These buttons remain operative for all the screens in the SYSINFO program.

- ◆ **Next** advances you to the next information screen. (It steps sequentially through all the items on the menus, described later.)
- ◆ **Previous** displays the previous information screen.
- ◆ **Print** displays the Print Current Information dialog box, shown in Figure 29.2.

Select **Printer** to print the currently displayed information. Select **File** to print the information to a disk file. Selecting this option will display a dialog box in which you can specify a path and file name where the information is to be saved. **Cancel** returns you to the System Information screen with no options selected.

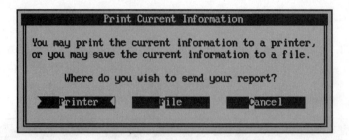

Figure 29.2 The Print Current Information dialog box

The Menu Bar

At the top of the System Information screen is a menu bar that contains six menus—File, System, Disks, Memory, Benchmarks, and Help—that provide direct access to specific System Information screens (rather than using the **Next/Previous** buttons). Press **Alt** or **F10** to access the menu bar.

The File Menu

The File menu allows you to view the contents of five files that, if present, have a significant effect on your computer's configuration and operation:

- CONFIG.SYS
- AUTOEXEC.BAT
- NDOS.INI (initialization file for the NDOS command interpreter, if installed)
- WIN.INI (initialization file for Windows 3.*x*, if present)
- SYSTEM.INI (another Windows 3.*x* initialization file)

The final item on the File menu, **Report**, allows you to print a complete report of *all* the SYSINFO options or selected options. Selecting **Report** opens the dialog box in Figure 29.3. You can scroll through the list of options in the scroll box and include or exclude individual options from the report by checking and unchecking them with the spacebar. You can print the report to your printer or save it to a file. Use the list box below the scroll box to select the destination for your report.

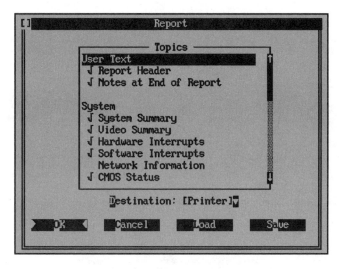

Figure 29.3 *The Report dialog box*

At the bottom of the dialog box are four buttons: **OK**, **Cancel**, **Load**, and **Save**.

- **OK** generates the report with the settings you have specified.
- **Cancel** exits the Report dialog box.
- **Load** loads a set of report options that you previously saved in a file.
- **Save** saves the current settings (i.e., the items in the scroll box that are checked) in a file.

The System Menu

The System menu contains five options that provide more detailed information about hardware and software use, and a summary of your system and network.

System Summary—displays the System Summary screen. (This is the same screen that is displayed when you first load the program.)

Video Summary—displays information about your display adapter, monitor type, current video mode, character resolution, and installed video RAM (see Figure 29.4).

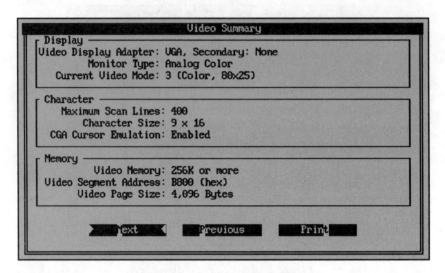

Figure 29.4 Video Summary dialog box

Even if your video card has more than 256Kb of video memory, SYSINFO will only show 256Kb. This is because IBM has defined a standard way to ask the video card how much memory is available, and it limits the answer to 256Kb or less.

Hardware Interrupts—displays a list of your system's hardware interrupts such as that in Figure 29.5, along with the devices or programs that "own" them, in a scroll box.

A hardware interrupt is a signal generated by a device such as the keyboard, mouse, or printer. Interrupts are usually generated when some input or output is required. When the CPU receives an interrupt signal, it stops what it's doing (i.e., running an application) and jumps to a block of code that "services" the interrupt. When this is done, it goes back to the previous task and picks up where it left off. All interrupts are prioritized. Those with highest priority are serviced first. Each hardware device is assigned its own signal so the computer can recognize it. The screen shows the interrupt (IRQ) number, the hex address of the interrupt code, the name of the device that generates the interrupt, and the program that uses the hardware.

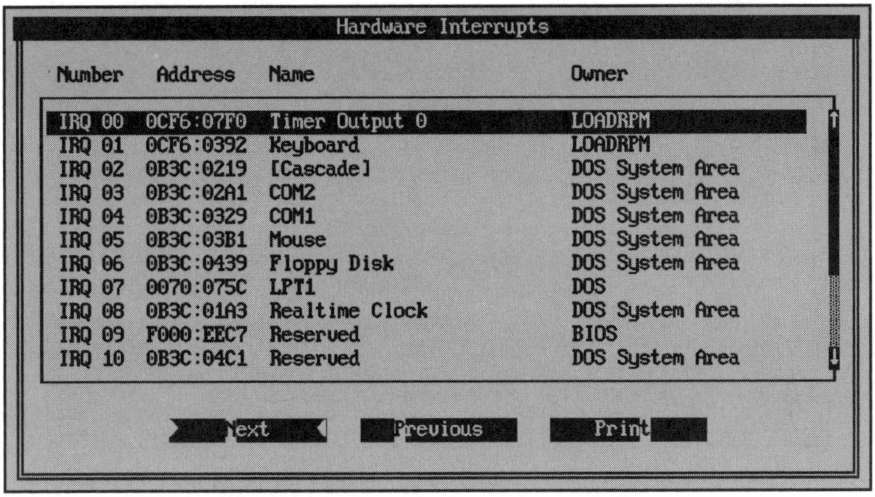

Chapter Twenty-nine: Norton System Information (SYSINFO) ■ 465

```
                    Hardware Interrupts
    Number    Address    Name                 Owner

    IRQ 00   0CF6:07F0   Timer Output 0       LOADRPM
    IRQ 01   0CF6:0392   Keyboard             LOADRPM
    IRQ 02   0B3C:0219   [Cascade]            DOS System Area
    IRQ 03   0B3C:02A1   COM2                 DOS System Area
    IRQ 04   0B3C:0329   COM1                 DOS System Area
    IRQ 05   0B3C:03B1   Mouse                DOS System Area
    IRQ 06   0B3C:0439   Floppy Disk          DOS System Area
    IRQ 07   0070:075C   LPT1                 DOS
    IRQ 08   0B3C:01A3   Realtime Clock       DOS System Area
    IRQ 09   F000:EEC7   Reserved             BIOS
    IRQ 10   0B3C:04C1   Reserved             DOS System Area


            Next          Previous          Print
```

Figure 29.5 Hardware Interrupts dialog box

The hardware interrupt list is useful when you want to install a new hardware device (e.g., an expansion board) in your system. These devices usually require hardware interrupts and can often be programmed by switches or jumpers or by software options to select one of several interrupts. Before installing a new device, check the hardware interrupt list to see what interrupts are available, so you don't create a conflict by selecting an interrupt that's already in use.

Software Interrupts—displays a list of the software interrupts such as that in Figure 29.6, with the interrupt number, interrupt name, interrupt handler address, and the owner. Software interrupts are similar to hardware interrupts except that they are generated by system software or application software. They are used for essentially the same purpose: controlling access to I/O devices. There are 256 possible software interrupts.

Software conflicts sometimes arise because different programs, drivers, and TSRs attempt to use the same software interrupt. (More than one program *can* use the same interrupt safely, provided that they behave properly and do not interfere with each other's interrupt-handler code.) If you are experiencing a possible software conflict, check the software interrupt list to see if two programs are sharing an interrupt. If so, check the programs' documentation to see whether you can change the interrupt usage of one of the programs.

466 ■ *Power Of...Norton Utilities*

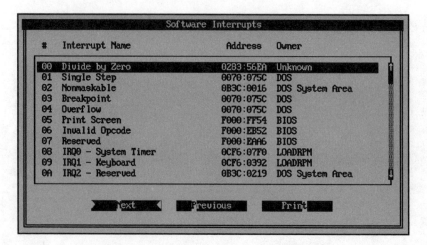

Figure 29.6 Software Interrupts screen

Network Information—is available only if you are using Novell NetWare. It provides user and network information.

CMOS Status—provides a summary of the configuration information stored in your CMOS setup memory. This includes information about your hard disk, floppy disk drives, and installed memory. Figure 29.7 shows a typical CMOS Values display. The setup program values are checked against the CMOS checksum to determine if values have changed. Incorrect values are shown in red or bold text. If the checksum values are wrong or there are other errors, you should run your Setup program to correct them. If you still have problems after running Setup, you may need to replace the battery.

The Disks Menu

The Disks menu contains three items:

Disk Summary—displays a list of the disks currently installed such as that in Figure 29.8, including floppy drives, hard drives and/or logical volumes, and the drive letter available for new drives. It also lists the active directory for each installed drive. When a drive letter is listed as available, it can be used either for a new hardware drive or for a "virtual disk" created by the DOS SUBSTITUTE command or the Norton Diskreet program.

Chapter Twenty-nine: Norton System Information (SYSINFO) ■ 467

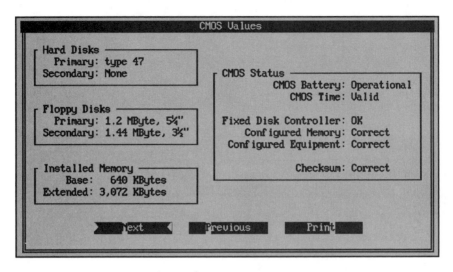

Figure 29.7 The CMOS Status screen

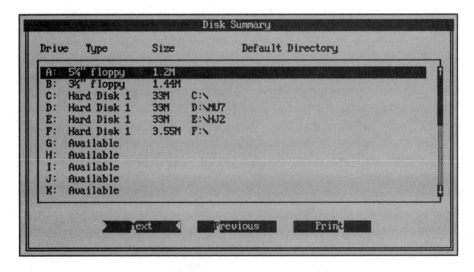

Figure 29.8 Disk Summary screen

Disk Characteristics—displays the logical and physical characteristics of the drive highlighted in the box at the right side of the screen (Figure 29.9). Use the arrow keys to select the drive you want, and the display will change to reflect the characteristics of that drive.

468 ■ *Power Of...Norton Utilities*

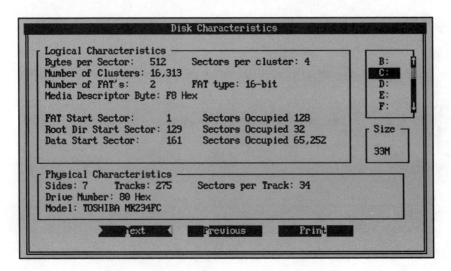

Figure 29.9 Disk Characteristics screen

NOTE
For a detailed discussion of the terms on the Disk Characteristics screen, refer to Chapter 23.

Logical characteristics are determined by the size of the selected disk partition (hard disks only), by the number of bytes per sector, and by the number of sectors per cluster. These, in turn, are determined by the disk type. The logical characteristics determine how many clusters are on a disk, which in turn determines the type of file allocation table (FAT) that is used: Disks with more than 4085 clusters require a 16-bit FAT, whereas those with fewer clusters can use a 12-bit FAT.

The physical characteristics section tells you the number of heads, tracks, and sectors per track on the selected disk. Some hard-disk controllers, including ESDI, IDE, or SCSI controllers, may "remap" the disk geometry so that the physical disk looks like a type that is supported by the computer's BIOS. If this is the case, the information displayed in this section will not accurately reflect the physical characteristics of the disk.

Partition Tables—displays information on the partition tables for your hard disks (Figure 29.10). The information includes whether a partition is bootable (only one partition on a physical disk can be so), the operating system that owns that partition and the type of FAT it uses, the starting and ending sectors, and the size of the partition in sectors. For more detailed information on partitions and partition tables, consult Chapter 23.

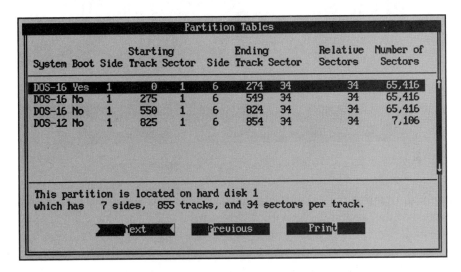

Figure 29.10 *Partition Tables screen*

The Memory Menu

The Memory menu includes six options for examining memory configuration and usage:

Memory Usage Summary—this screen (Figure 29.11) is divided into three sections. The top part shows DOS usage (how much of the 640Kb of conventional or DOS memory is allocated to DOS and resident programs and how much is free for applications). The next section displays overall memory. It lists the available amounts of main memory, display memory, extended memory, and expanded memory. The last section shows the location of any ROM BIOS extensions.

NOTE

The amount shown for display (video) memory may be different from that shown on the Video Summary screen, because video memory may be paged in and out of the display memory window.

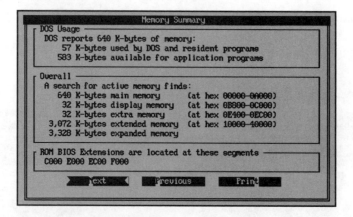

Figure 29.11 Memory Usage Summary screen

Expanded Memory (EMS)—this item is available only if you have expanded memory and an expanded memory manager installed. (For a detailed discussion of expanded and extended memory, consult Chapter 16.) The Expanded Memory screen (Figure 29.12) is divided into four areas: The area at the top left displays information on how much total expanded memory there is, how much is reserved by the system, how much is allocated (expanded memory is allocated in 16Kb pages), and how much is currently available.

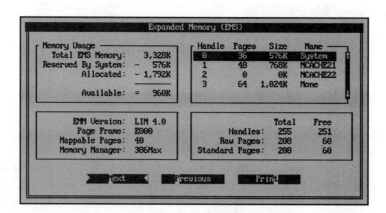

Figure 29.12 Expanded Memory screen

Below this is an area that lists the version of the Expanded Memory Specification your expanded memory manager (EMM) supports. (There are

Chapter Twenty-nine: Norton System Information (SYSINFO) ■ 471

only two versions: 3.2 and 4.0.) Under this are the hex address of the page frame, the number of mappable pages, and the name of the expanded memory manager, if known. The page frame is the 64Kb window used by expanded memory manager to pass information back and forth to programs.

The upper-right area lists the handles currently in use. Handles are values assigned to expanded memory blocks by the EMM and used by programs to identify the blocks they want to access. The number of pages assigned to the handle and the total memory comprised by the pages are listed, along with the name of the handle if it has one. (Version 4.0 of the LIM EMS allows names to be assigned to handles.)

At the bottom left are the total number of handles available (the default for LIM EMS 4.0 is 64), and the number that are free. Beneath that are the total pages and free pages, expressed as both "raw" and "standard" pages. A standard page is 16Kb, whereas a raw page can be a multiple of 16Kb.

NOTE

If the screen shows the same number of standard and raw pages, this indicates that raw pages are not supported on your system.

Extended Memory (XMS)—this item is available only if you have extended memory and have an extended memory manager (XMM) installed. The Extended Memory screen (Figure 29.13) is divided into four sections and is very similar to the Expanded Memory screen.

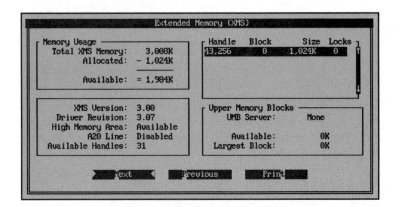

Figure 29.13 Extended Memory screen

The top left section of the extended memory screen gives information on the total XMS memory, the amount presently allocated (extended memory is allocated in blocks of 1Kb), and the amount available for allocation. The lower-left section shows the version of the Extended Memory Specification (XMS) being used, the driver revision, status of the A20 line (the CPU address line that controls access to the high memory area), and the number of available handles.

At the top right is a summary of the handle numbers, the blocks they are assigned to, the size of the blocks, and whether or not they are locked. As with expanded memory, the XMM assigns numerical values or handles to memory blocks so that applications can request access to particular extended memory blocks. With extended memory, a block can be locked by an application so that other applications can't access it. Normally, there will be no locks, so the lock value will be zero. (The block is unlocked.) When you are running in a multitasking environment, such as Windows or DESQview, locks may be set.

The last section deals with the upper memory blocks, or UMBs (unused memory areas in the 640Kb to 1Mb range). These are normally supported only on '386 or '486 computers, and they require a memory manager, such as QEMM386, to manage their use. (DOS 5.0 can also manage these blocks.) If your computer does not have UMB support, this will be set to None.

NOTE The newer versions of extended memory managers, such as QEMM386, 386MAX, or EMM386, can deal with both expanded and extended memory and can supply whatever type of memory is requested by a program. When using such managers, you may see EMB blocks followed by a number on the Expanded Memory screen. These blocks are actually extended memory blocks—blocks of extended memory that have been reallocated as expanded memory. You may notice some discrepancies between the Expanded and Extended Memory screens because expanded and extended memory are allocated in different block sizes. For example, if you set up a 68Kb NDOS swap file in extended memory, the memory manager may convert this to expanded memory, in which case it will allocate five pages or 80Kb (the closest higher value in 16Kb blocks). The Extended Memory screen will therefore show a different amount of allocated memory than you requested.

Memory Block List—displays the address (in hex), the size (in bytes), the owner, and the type of usage (data, program, or environment) of DOS memory blocks and upper memory blocks (see Figure 29.14).

Chapter Twenty-nine: Norton System Information (SYSINFO) ■ 473

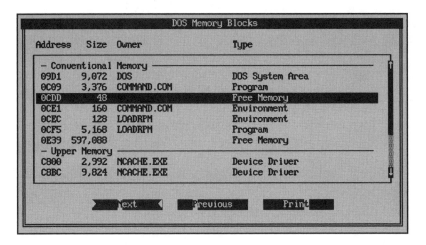

Figure 29.14 Memory Block List

TSR Programs—lists the address in memory, size of the program in bytes, the owner (the program that loaded the TSR), and hooked interrupt vectors for the loaded TSR programs (see Figure 29.15). In addition, the path and command-line options used to load the TSR and memory allocation blocks are shown at the bottom of the screen for the currently highlighted TSR (if possible). Some TSRs strip out the path and command-line data to save memory, so this information may not be available for all entries.

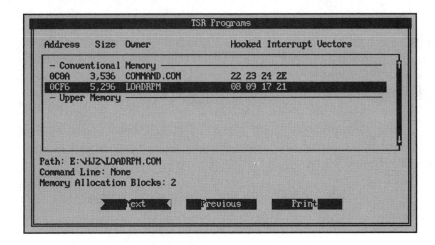

Figure 29.15 TSR screen

NOTE An interrupt vector is a value stored in the first 1024 bytes of conventional memory. It points to the address of an interrupt service routine. An interrupt service routine is a block of code that is executed by the CPU when a particular interrupt occurs. TSRs function by "hooking" interrupt vectors; that is, a TSR changes the pointer for an interrupt, such as the keyboard or system clock, to point to its own interrupt service routine. Hence, when an event like a keypress or timer tick occurs, the TSR can "wake up" and check whether the conditions for its activation are present. If they are, the TSR performs whatever task it is intended to do. Otherwise, the TSR passes control to the standard interrupt service routine and goes "back to sleep."

Device Drivers—shows the memory addresses (in hex), names, and descriptions of the device drivers currently installed in your system (see Figure 29.16). A device driver is a program that interfaces between DOS and some hardware device, such as a printer or mouse. The device drivers displayed on the screen are of two types: those that you install by adding a "DEVICE=" line in your CONFIG.SYS file and those (the majority) that are automatically installed by DOS. Those belonging to DOS are easily recognized by their familiar logical device names (e.g., CON, AUX, PRN, LPT1, and COM1).

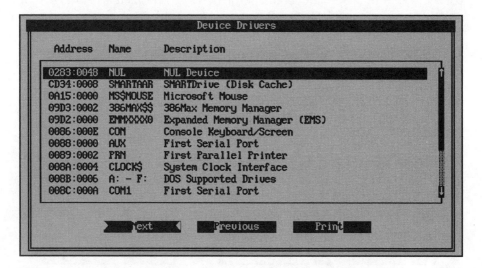

Figure 29.16 Device Drivers screen

The Benchmarks Menu

The Benchmarks menu contains three options that test the relative performance of your system. The reference for these tests is the 4.77-MHz 8088 IBM PC-XT (circa 1983). The XT is given a rating of 1, and the performance of your system is given a numerical rating in comparison to the XT.

CPU Speed—tests the central processing unit (the microprocessor) and gives it a numerical speed rating (see Figure 29.17). (You will sometimes see this rating listed in computer advertising as Norton S.I.) For comparison, the relative speeds of the XT, the original IBM AT (8-MHz '286), and the Compaq Deskpro '486–33 are also displayed.

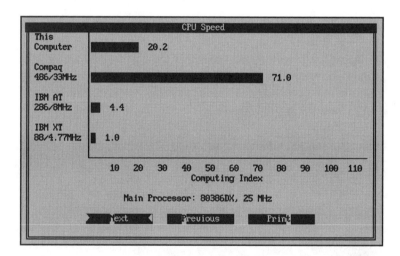

Figure 29.17 CPU Speed screen

NOTE CPU testing is an ongoing process as long as the CPU Speed screen is displayed. Therefore, the speed rating for your CPU may periodically change while you view the screen. Moving the mouse or typing on the keyboard may cause the CPU speed rating to drop noticeably.

Hard-Disk Speed—rates your hard-disk speed relative to the 10Mb hard disk in the original IBM XT and displays the average seek time, track-to-track seek time, and data transfer rate (see Figure 29.18). The relative speeds of the XT, AT, and Compaq '486–33 are shown for comparison.

476 ■ *Power Of...Norton Utilities*

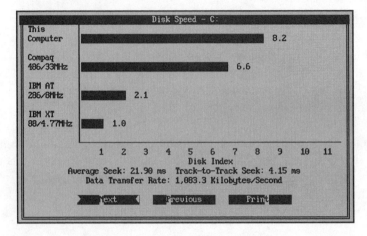

Figure 29.18 *Hard-Disk Speed screen*

 Starting with Norton Utilities 5.0, a more accurate method is used to determine the CPU and Disk Speed indices. In most cases, these numbers will be somewhat lower than those reported by earlier versions of System Information.

N O T E

Overall Performance Index—combines the CPU and hard-disk speed ratings to produce an overall system speed rating (see Figure 29.19). The speed ratings of the XT, AT, and Compaq '486–33 are displayed for comparison.

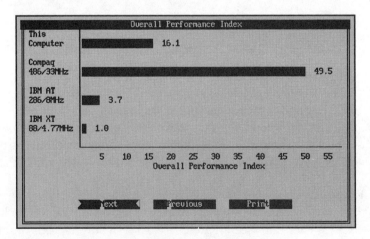

Figure 29.19 *Overall Performance screen*

Chapter Twenty-nine: Norton System Information (SYSINFO) ■ **477**

Network Performance Speed—available only if you are connected to a Novell NetWare network and have read and write privileges on a network drive. It measures throughput for reads and writes on the network.

RUNNING NORTON SYSTEM INFORMATION FROM THE DOS PROMPT

Most of SYSINFO's tests can be initiated from the DOS prompt, bypassing the menus. The command-line syntax for Sysinfo is

```
SYSINFO [drive] [options]
```

The following options are available:

/TSR	Check installed TSRs and display a report on the screen. (The report can be redirected to the printer or to a file with the DOS redirection character, ">".)
/N	Bypass the live memory probe. (Use this option if the program repeatedly locks the system when checking memory.)
/NOHDM	Do not attempt to detect hard-drive model.
/AUTO:*n*	Perform all tests sequentially, beginning with the system summary. Delay *n* seconds between screens. The tests will repeat indefinitely. Press **Esc** to halt testing.
/DEMO	Cycle through the benchmark tests and summary screen only.
/SUMMARY	Display the System Info summary screen only.
/SOUND	Beep between CPU tests.
/DI	Display the drive information (summary screen) only.
/REP:file1	Print a report to the specified file.
/SPEC:file2	Use the specified settings to generate a report.

You can view a list of the available options from the command line by typing **SYSINFO /?**

478 ■ *Power Of...Norton Utilities*

SUMMARY

The System Information program provides you with easy access to a wealth of information about your system. Among the things you can view are memory usage, information about your disks, CONFIG.SYS and AUTOEXEC.BAT files, and video characteristics. The program will also test your system and rate its performance against other computers.

30

TESTING HARDWARE SYSTEMS WITH NORTON DIAGNOSTICS (NDIAGS)

The Norton Diagnostics, a new feature of the Norton Utilities 7.0, performs extensive tests on all your hardware subsystems, including the system board, I/O ports, memory, disks, video, keyboard, and mouse. (The Norton System Information utility [SYSINFO.EXE] performs a more limited set of hardware tests.) You can start the diagnostics by selecting **Diagnostics** in the Command window or by typing `NDIAGS Enter` on the command line. The diagnostics can use a variety of command-line options, which will be explained later.

NOTE The Norton Diagnostics will not run under a multitasking environment, such as Windows or DESQview. If you attempt to load the diagnostics under such an environment, a message box will appear to inform you of this fact and to instruct you to switch to a single-task environment (i.e., DOS) before starting the program.

When you first load the diagnostics, the program displays a message indicating that it is determining the contents of the system. When it is finished, it displays an information screen (Figure 30.1) identical to that displayed by the System Information program (see Chapter 29), indicating the make and model of the system, the type and date of the BIOS, the type and speed of the CPU, the type and speed of the math coprocessor (if installed), the type of video display adapter, and the type of mouse. It also displays the number and type of installed disks, the amounts of DOS (conventional) memory, expanded memory, and extended memory; the bus type; the number of serial and parallel ports; the keyboard type; and the operating system version.

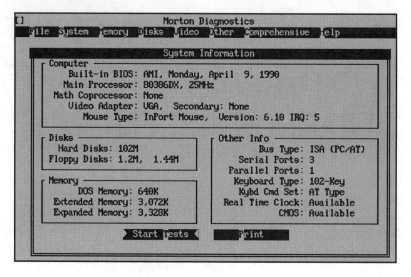

Figure 30.1 *System Configuration screen*

Once you have loaded the diagnostics, you can run the tests in a number of different ways:

- ◆ Select any individual test from the pull-down menus at the top of the screen.
- ◆ Use the **Next** button at the bottom of the test results screen to step sequentially through the available tests. (This method begins with the tests on the system menu and bypasses the "comprehensive" tests, described later.)

Chapter Thirty: Norton Diagnostics (NDIAGS) ■ **481**

◆ Use **Report** on the File menu to specify which subsystems to test and to create a report on the results.

THE FILE MENU

Hardware Configuration

The **Hardware Configuration** item on the File menu displays information about the configuration of your serial and parallel ports and your type of keyboard (Figure 30.2), and allows you to change this information if it is incorrect. For the serial ports, the dialog box displays the port address, interrupt (IRQ) level, and type of serial port chip for each installed port. For the parallel ports, it displays the port address and has a space for the IRQ level, which initially shows a question mark. (The diagnostics cannot determine the interrupt level a parallel port uses unless you perform the loopback plug tests. See later.) The keyboard is identified as one of four types: 83-key and 84-key (10 function keys on the left, with cursor keys also serving as a numeric keypad), 101-key and 102-key (12 function keys, usually at the top, with separate numeric and cursor keypads).

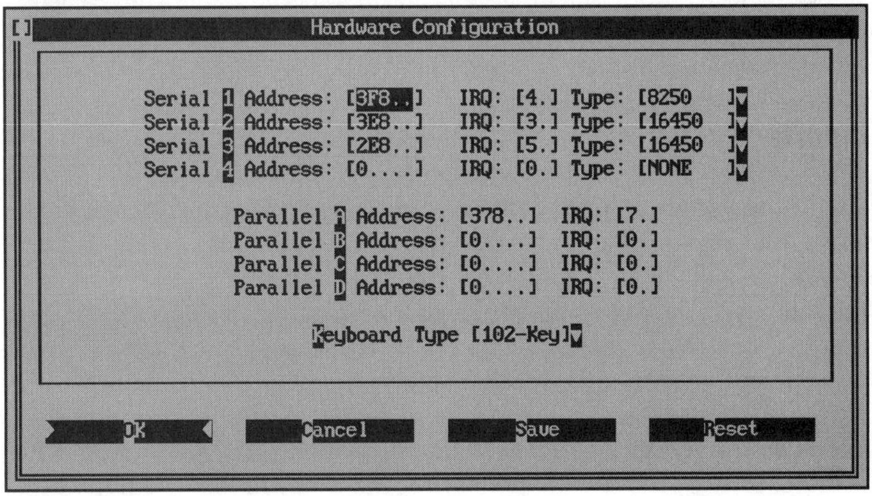

```
┌─[ ]────────────────── Hardware Configuration ──────────────────┐
│                                                                │
│   Serial 1 Address: [3F8..]   IRQ: [4.] Type: [8250   ]▼       │
│   Serial 2 Address: [3E8..]   IRQ: [3.] Type: [16450  ]▼       │
│   Serial 3 Address: [2E8..]   IRQ: [5.] Type: [16450  ]▼       │
│   Serial 4 Address: [0....]   IRQ: [0.] Type: [NONE   ]▼       │
│                                                                │
│       Parallel A Address: [378..]   IRQ: [7.]                  │
│       Parallel B Address: [0....]   IRQ: [0.]                  │
│       Parallel C Address: [0....]   IRQ: [0.]                  │
│       Parallel D Address: [0....]   IRQ: [0.]                  │
│                                                                │
│             Keyboard Type [102-Key]▼                           │
│                                                                │
│   ► OK ◄      Cancel        Save          Reset                │
└────────────────────────────────────────────────────────────────┘
```

Figure 30.2 Hardware Configuration screen

482 ■ *Power Of...Norton Utilities*

If you know that the information shown on the hardware configuration screen is incorrect, you should change it before running serial, parallel, or keyboard tests. Most users, however, will be unlikely to know the hardware addresses, interrupt levels, or chip types of their serial or parallel ports. If this is the case, it is best to accept the findings of the Norton Diagnostics and go ahead with the tests. If one of the serial or parallel port tests fails, check your system documentation or consult the manufacturer of your system to make sure that the port configuration information displayed by the Norton Diagnostics is correct.

Options

The **Options** item on the File menu allows you to turn two aspects of the diagnostics on or off: loopback tests and introductory messages. Loopback tests are part of the serial and parallel port tests; they require installing a loopback plug (also called a wrap plug) on the port. If you don't have one or don't intend to install it, turn these tests off so you won't be bothered by the message asking you to install the plug every time you run the serial or parallel port test.

When you first run the diagnostics, the program displays detailed introductory messages before each test, indicating what the test does and any actions you need to take in running it. These messages can be useful the first few times you run the diagnostics, After that, they begin to become annoying. When you reach this stage, turn them off.

Reports

As with the System Information program, Norton Diagnostics can create a report containing the results of its various tests. The **Reports** option on the File menu opens a dialog box like that in Figure 30.3, with a scroll box listing the available tests. Use the spacebar to check or uncheck items on the list to include or exclude them from the report. Interactive items in the list (i.e., those that require keyboard input or other actions by the user) are marked with an asterisk (*). If you want to create a set of tests that can be run automatically without your intervention, uncheck the interactive options. (You can achieve the same result by starting the program at the command line with the /AUTO option. See later.)

Chapter Thirty: Norton Diagnostics (NDIAGS) ■ 483

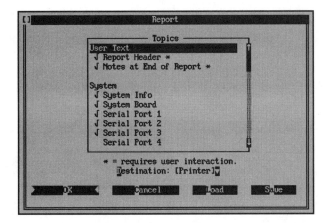

Figure 30.3 *The Reports dialog box*

Below the scroll box is a list box where you can specify the destination for the report. The report can be sent to the screen, to the printer, or to a file. If you specify a file as the destination, you will be prompted for a file name when you start the tests. If you don't enter a file name, the default name NDIAGS.RPT will be used. At the bottom of the report dialog box are four buttons: **OK**, **Cancel**, **Load**, and **Save**. Selecting **OK** performs the selected tests and creates a report. **Cancel** exits the dialog box without saving the selections or performing any tests. **Save** saves the current settings (the selections checked in the scroll box) in a file for future use, and **Load** loads a list of options previously saved with the **Save** button.

System Tests

The system tests include tests of your system board (motherboard), up to four serial ports and four parallel ports, and examines the contents of your CMOS setup memory.

System Board Test

The System Board test checks the performance of various components on your system board. It tests the registers and functions of your microprocessor (CPU) and of your math coprocessor (NPU), if one is installed. The Protected Mode test checks the ability of your processor to switch between real mode and protected mode. Other system board components—including the direct-memory access (DMA) controller, interrupt controller, and the timer chips—are also tested. The results of these tests are displayed on a screen such as that in Figure 30.4.

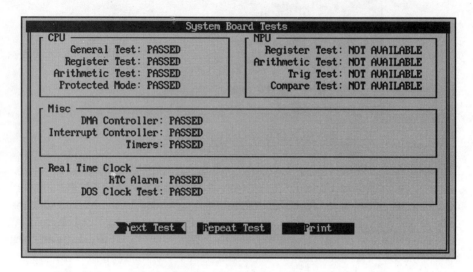

Figure 30.4 System Board tests screen

CPU Tests

The following tests are performed on the CPU:

General Test—tests register shifts and rotate functions, 16-bit arithmetic, and conditional branching instructions.

Register Tests—performs bit-pattern tests on the internal registers of the CPU.

Arithmetic Test—tests integer arithmetic functions.

Protected Mode—tests the ability of the CPU to switch into protected mode.

NPU Tests

If you have a numeric processor (math coprocessor) installed in your system, the following tests are performed:

Register Test—performs bit-pattern tests on the internal registers of the NPU and also checks for CPU and NPU clock-speed deviations.

Arithmetic Test—tests floating point addition, subtraction, division, and multiplication operations.

Trig Test—tests the NPU's performance of sine, cosine, and tangent functions.

Compare Test—compares the results of 32-bit arithmetic operations performed by the CPU and NPU.

The Misc Test

The following tests are also done:

DMA Controller—tests both 8237 DMA-controller chips to verify that data transfers between the CPU and peripherals are performed correctly.

Interrupt Controller—tests the 8259A interrupt-controller test to verify that they are working properly.

Timer—tests the timer chips that operate the system clock and the speaker.

Real-Time Clock Test

The Real-Time Clock test checks the real-time (hardware) clock and the DOS (software) clock and verifies that they are in sync.

Serial Port Tests

The Serial Port tests check the operation of up to four serial ports (COM1–COM4). The test first checks the internal registers of the serial port controller chip, using the chip's internal loopback feature. This test does not send any data through the port. To perform more extensive tests, you must attack a loopback plug (also known as a wrap plug) to the port. If you don't have a loopback plug and want to perform these tests, a qualified technician can make a loopback plug for you. Unless you are experiencing problems with your serial ports, it is probably unnecessary to run the loopback tests. If you don't intend to perform the loopback tests, you can disable this portion of the serial and parallel port tests using the **Options** selection on the File menu.

486 ■ Power Of...Norton Utilities

WARNING
Before attaching the loopback plug (or before connecting or disconnecting *any* peripheral device, for that matter), turn off your computer and any peripheral device currently connected to the serial port, then disconnect the serial cable and connect the loopback plug. Now you can turn the system back on and perform the test. When you are through with the test, turn the system off again before removing the loopback plug and reconnecting the serial cable. Connecting and disconnecting devices connected to serial or parallel I/O ports while the system unit and peripheral devices are turned on may cause hardware damage.

NOTE
You may be unable to perform loopback plug tests on all the serial ports that the diagnostics detect in your systems because some of those ports may belong to internal devices, such as internal modems or bus mouse cards.

Parallel Port Tests

The Parallel Port test is similar to the serial port test. It tests the operation of up to four parallel printer ports (LPT1–LPT4). It first tests the parallel port control and data registers. Then it prompts you to install a loopback plug (also known as a "wrap plug") in order to perform more extensive tests. If you don't have a loopback plug and want to perform these tests, a qualified technician can make a loopback plug for you. Unless you are experiencing problems with your parallel ports, it is probably unnecessary to run the loopback tests. If you don't intend to perform the loopback tests, you can disable this portion of the serial and parallel port tests using the **Options** selection on the File menu.

WARNING
Before attaching the loopback plug (or before connecting or disconnecting *any* peripheral device, for that matter), turn off your computer and any peripheral device currently connected to the parallel port, then disconnect the parallel cable and connect the loopback plug. Now you can turn the system back on and perform the test. When you are through with the test, turn off the system again before removing the loopback plug and reconnecting the parallel cable. Connecting and disconnecting devices connected to serial or parallel I/O ports while the system unit and peripheral devices are turned on may cause hardware damage.

CMOS Status Test

The CMOS Status test checks the contents of your nonvolatile setup memory and checks that the information there accurately reflects current configuration of the system. The CMOS Status screen is shown in Figure 30.5. The information includes the types of hard disk(s) and floppy disk drives installed, the amount and type(s) of memory installed, the status of the battery powering your setup memory, and your hard-disk controller. It also confirms that the memory configuration and equipment configuration indicated are valid. The CMOS Checksum is a value generated by your computer to verify that the settings in CMOS memory have not been changed (e.g., by a software error). If the CMOS Checksum is incorrect, run the setup program that came with your computer to correct the values. If you are uncertain about the values, consult the documentation that came with your system or contact your dealer or the manufacturer. (If you have a rescue disk [see Chapter 7] that was made before the CMOS settings were corrupted, you can probably restore the settings from the rescue disk.)

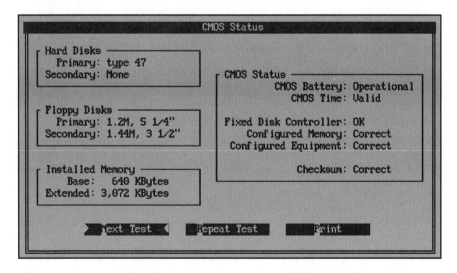

Figure 30.5 *CMOS Status screen*

 Do not alter the hard-disk-type setting in your CMOS setup unless you know what you are doing. If the hard-disk setting in your CMOS setup is incorrect, your system will probably not be able to access the hard disk.

Memory Tests

The memory tests perform extensive tests of your base memory (memory in the first 640Kb of the PC's address space) and of extended and/or expanded memory, if they are present. All three memory tests operate similarly; they differ only in the areas of memory they test. Each test writes a variety of different patterns to an area of memory (Figure 30.6), then reads them back to verify the integrity of that memory area. If any errors are discovered, the program reports the hexadecimal address of the area(s) where the error occurred. This information will help a qualified technician locate the memory chips responsible for the problem. The expanded memory test describes the area of memory being tested in terms of pages and handles, rather than of hex addresses.

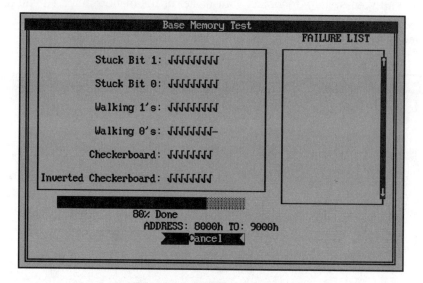

Figure 30.6 *Base Memory Tests screen*

NOTE To perform the *expanded* memory test, an expanded memory driver or expanded memory manager must be loaded. Conversely, to perform the *extended* memory test, an expanded/extended memory manager *must not* be loaded. An exception to this rule is the HIMEM.SYS driver supplied with DOS 5.0 or above and Windows 3.x.

Disk Tests

The disk tests check all installed floppy drives and one or two *physical* hard disks (not logical disks).

Hard-Disk Tests

The Norton Diagnostics performs three tests on hard disks, as shown in Figure 30.7:

Sequential Read Test—reads the first sector on each track to verify that the head mechanism can be accurately placed over every track.

Random Read Test—reads random sectors to verify that the seek mechanism works properly.

Effective RPM—measures the speed of hard-disk rotation in rpm. Normal operating speed for most hard disks is around 3600 rpm.

NOTE

If you have a disk cache installed, you may get an incorrectly high figure for Effective RPM.

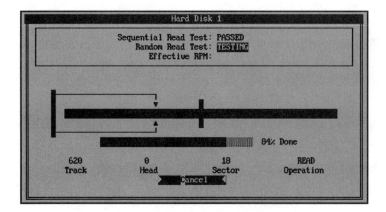

Figure 30.7 Hard-Disk Test screen

Floppy Disk Tests

The Floppy Drive test (Figure 30.8) consists of five different tests. A formatted floppy of the correct size and capacity is required. (You can't use a double-density disk to test a high-density drive, even though the drive can read and write such disks.)

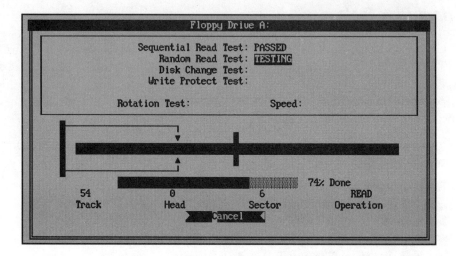

Figure 30.8 Floppy Disk test screen

NOTE Do not use a floppy disk with valuable files for the floppy disk tests. Even though the test does not intentionally write to the disk, a malfunctioning drive could damage the disk.

Sequential Read Test—reads the first sector of every track to verify that the disk heads can be correctly positioned over every track.

Random Read Test—reads random sectors all over the disk to verify that seek operations are performed correctly.

Disk Change Test—tests the ability of the drive to recognize that the disk has been removed and replaced. (The program prompts you when to remove and replace the disk.)

Chapter Thirty: Norton Diagnostics (NDIAGS) ■ 491

Write Protection Test—tests the ability of the drive to recognize write-protected and non-write-protected disks. You are prompted to remove the disk and set or place a write-protect tab, then return it to the drive.

Rotation Speed Test—checks and displays the rotation speed of the disk. The correct rotation speed for a floppy disk is around 360 rpm.

N O T E Some new users might be unfamiliar with write-protect tabs. On a 3.5" drive, the tab is a small piece of plastic that slides to open or close a square hole in one corner of the diskette. When the hole is closed, the disk is writable; when the hole is open, the disk is write-protected, and neither DOS nor any other program can alter the contents of the diskette. On a 5.25" diskette, there is a notch near the upper-right corner of the disk (viewed with the disk label facing you). To write-protect a 5.25" disk, you must cover this notch with a small piece of metallic tape known as a write-protect tab. A sheet of write-protect tabs comes in each box of new floppy disks.

VIDEO TESTS

The video tests check video memory (the memory located on your display adapter and used for frame buffer purposes), character video modes, and the ability of your display adapter to display patterns and colors in the various graphics modes.

Memory Test

The test of the memory writes various patterns to your video memory, then reads them back to verify that the memory is operating properly. This operation requires several seconds, during which your screen will flash rapidly in a variety of colors and patterns. When this operation is completed, the program will report whether any problems were encountered.

Mode Test

The Video Mode test checks the various character modes of your display adapter. This test requires user participation: You will be shown a series of screens with a line or two of text and will be asked to confirm that they are displayed properly. When this operation is completed, the program will report which modes were displayed properly and which, if any, failed. The modes are referred to by the hexadecimal mode numbers assigned by IBM to its standard video display adapters (i.e., the CGA, EGA, and VGA).

Grid Test

The Grid test is similar to the Video Mode test: screens showing a grid of horizontal and vertical lines are displayed, and you are asked to confirm whether each is displayed properly (i.e., free of distortions, gaps, or other anomalies). At the end of the test, the program displays a report of which modes were displayed properly and which failed. As earlier, video modes are referred to by their IBM-standard mode numbers.

NOTE

If horizontal or vertical lines are distorted, try adjusting the horizontal and/or vertical sync and placement controls on your monitor, if present.

Color Test

The Color test is similar to the previous two tests: it displays a series of screens with a group of colored blocks, with labels indicating the proper colors. You are asked to confirm whether the indicated colors are displayed. Once again, the program reports which modes were displayed properly and which failed, using standard mode numbers.

NOTE

If some colors on your monitor do not display properly, try adjusting the brightness, intensity, or saturation controls on your monitor, if present.

Other Tests

The **Other Tests** option includes mouse, speaker, and keyboard tests.

Mouse Test

The test of the mouse prompts you to click your left and right mouse buttons and to move the mouse pointer to the top, bottom, left, and right edges of your screen. The program confirms that you have performed these actions successfully (or have failed to do so). The screen coordinates for the mouse position are displayed as you move the mouse.

Speaker Test

The test of the speaker plays a digitized voice message over your speaker and asks you to confirm whether you hear the message.

Keyboard Tests

There are two keyboard tests, a Key Press test and a Keyboard Light test. The Key Press test displays a map of your keyboard and asks you to press each key. As you do so it displays the scan code for that key (the code that the keyboard controller sends to the CPU, not the same as the ASCII code) and indicates what key it believes was pressed. Watch this display and make sure it corresponds correctly for each key. Every key must be pressed for the test to be considered a pass. Do not press multiple keys at once, as this may cause the test to believe that a key is stuck or has a defective auto-repeat mechanism. Pressing any key three times in succession ends the test.

NOTE

You don't really need to know the scan codes to use the Key Press test. In most cases just seeing that the test agrees as to what key you are pressing is sufficient.

494 ■ *Power Of...Norton Utilities*

The Keyboard Light test alternately turns your number lock, caps lock, and scroll lock lights on and off and asks you to confirm when they are on and off.

COMPREHENSIVE TESTS

The tests listed on the Comprehensive Tests menu check disk subsystems and memory in a much more detailed way than those on the Disks or Memory menus. Tests are available for any floppy disks that are installed, for the hard disk, for memory, and for 16550 serial-port chips, if present.

Floppy Disk Tests

The floppy disk tests require a blank, formatted floppy of the appropriate type. Sequential and random read/write tests are performed on every sector and track. This process can take up to 45 minutes on a 1.2Mb, 5.25" drive.

Hard-Disk Tests

The comprehensive hard-disk test consists of running the Norton Calibrate utility (CALIBRAT.EXE), which performs extensive tests on the disk surface, determines the optimal interleave factor, and, if necessary, performs a nondestructive low-level format to change the interleave. This program is the subject of Chapter 15, so we won't repeat that information here.

Memory Test

For the Comprehensive Memory test, NDIAGS reboots your system with a minimal configuration (i.e., without unnecessary TSRs or drivers) and then performs exhaustive read, write, and verify tests on all the installed memory. When you select this option, the program displays a dialog box such as that in Figure 30.9, indicating the memory ranges it will test and the size of the memory blocks it will work on (increment). At the bottom of the dialog box is the program's estimate of how long the tests will take. This may be several

Chapter Thirty: Norton Diagnostics (NDIAGS) ■ 495

hours or even days, depending on the speed of your system and how much memory is installed, so be sure to allow sufficient time. Select **OK** to begin the tests or **Cancel** to return to the NDIAGS main screen. If you choose to proceed with the tests, a prompt box will appear warning you that the system is about to be rebooted and giving you one more opportunity to cancel or confirm the tests. When the comprehensive memory test is completed, the program will display a list of any errors found. NDIAGS restores your bootup configuration (AUTOEXEC.BAT and CONFIG.SYS files) to their normal state, so that you can reboot your system to return to your normal working configuration.

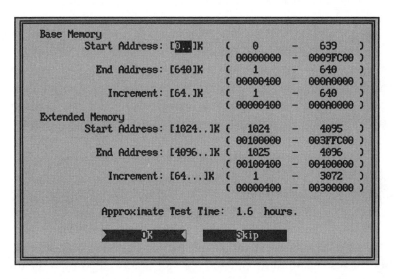

Figure 30.9 *Comprehensive Memory Test configuration screen*

16550 Tests

The 16550 tests are extensions of the serial-port tests. The 16550 is a relatively new serial-port controller chip (UART) and is not installed in most current systems. Most systems now use the 8250 or 16540 serial-port chips. (To see what kind of serial-port chips are installed in your system, check the **Hardware Configuration** item on the File menu.) If your system doesn't use the 16550, this test will be "grayed out" on the menu (or shown in parentheses on monochrome screens) to indicate that the test is unavailable.

496 ■ *Power Of...Norton Utilities*

Unlike the earlier serial-port chips, the 16550 is equipped with two 16-character first-in, first-out (FIFO) buffers. These buffers allow the 16550 to send or receive larger groups of characters (up to 16) between CPU interrupts. The 16550 tests check the effective baud rate of the chip at various settings and the buffer usage at four different interrupt settings (2, 4, 8, or 14 characters). A loopback plug is required for the 16550 tests.

WHAT IF MY SYSTEM FAILS THE DIAGNOSTICS?

If your system fails one or more of the tests in the Norton Diagnostics, *don't panic*. Use your common sense and the following procedures to verify that the test results are valid. Don't schedule surgery before you get a second opinion.

How you should interpret the tests depends partly, on the circumstances in which you are using them. If you're running a particular test to diagnose the cause of a problem (e.g., you are running the floppy disk tests because you have recurrent problems with floppy disk reads or writes) and the system fails the tests, it is reasonable to assume that the test result is correct, as it coincides with your observations.

But what if you haven't experienced any problems, you run the diagnostics as a check-up, and an error turns up in some area that you don't know much about and don't have any other means to test, such as the DMA or interrupt controller chip? Again, don't panic. You may or may not have a serious problem. Try the test again under different circumstances. If you ran the test when your computer was first turned on in the morning, try it again when the system has warmed up for several hours. If you ran the test with a full set of device drivers and TSRs loaded, try again with a stripped-down configuration. Do whatever you can to isolate the conditions in which the system fails the particular test. Contact your dealer and/or the manufacturer of your system and ask them for a possible explanation. Contact the Symantec/Norton tech support department to see if they know any reason why the diagnostics might not work correctly with your particular system and configuration. (You might, for example, have some nonstandard component in your system that confuses the diagnostics.) If all these methods fail to provide a solution, and your system continues to fail the test while operating properly, there are several approaches you can take:

Chapter Thirty: Norton Diagnostics (NDIAGS) ■ 497

1. *Swap components*. If you work in an environment where there are several similarly configured PCs and if the component that is failing the diagnostics is one that can easily be moved from one system to another (e.g., a keyboard, a display adapter and/or monitor, a serial or parallel card, or a floppy drive), try swapping the component into another system and/or swapping an identical component into yours. If the problem travels with the removable component (e.g., a floppy drive continues to fail the test when installed in a different system with a different drive controller card), then there probably is a real problem. If, on the other hand, a second component also fails the test when installed in your system, then most likely the problem lies elsewhere. In the case of a drive, for example, either there is a problem with your drive controller card or some other component in your system is preventing the test from working correctly. Try swapping the drive controller card to see what effect that has on the situation. It's simply a matter of using a little common sense to close in on the most likely source of the problem. This approach is not for everyone; you have to feel comfortable working inside your system. But if you can get over your fear of messing with the innards of an expensive machine, you may find the experience empowering (to use a PC buzzword). See the following tips for working inside your system.

2. *Get professional assistance*. If your dealer has a service department or you have an on-site service contract, by all means have a qualified service technician check the machine. A service technician should be able to use more sophisticated hardware and software tools to check the diagnosis provided by Norton Diagnostics.

3. *Wait until something breaks*. If your system isn't under warranty and you don't want to spend the money or endure the down-time to have it professionally tested, wait. If the problem is the beginning of a real hardware failure, it will probably get worse over time and begin to manifest itself with recognizable symptoms. If it doesn't, then it is probably not a real problem, or at least not a very serious one. If it does manifest itself, you will have relatively little risk, provided that you back up your data regularly, as you should. (Of course, whatever the component is, it will fail at the most inconvenient time, but there's no escaping that law.)

4. *Protect your warranty rights*. If your system is under warranty and your dealer or the manufacturer cannot resolve the problem or fails to take it seriously, you might consider writing a letter to the manufacturer and/or

498 ■ *Power Of...Norton Utilities*

dealer explaining the diagnostic results and the steps you have taken to try to solve the problem. Keep a copy for your files. Then, if your system should fail later for the reason detected by the diagnostics, you will have an adequate record that the problem began within the warranty period and you took reasonable steps to inform the dealer and to solve the problem.

Some Tips on Working Inside Your System

To check the results of some of the tests, it is necessary to open your system and examine certain components. If you have never opened your PC before, you may find this prospect intimidating, but it really is not hazardous (either to you or the computer) if you go about it sensibly. Use the following steps:

1. Park your hard-disk heads. This can be done using the Norton Disk Monitor program (see Chapter 6).

2. Turn off your PC and all peripheral devices connected to it (e.g., printer, monitor, external modem, and storage devices) before you attempt to open the case. As an extra precaution, disconnect the power cable. If you're connected to a network, consult your network administrator or technician about disconnecting network cables.

3. If you have a desk-top case, remove your monitor and put it somewhere safe. Clear some space around your system so that you can work without obstacles. (Good luck!)

4. Consult the manual that came with your system to see how to open the case. A lot of different PC case styles are in use today. Some can be opened by removing one or two thumb screws; others are built like tanks and are about as easy to open. If your documentation doesn't explain how to open the case (or if, as in the case of some clones, you don't have any system documentation), you will probably want to begin by removing four screws located at the corners of the back panel of the case, and possibly a fifth in the center. *Put the screws somewhere safe!* You definitely *do not* want to unscrew your power supply from the case. The power supply is a box within your computer that converts AC current from the wall socket to the low-voltage DC needed by your computer's components. The power supply is located where you see the cooling fan at the back of your system. You will probably see a group of screws forming a smaller rectangle at one side or

Chapter Thirty: Norton Diagnostics (NDIAGS) ■ **499**

the other of the back panel of your case surrounding the fan. These are the screws that hold the power supply in place. Do not remove them.

5. When you have removed what you think are the right screws, try to remove the case. Some cases slide straight forward, others are hinged at the front and lift upward. Be firm but gentle and use common sense. Depending on the design of the system, there will be only one or two directions in which the case top can reasonably be expected to move. If it will not budge, look around for other screws that you might have missed.

6. Assuming that you have succeeded in opening the case, beware of static electricity. Static charges from your body can damage or destroy sensitive components. Before you touch any components on the system board or expansion boards, touch the power supply case or the back panel, which, at least in theory, is grounded, to discharge yourself. If it's one of those cold, dry days when you get a shock whenever you touch the doorknob, it is probably best to wait for another day to work inside your system, unless the matter is urgent. If your work space is one in which you get static shocks regularly, regardless of the weather, you might consider getting anti-static floor mats (available from most computer supply dealers) or using an antistatic spray on your carpet.

7. Depending on what case style you have and how many expansion boards you have in your system, it may or may not be easy to get at the components you want to check. For example, ribbon cables from hard disks and floppy drives may run over the tops of expansion boards, and the expansion boards themselves may cover up some components on the system board. If you have to disconnect cables to get to the components you want to check, make *careful* notes of how things are connected so that you can restore them to their former state afterwards. If you remove expansion boards, be very *careful* in removing the screws that attach the expansion boards to the back panel of the case. *Do not drop the screw into the case. You won't know what trouble is until you drop a screw into the case and it rolls under the system board and gets stuck there.*

8. When you're done, follow the preceding steps in reverse order to reassemble your system.

If all this is too intimidating to cope with, then by all means get a more experienced person to open your system, but be sure to watch so that you can do it yourself next time.

500 ■ *Power Of...Norton Utilities*

Checking and Confirming Test Results

CPU and NPU Tests

If either the CPU or NPU tests fail, run the base memory test three or more times to make sure that a memory problem is not interfering with the CPU or NPU tests. If you find no memory problems, you may want to check to be sure that the CPU and/or NPU are properly socketed and that no stray wires or foreign objects are touching the CPU/NPU pins. To do this, you must open your system. (See the tips on the preceding pages.) The CPU and NPU are large, square, socketed chips, usually located on the system board (motherboard). A few systems place the CPU and NPU on a small plug-in expansion board. The CPU and NPU are normally clearly marked with their model numbers on the chip surface (e.g., 80286 and 80287, 80386 and 80387, and so on). If you have an 80486DX system, the '486 chip functions as both the CPU and NPU. The chips should be seated levelly in their sockets. Press firmly and evenly down on the center of the chips to make sure they're properly socketed. (Don't press *too hard*, or you could crack the traces on your system board.)

DMA and Interrupt Controller Tests

There is no way for a user without special test hardware to verify or cross-check the results of these tests. However, if your system runs reliably and you don't experience mysterious crashes or errors when accessing peripheral devices, it is unlikely that you have a serious problem with the interrupt or DMA controller chip. Consult a qualified technician if you want to make certain.

Timer Tests

If the timer test consistently fails, try the speaker test. If this also fails it is likely that the timer that controls the speaker is defective. If it doesn't, check the DOS clock test results; the other timer controls the DOS clock.

Real-Time Clock Tests

If the RTC alarm subtest fails consistently, you may have a defective or nonstandard real-time clock chip. There is no cross-check for this test. If the DOS clock test fails but the RTC test doesn't, the timer chip may be defective. Try the timer test for confirmation. Also, check the CMOS status test to be sure the CMOS

Chapter Thirty: Norton Diagnostics (NDIAGS) ■ **501**

battery is operational and the CMOS time is valid. If not, reset the CMOS time with your setup program or the Norton Control Center (see Chapter 25) and/or replace the battery. If you replace the battery, you will need to restore your CMOS settings from your rescue disk (see Chapter 7) in order to access your hard disk.

Serial Port Tests

If the internal register tests fail, unplug any device(s) connected to the port(s) and repeat the test. If the test still fails, run Norton SYSINFO (see Chapter 29) and check the hardware interrupts screen to be sure that there are no interrupt conflicts between the serial ports (listed on the screen as COM1, COM2, etc.) and any other hardware devices. Again, use your common sense. Do the devices connected to your serial ports (e.g., your modem or mouse) normally perform correctly? If so, it is unlikely that the port has any serious defect.

If your system fails one or more of the loopback tests, be sure that your loopback plug is wired properly and that the connections are good. Do not be surprised if your system cannot achieve the highest speeds on the loopback tests. Only the fastest '386 and '486 machines and/or those equipped with the 16550 serial-port chip can achieve speeds of 115,200 baud. Most '386s can reach 57,600 baud, but earlier systems may be unable to exceed 4800 baud.

Parallel Port Tests

If the internal register tests fail, unplug any device(s) connected to the port(s) and repeat the test. If the test still fails, run Norton SYSINFO (see Chapter 29) and check the hardware interrupts screen to be sure there are no interrupt conflicts between the parallel ports (listed on the screen as PRN, LPT1, and so on) and any other hardware devices.

If your system fails one or more of the loopback tests, be sure that your loopback plug is wired properly and that the connections are good.

CMOS Tests

If the contents of the CMOS memory are invalid, run your setup program and reset the correct values. (*Caution:* Do not change the data for your hard disk unless you're sure of the correct values. Incorrect data could make your hard disk inaccessible to DOS.) Turn your system off, wait 60 seconds, then turn it

502 ■ *Power Of...Norton Utilities*

on again and check the CMOS again to be sure that the correct data is retained. If it is not, you may need to replace the battery. If replacing the battery does not correct the problem, you may have a defective CMOS memory chip. Consult a qualified technician.

Memory Tests

If one or more of the memory tests fail, restart your system with a minimal configuration (no unnecessary TSRs or device drivers) and repeat the test. (Of course, you will need to have your expanded memory manager installed to perform the expanded memory test.) If the test still fails, note the addresses of the failures and run the Comprehensive memory test. If this test fails and shows the same bad addresses, you probably have some defective memory chips. Consult a qualified technician.

Hard-Disk Tests

If only the rotation speed test fails, you may have a hard disk that runs at a nonstandard speed. If any of the other tests fail, reboot your system with a minimal configuration (no unnecessary TSRs or device drivers). If the test still fails, run the Comprehensive Hard Disk test (the same as the Norton Calibrate utility, see Chapter 15). Allow several hours for the completion of this test.

Floppy Disk Tests

If your drive fails one of these tests, don't panic. It may be the result of a defective diskette. Try the tests again with a different diskette. You should try the test several times with different diskettes before concluding that you have a defective drive. If the drive does appear to have a problem or if you have been having problems with disks but the test *doesn't* reveal any problems, try the Comprehensive Floppy Disk tests, which test sequential and random read, write, and seek operations for every sector/track/head combination.

If your drive consistently fails the read test, you may need to clean, recalibrate, or replace the read/write heads. You can easily clean the heads with a cleaning kit (available from most computer supply dealers). For the do-it-yourself types, there are programs on the market that allow you to check and adjust diskette drive head alignment without special tools. If this doesn't appeal to you, consult a qualified technician. A technician is also required to replace the

Chapter Thirty: Norton Diagnostics (NDIAGS) ■ 503

drive heads, but with prices on floppy drives as low as they are today, it may be cheaper to replace the whole drive (a task you can probably perform yourself).

If your drive fails the disk-change, write-protect, or rotation-speed tests, this also may be a sign of a defective drive. Try swapping a drive from another system if one is available. Again, floppy drives are neither expensive or difficult to replace, so don't spend too much time trying to troubleshoot a bad drive.

Video Test

If the color tests fail, first try to adjust the brightness and saturation controls on your monitor, if available. If you cannot correct colors this way, try swapping monitors, if possible, to see whether the problem is with the monitor or the display adapter. Try the same approach if you have trouble with the grid tests: First, try to adjust your monitor's horizontal and vertical sync and position controls. If this does not solve the problem, try swapping the monitor or the display adapter, if possible, to see which of these devices is the problem. If you have an exotic video adapter (e.g., something that is not a standard VGA), contact the manufacturer to be sure that it supports the modes in which the Norton Diagnostics is trying to test it. Your display adapter may have come with a utilities diskette that included diagnostic software better suited to that particular adapter. If not, contact the manufacturer to see if such software is available.

Mouse Tests

If your mouse does not perform correctly in the tests, first clean it according to the manufacturer's instructions. Second, run Norton SYSINFO (see Chapter 29) and check the hardware interrupt page to verify that there is not an interrupt conflict between the mouse and another hardware device. If the mouse is connected to a serial port, check the results of the serial port tests for that port and/or try connecting the mouse to another serial port. If the mouse is connected to its own expansion card, open the system and make sure the card is properly seated in the expansion slot. If none of these steps improve mouse performance, the mouse is probably defective.

Speaker Test

If you do not hear the message from the speaker, compare the results of the timer subtest on the system board test. (The speaker is operated by one of the

504 ■ *Power Of...Norton Utilities*

two timers.) If the timer test is okay, then the speaker may be disconnected. Open the system and check. If the speaker is connected properly, it is probably defective and should be replaced.

Keyboard Test

If some of the keys don't perform properly on the Key Press test, check to be sure that the keyboard is properly plugged into the keyboard port and that the cable is not damaged. Check to see that the key that creates the problem is not physically damaged. If your keyboard has a switch to configure it for operation with XT- and AT-type systems, make sure the switch is set correctly.

If the keyboard-light test does not perform correctly, either the LEDs are burned out or the driving circuitry is defective.

RUNNING THE NORTON DIAGNOSTICS FROM THE COMMAND LINE

Those options in the Norton Diagnostics that do not require user participation can be run automatically from the command line with a variety of settings. The command-line syntax for the Norton Diagnostics is as follows:

```
NDIAGS [options]
```

where [options] are one or more of the following:

/AUTO:*n*	Automatically cycle through all the noninteractive tests, pausing *n* seconds between screens. (The comprehensive tests are not used with this option.)
/REP:file	Print a report to the specified file.
/SPEC:file	Run the noninteractive tests listed in the specified file (created with the **Report** option on the File menu).
/COMP	Run the comprehensive memory test.
/RESET	Check the system and reset the information stored in the SYM-CFG.BIN file. (Use this option if you have changed the hardware configuration of the system since installing the Norton Utilities.)

Chapter Thirty: Norton Diagnostics (NDIAGS) ■ **505**

/BURNIN:x   Cycle through all noninteractive tests *x* times. This can be used in conjunction with the /SPEC option.

To see a list of available options at the DOS prompt, type **NDIAGS /?**

SUMMARY

The Norton Diagnostics perform extensive tests of all your hardware subsystems. Tests can be selected individually from the menus or stepped through sequentially, or a selected group of tests can be run from a report spec file.

INDEX

A

/A20 switch (Diskreet), 161
accidental erasure, protecting against, 41-51
    with Disk Monitor, 50
    with Diskreet, 50
    with File Attribute, 48-50
    with SmartCan, 42-47
accidental formatting
    protecting disks from. See Image utility; Safe Format
        utility
    restoring accidentally formatted disks. See
        UnFormat utility
Add menu item option (Menu menu), 9
ADJUST (Line Print option), 437
Advanced Recovery Mode option (Disk Editor), 380-
    381, 381
Advanced Search option (File Find), 293-294
All Clusters option (Manual UnErase), 100
All Graphical Controls option (Configuration), 24
alternate program names for utilities, 31-32
AM|PM (Line Print option), 451
Append To option (UnErase), 95-96
application programs, 3
Archive attribute bit, 282, 334
ASCII files
    as batch files, 453-454
    printing. See Line Print utility
ASCII Table option (Disk Editor), 382
ASK command (Batch Enhancer), 436-438
attribute bits, 281-282
/AUTO switch
    with Norton Diagnostics, 504
    with System Information, 477
Auto-Close Timeout option (Diskreet), 173
AUTOEXEC.BAT
    configuration of, 28-31
    deleting FASTOPEN from, 213
    Disk Doctor in, 130-131
    Disk Monitor in, 70
    Image command in, 55-56
    installing Norton Cache to, 222-223
    for minimal configuration, 199
    on rescue disk, 83
    SmartCan in, 42
Auto View option (Disk Editor), 355
average seek time, 203

B

backup files, locating, 181
backups, hard-disk, 38-39, 42
/BATCH switch
    with Calibrate, 208
    with File Find, 300
    with Norton Change Directory, 271
    with Wipe Info, 189
Batch Enhancer utility (BE), 433-457
    in batch files, 435
    command-line execution of, 435
    creating and editing batch or script files with, 453-
        457
    script files, 435-436
    subcommands, 436-452

batch file(s), 433-434
    Batch Enhancer commands in, 435
    creating and editing, 453-454
    in File Find, 296-297
    sample, 454-457
Baud rate option (Norton Control Center), 405
BEEP command (Batch Enhancer), 439-440
BE.EXE, 200
Benchmarks menu (System Information), 475-477
binary numbering, 383
.BIN files, 72
BIOS seek overhead time, 202
/BLANK switch (Calibrate), 208
BLINKING (Line Print option), 447
/BLOCK switch (Norton Cache), 233
Block Cursor check box (Configuration), 24
Bold Header option (Configuration), 28
BOOK.LOG, 408-409
bootable disk, making a, 152-153
Boot Record option (Disk Editor), 362, 363, 373
boot-sector viruses, 68-69
BOX command (Batch Enhancer), 440-441, 452
BRIGHT (Line Print option), 447
Browse option (Manual UnErase), 101
buffers, 212-213, 226-227
/BURNIN switch (Norton Diagnostics), 505
Button Arrows check box (Configuration), 24
/BW80 switch (Norton Control Center), 417
bytes, 383

C

Calculator (Disk Editor), 380
Calibrate utility (CALIBRAT), 193-208
    for head alignment problems, 196
    interleave testing modification with, 194-195
    interrupting, 206
    limitations of, 196-197
    preparing to use, 198-200
    procedure for running, 200-206
    report, 207
    running from DOS prompt, 207-208
    screen blanking, 206
    starting, 200, 207-208
    testing with, 196, 201-206
    track sector ID and data "refreshment" with, 195
Change Directory option (UnErase), 94
Change Disk option (Norton Change Directory), 262
check boxes, 15
CHKDSK command (DOS), 118
/CLEAR switch
    with File Attributes, 284
    with File Find, 300
Clipboard option (Disk Editor), 364-367
/CLOSE switch (Diskreet), 177
/CLS switch (Line Print), 448
CLS command (Batch Enhancer), 441
Cluster Chain option (Disk Editor), 371
Cluster Number option (Manual UnErase), 101-102
Cluster option (Disk Editor), 358-359, 359, 391
cluster(s), 328
    Manual UnErase and, 99-104

507

marking, with Disk Tools, 151-152
recovering lost, 118-119
sizes of, 306
CMOS battery failure, 80
CMOS Status option (System Information), 466, 467
CMOS Status test (Norton Diagnostics), 487
/CO80 switch (Norton Control Center), 417
code pages, 412-415
Color selection dialog box, 22, 23
Color test (Norton Diagnostics), 492
.COM files, 252
COMMAND.COM, 153, 434
Commands menu (File Find), 297-299
command window, 7-8, 16
/COMP switch (Norton Diagnostics), 504
Compare Windows option (Disk Editor), 378-379
COM ports, 404
Compressed Print option (Configuration), 26
computer numbering, 382-384
/CON switch (DOS COPY command), 453
CONFIG.SYS, 80
    BUFFERS setting in, 212-213
    configuration of, 28-31
    COUNTRY configuration command in, 411
    deleting FASTOPEN from, 213
    "DEVICE=" line in, 474
    encryption driver in, 158
    installing Diskreet to, 160-164
    installing Norton Cache to, 222
    for minimal configuration, 199
    on rescue disk, 83
configuration, minimal, 199-200
Configuration utility (NUCONFIG), 19-35
    alternate program names, 31-32
    dialog box, 20, 20
    installing Norton Cache with, 220
    menu, 11, 11, 20, 20
    menu editing with, 34-35
    mouse, 21, 24-25
    passwords, 32-34
    printer, 25-28
    screen, 21-24
    startup programs, 28-31
Configure menu (Speed Disk), 250-252
Configure option (Norton Change Directory), 269
context-sensitive help, 12-13
Continue Search option (UnErase), 97
control buttons, 15
conventional (DOS) memory, 214-215, 230-231
/CONVERT switch (SmartCan), 46
COPY command (DOS), 422, 453
COPY command (Norton Change Directory), 270
copying floppy disks with Disk Duplicator, 419-423
Copy option (Disk Editor), 368
copy-protection, Speed Disk and, 245-246
Copy Tree command (Norton Change Directory), 266-267
Country Info option (Norton Control Center), 410, 410-411
COUNTRY.SYS, 411
CPU Speed option (System Information), 475, 475
CPU tests (Norton Diagnostics), 484
Create Batch option (File Find), 296, 296-297
Create option (Diskreet), 167-168
cross-linked files, 119
/CS switch
    with File Find, 300
    with Text Search, 313
cursor, 24, 446-447
/CURSOR switch (Norton Control Center), 417

Cursor Size option (Norton Control Center), 398, 398-399
customization. See Configuration utility
Customize Colors dialog box, 22, 22
Custom Message option (Norton Disk Doctor), 123
cylinders, 327, 329

D

Data bits (Norton Control Center), 406
Data Clearing Method option (Diskreet), 174-175
Data Encryption Standard (DES), 159
Data Format option (Configuration), 28
Data Search option (Manual UnErase), 100
date, marking file. See File Date utility
DATE command (DOS), 414
/DEBUG switch (Line Print), 437, 443, 444, 450, 451
DEFAULT (Line Print option), 437
defective diskettes, using Disk Tools to revive, 150-151
/DELAY switch (Norton Cache), 232
Delay Before Sectors Are Written option (Norton Cache), 227
DELAY command (Batch Enhancer), 441-442
DELETE command (DOS), 187
Delete command (Norton Change Directory), 265
Delete menu item option (Menu menu), 10
Delete option (Diskreet), 171
Delete Tracking (Mirror program), 89
/DEMO switch (System Information), 477
Description option (Diskreet), 170-171
description window, 7-8
Device Drivers option (System Information), 474, 474
/DI switch (System Information), 477
Diagnose Disk option (Norton Disk Doctor), 120-121, 123-126
diagnostic cylinder, 198-199, 392
/DIR switch (File Attributes), 283
DIR command (DOS), 281, 390
directory, changing. See Norton Change Directory utility
directory attribution bit, 335
Directory menu (Norton Change Directory), 264, 264-269
Directory option (Disk Editor)
    Link menu, 371
    Object menu, 357, 357-358
    View menu, 373
Directory Order option (Speed Disk), 250-251, 252
Directory Sort utility (DS), 273-279
    command-line usage, 277-279
    dialog box, 275
    full-screen mode, 274-277
    network usage, 274
Disk change test (System Information), 490
Disk Characteristics option (System Information), 467-468, 468
DISKCOPY command (DOS), 99, 419-420, 422
Disk Duplicator utility (DUPDISK), 419-423
Disk Editor utility (DISKEDIT), 351-392
    Clipboard, 364-367
    configuration of, 354-356
    Edit menu, 367-370
        Copy option, 368
        Discard Changes option, 370
        Fill option, 369, 369
        Mark option, 368
        Paste Over option, 368
        Undo option, 367-368
        Write option, 369
    Info menu, 374-375
        Drive Info option, 375

Index ■ 509

Map of Object option, 375, *375*
Object Info option, 375
initial display, *353*
Link menu, 370-371
    Cluster Chain option, 371
    Directory option, 371
    File option, 370
    Partition option, 371
    Window option, 371
Memory Dump option, *365*, 365-367, *366*
Object menu, 356-364
    Boot Record option, 362, *363*
    Cluster option, 358-359, *359*
    Directory option, *357*, 357-358
    Drive option, 356-357
    File option, 358, *358*
    1st copy of FAT option, 362-364, *363*
    Partition table option, *361*, 361-362
    Physical Sector option, 360, *360*
    2nd copy of FAT option, 364
    Sector option, *359*, 359-360
running from DOS prompt, 382
starting, 353, 382
Tools menu, 375-382
    Advanced Recovery Mode option, 380-381
    ASCII Table option, 382
    calculator, 380
    Compare Windows option, 378-379
    Find Again option, 376
    Find Object option, 376
    Find option, 376
    Print As option, 377-378
    Recalculate Partition option, 378
    Set Attributes option, 379
    Set Date/Time option, 379-380
    Write To option, 376-377
View menu, 371-374
    Boot Record option, 373
    Directory option, 373
    FAT option, 373
    Grow Window option, 374
    Hex option, 372, *372*
    Partition Table option, 373
    Shrink Window option, 374
    Split (Unsplit) Window option, 373-374
    Switch Windows option, 374
    Text option, 373
Disk Light (Disk Monitor), 76
Disk menu (Norton Change Directory), 262-264, *263*
Disk Monitor utility (DISKMON), 50, 67, 69-78
    controlling disk writes with, 69-74
        automatic installation, 70
        configuration, 70-73
        graphics mode, 73-74
        network usage, 74
        text mode, 73
    hard-disk head parking with, 75-77
        command-line options, 76-77
        Disk Light feature, 76
DISKREET.INI, 163
DISKREET.SYS, 158, 160-164
Diskreet utility (DISKREET), 50, 157-178
    decrypting a single file with, 165-166
    dialog box, 164, *164*
    encrypting a single file with, 165
    encryption methods of, 158-159
    files menu, 165-166
    installing DISKREET.SYS driver, 160-164
    NDisks, working with, 175-176

NDisks menu, 167-172
    Create option, 167-168
    Delete option, 171
    Description option, 170-171
    Edit option, 169
    Password option, 171
    Prompt and Prompt At options, 169-170
    Search option, 172
network usage, 159
Options menu, 172-175
    Driver menu, 172-174
    Files option, 174
    Global menu, 174-175
passwords in, 159-160, 165
running from DOS prompt, 176-177
starting, 164, 176-177
/DISKRESET switch (Norton Cache), 237
Disks menu (System Information), 466-469
Disk Statistics option (Speed Disk), 253, *253*
Disk Summary option (System Information), 466, *467*
Disk tests (Norton Diagnostics), 489-491
    floppy drive, *490*, 490-491
    hard-disk, 489, *489*
Disk Tools utility (DISKTOOL), 147-153
    making a disk bootable with, 152-153
    marking a cluster with, 151-152
    recovering from DOS RECOVER command with, 148-150
    starting, 148-149
display. See screen
Display Lines option (Configuration), 23-24
Display Mode option (Configuration), 24
DM.INI, 73
.DOC files, 48
/DOS switch (Norton Cache), 230-231
DOS boot records (DBR), 343, 388, *389*
DOS buffers, 212-213
/DOSCOLOR switch (Norton Control Center), 417
DOS Colors option (Norton Control Center), 399, *399*
DOS Format option (Safe Format), 58
DOS=HIGH command, 162
DOS memory. See conventional memory
Drive Letters to Reserve option (Diskreet), 172-173
Drive option (Disk Editor), 356-357
drive RPM, 203
drives. See Floppy drives; Hard-disk
Drives option (Wipe Info), 186-188
DS. See Directory Sort utility
/DT switch (Norton Disk Doctor), 130
/DUMP switch (Norton Cache), 237

E

E (Sortkey), 278
/EBCDIC switch
    with Line Print, 428
    with Text Search, 313
EBCDIC format, 425
Edit menu (Disk Editor), 367-370
Edit menu item option (Menu menu), 10
Edit option (Diskreet), 169
EDLIN line editor (DOS), 453
EDSI controller, 468
EMM386, 162, 472
Enable/Disable Menu Editing (Configuration menu), 10
encoding type, 203
encryption, 157-159
End key, 14
Enter key, 14

510 ■ *Power Of...Norton Utilities*

Enter Moves Focus check box (Configuration), 25
EP (Line Print option), 428
ERASE command (DOS), 187
erased/erasing files
  permanently erased files. See Wipe Info
  protecting against accidental erasure, 41-51
    with Disk Monitor, 50
    with Diskreet, 50
    with File Attributes, 48-50
    with SmartCan, 42-47
  recovering erased files. See UnErase utility
  technical background, 87-88
Erase protect utility. See SmartCan utility
errorlevel codes, 438
error messages
  DOS, 4
  Norton Advisor, 11-12
Escape key, 14
ESDI interface, 345
.EXE files, 48-49, 72, 252
EXIT command (Batch Enhancer), 442
/EXP switch (Norton Cache), 231
expanded memory, 215-216, 231
Expanded Memory Manager (EMM), 215
Expanded Memory option (System Information), *470*,
  470-471
Expanded Memory Specification (EMS), 215
/EXT switch (Norton Cache), 231-232
extended memory, 216-218, 231-232
Extended Memory Manager (XMM), 217, 471
Extended Memory option (System Information), *471*,
  471-472
Extended Memory Specification (XMS), 217
extended partition tables, 388

F

/FAST switch (Norton Control Center), 417
Fast Mouse Reset check box (Configuration), 25
FASTOPEN (DOS), 213
Fast Wipe, 180
FAT option (Disk Editor), 373
/FD switch (Speed Disk), 255
FDISK command (DOS), 331, 378
/FF switch (Speed Disk), 255
file allocation tables (FATs), 333, 337-340, 343, *389*
  cross-linked files and, 119
  erasure of files and, 87-88
  FASTOPEN and, 213
  Fill option (Disk Editor) and, 369
  logical characteristics and, 468
  lost clusters, 118
  protection of, by Disk Monitor, 71
  Repair option (Norton Disk Doctor) and, 122
  12-bit vs. 16-bit, 338
  viewing, with Disk Editor, 362-364, 388-390
file attributes, 281-282, 379
File Attributes utility (FA), 35, 41, 48-50, 281-285
File Date utility (FD), 310-312
File Find utility (FILEFIND), 287-301
  Commands menu, 297-299
  File menu, 292
  full-screen operation, 288-291
  Help menu, 299
  List menu, 294-297
  main dialog box, 288, *289*
  Mode menu, 299
  network usage, 288
  running from DOS prompt, 299-301

Search menu, 292-294
  Viewer menu, 299
File Fix utility (FILEFIX), 133-146
  compatibility considerations, 133-134
  dBASE files, 136-144
    damaged file headers, 139-140, *140*
    damaged record dialog box, 138-139, *139*
    main dialog box, 136-137, *137*
    manually repairing file headers, 140-144
  running from DOS prompt, 146
  spreadsheet files, 135-136
  starting, 134, 146
  WordPerfect files, 144-146
File List option (Norton Change Directory), 265
File Locate utility (FL), 287, 301-304
File menu
  File Find, 292
  Norton Diagnostics, 481-483
  System Information, 462-463
  Unerase, 94-96
File option (Disk Editor), 358, *358*
File Size utility (FS), 306-309
Files option (Wipe Info), 183-186
File Sort option (Speed Disk), 251
Files to Place First option (Speed Disk), 252
Fill option (Disk Editor), 369, *369*
Find Again option (Disk Editor), 376
Find Object option (Disk Editor), 376
Find option (Disk Editor), 376
1st copy of FAT option (Disk Editor), 362-364, *363*
FIXED.DBF, 136-137
Fix Shifted Data Automatically option (File Fix), 137
/FIXSPACES switch (Norton Disk Doctor), 130
FL. See File Locate utility
  caching of, 224
  copying, with Disk Duplicator, 419-423
  formatting, 59-62, 72
  hard-disk vs., 325-326
floppy drives
  diagnostics tests, 489-490, *490*
  protection of, with SmartCan, 44
  Safe Format configuration for, 63
FM recording, 347
For Data Types option (UnErase), 96
For Lost Names option (UnErase), 96
FORMAT.COM, 54, 57-58, 107
FORMAT command (DOS), 106, 331
formatting, 54, 105-106, 330
  of floppy disks, under Disk Monitor, 72
  levels of, 54
For Text option (UnErase), 96
Fragmentation Report option (Speed Disk), 254, *254*
fragmented disks, 243-244
FRECOVER.DAT, 56, 109
Free Space option (Norton Change Directory), 263
FS. See File Size utility
Full Optimization option (Speed Disk), 248
full stroke time, 203
Full with Directories First option (Speed Disk), 248
Full with File Reorder option (Speed Disk), 248-249
Fully Automatic option (File Fix), 138

G

GE (Line Print option), 428
GOTO command (Batch Enhancer), 442-443
/GOV switch (Wipe Info), 189
Government Wipe, 180-181, 182-183
GRAFT command (Norton Change Directory), 270

Index ■ **511**

Graphical Mouse check box (Configuration), 25
Grid test (Norton Diagnostics), 492
Grow Window option (Disk Editor), 374

H

hard-disk controllers, 344-349
    in Calibrate, 203
    decorative vs. useful, 211
    encoding techniques, 347-349
        FM recording, 347
        high density, 348
        MFM recording, 348
        Run Length Limited recording, 349
    interface types, 344-347
        ESDI, 345
        IDE, 345
        SCSI, 346
        ST506, 344
hard-disk(s), 325. See also hard-disk controllers
    access times of, 209-210
    backing up, 38-39, 42
    bad areas on, 122
    diagnostics tests, 489, *489*
    floppy vs., 325-326
    formatting in DOS, 106-107
    head parking with Disk Monitor, 75-77
    improving access speed of. See Norton Cache utility;
        Speed Disk utility
    improving sub-system performance of. See Calibrate
        utility
    low-level formatting of, 330
    partitioning of, 340-343
    physical layout of, 343
    unfragmenting. See Speed Disk utility
    using rescue disk to gain access to, 84
    viewing, in Disk Editor, 385-392
        clusters, 391
        diagnostic cylinder, 392
        DOS boot records, 388
        file allocation tables, 388-390
        master boot record and partition tables, 385-388
Hard-Disk Speed option (System Information), 475-
    476, *476*
Hardware Configuration option (Norton Diagnostics),
    480, 481-482
Hardware Interrupts option (System Information), 464-
    465, *465*
head alignment, Calibrate adjustment for, 196
head crash, 326
/HEADER switch (Line Print), 427, 429, 430
Header option (Configuration), 27
heads (hard-disk), 75, 322, 324, 326
help
    context-sensitive, 12-13
    on DOS command line, 17
Help menu, 11-12, *12*
hexadecimal numbering system, 383-384
Hex option (Disk Editor), 372, *372*
Hex Strings option (File Find), 294, *295*
/HI switch (Line Print), 427
/HID switch
    with File Attributes, 283
    with File Find, 300
Hidden attribute bit, 282, 334
/HIDE switch (Diskreet), 177
high density recording, 348
High DOS Memory. See Upper memory blocks
high-level formatting, 54, 106, 330

High Memory Area (HMA)
    loading DISKREET.SYS driver in, 161-163
    Norton Cache and, 218, 223-224
HIMEM, 162
HMA. See High Memory Area; High memory area
Home key, 14
hot keys, 14
Hot Keys—Quick Close All option (Diskreet), 173-174

I

IBMBIO.COM, 152, 343, 390
IBMDOS.COM, 152, 343, 390
IDE controller, 197, 345-346, 468
/IMAGE switch
    with UnErase, 98
    with UnFormat, 115
IMAGE.BAK, 56, 112
IMAGE.DAT, 55-58, 106, 108-110, 112, 248
IMAGE.IDX, 55
Image utility, 29, 53, 55-57, 106
    command-line options, 56
    daily running of, 55-56
    Mirror vs., 88-89
    network usage, 56
    running from DOS prompt, 56-57
Include Non-erased files option (UnErase), 97
Info menu (Disk Editor), 374-375
Information menu (Speed Disk), 252-254
/INI switch (Norton Cache), 233
/INSTALL switch (Norton Cache), 223, 229-230
IntelliWrites, 224, 227, 232
interface standards, 344
interleave factors, 194, 331-332, 333
interleave testing modification with Calibrate, 194-195,
    204
interrupts, 464-465
IO.SYS, 152, 343, 390

J

JUMP command (Batch Enhancer), 443

K

key, encryption, 158
KEYB command, 413
keyboard
    changing settings of, with Norton Control Center, 413
    diagnostics tests, 493-494
    usage, 13-16
        check boxes, 15
        Command window, 16
        control buttons, 15
        pull-down menus, 13-14
        radio buttons, 15
        special keys, 14
        text boxes, 16
Keyboard Light test, 493-494
Keyboard Speed option (Norton Control Center), 402, *402*
KEYBOARD.SYS, 413
Key Press test, 493
KEYSTACK.SYS, 29

L

label attribute bit, 335
LABEL command (DOS)

512 ■ *Power Of...Norton Utilities*

LA (Line Print option), 428
Left-Handed Mouse check box (Configuration), 25
/LIGHT+(-) switch (Disk Monitor), 77
Line Print utility (LP), 425-432
    command-line operation of, 426-428
    printing, 428-431
Line Spacing option (Configuration), 27
Link menu (Disk Editor), 370-371, 390
List menu (File Find), 294-297
/LOG switch (Text Search), 314
logical drives, 340-343
Logical Drives option (Disk Editor), 356-357
lost clusters, recovering, 118-119
low-level formatting, 54, 106, 205, 322, 330

M

magnetic recording media, 321-322
Maintenance option (Disk Editor), 392
Make a Disk Bootable option (Disk Tools), 152-153
/MAKEBOOT switch (Disk Tools), 153
Make command (Norton Change Directory), 266
Manual UnErase, 96, 98-104
Map Legend option (Speed Disk), 253
Map of Object option (Disk Editor), 375, *375*
Margins option (Configuration), 27
/MARKCLUSTER switch (Disk Tools), 151
Marking a Cluster option (Disk Tools), 151-152
Mark option (Disk Editor), 368
master boot record (MBR), 329, 341, 343, 361, *386*
    viewing, with Disk Editor, 385-386
MD command (Norton Change Directory), 271
memory
    disk caches and, 210-211
    map, *217*
    Norton Cache and, 211-212, 224-225, 230-236
    video memory test, 491
Memory Block List option (System Information), 472, 473
Memory Dump option (Disk Editor), *365*, 365-367, *366*
Memory menu (System Information), 469-471
memory-resident programs (TSRs), 163, 473-474
Memory tests (Norton Diagnostics), 488, 491
Memory Usage Summary option (System Information),
    469, *470*
menu bar, 8-12
menu editing, configuration of, 34-35
Menu menu, 8-10, *9*
menus, pull-down, 13-14
menu screen, 7-13, *8*
MFM recording, 348
Minimal Pattern Testing option (Calibrate), 205
/MIRROR switch
    with UnErase, 98
    with UnFormat, 115
MIRROR.FIL, 106
Mirror utility (DOS), 88-89, 106
Misc test (Norton Diagnostics), 485
MODE command (DOS), 396
Mode menu (File Find), 299
Mode test (Norton Diagnostics), 492
MONTHDAY command (Batch Enhancer), 444
mouse
    configuration of, 21, 24-25
    diagnostics test, 493
    usage, 13-16
        check boxes, 15
        Command window, 16
        pull-down menus, 14
        radio buttons, 15

        text boxes, 16
Mouse Speed option (Norton Control Center), 402-403
MSDOS.SYS, 152, 343, 390
/MULTI switch (Norton Cache), 237
    Calibrate, 200
    Disk Editor, 353
    Disk Monitor, 73-74
    Diskreet, 161
    Norton Disk Doctor, 120
    UnFormat, 108

N

National Language Support Function file
    (NLSFUNC.EXE), 411
NCACHE2. See Norton Cache utility
NCACHE.INI, 222, 229
NDDUNDO.DAT, 126
NDIAGS. See Norton Diagnostics utility
NDisks, 50, 158-159
    passwords for, 159-160
    working with, 175-176
NDisks menu (Diskreet), 167-172
    Create option, 167-168
    Delete option, 171
    Description option, 170-171
    Edit option, 169
    Password option, 171
    Prompt and Prompt At options, 169-170
    Search option, 172
NDOS.COM, 29
/NET switch (Norton Change Directory), 271
Network Performance Speed option (System
    Information), 477
networks
    Directory Sort on, 274
    Disk Doctor on, 119
    Disk Monitor on, 74
    Diskreet on, 159
    File Find on, 288
    Norton Change Directory on, 260
    purging files from, 45
    System Information on, 460
    UnFormat on, 107
    Wipe Info on, 181
Next Probable option (Manual UnErase), 100
/NG switch (Norton Change Directory), 270
NLSFUNC.EXE, 411
/NOCOPY switch (Calibrate), 208
/NOFORMAT switch (Calibrate), 208
/NOHDM switch (System Information), 477
/NOHMA switch (Diskreet), 161
/NOINFO switch (UnErase), 98
NORMAL.BAT, 199-200
NORMAL (Line Print option), 447
Norton Advisor, 11-12
Norton Backup, 214
Norton Cache utility (NCACHE2), 209-241
    compatibility considerations, 213
    conventional (DOS) memory and, 214-215
    DOS buffers and, 212-213
    drive options, 238-240
    expanded memory and, 215-216
    extended memory and, 216-218
    FASTOPEN and, 213
    high memory area and, 218
    installing, 219-228
        advanced options, 226-228
        in AUTOEXEC.BAT, 222-223

Index ■ **513**

in CONFIG.SYS, 222
from DOS prompt, 241
floppy disk caching, 224
in high memory, 223-224
memory usage, 224-225
options, 229-236
from Startup Programs, 220-221
optional parameters for, 229
reconfigure options, 236-238
status report, 234, 234-236
system requirements, 211-212
technical background, 209-211
upper memory blocks and, 218-219
Norton Change Directory utility (NCD), 114-115, 149,
259-285
Directory menu, *264*, 264-269
Configure option, 269
Copy Tree option, 266-267
Delete command, 266
File List option, 265
Make command, 266
Prune and Graft option, 267-269
Remove Tree option, 267
Rename command, 265
Tree Size option, 266
Disk menu, 262-264, *263*
Change Disk option, 262
Free Space option, 263
Print Tree option, 263-264
Rescan Disk option, 263
Volume Label option, 263
Help menu, 269
network usage, 260
running from DOS prompt, 269-272
starting, 261
TREEINFO.NCD file and, 261
View menu, 269
Norton Control Center utility (NCC), 395-418
code pages, 412-415
keyboard, 413-414
outside DOS, 412-413
time and date, 414-415
Country Info option, 410, 410-411
Cursor Size option, *398*, 398-399
DOS Colors option, 399, *399*
Keyboard Speed option, 402, *402*
main screen, *397*
Mouse Speed option, 402-403, *403*
Palette Colors option, 400, *400, 401*
running from DOS prompt, 416-418
saving settings, 415-416, *416*
Serial Ports option, 404-410, *405*
baud rate, 405
data bits, 406
parity, 405-406
stop bits, 406
Watches option, 406-410, *410*
starting, 397-398, 416-417
Video Mode option, *401*, 401-402
Norton Diagnostics utility (NDIAGS), 479-505
comprehensive tests, 494-496, *495*
configuration screen, 480, *480*
disk tests, 489-491
floppy drive, *490*, 490-491
hard-disk, 489, *489*
File menu, 481-483
Hardware Configuration option, *480*, 481-482
Options item, 482
Reports option, 482-483, *483*

keyboard tests, 493-494
memory tests, 488
mouse test, 493
speaker test, 493
starting, 479-480
system tests, 483-487
CMOS Status test, 487
Parallel Port test, 486
Serial Port tests, 485-486
System Board test, 483-485, *484*
video tests, 491-492
color test, 492
grid test, 492
memory test, 491
mode test, 492
Norton Disk Doctor utility (NDD), 117-131, 134
after UnFormat, 111-112
compatibility considerations, 119
Diagnose Disk option, 120-121, 123-126
DOS RECOVER, as preferable alternative to, 148
lost clusters, recovering, 118
main menu, 120, *120*
network usage, 119
running from AUTOEXEC.BAT, 130-131
running from DOS prompt, 129-130
setting options for, 123
starting, 119-120, 129-131
Surface Test option, 121-122, 127-129
Passes option, 121-122
progress screen, 127, *127*
Repair option, 122
sample report, 128
Test Type option, 121-122
Undo Changes option, 122-123
NORTON.INI, 10, 35
/NOSEEK switch (Calibrate), 208
/NOSMARTCAN switch (UnErase), 98
/NOTRACK switch (UnErase), 98
/NOW switch (File Find), 300
NPU tests (Norton Diagnostics), 484-485
NUCONFIG, 20
numbering, computer, 382-384
Number Lines option (Configuration), 26

O

Object menu (Disk Editor), 356-364
/OFF switch
with Diskreet, 177
with SmartCan, 46
/ON switch
with Diskreet, 177
with SmartCan, 46
Optimization option (Norton Cache), 228
/OPTIMIZE switch (Norton Cache), 232-233
Optimize menu (Speed Disk), 249-250
Options item (Norton Diagnostics), 482
Options menu (UnErase), 97
Orientation option (Configuration), 28
Output Destination option (Configuration), 28
Overall Performance Index option (System Information),
476, *476*
.OVL files, 72

P

/PA switch (Line Print), 427
Page Down key, 14
Page Size option (Configuration), 27

514 ■ Power Of...Norton Utilities

/PALETTE switch (Norton Control Center), 417
Palette Colors option (Norton Control Center), 400
Parallel Port test (Norton Diagnostics), 486
Parity option (Norton Control Center), 405-406
/PARK switch (Disk Monitor), 77
    command-line options, 76-77
    Disk Light feature, 76
Partition option (Disk Editor), 371
partitions, 340-343
partition tables, 341-342, 343, 387
    viewing, with Disk Editor, 385-388
Partition Table(s) option
    Disk Editor, *361*, 361-362, 373, 387
    System Information, 468-469, *469*
Password option (Diskreet), 159-160
passwords
    configuration of, 32-34
    in Diskreet, 165, 171, 175
    lost or forgotten, 34
Passwords option (Configuration), 32-33
Paste Over option (Disk Editor), 368
PATH statement (DOS), 29-30, 200
/PATTERN switch (Calibrate), 208
Physical Drives option (Disk Editor), 357
Physical Sector option (Disk Editor), 360, *360*
PO (Line Print option), 428
ports, serial, 404
/PR switch (Line Print), 428
Print As option (Disk Editor), 377-378
PRINTCHAR command (Batch Enhancer), 444-445
Printer Configuration option, 25-28, 427, 429
printer setup strings, 430-431
Printer Type option (Configuration), 26-27
printing ASCII files. See Line Print utility
Print List option (File Find), 295, *296*
Print Tree option (Norton Change Directory), 263-264
PR (Line Print option), 428
Prompt and Prompt At options (Diskreet), 169-170
/PROTECT+(-) switch (Disk Monitor), 77
protected mode, 216-217
Prune and Graft command (Norton Change Directory), 267-269
purging files (SmartCan), 44-45

Q

/QUICK switch (Norton Cache), 233-234
Quick Format option (Safe Format), 58
Quick Links option (Disk Editor), 355
Quick Move option (Disk Editor), 355
/QUIET switch
    with Diskreet, 161
    with Norton Cache, 237

R

RAM, disk caching and, 209-211
random access media, 322
Random read test (System Information), 490
RD command (Norton Change Directory), 271
/READ switch (Norton Cache), 232
Read-Ahead Buffer option (Norton Cache), 226-227
read-only attribute bit, 48-49, 282, 335
read-only files, wiping, 184
Read-Only mode (Disk Editor), 353, 354, 367, 385
REBOOT command (Batch Enhancer), 200, 445-446
/REBUILD switch (Norton Disk Doctor), 130
Recalculate Partition option (Disk Editor), 378
RECOVER command (DOS), 147-150

Recover from DOS's Recover option (Disk Tools), 148-150
recovering
    erased files. See UnErase utility
    formatted disks. See UnFormat utility
    lost clusters, 118-119
Remove Tree command (Norton Change Directory), 267
Rename command (Norton Change Directory), 265
Rename option (UnErase), 95
repartitioning, 343
/REPORT switch (Norton Cache), 234-236
Report dialog box (System Information), 462-463, *463*
Reports option (Norton Diagnostics), 482-483, *483*
Rescan Disk command (Norton Change Directory), 261, 263
rescue disk, 79-86
    creating, 81-84
    restoring, 84
    updating, 84
/RESET switch
    with Norton Cache, 236-237
    with Norton Diagnostics, 504
REVERSE (Line Print option), 447
Review Damaged Records option (File Fix), 138-139
/REVIVE switch (Disk Tools), 150
Revive a Defective Diskette option (Disk Tools), 150-151
Rigorous Pattern Testing option (Calibrate), 205
RMTREE command (Norton Change Directory), 271
Rotation speed test (System Information), 491
ROWCOL command (Batch Enhancer), 446-447
Run Length Limited (RLL) recording, 349

S

Safe Format utility (SFORMAT), 54, 57-65, 106, 107
    alternate program names, 31-32, 58
    configuration of, 62-64
    DOS Format option, 58
    floppy disk format, 59-62
    Quick Format option, 58
    running from DOS prompt, 64-65
    Safe Format option, 57-58
    starting, 58-59
/SAVE switch (Norton Cache), 237
script files, 435-436, 442-443
SCSI controller, 197, 346-347, 468
Search Drives option (File Find), 292-293
searches, case-sensitive, 290
searching for text. See Text Search
Search menu
    File Find, 292-294
    Unerase, 96-97
Search option (Diskreet), 172
Sector Angle, 203
sector IDs, fading of, 195
Sector option (Disk Editor), *359*, 359-360
sector(s), 322-325, 329-330
Select Group option (UnErase), 95
Select (Spacebar) option (UnErase), 94
Serial Ports option (Norton Control Center), 404-410, *405*
Serial Port tests (Norton Diagnostics), 485-486
/SET switch
    with Line Print, 428, 431
    with Norton Control Center, 417
Set Attribute(s) option
    Disk Editor, 379
    File Find, 297-298, *298*
SET command (DOS), 30

Index ■ 515

Set Date/Time option
 Disk Editor, 379-380
 File Find, 298, *298*
Set List Display option (File Find), 294, *295*
Set Search Range option (UnErase), 97
setup memory, 80
SHIFTSTATE command (Batch Enhancer), 450
Shift+Tab, 14
/SHOW switch (Diskreet), 153, 176-177
Show All Characters option (Disk Editor), 355
Show Static Files option (Speed Disk), 253
Shrink Window option (Disk Editor), 374
SIZE command (Norton Change Directory), 271
Size of Cache Buffer Blocks option (Norton Cache), 227
size of file(s), determining. See File Size utility
/SKIPHIGH switch
 with Disk Editor, 382
 with Disk Monitor, 77
 with Diskreet, 161
 with Norton Disk Doctor, 130
 with SmartCan, 46
 with Speed Disk, 255
 with UnErase, 98
/SMARTCAN switch (UnErase), 98
SmartCan utility, 41-47
 advantages and disadvantages of, 46-47
 command-line options, 45-46
 configuration of, 42-44
 Delete Tracking vs., 89
 files suited for, 41-42
 purging files, 44-45
SMARTDrive disk cache program, 213
Sort by name option (Menu menu), 8-9, 14
Sort by prognosis option (UnErase), 97
Sort by topic option (Menu menu), 8-9
/SOUND switch (System Information), 477
/SP switch (Line Print), 427
speaker diagnostics test, 493
/SPEC switch
 with Norton Diagnostics, 504
 with System Information, 477
Speed Disk utility (SPEEDISK), 243-256
 Configure menu, 250-252
 copy-protection and, 245-246
 Information menu, 252-254
 network usage, 244
 optimization with, 246-249
 Optimize menu, 249-250
 precautions, 244-245
 running from DOS prompt, 255-256
 starting, 246
standard display mode, 24
/START switch (Norton Control Center), 407, 417
starting Norton Utilities, 7
 from DOS command line, 16-17
 from menus, 12
startup programs, configuration of, 28-31. See also
 AUTOEXEC.BAT; CONFIG.SYS
Startup Programs option (Configuration menu), 70
/START:WATCH switch (Norton Control Center), 407
/STATUS switch
 with Disk Monitor, 77
 with Diskreet, 177
 with Norton Cache, 236
 with SmartCan, 46
/STOP switch (Norton Control Center), 407, 418
Stop bits option (Norton Control Center), 406
Strict Character Checking option (File Fix), 137
subdirectories, 335-337

SUBSTITUTE command (DOS), 196, 466
/SUMMARY switch (System Information), 477
Surface Test option (Norton Disk Doctor), 121-122, 127-129
 Passes option, 121-122
 Repair option, 122
 Test Type option, 121-122
Switch Windows option (Disk Editor), 374
/SYS switch
 with File Attributes, 283
 with File Find, 300
SYS command (DOS), 153
.SYS files, 72
system area, 70, 71, 87, 105-106, 330
system attribute bit, 282, 335
System Board test (Norton Diagnostics), 483-485, *484*
System Information utility (SYSINFO), 459-478
 Benchmarks menu, 475-477
 CPU Speed option, 475, *475*
 Hard-Disk Speed option, 475-476, *476*
 Network Performance Speed option, 477
 Overall Performance Index option, *476*, 476
 Disks menu, 466-469
 Disk Characteristics option, 467-468, *468*
 Disk Summary option, 466, *467*
 Partition Tables option, 468-469, *469*
 File menu, 462-463
 Memory menu, 469-474
 Device Drivers option, 474, *474*
 Expanded Memory option, 470, *470*-471
 Extended Memory option, *471*, 471-472
 Memory Block List option, 472, *473*
 Memory Usage Summary option, 469, *470*
 TSR Programs option, *473*, 473-474
 network usage, 460
 running from DOS prompt, 477
 starting, 460
 summary screen, 461, *461*
 System menu, 463-466
 CMOS Status option, 466, *467*
 Hardware Interrupts option, 464-465, *465*
 Network Information option, 466
 Software Interrupts option, 465, *466*
 System Summary option, 463
 Video Summary option, 464, *464*
System menu (System Information), 463-466
System tests (Norton Diagnostics), 483-487
 CMOS Status test, 487
 Parallel Port test, 486
 Serial Port tests, 485-486
 System Board test, 483-485, *484*

T

/TAB switch (Line Print), 427
Tab key, 14
Tabs option (Configuration), 27
/TARGET switch (File Find), 300
Target Fit option (File Find), 299
temporary files, locating, 181
Tests to Skip option (Norton Disk Doctor), 123
text boxes, 16
Text option (Disk Editor), 373
Text Search utility (TS), 312-317
time, marking file. See File Date utility
Time and Date option (Norton Control Center), *414*, 414-415
TIME command (DOS), 414
TO (Line Print option), 428

516 ■ *Power Of...Norton Utilities*

tones, producing, 439-440
Tools menu (Disk Editor), 375-382
topics, 9
track IDs, fading of, 195
tracks, 322-325
track-to-track time, 202
TREEINFO.NCD, 260, 261-262
Tree Size option (Norton Change Directory), 266
tree-structured directory system, 335-336
TRIGGER command (Batch Enhancer), 450-451
TS. See Text Search utility
/TSR switch (System Information), 477
TSR Programs option (System Information), *473*, 473-474
TSRs. See memory-resident programs
TT (Line Print option), 428

U

UMB. See upper memory blocks
/UNDELETE switch (Norton Disk), 130
/UNDO switch (Norton Disk Doctor), 130
Undo Changes option (Norton Disk Doctor), 122-123
UnDo files, 125-126
Undo option (Disk Editor), 367-368
UnErase To option (UnErase), 93, 95
UnErase utility (UNERASE), 88-104
    dialog box, 90-91, *91*
    emergency situations, 89-90
    File menu, 94-96
    Options menu, 97
    running, after installation, 90-97
    running from DOS prompt, 97-98
    Search menu, 96-97
    simple recovery, 92-93
    using Manual UnErase, 98-104
    view box, 92, *92*
UnFormat utility (UNFORMAT), 53, 62, 105-115
    drive selection box, 108, *109*
    emergency situations, 107
    files on disk warning, *109*, 109-110
    introductory screen, *108*, 108
    on networks, 107
    running, after installation, 108-115
        command-line options, 115
        recovering disk without IMAGE.DAT file, 112-115
        when two image files exist, 112
    successful recovery message, *111*
    technical background, 105-107
Unfragment Files Only option (Speed Disk), 249
Unfragment Free Space option (Speed Disk), 249
/UNINSTALL switch
    with Disk Monitor, 77
    with Norton Cache, 223, 237
    with SmartCan, 46
Unmovable Files option (Speed Disk), 252
upper memory blocks (UMBs), 218-219
    loading DISKREET.SYS driver in, 161-163
    location of, *219*
/USEHIGH switch (Norton Cache), 233
/USEHMA switch (Norton Cache), 233
utilities. See also starting Norton Utilities
    definition, 3
    DOS, 4, 396

V

VANILLA.BAT, 199-200

Version 7.0, new features of, 5
Video Mode option (Norton Control Center), *401*, 401-402
Video Summary option (System Information), 464, *464*
Video tests (Norton Diagnostics), 491-492
    color test, 492
    grid test, 492
    memory test, 491
    mode test, 492
Viewer menu (File Find), 299
View menu
    Disk Editor, 371-374
    Norton Change Directory, 269
View WordStar Files option (Disk Editor), 355
viruses, 67-69, 70
Volume Label option (Norton Change Directory), 263

W

    with Disk Editor, 382
    with File Locate, 302
    with Line Print, 427, 439
    with Norton Cache, 239
Walk Map option (Speed Disk), 253, *254*
WEEKDAY command (Batch Enhancer), 451
wild-card characters (with Line Print), 429
WINDOW command (Batch Enhancer), 452
Window option (Disk Editor), 371
Windows, Norton Cache and, 213, 216, 218, 225
Wipe Info utility (WIPEINFO), 179-190
    configuration of, 182-183
    drives, 186-188
    files, 183-186
    hidden data, 181-182
    levels of information wiping in, 180-181
    network usage, 181
    running from DOS prompt, 188-190
    starting, 182, 188-189
WordStar files, 355
Wrap Lines option (Configuration), 26
/WRITE switch (Norton Cache), 232
Write-Back Buffer option (Norton Cache), 227
Write option (Disk Editor), 370
Write protection test (System Information), 491
Write To option (Disk Editor), 376-377
writing to disks
    controlling, 69-74
        automatic installation of Disk Monitor, 70
        configuration of Disk Monitor, 70-73
        graphics mode, 73-74
        networks, 74
        text mode, 73
    problem disks, 86
    recovering erased files and, 88

X

    with Calibrate, 208
    with Disk Editor, 382
    with Norton Disk Doctor, 130
XCOPY command (DOS), 422
XFORMAT, 32, 58, 107

Z

Zooming Boxes check box (Configuration), 24
ZOOM option (Line Print), 452